Also by Peter Englund

The Beauty and the Sorrow:
An Intimate History of the First World War

The Battle That Shook Europe:
Poltava and the Birth of the Russian Empire

November 1942

November 1942

An Intimate History of the
Turning Point of World War II

Peter Englund

TRANSLATED FROM THE SWEDISH BY
Peter Graves

Alfred A. Knopf | New York 2023

THIS IS A BORZOI BOOK
PUBLISHED BY ALFRED A. KNOPF

www.aaknopf.com

Library of Congress Cataloging-in-Publication Data
Names: Englund, Peter, [date] author. | Graves, Peter, [date] translator.
Title: November 1942 : an intimate history of the turning point of
World War II / Peter Englund ; translated from Swedish by Peter Graves.
Other titles: Onda nätters drömmar. English | Intimate history of the
turning point of World War II
Description: First American edition. | New York : Alfred A. Knopf, 2023. |
"Originally published in Sweden as Onda nätters drömmar by Natur &
Kultur, Stockholm, 2022." | Includes bibliographical references and index.
Identifiers: LCCN 2023001804 (print) | LCCN 2023001805 (ebook) |
ISBN 9781524733315 (hardcover) | ISBN 9781524733322 (ebook)
Subjects: LCSH: World War, 1939–1945.
Classification: LCC D743 .E54 2023 (print) | LCC D743 (ebook) |
DDC 940.53—dc23/eng/20230117
LC record available at https://lccn.loc.gov/2023001804
LC ebook record available at https://lccn.loc.gov/2023001805

Jacket photograph by PAP / Alamy
Jacket design by Chip Kidd

Manufactured in the United States of America
First American Edition

Dedicated to the memory of
Józef Lewandowski
and all those others I've met through the years
who were there and took part

We dreamed in the savage nights
Dense violent dreams
Dreamed with soul and body:
To return; to eat; to tell the story.
Until the dawn command
Sounded brief, low:
"Wstawac":

And the heart shattered in the breast.
Now we have found our home again,
Our bellies are full,
We've finished telling the story.
It's time. Soon we'll hear again
The strange command:
"Wstawac."

—PRIMO LEVI, "ALZARSI"*

---

* Levi wrote this poem on January 11, 1946, when the first anniversary of his liberation from Auschwitz was approaching. In the original Italian of the poem he uses the Polish word for "Wake up" that was used in the camp: "*Wstawac.*"

Contents

A Note to the Reader

This is a book about November 1942, the month that marked the turning point of the Second World War. At the start of that month many people still believed that the Axis powers would be victorious. By the end of that month it had become clear that it was only a matter of time before they would lose. This book, however, will not attempt to describe *what* the war was during these four critical weeks—its opportunities, plans, course of events and consequences—but will try to say something about *how* it was.

A phenomenon like the Second World War will in some sense always elude us. To a great extent it's a question of scale. It's self-evident that a conflict that lasted so long, covered so much of the world, caused such great destruction and cost so many lives will be impossible to grasp as a whole. It is to some extent unknowable in that it involved such terrible events that our comprehension, judgment, language even, struggles and proves insufficient. And there is a further complication. Primo Levi writes that "those who have seen the face of the Gorgon did not return, or returned wordless." My own impression, having met many of those involved, is that they all had their secrets, repressed or unspoken, and that their secrets died with them.

The fact that what happened is difficult to grasp is no argument for not trying. Quite the reverse: the effort must be made, both for our own sakes and for all those who succumbed. This book is an attempt to do that, its motivation being to try to do it in a different way. It does not have an overarching framework and it tries to avoid what Paul Fussell called "the adventure story model" that ascribes "clear, and usually noble, cause and purpose to accidental or demeaning events."

Like my earlier book on the First World War, this book takes the form
of interwoven biographies. At its center stands the individual human
being, his or her experiences and, not least, his or her feelings; all the
things that may perhaps be found in footnotes, or that may sometimes
emerge as passing flashes of color in the heavy flow of the grand narrative, but which are for the most part invisible. And if you are wondering
what I've added to these frequently intimate descriptions, the answer
is: nothing. My sources are quite rich enough in themselves.

Viewed as historiography, this form is experimental and arises from
a sense that the complexity of events emerges most clearly at the level
of the individual. There is a dark paradox here. Many of those who
went to the First World War were driven by an idealism that lacked any
basis in reality: they were fighting for fantasies. Idealism of that kind
was largely absent in the Second World War, in spite of the fact that
there was so much more at stake. This created a remarkable tension
between the purpose of the war and how it was experienced, between
its grand aims and a reality that more often than not was a "crazy hysterical mess," as the Nobel Prize winner John Steinbeck later summed
up his own experiences.

At the same time, though, not everything was like that. We know that
it really did come down to a struggle between barbarity and civilization
and that November 1942 witnessed the crux of that struggle. Many of
the people involved probably understood that too. The sacrifices it
demanded are obvious. And it would be a mistake to see the outcome
of the struggle as a given, not just because that would make the sacrifices a sort of historical technicality, but also because it would change
an uncertain, unpredictable human catastrophe that was beyond comprehension at the time into an exciting but essentially non-dangerous
narrative. That, in turn, could feed the dangerous illusion that all this
could not be repeated, but with a diametrically opposite result this
time round.

P.E., Uppsala, March 2022

Dramatis Personae

Mansur Abdulin, private,
infantry, outside Stalingrad,
age nineteen

John Amery, fascist and
defector, in Berlin,
age thirty

Hélène Berr, university
student in Paris,
age twenty-one

Ursula Blomberg, refugee in
Shanghai, age twelve*

Vera Brittain, author and
pacifist in London,
age forty-eight

John Bushby, machine-
gunner on a Lancaster
bomber, age twenty-two*

Paolo Caccia Dominioni,
major, paratroopers, in
North Africa, age forty-six

Albert Camus, author from
Algeria, in Le Panelier,
age twenty-nine

Keith Douglas, lieutenant, in
tanks, in North Africa,
age twenty-two

Edward "Weary" Dunlop,
military doctor and prisoner
of war on Java, age thirty-five

Danuta Fijalkowska, refugee
and mother of one child, in
Międzyrzec Podlaski,
age twenty

Lidiya Ginzburg, university
teacher in Leningrad,
age forty

Vasily Grossman, reporter
for *Krasnaja Zvezda* in
Stalingrad, age thirty-six

Tameichi Hara, commander
of a destroyer off
Guadalcanal, age forty-two

Adelbert Holl, lieutenant,
infantry, in Stalingrad,
age twenty-three

Vera Inber, poet and
journalist in Leningrad,
age fifty-two

Ernst Jünger, army captain
and writer, on a journey to
the Eastern Front,
age forty-seven

Ursula von Kardorff,
journalist in Berlin,
age thirty-one

Nella Last, housewife in
Barrow-in-Furness,
age fifty-three

John McEniry, dive-bomber
pilot at Guadalcanal,
age twenty-four

Mun Okchu, comfort woman
in a Japanese brothel in
Mandalay, age eighteen

Nikolai Obrynba,
partisan in White Russia,
age twenty-nine

John Parris, journalist
covering the landing in
Algeria, age twenty-eight

Poon Lim, second steward on
a British merchant ship,
age twenty-four

Jechiel "Chil" Rajchman,
inmate in the Treblinka
extermination camp,
age twenty-eight*

Willy Peter Reese, private,
infantry, on the Eastern
Front, age twenty-one

Dorothy Robinson,
housewife on Long Island,
age forty

Ned Russell, journalist
covering the campaign in
Tunisia, age twenty-six

Sophie Scholl, university
student in Munich, living
in Ulm, age twenty-one

Elena Skrjabina, refugee and
mother of two in Pyatigorsk,
age thirty-six

Anne Somerhausen, office
worker and mother of three
in Brussels, age forty-one

Leonard Thomas, engineer
in a vessel on an Arctic
convoy, age twenty

Bede Thongs, sergeant,
infantry, in New Guinea,
age twenty-two

Vittorio Vallicella, private,
truck driver, in North Africa,
age twenty-four

Tohichi Wakabayashi,
lieutenant, infantry, at
Guadalcanal, age thirty

Charles Walker, second
lieutenant, infantry, at
Guadalcanal, age twenty-two

Kurt West, private, infantry,
on the Svir Front,
age nineteen

Leona Woods, doctoral
student in physics in
Chicago, age twenty-three

Zhang Zhonglou, civil
servant on an inspection
journey in Henan,
age unknown

* Photograph taken after the war.

November 1942

NOVEMBER 1–8

Plans, Great and Small

"Compassion and brutality can exist in the same individual and in the same moment, despite all logic."

"Death can be successfully suppressed for the very reason that it is not susceptible to experience."

"Just a week earlier the destruction of a battalion had taken half a day; now the whole regiment was wiped out in three-quarters of an hour."

Strong winds sweep in from the East China Sea and the Huangpu River, sweeping past the junks, steamships and sailing vessels in the harbor, over the crowds of people, animals and vehicles on the wide promenade, past rickshaws, carts, cyclists—hordes of cyclists—overcrowded streetcars, wood-gas buses and military trucks. They sweep past the rows of tall, imposing, Western-style buildings of the Bund—"the Million Dollar Mile"—past its colonnades, domes, ledges, balustrades and spires, and over the never-diminishing groups of beggars below them. They move on via Pootung Point into the narrow streets and low houses of Hongkou, many of which still lie in ruins after five years; then on towards Zhabei, winding their way up through the walls and clusters of crenelated wooden roofs of the old Chinese town and on over the empty racecourse with its ten-story tower and silent, deserted multistory grandstand. And so into the international district, along crowded straight streets and tree-lined avenues (Gordon Road, Bubbling Wells Road, Avenue Foch, Avenue Joffre, Avenue Pétain), past temples and cathedrals, hospitals and universities, department stores and theatres, road blocks and barbed wire, cafés, bars and brothels. Then they proceed on up through parks where the trees become ever darker and barer as the chill winds sweep away their warm-colored leaves before finally disappearing eastwards towards the Wusong River and the surrounding countryside with its small towns, villages and rice fields, away towards distant Jiangsu, Anhui and Henan. It's late autumn in Shanghai.

Under these grey autumn skies, a girl named Ursula Blomberg lives in the southern part of the French concession. She has just had her twelfth birthday. She lives with her parents on the bottom floor of a house surrounded by a wall on the small Place de Fleurs, right by Rue de Kaufmann. The family are refugees from Germany and they rent a room and kitchen from a Russian woman. A number of other refugees from Leipzig live upstairs, and two men from Berlin live in a room that looks out on the yard, but they are seldom there. Ursula and her parents consider themselves fortunate: the district is safe, the street is quiet, the room light and airy, the kitchen clean and equipped with two hot plates and an icebox. They even have access to a bathroom, lined with blue tiles, where for a few cents they can take a hot bath. (This is very different from the refugee camps in Hongkou where many of those who arrived on the same vessel are still living, crowded together in filthy, stinking conditions behind curtains hung above rough concrete floors.)

The family, like millions of others, follows the course of the war on maps torn out of newspapers and stuck up in the hall on a piece of white cotton cloth. Ursula has made small, colored paper flags which they pin up to mark the advances and retreats of the different sides— red for Great Britain, blue for the United States, green for the Netherlands, yellow for Japan and so on. (In the memoir she wrote much later, she doesn't mention what color the flags of Germany were, so we will have to guess. Black?) Over the last year these flags have been moved again and again, because the news has been "devastating," as she writes in her diary. (That is the word she uses again and again to describe the effect the narrative of the events of the war has on her.) She has had to look for islands she didn't know existed, place names she doesn't know how to pronounce. Corregidor. Rabaul. Kokoda. Alam el Halfa. Majkop. Stalin-grad. *Gua-dal-canal.* The green flags have disappeared.

The lines of small holes on the paper maps show how the area under the control of the Axis powers has grown and grown. The discussion among refugees is whether Australia is likely to be the next country invaded. Three clusters of flags are particularly frightening: those in North Africa pointing eastwards towards Egypt, those in the Caucasus pointing down towards Persia and Axis-friendly Iraq,* and those

---

* The previous year, a Nazi-inspired nationalist coup had taken place in Iraq with direct military support from Italy and Germany. (It also sparked massacres of the Jewish population of Baghdad.) In a short war, the outcome of which was by no means assured, British forces had succeeded in reestablishing the pro-British regime.

in Burma pointing westwards to India. If the Axis powers continue to advance, those lines of flags are going to join up somewhere. Where? Afghanistan? Western India?*

"We were scared. Was it possible for a puny little nation like Japan, and for Germany with its overly inflated ego…to win a war against the whole western world? America included?"

At the moment it seems more than likely. Ursula finds life in unfamiliar Shanghai a "dreamlike experience." They live in oppressive isolation, shut off from the world, at the back of the moon, knowing only what the strictly censored newspapers and Japanese radio tell them and rumor claims. Which is why it was possible for a long time to comfort themselves with the thought that this dreadful news was all propaganda, exaggeration and disinformation. But a friend of a friend has a hidden radio and sometimes, through a wall of crackles and roars and whistles, he can pick up news from the BBC. "No longer rumors, many of the devastating war reports were true, and the future haunted us all."†

· · ·

The damp gets everywhere. His trousers and coat are sodden, as is his bread. Mold attacks the one as much as the other. His boots sink in with every step he takes. He and all the others totter through the sticky mud of the trenches "like tightrope walkers." His name is Willy Peter Reese and he writes:

---

* There was an agreement between Japan and Germany that they would divide up Asia and the Soviet Union along the 70th meridian. There was even a German military plan for this—Fall Orient—which, after success in Egypt and the Caucasus, and after securing the oil resources of the Middle East, would continue eastwards and link up with Japanese forces in Afghanistan or nearby.

† If you had access only to controlled media, it was easy to conclude that support for Japan was widespread in Asia. At the beginning of the year, Thailand had entered into an alliance with Japan; there were two quite large vassal states in China—Manchukuo, which had been in existence for ten years, and Mengkukuo; further vassal states were in the process of being formed in the Philippines and in Burma; and the Indian independence movement was stronger than ever. (At this point, there were both Burmese and Indian troops fighting for Japan in order to win independence for their countries from the British.) And in all the countries, there were plenty of opportunists willing to cooperate with the apparently invincible Japanese empire.

We found the trenches boggy and often flooded. Water dripped in to the temporary bunkers and primitive gunports, and the horses collapsed on the roads. A horse was more valuable than a soldier and we accepted our lot as it came, living in our memories and dreaming of getting back home. We soon got used to things again, as if nothing had changed since last year's rainy season.

Reese and the rest of his group are living in an extended trench, roofed with dripping wooden beams and with a piece of tent cloth as the door. They get their heat from a cast-iron stove and food comes from a field kitchen hidden away in a ravine some distance away. Anyone fetching food has to run there under cover of twilight. There is no way he can wash and he can't even change his sodden boots and socks. Short sunny spells are followed by yet another downpour. The wooded landscape is becoming increasingly empty, naked, waterlogged, its once vibrant hues washed out to a weak watercolor. Rainwater runs along the roads and the tall grass is bent, as if expecting frost and snow.

During the day Reese and the rest of the soldiers dig out the water-logged trenches, clean their personal weapons and ammunition as well as one of the machine guns and the light anti-tank gun they are manning. At night he stands guard for about an hour, then he is allowed to rest for three. That's what he does most of the time. Stands guard "exhausted, freezing, longing and powerless." His nights are sliced up in that way and the lack of sleep adds one more level to the dulling that numbs his body and soul. Things that frightened the life out of him a year ago hardly affect him these days—a kind of blessed indifference has taken over instead. Reese doesn't know whether the feeling comes from "fatalism or trust in God." The danger of death has become an everyday matter, as has death itself.

Willy Peter Reese is a twenty-one-year-old private in the 14th Company, 279th Regiment, 95th Infantry Division of the German army. He is of slim build and wears rimless glasses which emphasize his already rather shy appearance. (He reads and writes a lot, and since both activities need light, this is a frequent source of complaint from his comrades who want darkness so they can get to sleep. He sometimes ends up reading or writing by the glow of a cigarette.) His helmet and uniform both give the impression of being a bit too big for his thin body. He still gets adolescent blemishes. His eyes are hard and watchful, considerably older than his face.

Some 320 yards away, on the other side of a wide hollow, behind coils of barbed wire and among spruce trees and bare alder thickets, there's a glimpse of the Soviet lines. The place is called Tabakovo after the destroyed village a short distance behind them. Very little of it is left apart from piles of burned timbers crowned with the remains of chimney stacks and gardens with frosted, withered vegetables.

When Willy Peter Reese has to explain it to others, he says they are located "at Rzhev."* Things are quiet at the moment, which means that there aren't any mass attacks by the Soviet army, but they are under almost continuous fire from snipers and light grenade launchers. They can't use the stove during the day as smoke from the green wood immediately stirs the interest of enemy spotters. When they are in the trenches, there is no protection against projectiles plumping down from above, not when they are in close proximity. Reese was present when they found a comrade who'd been the victim of a direct hit during the night. The trench was plastered with frozen intestines, pieces of cloth, brain and flesh, and the dead man was totally unrecognizable.

There's another night when what Reese calls "the god of dreams" briefly and deceptively takes him home and away from all this. (It's not hard to imagine what it is like to wake from that.) The darkness becomes morning. Dawn light is still hanging over no-man's-land, over copses and bogs and the withered yellow-brown grass. It's quiet and he writes: "The beauty of these hours is worth many a night filled with terror and toil."

. . .

Back to Ursula Blomberg. She and her parents are only temporarily residents in Shanghai and they have no choice but to wait for peace and

---

* "At Rzhev" is a kind of typographical abbreviation for a 120-mile-long bulge in the German lines, a remnant of the failed attempt to take Moscow in 1941. It was so obvious even on large-scale maps that it always attracted the attention of strategists on both sides. Its proximity to Moscow meant that Hitler wanted to hang on to this geographical anomaly and, for the same reason, Stalin wanted to eliminate it. Both of them demanded that this be done "at any price," the military cliché that had its fullest and most horrific realization in these two dictators.

the possibility of travelling onwards to their final destination, America. There's no great mystery about their ending up in Shanghai. In the spring of 1939, which is when the family set out on their voyage, this cosmopolitan metropolis was almost the only port in the world that still unconditionally welcomed Jewish refugees from Germany. The reputation that Shanghai had as depraved, sinful, confusing and dangerous was unimportant, and about eighteen thousand Jews have arrived in recent years.

There are times when she is visited by dark thoughts—when, for instance, she thinks of all the British, American, Dutch and French civilians who have disappeared and been interned by the Japanese in a big camp in the direction of Wuzong, or when she thinks of her relatives who remained in Germany and she wonders how things are for them. Much later, when, as an adult, she looks back on this time, she realizes that "for a while our lives went on outwardly undisturbed, and we were lulled into a counterfeit mode of purely selfish contentment." It helps that everything here is so peaceful and that the Japanese soldiers treat them with respect—courtesy, even. They are, when all is said and done, Germans and consequently allies.

But anxiety still lurks beneath the surface.

In spite of it all, Ursula enjoys a paradoxical and unexpected degree of freedom. The fact that it is late autumn doesn't bother her—it's nice to have the heavy, damp heat of summer out of the way. Her father's painting and decorating business is going well and her mother does seamstress work at home. She herself brings in a little money by trying to teach English to three young, pretty, giggling Asian women, the "sisters" of a wealthy Chinese man; she has come to recognize that they are his concubines. When the weather permits, she plays croquet and table tennis with the "sisters," and now with the start of the month being cold and wet, they play cards.

. . .

Musical intermezzo: the day has begun to grow cooler and they are standing in the low desert sun singing hymns to the quite unusual accompaniment of a saxophone. Their voices are unpracticed and unsteady. The song fades away and all the more familiar sounds come in: the rumble of the engines, the clank of metal against metal, the vague thud of distant detonations. Regimental prayers are coming to an end and the thin chaplain with the cultured accent raises his hand

and gives them the Lord's blessing. They bow their heads. The man sees that the regimental commander has slipped to the front and he studies him surreptitiously. The commander, as ever, is irreproachably dressed: his buttons and insignia of rank and unit are gleaming, his moustache waxed and his swagger stick under his arm. It looks as if even their commander is bowing his head, but it seems more likely that he is studying his suede desert boots, tied with such precision that equal lengths of lace hang down on each side.

The individual studying his commander so carefully is a dark-haired, twenty-two-year-old lieutenant with an aquiline nose, shy smile and thick glasses. His name is Keith Douglas. He has good reason to look around inquisitively, since he is new to the unit and only arrived a couple of days ago. He is actually on the divisional staff, which is located some twenty-five miles away, but he could no longer tolerate the inactivity, the rigid military bureaucracy, the meaningless deskwork and the shame of not having a combat role, particularly now that a major battle has begun: "The experience of battle is something I must have." So, without permission, he left his post three days ago, dressed in a clean uniform, and commandeered a truck. Now he is here, having more or less bluffed his way into being given command of a troop of two tanks.* Not that it proved too difficult: the regiment had already lost many officers in the lower ranks since it all started nine days earlier. Today is Sunday, November 1.

The colonel in command makes a speech.

> Tomorrow we shall go forward to fight the second phase of the battle of Alamein. The first phase, the dislodgement of the enemy from his position along the whole of his line of battle, is complete. In that phase this Division, this Brigade, did sterling work. The Divisional General and the Brigadier are very pleased.

It's obvious that he is used to speaking. (He is, after all, a member of Parliament, a Conservative.) He then adds personal comments to selected individuals.

So what does Douglas feel about his commander? A contradictory

---

* He hasn't had any training in the Crusader Mark III, the type of tank used by the squadron; at most, he has taken a look at an older model.

mixture of admiration and envy, pride and irritation. The colonel represents what he himself has never had: money, traditions, good family, private schools, cricket, fox-hunting in red coats—above all, the charm and self-confidence that comes from being born into the elite. The colonel's physical courage is renowned.

At the same time, however, the colonel is a representative of everything that is anachronistic, wooden-headed and antiquated in the British army—an important part of why they have lost time after time since 1940, frequently in a heroic and stylish manner, but lost nonetheless. When this unit arrived in the Middle East more or less two years ago, it was still a mounted cavalry regiment and many of the officers of the regiment adhere strictly to those traditions. This manifests itself, for instance, in their scorn for too much technical expertise. This is something that has caused problems for Douglas from his very first day in the Middle East a year ago. He was already a trained tank officer whereas the rest of the unit had scarcely seen a tank, which meant that he was regarded as an unbearable know-it-all right from the start. Not without some cause. Given his ordinary background, he finds it difficult to keep his mouth shut and put up with snobbery and upper-class affectation. He frequently becomes opinionated.

Douglas is a little odd. He writes modernist poetry and more than once he's been caught sketching rather than paying attention during briefings.

The colonel is coming to the end of his speech:

> Now this time, in the second phase, we shall not have quite so much duty work to do; other people ... er ... are to be allowed to look in. General Montgomery is going to divide the enemy's forces up into small pockets. Tonight the New Zealanders will attack and after them will go the Ninth Armoured Brigade and other armoured formations. When General Montgomery is ready we shall move in behind them, to administer the *coup de grâce* to the German armor. That is a great honor and you can take credit to yourselves that it has been granted to this Brigade. When we've destroyed the enemy's armor and routed his forces, we shall then go back to Cairo and ... er ... have a bath, and leave the other buggers to do the chasing for us.

The speech goes down well with the men and the officers. In spite of his skepticism, even Douglas is impressed.

The group of men disperses into the quickly falling twilight. A great deal of work remains to be done if they are to be ready to attack early tomorrow. All the tanks must be filled with gasoline, oil, water, ammunition and food. A sure sign that things really are serious now is that the quartermaster distributes socks, coats and other bits of uniform without demanding they be signed for. It's another clear, starlit night.

The question is whether Douglas is, in a sense, just as anachronistic as his regimental commander, but in a different way. Many of the psychological preconditions of this war were set by what happened earlier and this shows not least in a fear of the beautiful but notorious illusions of the last war. In many ways, this twenty-two-year-old lieutenant resembles the young men of 1914 more than his contemporaries. He wants combat, it's an experience he *must* have, a test he *must* undergo. For him, war is to some degree an aesthetic experience that gains its meaning because of the literary and poetic images. He sees the absurdities of war quite clearly but, given his complex character, he is receptive to its ambiguity in a way that was much more common, perhaps, twenty years before rather than in this more disillusioned age.*

Douglas writes:

> It is exciting and amazing to see thousands of men, very few of whom have much idea why they are fighting, all enduring hardships, living in an unnatural, dangerous, but not wholly terrible world, having to kill and to be killed, and yet at intervals moved by a feeling of comradeship with the men who kill them and whom they kill, because they are enduring and experiencing the same things. It is tremendously illogical—to read about it cannot convey the impression of having walked through the looking glass which touches a man entering a battle.

·   ·   ·

---

* There is an interesting link with the past. Edmund Blunden, author of *Undertones of War,* a poetic and harrowing memoir of the First World War, was Douglas's tutor at Oxford. Blunden encouraged Douglas to write poetry and showed a number of his poems to T. S. Eliot.

That same Sunday in Berlin has been a reasonably warm but showery
autumn day. It's now evening and a party is being held—yet again—on
the fourth floor of Rankestrasse 21. The building is in the neo-romantic
style, with mirror walls and marble caryatids in the entrance hall. It's
close to the city center, just a couple of blocks away from the Zoo-
logical Gardens and the breathtakingly tall Kaiser Wilhelm Memorial
Church. The apartment itself is beautiful: gleaming parquet floors,
heavy furnishings, pictures in gold frames and masses of books. It's full
of people at the moment, fifty or more anyway, and through the cigarette smoke and chiaroscuro lighting you can hear laughter and voices
and happy gramophone music. The dining table in the reception room
has been moved to one side to make space for people to dance. Ursula
von Kardorff loves dancing and she loves parties.

   She is thirty-one years old. Her two brothers are also there—Jürgen,
the younger, and Klaus—wearing their uniforms as army officers. Many
of the other young men at the party are also in uniform, and six of them
are convalescents. One has had an arm amputated at the shoulder, a
second is on crutches, a third can only sit on an inflatable cushion,
even then with difficulty. A fourth man is still recovering from having
large parts of his feet amputated as a result of frostbite: despite that, he
is doing his best to dance. But it's not only the uniforms and crutches
that bring the war to mind: as has become normal now, the hostess—in
this case Ursula—only provides the glasses and it's up to the guests to
bring the refreshments. And there are plenty of bottles. Something else,
too: all the windows are covered with curtains and sheets of paper, as
the blackout starts at 5:30 p.m. and continues until 6:29 a.m.* Should
any of the guests look out, there is very little to see in the thorough
blackout on Rankestrasse apart from the small, swaying pricks of light
made by the pocket torches of occasional pedestrians and the ghostly,
blue-green lights of streetcars clanking past.

   Those carefully covered windows are not only a reminder of what is
going on in Europe and the world; they also reflect an attitude. Ursula
von Kardorff, like many Germans, prefers to keep the war and politics

---

* The rules bear out our preconceived ideas of German thoroughness: on the
night between November 3 and 4, blackout hours are 7:28 p.m. to 6:31 a.m. On
the whole, blackout is adhered to pretty well, though there have been official
complaints this month about the "lack of street discipline" of pedestrians and
cyclists—not all traffic regulations are respected in the darkness.

at arm's length. She shuts out these phenomena and retreats into private life. This is meant to be a happy party, far from the troubles of the world.

But the proper mood just doesn't emerge. She is disappointed to see that many guests don't join in the dancing, retiring instead to one of the other rooms in order to talk. To a great extent it's the young officers who set the tone, a tone that is both disillusioned and critical in a new and more open way. And that is true in general. Just two years ago, after the victories in the west, many of these uniformed young men were still enthusiastic. Like many others in their situation, their faith in the Führer, Germany and the Final Victory had been reinforced by the quick and brutal success. (And we can assume that they were the envy of many of their generation who hadn't been involved and had begun to fear that the war might be over before they'd had their chance.)

One might think that even these young officers, like the majority of their countrymen, had had their confidence shaken by their failure to knock out the Soviet Union quickly in 1941 as Hitler had publicly forecast, but that their faith had been restored at least for the time being by the famous speech he gave in March, in which he promised victory *this* summer instead. Because up until now, the Führer has always been right. But summer is now long past, winter will soon be here, and uncertainty is growing.* Not, of course, among the faithful, since, for them, fantasy is always more powerful than reality.

For civilians like Ursula, however, who are living in a city where bombed-out houses are still a rarity and who can retreat into a private life and private pleasures, things are different than for these young men in uniform. And it's not just their experiences and the alcohol that tempt them to talk critically; they can do so because, to some extent, they are protected by their wounds, their medals and their status as Frontkämpfer, warriors at the front.† She is clearly shaken by their

---

* Detlev Peukert and Ian Kershaw have both shown that what they call the Hitler Myth—which made it possible for many people to be both critical of the Nazi Party and yet trust the Führer—rested above all on the fact that the forecasts he made in his radio speeches came to pass time after time. When things began to go in the opposite direction and Hitler's forecasts turned out to be wrong, the myth began to be weakened. So when Hitler insisted against all military logic that Stalingrad should be taken, it wasn't only to uphold his own personal prestige but also that of his regime. The two things were interlinked.

† One of the highest accolades in the Nazi vocabulary, along with concepts such as willingness to sacrifice oneself, duty to the community, will, purity, fanaticism.

bitterness. Up until now the reverse has been true: returning soldiers have been full of confidence whereas the civilians had their doubts. So what is happening now?

When Hans Schwarz van Berk rings the doorbell the party quickly sinks from merely disappointing to being an utter disaster. He is one of Ursula von Kardorff's old acquaintances and they've known each other since the time she worked for *Der Angriff,* the Nazi newspaper. He is someone she both appreciates and respects. Schwarz van Berk is forty years old and has long been one of Goebbels's people, but is neverthe-less regarded as a competent journalist, despite being a convinced Nazi and member of the Waffen-SS. In one of the rooms an increasingly heated exchange soon breaks out between the SS man and several of the young officers. Someone says, "We are all like rats on a sinking ship, with the difference that we can no longer get off." Schwarz van Berk is shocked and disagrees, yet nevertheless tries to discuss things calmly. But when another guest says to him, "Someone like you does everything he can to suppress the truth," he has had enough. He gets to his feet angrily and heads for the door. Ursula and her big brother, Klaus, rush after him, making excuses and trying to smooth things over. And with some difficulty, they succeed.

Afterwards, however, this woman—normally so self-confident—is a little afraid. "That sort of talk can be dangerous for everyone involved." And she's disappointed. She writes: "The best part of the evening was when I was dancing with each of my two brothers in turn in the empty dining room before our guests arrived."

The following day Schwarz van Berk calls Ursula's mother, Ina. She has long been a convinced and loyal supporter of the regime. He says he is "sickened to hear all that defeatist talk."

.   .   .

No one likes the smell of victory in the morning. This is particularly true when the final victory had been four days earlier and there's been no letup in the tropical heat both night and day.

Japanese troops attacked for three nights and were beaten back each time. There's no way of knowing exactly how many dead Japanese soldiers are lying out there. Someone says there must be a thousand or more. Charles Walker, never called anything but Chuck, is a tall, bespectacled second lieutenant in H Company, 2nd Battalion, 164th Infantry Regiment of the American army. He has heard the number

3,500, but no one can or wants to count them all. In some places there are heaps of them three or four deep, piled up and tangled together. The corpses have begun to swell in the heat, filling their uniforms, changing color and turning black. Their faces are twisted into grotesque masks and swarms of greyish-white maggots crawl out of every bodily orifice. The place has earned its name: Bloody Ridge.

Walker and his battalion have been on Guadalcanal since October 13. For him and for the others, it's a new world, unknown, strange and frightening. The majority of the men in the battalion come from North Dakota, quite a few from Minnesota—there are many Scandinavian names in the muster rolls—and many of them are miners, lumberjacks, cowboys, joiners, mechanics and farmers. They are strong, tall young men. It was snowing on that cold February evening last year when they boarded the train in Fargo, North Dakota, to be transported to a training camp in Louisiana, where they would be turned from National Guard soldiers into a fighting unit. And here they are now in the tropical rain forest on an island in the Pacific. It's as if they are on a different planet.

Their senses have been pretty well overwhelmed by all the new impressions, not least the smells. A rain forest reeks of hot, damp foliage, of motionless, slimy green water, of mold and decay. For the sake of survival, they very quickly learn to hone their senses—sight, hearing and particularly smell—in a new way. For when the night is pitch-black and the cotton grass unusually thick, it is sometimes possible to smell the proximity of Japanese soldiers: their fine, new leather equipment gives off an odd, slightly sweetish odor.* And they have already learned that the body odor of living Japanese soldiers differs from that of Americans. It's not clear whether it's their situation or fear, but after weeks crowded together in narrow trenches many of them find they can pick out the individual smell of their fellow soldiers. That can sometimes mean the difference between life and death.

But all the other smells have disappeared now, blocked out by the thick, sickeningly sweet stench of the fallen. Walker and the rest of them can't put up with it. The clearing of the battlefield has already been started. The bodies must be buried. The corpses of the fallen are particularly numerous in front of the position Walker's company

---

* This phenomenon worked both ways. Their adversaries could smell the proximity of American soldiers from the scent of their excellent cigarettes.

has been holding: this is probably when it gets its nickname—Coffin Corner.

Wave after wave of Japanese attack for three nights in succession,* screaming, shouting, howling, ranting. Carrying simple wooden ladders to surmount the barbed wire, the attackers—bayonets fixed, officers with drawn swords—are determined to break through and capture the new airfield[†] that lies a short way behind the American defenses. That's why they are all here and that's why all this is happening.

The fact that it has ended up being such a slaughter is the result of two factors: the discipline, tenacity and scorn for death that makes the Japanese infantrymen so formidable in defense can make them virtually self-destructive when they are attacking. Irrespective of losses, they continue to come on, carried by courage, arrogance, a desperate bravery—as if they were attempting to use their bodies to prove the idea that spirit trumps matter.[‡] And then there is the fact that their opponents are raw recruits who have never been in battle before—they are National Guardsmen and thus, by definition, amateurs.[§]

The majority of the newly formed units of the American army on their way to Great Britain, North Africa and the Pacific at this time have a similar background: their training has usually been too short and those in command too inexperienced to turn them into professionals rather than amateur soldiers. (They will pay dearly for these things.)

---

* The nights in question were October 24–25, 25–26, and 26–27. Sniping and clashes with small groups of roving Japanese continued over the following days, but the battle as such was decided by then.

[†] In a fairly typical example of the Japanese army's overestimation of its own ability and underestimation of its opponent, the commander had guaranteed the airfield would be taken by October 25. He had even reported it, so several Japanese planes attempted to land there that morning. The pilots quickly learned their mistake.

[‡] This idea of the primacy of will over matter is a fascistic and militaristic notion cherished by all three Axis powers, with ever-diminishing returns.

[§] This is particularly so in comparison with the experienced Marine Corps soldiers who were holding the line immediately to the right of Walker's company. The reason why this battalion of the 164th Infantry Regiment was positioned here (replacing a battalion of Marines) was that American commanders on Guadalcanal judged that the next Japanese attack on the airfield would occur elsewhere and thus concluded this was a "quiet sector" suitable for newcomers. It should be mentioned that Walker's battalion was the very first American army unit to take part in a full battle.

The 164th Infantry Regiment might have been better trained than most, but Walker's previous battalion commander was permanently drunk and he cut back on their weapons training in order to hoard ammunition, which he then used to lay on displays for his superiors. They did, however, have time for a certain amount of jungle training in New Caledonia.

Many of the old officers, who were inexperienced or unsuitable or both, occupied their positions as a result of political contacts. The turnover was considerable in the months before they reached Guadalcanal. The former commander of the regiment had been a banker in civilian life and has been replaced by a professional officer; the drunken battalion commander referred to above has been hastily replaced by one of the company commanders; the earlier company commander was an incompetent and violent bully who was busted after fights and a revolt among his men, and he has been replaced by a new captain. The final weeding out occurred when news came through that they were to be sent to the island: at that point, no fewer than *eleven* officers suddenly discovered they were suffering from a variety of serious ailments and quickly reported themselves sick—among these being both the previous battalion commander and his replacement. Witnessing so much incompetence and cowardice among their officers has had a demoralizing effect.

Walker's battalion is, however, well-equipped. Before leaving for the island, they were provided with twelve more heavy machine guns, two extra mortars and a variety of extra small arms, such as sub-machine guns and pump-action shotguns, particularly suitable for close combat in the jungle. The whole battalion, unlike the Marines holding the ridge to their right, has been equipped with the new M1 semi-automatic rifles.* (Many of the soldiers are already excellent marksmen from their civilian days.) And the position they are sent to take over is well-designed and well-constructed—quite exemplary, in fact, with

---

* They are much desired, particularly by the Marines, who are still armed with Springfield rifles from 1903. It wasn't unknown for them to steal rifles from the ordinary soldiers. The adjoining Marine battalion—immortalized with considerable poetic license in the TV series *The Pacific*, centering on John Basilone, who was awarded the Medal of Honor—actually came close to collapsing under the pressure. The terrain they were defending was more difficult and their field of fire much more limited—no more than about 120 yards. Added to which, they were already weakened by losses and had fewer automatic weapons.

wide barbed-wire entanglements seventy yards out from their firing positions.

So, time after time, the tough Japanese* have hurled themselves at the kind of defense that made attacks virtually impossible in the last war: solid walls of flanking fire. And a storm of automatic and semi-automatic fire of a density never witnessed before, together with hand grenades, light artillery shells and a hail of projectiles from mortars of various calibres, had proved beyond all doubt that matter always trumps spirit, however strong the latter may be—sometimes, perhaps, precisely *because* the spirit is strong.

But it had been a hard battle. In the darkness and confusion, one or two groups of Japanese soldiers had broken through the lines and reached the airfield by following the narrow, rough jeep track immediately behind the defenses. Given their utter exhaustion and the absence of orders about what to do next, they lay down to sleep. When they were found the following morning, some of them were killed while they slept. And every so often stray Japanese soldiers are sighted, hunted down like rabbits and shot without further ceremony.

It's over now, and the only thing left is the stench.

They bury 150 or more bodies in a mass grave the men of Charles Walker's battalion dig in the hard clay in front of Coffin Corner. It's nothing like big enough and more mass graves have to be dug. This particular day, they use explosives to create an enormous crater just east of the first grave. Walker and his fellows soon find the business of collecting the shattered remnants of what had been living beings too nauseating and they hand the task over to the Korean slave laborers the Japanese brought to the island to construct the airfield and left there when the Americans landed.[†]

Well, it's over now. He can tell it is because of the arrival of souvenir hunters from their baggage train and senior officers sightseeing, many of them with cameras.[‡]

---

* They weren't novices, by any means. The division had seen action in China as early as 1931 and then again after 1937. And they had also taken part in the notorious Nanking massacre.

[†] The Koreans had been used for jobs of that kind ever since the Battle of the Tenaru at the end of August.

[‡] It is worth noting that even combat troops were keen to collect souvenirs such as pistols, swords, pennants and wristwatches. The senior officers' cameras caused

.   .   .

RAF Wyton is an air station in Huntingdonshire in eastern England, about twelve miles north of Cambridge. Whenever the airmen get an opportunity they take the bus in to the beautiful university town to live it up and chase girls. Afterwards, happy, seriously intoxicated and possibly even sexually satisfied, they can always find some shady taxi driver to help them out. It's expensive because they are using black-market fuel, but it's worth it. No one says it straight out, but they could all be dead tomorrow. The official expression is *Missing.* The expressions they use themselves when someone is killed or fails to return are a pot-pourri of euphemisms: someone has "got the chop," "bought the farm," "bought it," "hopped the twig," "gone for six," "gone for a Burton."

His name is John Bushby, a twenty-two-year-old machine-gunner in 83 Squadron, RAF Bomber Command. In civilian life he was a typographer but he's been interested in flying ever since he was a child. When he first joined, he was a parachute packer, but he managed—thanks to a considerable degree of stubbornness—to be transferred to combat duties, in his case as gunner on a bomber. He was already fully aware of how dangerous it was. (They all are, and they are all volunteers.) He writes: "It was probably from that moment* that I first assumed the state of mind which protects all fighting men from the prospect of their own death: 'It happens, of course, but never to me.'"

And that's the way it has been so far. Barely ten months ago Bushby flew his first combat mission and, since then, luck has been on his side on a number of occasions. There has been engine trouble, inclement weather, a crash landing, anti-aircraft rounds that explode unpleasantly close or a German night fighter that flashes past with no more than a yard or so to spare. On one occasion, luck itself was literally on his side: he and another gunner tossed a coin to see which of them would go on a particular flight they were both keen on. Bushby lost the toss and the bomber took off without him. The plane was shot down and all its crew killed. (Bushby has kept that coin.) Or there was the time in May when he was sent off on a course and so, to his great frustration, missed the initial "thousand-bomber raids" on Cologne and Essen. When he

---

bad feelings because that was strictly forbidden and the ordinary soldiers had been compelled to hand in their cameras.

* When he made his application to be a machine-gunner on a bomber.

returned to base after the course, he discovered that the bomber he usually flew with had been shot down and all the crew killed.

John Bushby has shrugged that off, as young men do, but also because that's what you are expected to do. It's part of Bomber Command culture, just as much as drinking, joking, indecent songs and casual sex: of all categories of service personnel, bomber crews have far more cases of sexually transmitted infections than the rest.* And you must never boast about medals or question an order or show you are afraid.

So Bushby has carried on flying, outwardly unconcerned, usually worried and often afraid, but without ever showing it or voicing it. His is an existence that, given its complete contrasts, can seem unreal: one evening drunk and noisily happy, the next in utter mortal terror—and then home again, safe at a party or wrapped in someone's naked embrace.

Reality caught up with him a short time ago, when at a briefing in preparation for another raid over Germany, he looked around the room and studied all the faces. He began counting, and then he realized that there were only two left of all the pilots and crewmen in 83 Squadron he'd started his service with in January. One of them was Bill Williams, his pilot, a young man of Bushby's own age, immediately recognizable by his neat, waxed moustache—the other was himself. Bushby writes:

> It had never come home to me as starkly as at that moment, and I had a feeling of near panic, of being trapped, suffocated by something which was closing in around me and which I was powerless to prevent. This couldn't last. I was here, with blood coursing through my veins, my senses working and fibres, muscle and brain intact. I was alive, yet so many were not. It couldn't last. The odds were against it.† Why me? Why

---

* This worried the commander-in-chief of Bomber Command so much that a few months later (January 1943) he introduced a rule that if any member of an aircrew became infected with venereal disease before completing his "tour" of thirty missions, he would have to start over from zero. That was more or less a death sentence at that point. When the Air Ministry got word of this draconian directive, it was immediately rescinded.

† The odds of survival at this particular period were especially appalling. Over the course of the war, 46 percent of Bomber Command crews were killed, but out of every one hundred crewmen who joined Bomber Command during 1941

me when so many others just the same as me had gone out
and not come back?

Did he hesitate to continue? Possibly. Did Bushby continue flying? Yes,
he did. He went so far as to volunteer for fifteen more missions.

It's the start of November now and the weather has been dreadful
for several days. A lot of rain, strong winds and even occasional thunder. So the big four-engine bombers, their undersides painted black,
stand waiting in the three hangars and out along the runway, wet and
gleaming in the rain, like sleeping prehistoric beasts. Maybe Bushby
and the others grab the chance for another celebration in a smoky pub
in one of the small towns close to the airfield, St. Ives or Huntingdon,
or go to a dance hall in Cambridge? Or perhaps they play cards or sleep
in the small wooden hut with seven beds they call their home? After
all, when nothing else works, there is always the oblivion that sleep
brings. Bushby knows that once the weather clears up it will be time
for them to go.

.   .   .

There are many different ways of measuring the seriousness of the situation of the Italian army on the el-Alamein front. One clear indication
is that battlefield tourists no longer appear. Everyone, even the people
back home, know the phenomenon: Fascist Party bosses, major and
minor, tend to be given vague orders to visit the front when there is any
scent of victory. They snoop around in their pristine new uniforms for
a while and then, once journalists have photographed them in heroic
poses and they've been awarded medals to boost their egos and their
careers, they quickly pack their bags and set off home. As if blown by
the wind. That's how bad it is. Paolo Caccia Dominioni snorts.

He is an elegant forty-six-year-old major who, in spite of the fact
that he formally belongs to a paratroop unit in the elite Folgore Division, wears one of those peaked Alpine Jäger hats with a feather in it. He
often smokes a pipe. Ever since the British offensive started on October
23, the 31st Pioneer Battalion and the rest of the Folgore Division have
been under hard pressure in the southern sector. Very hard pressure.

---

and 1942, only about twelve completed their first "tour" of thirty missions; "and
of these twelve, only three would survive thirty more missions."

Like all senior officers on both sides, Caccia Dominioni is a veteran of the 1914–1918 war. He was decorated, as well as being wounded several times on one of the most feared of all the battlefields, the Isonzo front. Here at el-Alamein there is much that reminds him of the last war at its worst: the blocked, immobile situation, the barbed wire, the trenches—all made even more blocked by the hundreds of thousands of mines, millions even, laid by both sides in an elaborate attempt to protect their lines. Once the battle got underway, the rolling fire, the hail of shells, the storm of steel, were all at a level not seen since 1918 and followed by waves of infantry supported by dust-covered steel colossi.

They were dug in along an extended ridge and have defended themselves surprisingly well hitherto. The infantry attacking them was mowed down, once again in a way more reminiscent of the last war than of the present one. In spite of an acute shortage of heavy guns they have even managed to hold back the tanks, mainly with the help of gasoline bombs, flamethrowers, mines and German gunners. But they have paid for it. Losses have been great, even in the 31st Pioneer Battalion. (He remembers three of them, in particular: Rota Rossi, the second lieutenant with the big dog—he died alone, out on an extremely dangerous mission in one of the minefields in no-man's-land; Santino Tuvo, a bearded corporal who despite suffering severe wounds to his throat and stomach still managed to drag a man whose legs had been blown off for three-quarters of a mile; the quartermaster, Carlo Biagioli, who for some inexplicable reason, when they were being attacked from the air yet again, leaped out of his bunker and began shooting at an approaching fighter plane with his sub-machine gun—he was, of course, killed instantly by a hail of bullets, but "upright and proud, with a cigarette clenched defiantly between his lips.")

Well, Caccia Dominioni has seen all this before. This is a battle to exhaustion, a battle of materiel, a battle of attrition. There is no finesse here, no smart moves. It's all about pounding away and seeing who can hold out longest.

At the moment, however, it's quite calm down here in the south. Up to this point, all attacks have been repulsed. What's going to happen next? Maybe they have won. Caccia Dominioni looks from the ridge out over no-man's-land where the wrecks of British tanks glint like gold in the broken beams of the setting sun.

. . .

It's another world: dark, narrow, enclosed, claustrophobic and dominated by two senses: hearing and smell. Smell because the air is thick with the stench of unwashed bodies, sweat and cooking—all mixed with the sticky, fat odor of diesel oil. Hearing because, once underwater, a U-boat is blind in every way, and just as hearing seeks to compensate for the absence of sight in human beings, every sound coming from outside down here becomes meaningful, something to be interpreted, whether in fear or hope. All of them stay quiet, perk up their ears, listen, move around cautiously.

The hydrophone operator in his little cubby-hole reports that he can hear the dull, slowly fading whirr of the propellers of a cargo ship, mixed with increasing, higher-pitched propeller sounds. That can only mean one thing: their potential prey is disappearing and a destroyer is approaching. The operator reports this to the commander of the U-boat, Captain Lieutenant Horst Höltring, but he uses the word "vessel" rather than "destroyer," that being the euphemism the two of them use in order not to worry the crew unnecessarily: the approach of a destroyer is always bad news.

It is Sunday, November 1. Somewhere out in the Atlantic between the coast of Portugal and the Azores, U-604 has been underwater since 8:23 a.m. It was forced to submerge because of yet another aircraft alert. Increasing numbers of Allied planes are being sighted as the convoy U-604 is attacking steams north along the coast of Africa.

For five days now U-604 and seven other U-boats have been continuously circling the convoy, like wolves around a flock of sheep. (That's also the metaphor the U-boat crews themselves like to use, loaded as it is with the pseudo-Darwinian imagery Nazism is fond of: in nature the strong rule and the weak go under, and they *should* go under. To attack as a group is known as the Wolfrudeltaktik, the "wolf pack tactic," and German newspapers have christened their U-boat crews *graue Wölfe*, "grey wolves of the sea.")* U-604 alone has recently sent three of this convoy's ships to the bottom. The first was a tanker, torpedoed

* When it forms, each "wolf pack" is given a unique temporary code name: this one has been named *Streitaxt*, "battleaxe." The name of the convoy is SL125, which refers to the fact that it's on its way from its gathering point in Sierra

southwest of the Canary Islands on October 27, followed—in heavy weather three days later—by a large troopship and a small steamship. It's impossible for them to know how many of those on board these ships were killed* and it's doubtful whether they even think about it. Without suffering losses themselves, they have sunk twelve of the thirty-seven ships in the convoy, but now they have received orders from BdU† to discontinue the attacks.

That slightly higher-pitched propeller sound falls silent. Höltring orders his U-boat up to periscope depth: a destroyer is lying roughly a thousand yards away. Immediately after that, they all hear the weak, pinging sound of the enemy vessel's sonar—now, as the cliché has it, the hunter has become the hunted. Then it happens. The sonic waves encounter the hull of the U-boat and the pinging sound becomes a slightly lower and more toneless bing. They have been located. Höltring gives the order to dive.

Commands and procedures are well-practiced. The bow planes are set to fast dive, the stern planes to zero; the vents are opened; water pours into the ballast tanks; the nose of the boat is pulled more and more steeply downwards; everyone hangs on so as not to lose footing because of the steep diving angle; they are on their way "down to the cellar," as U-boat slang puts it. Meanwhile, the sonar pings and bings of the destroyer are repeated at ever shorter intervals—the destroyer is coming straight for them.

The U-boat commander, Horst Höltring, has been in the U-boat service for no more than two years and is not one of those famous and much acclaimed "U-boat aces" who feature so often in newsreels. But he is competent and popular with his crew because he doesn't take unnecessary risks, unlike many young U-boat commanders who are eager to win fame and the coveted Knight's Cross. Höltring is, however,

---

Leone to Liverpool. It was carrying a mixed cargo, including iron ore and frozen meat, from South America, India and Africa.

* The whole crew of the tanker *Anglo Maersk* survived, and the same is true of the small steamer *Baron Vernon*. *Président Doumer*, the troopship, had a crew and passengers numbering 345 people, of whom 260 died, the fifty-one-year-old captain among them.

† BdU—Befehlshaber der U-Boote—that is, Admiral Karl Dönitz himself and his small staff located in a large house in Lorient. The primary reason was the huge increase in numbers of Allied planes. Also, by this point many U-boats were damaged or limited by a shortage of fuel and torpedoes.

restless and he drinks too much—which hints at strong inner tension. A
personal quirk of his is the habit of always wearing a weapon, which is
unusual. The story circulates among the crew that one time, in a state
of intoxication, Höltring managed to shoot himself in the foot.

But if Höltring is quite popular in spite of everything, another of
the officers is positively loathed. His name is Hermann von Bothmer,
a former SS man with a doctorate from the University of Berlin and
a talented amateur flautist. The fact that von Bothmer is a convinced
Nazi is not a problem: the majority of U-boat crewmen of whatever
rank are volunteers, loyal to the regime and besotted by the concept of
war as the highest good. No, it's his pedantic and bullying streak that
gets to them. In the smelly interior of a U-boat, where it's so tight that
few men can actually walk upright and where they are all living cheek
by jowl, a quasi-democratic community develops that, if it is to function, needs goodwill and indulgence. (Dress is some kind of reflection
of this: few of them wear strict uniforms. Naval issue is mixed and
supplemented by civilian clothing, and visible badges of rank are rarely
seen.) In an environment of this kind, constant admonishment about
trivial issues has a corrosive effect.

At a depth of about 300 feet the order is given to blow the ballast
tanks. The familiar roar of compressed air temporarily drowns out all
other sounds. The vessel is balanced in zero trim. The command is
now Slow Ahead. It's a case of saving battery power. Above them, the
destroyer makes a first pass and drops depth charges.

Photographs of similar occasions reveal how most crew members
instinctively look upwards when this happens. As if there was something
to see. Then they hear and feel one, two, three, four … seven explosions.
Sound being carried better by water than by air, the noise is deafening.
Depth, 425 feet. Höltring gives the command for more twists and turns.
The U-boat turns and moves carefully upwards. Then the destroyer
makes another run. More depth charges. The seconds stretch out and
become painfully long. Depth, 360 feet. One, two, three … seven more
explosions. The noise is even louder, the pressure harder. The electric
bulbs shatter. Lights flash on and off. Silence. Darkness. Everyone's on
the alert, everyone's listening.

The U-boat moves on slowly through the water. Another destroyer
moves in. More depth charges.

Four hours later, U-604 surfaces, still in one piece apart from a damaged bilge pump and some minor damage to the air ventilators. The

destroyers have departed. There is an enormous sense of relief among the men on board when the hatch in the conning tower is opened and a powerful current of fresh air rushes in. They have survived their first depth charge attack.

.   .   .

When Warner Bros. started work on the film at the beginning of the year, there had been nothing out of the ordinary about it, whether in terms of expectation, budget or approach. The intention was just to produce another B movie, a story with romance and excitement as the main ingredient, the war as the backdrop, and B actors taking the main roles. Since April the American film industry has released twenty-eight films about spies, saboteurs and traitors, and a further nineteen are on the way. Hollywood has taken to the war with a vengeance—this despite the sudden and unexpectedly successful moves to put the U.S. economy onto a war footing. That has entailed many limitations, both great and small, significant and less significant.

So, for instance, the rationing of gasoline and rubber has meant that the stars and the directors are no longer driven to the shoots in limousines, but have to be prepared to travel in a bus along with the other studio operatives. And clothes rationing means that the costume department has to cut down on expensive fabrics: this film is the first in which all the characters, with no exceptions, wear cotton clothing. The footage of film used per production has been reduced by 25 percent and the authorities insist that the maximum cost of individual film sets be limited to $5,000. Doing any filming outdoors has become more difficult: one example is that there are now anti-aircraft batteries on the dry hills around the town where for years dozens of cowboys used to gallop in front of the cameras, so with the exception of one scene, the whole film has to be shot in the studio.* Another problem was that immediately after shooting started in May, a curfew was introduced forcing foreign citizens from enemy countries such as Germany to remain indoors between eight in the evening and six in the morning: what makes this particularly difficult is that the majority of the actors

---

* On several occasions, reports of unidentified planes led to a complete blackout in Los Angeles. This happened, for instance, on the night of May 25, the first day of filming. That shows how tense the mood was.

in the film are immigrants from Europe, quite a few of them refugees from Hitler and the war.*

The biggest restriction, however, is that the film, like all the other films, has to be approved by the newly established censorship office, the Bureau of Motion Pictures, which in turn is directly under the Office of War Information, the powerful and newly established propaganda office. Before any film is made, those responsible for it will be asked seven questions, the first of which is "Will this picture help win the war?" and the second question is "What war information problem does it seem to clarify, dramatize or interpret?" The films are then sorted into six categories considered to be helpful in various ways for public information or the conduct of the war. The said bureau classified this film as belonging to Category IIIB—that is to say, it deals with Allied nations and B means they are occupied nations; there is also the subordinate theme II C3 ("Enemy—Military").

The film is now ready and was shown to four inspectors just a week ago. They gave it their approval—with some enthusiasm. Among other things, they wrote in their report that the film emphasized that "personal desires must be subordinated to the task of defeating fascism," and that it "graphically illustrated the chaos and misery which fascism and the war has brought." The fact that it portrayed the U.S. as "the haven of the oppressed and the homeless" was especially worthy of praise. They also approved of the American male protagonist in the film being presented as a man who had even been an opponent of fascism before 1939, which demonstrates to the public "that our war did not commence with Pearl Harbor, but that the roots of aggression reach far back."

No problems. It gets the green light. The film can be given a premiere. And according to plan, that is to happen in two months. It's

---

* Only three of the fourteen actors whose names appear in the opening and closing credits were born in the U.S., and almost all the small parts were played by people who were immigrants and refugees from Europe. The film's director was a Hungarian, Manó Kaminer, who had changed his name to Michael Curtiz, but his extremely idiosyncratic English gave away his origin. Kaminer/Curtiz, who was undoubtedly talented, had a personal style that was virtually a parody of a Hollywood director: he wore riding breeches and boots, swore and yelled and took every possible opportunity to coerce the women who worked for him into sex.

almost exactly a year since Warner Bros. bought the rights to the stage play the film is based on—*Everybody Comes to Rick's*. Hal Wallis, the producer of the film, has, however, changed its name to the shorter and hopefully more marketable title *Casablanca*.

．　　．　　．

First comes an ordinary dirt road running through an open landscape of fences and grey, unpainted wooden houses. The road is not that wide, but it's quite usable by motor vehicles of various kinds. Then comes a section of corduroy road, logs laid transversely above swampy ground, followed by a narrow, muddy forest road, which winds its way through a dense woodland of deciduous saplings until, on a wooded slope on the left, you see the first bunkers—that's where company supplies are kept.

The terrain is now low and quite open, big areas of boggy ground and bare birch thickets that rustle in the cold wind. The forest road becomes narrower and narrower as it swings in a wide arc by some low mounds, past the company command bunker, where it turns into little more than a path and splits. The right-hand fork disappears down into a trench system that leads up to a hillock to where, among thickets and scattered pines above a boggy river, the base, the Black Grouse, is located. It is manned by half of the 1st Platoon, thirty-five men in all, part of the 9th Rifle Company, 3rd Battalion, 61st Infantry Regiment. It is the beginning of November—early winter in East Karelia.

The soldiers don't use the word "front." That's an expression for journalists and the people back home. As a concept the "front" is semantically vague. "The front is a society, many miles deep. And there is a home front in many zones. The company calls the battalion the home front, the battalion calls the regiment the home front, the regiment calls the division the home front—one by one until you eventually get to Helsingfors. But there is one word that carries all the harshness of war, and that word is the *line*."* And this is the Line.

One of the young men in the half-platoon is named Kurt West and he has been living on this patch of ground for a month and a half. The place doesn't have a name apart from Orren (Black Grouse); to the east of it lies Ugglan (Owl); to the west Järpen (Hazel Grouse),

* Gunnar Johansson, Finland Swedish lieutenant and war reporter, killed on the Svir River, May 15, 1942.

Dammen (Pond), Slussen (Lock), Tröskeln (Threshold) and so on. The names refer to strongpoints, laid out like a string of pearls with a hundred yards or so between each, usually within sight of the Svir, the forest-lined river which gave its name to the front. Nothing has moved there for about a year, not since the autumn of last year.

What happens here seldom gives rise to more than a brief notice in the newspapers, if that. The young men often feel they have been forgotten. Tens of thousands of Finnish soldiers live a virtually anonymous existence out here in the wilds, far from the apparently unconcerned life still continuing back at home: shop windows, trams, cinemas, farces at the theatre, dancing the tango at dance restaurants, cafés open in the evening, swing clubs, debates, concerts, handball tournaments—back where people still find time to worry about whether stockfish, a special type of conserved white fish, will still be available at Christmas.

The Finnish troops have every reason to feel forgotten. They are rarely given leave. It has been so long since they received fresh clothes that their grey army uniforms are filthy, torn and patched, which is why they wear more and more civilian clothing, which gives a non-military impression. Food is monotonous—usually gruel, made of whatever happens to be available. (West has already discovered that, in some strange way, all the more palatable food remains back in rear areas and soldiers in the front line always get the worst food.) As if that weren't enough, the regiment has been given a new commanding officer, a Finnish-speaking lieutenant colonel by the name of Marttinen, with a reputation for being both demanding and hard.

The fact that the new commanding officer is a Finn has boosted their silent resentment, for the 61st Infantry Regiment comes from the Swedish-speaking western parts of Finland, its working language is Swedish, all the paperwork is done in Swedish, and Swedish is the language spoken in the trenches and bunkers. West himself is a nineteen-year-old farmer's son from Esse, in Österbotten, and, like the rest of his regiment, a Finland Swede. Discipline is fairly informal, as is the way of addressing officers. Saluting is often not bothered with.

. . .

Mandalay, on the east bank of the Irrawaddy River, had once been the royal capital of Burma. Before the war it had settled into romantic decay, but the war has turned decay into devastation. Before marching into the city in May 1942, the Japanese bombed the defenseless city. About two thousand civilians were killed and three-fifths of the buildings burned down. Parts of the city are now deserted and full of ruins. That is where Mun Okchu is. Not that she gets to see very much of what is left of the magnificent places with their spires, picturesque cloisters, Buddhist belfries and crenelated defensive walls. She and seventeen other young Korean women are effectively prisoners, isolated in a dilapidated, two-story house in the outskirts of the city and kept out of contact with the general population. As though they were infectious. The establishment has a name that is both informal and euphemistic: the Taegu Inn.

On the ground floor of the house there is a large bathroom and the office where the two managers, the Korean couple Mr. and Mrs. Matsumoto, live and work. (Their real name is Song, but like many people who work for the Japanese, they have adopted a Japanese name.) Mr. Matsumoto frequently wears Western clothes—a suit and tie and, weather permitting, smart leather shoes. Mun and the other young women eat on the ground floor. The food prepared by a Burmese woman is pretty monotonous. No *ngapi, mohinga, nan gyithoke* or local dishes of that kind; it is mainly rice or soup, sometimes with meat but usually with wild vegetables gathered in the surrounding countryside. The man in charge of the communal food supplies is a certain Mr. Hondamineo and since being in China Mun has learned that someone in that position can be your savior in an emergency, so she makes sure she keeps on his good side.

A wooden staircase leads to the upper floor, where there is a hall and eighteen booths. The walls between the booths consist of hanging fibre mats that do not reach all the way to the ceiling. The doors are no more than cloth curtains and the booths are so small that they don't have room for much more than a bucket, a basket and a mattress. There's also a bottle of something pink that has the strange, slightly pungent smell of a mixture of disinfectant and ... something else.

By breakfast time, Mun Okchu and the other girls can see that a queue of expectant soldiers has already begun to form outside the house. Once the young women have finished eating, they go upstairs to their booths and at about nine o'clock the doors are opened to allow the uniformed men in. A man enters Mun Okchu's booth and gives her a brown card marked with a number. She checks that he is wearing a condom and then she lies down on the mattress and spreads her legs. She is eighteen years old.

. . .

They are deep in virgin forest and this is where they will spend the winter. They only came here a couple of weeks ago: where they were before had become too dangerous, too close to German garrisons. This new place is southwest of Antunovo in central White Russia and the "they" is a large group of partisans.

One of them is Nikolai Obrynba, a Ukrainian, formerly an art student, before that a state artist in Moscow, before that a soldier in the Red Army, before that a prisoner of war, and now a guerrilla fighter and medical orderly in what is known as the Dubrovsky Brigade—a rather grandiose name for a band only a couple of hundred strong. The majority of them are men but there are also quite a few women of various ages. Obrynba, at twenty-nine, is one of the older ones there and some of them are as young as thirteen or fourteen. Most of them are dressed in a shoddy mixture of civilian and military clothes, and not all of them have weapons.

Appearances can be deceptive, however. The group is stronger than ever and its organization is becoming ever more sophisticated. (In the course of one year, the number of active partisans in White Russia has increased from about 7,000 to about 47,000.) It has a small general staff; a section that deals with the gathering of information; a group responsible for spreading propaganda; another group for dealing with the underground young communist committees in the region. They are in direct radio contact with the central partisan staff in Moscow, and that, in turn, is under the direct command of Stavka, the headquarters of the Soviet military.

What is growing up here in the virgin forests of White Russia does not bear any resemblance to the well-camouflaged underground bunker where the sadly decimated remnant of the original partisan group hid last winter. This looks more like a village. Along the sandy road that runs through the camp, rows of earth-walled cottages—many of them with windows—are going up for people to live and sleep in. And there are specialist buildings too. They already have a smithy, a bakery and a dining room with kitchen. They are working on a cottage hospital, an armory and a sauna. An electricity generator has been installed, and the intention is to erect an arch in the middle of the camp and decorate it with an improvised Soviet banner. (Obrynba has already painted the banner on an old bedsheet.) The sounds of axes and hammers ring through the air and the smell of smoke hangs between the trees.

Obrynba is in a good mood. A good two months have passed since he escaped from the German prisoner-of-war camp and nothing can be as awful as life was there. Admittedly, the guerrilla operations he has taken part in have been pretty clumsy affairs, but losses were small and the autumn has been quite warm and fairly dry. (Important when you are living and sleeping in the open air most of the time.) He writes: "I was beginning to have the joyful conviction that we could get back everything the war had robbed us of."

The longing for what they have lost shows itself in many ways. Obrynba writes:

> Partisans often displayed a craving for pre-war things, mundane things—anything that reminded them of a time unburdened by war and many of their deeds, which may seem naïve and funny, become understandable when we remember. For example, when I photographed the female Partisans of our women's platoon, they would wear their carefully preserved blouses and skirts, instead of a fighter's uniform with firearms.

The earth-walled cottage he shares with three companions is well-equipped. There are two beds made of planks—they sleep in these in pairs. There is a small table with an electric lamp by the window to the right of the door. He often sits there working: drawing, painting posters, forging documents. Over to the left there is a small iron stove and an arrangement of shelves that goes right up to the low ceiling. That's where he stores his equipment: weapons, underclothes, paper, tubes of paint and his camera.

Obrynba has also acquired a dog, an Alsatian. It used to belong to a man whom the Germans chose to be village elder in a village not far away. They snatched him one night in September and after interrogating him, they killed him. We don't know how justified that was, and it seems that Obrynba didn't know either. Anyway, the Alsatian accompanied them from there and it sleeps in the cottage with him at night. He has named it Tass.

· · ·

Savannah, Georgia, is one of the harbors on the American East Coast that had to close for a while last spring because of the number of vessels sunk by German U-boats. Many of the wrecks were visible from the shore. Since then the city and its surroundings have had a blackout. That is now being questioned on grounds that whereas residential areas are carefully blacked out at night, the new shipyard a short distance downstream from the city is brightly lit by floodlights and by a twinkling galaxy of blue lights from hundreds of welding torches: work in the shipyard continues day and night, three shifts a day, seven days a week, week in, week out.

Only eighteen months ago there was nothing here but scrubby, low-lying and in places boggy riverbank, and now it's a shipyard with ten thousand workers, clusters of big and small buildings, gigantic cranes and miles of railroad tracks. As in a host of other wartime industries in the U.S., this enormous complex shot up in an amazingly short time and has been producing in ever-increasing quantities. Here, the Southeastern Shipbuilding Corporation is building transport vessels, a category that might come over as grey and lacking glamor, but one which is to be of utterly decisive significance.

Most of the people at the shipyard are well aware of what is at stake. The oil spills, bits of wreckage and bloated bodies that are still being washed up along the Savannah shoreline from the ships sunk last spring make that quite clear. It's all about one simple calculation—the magic word "tonnage." So far this year German U-boats have sunk many more transport vessels than the British and the Americans have been able to replace, and if this continues next year Great Britain will suffer a famine and the war will be lost. But if the equation can be reversed and more transport ships are built than the Germans are able to sink, then everything becomes possible.

To put it mildly, the chances of this occurring have not seemed auspicious. It can take up to a year to build an ordinary transport ship, which can then be sunk in a few minutes. But what they are building at Savannah and a string of other shipyards are not ordinary transport ships: the construction and design has been simplified in order to produce the greatest possible number of ships in the shortest possible time at the lowest possible cost.

Liberty ships, as they are called, consist mainly of large modules manufactured elsewhere and then put together at the shipyard here, as if the whole thing was a gigantic kit.* A further innovation is that the vessel is welded together without rivets—using rivets would be more secure but is also more complicated. Welding is not only faster, it's also a skill that is simpler to teach and less demanding in terms of physical strength, which means that accessing new workers becomes easier. Many of the welders are women, an innovation that was previously unheard of and, to some people anyway, shocking.

On Slipway No. 2 lies what is to be the first Liberty ship launched by the Southeastern Shipbuilding Corporation. She will be ready for launch in less than three weeks. Her keel was laid on May 22, a day when the newspapers were reporting further Japanese advances in China and the Philippines, renewed hard fighting on the Eastern Front, the execution by firing squad of fifteen Norwegians planning to flee to Great Britain, and dissatisfaction on the part of the American military authorities with the blackout in and around New York.

The ship will be ready a full month before the projected date, which is both astonishingly fast by the normal timescale of the pre-war shipbuilding industry and also almost two months faster than when the first vessel of this type was built. Things will get even faster and, in extreme cases, building time from laying the keel to launch will be slashed to forty-two days.

The shipyard workers on the banks of the wide, muddy-green Savannah River have weather on their side. Down here in Georgia the start of November has been dry and warm, the temperature rising on some days to the high sixties and above.

. . .

The reason why Kurt West and his companions find themselves here on the Svir River in this nothingness of bog and waterlogged mosses between Lakes Ladoga and Onega is to a considerable extent the result of the idea of a Greater Finland which nationalistically inclined Finns had been dreaming of for many years. There had seemed a chance of it becoming reality when, the summer before, Finland entered the war

---

* As Tony Cope, author of the excellent *On the Swing Shift*, points out, a shipyard like this was actually "an assembly plant, where, for the most part, hastily trained workers following very simple instructions and doing the same job over and over pieced together more than 30,000 parts of a Liberty ship, that were brought in on freight cars from 500 plants in 32 states."

on the side of Germany.* It was as natural for Finland Swedes as for Finns to defend the country when the Soviet Union invaded in 1939, and similarly natural for them to take advantage of the new situation in 1941 to try to regain the parts of Finland that Stalin seized in 1940. As to the notion of a Greater Finland, its glow has dimmed among Finland Swedes, and there is no enthusiasm for the attempts to Fennicise the country, the people and the geography that is going on in East Karelia.† Very few road signs with invented Finnish names for old Russian places are being erected in the 61st Infantry Regiment's district.

Kurt West's current home is Garrison Bunker No. 2 up at Orren. His bed is made of rough planks and located over in the far left corner. He has slowly begun to get to know the others. All of them are Finland Swedes, most of them—like the red-haired man in charge of his half-platoon—a little older than him. The other half-platoon is made up entirely of farmers' sons, steady and reliable, but the men crowded in with West in his dark and earth-smelling bunker are a more mixed bunch—many farm boys, of course, but also a couple of workers and some young academics. Hans Finne, who is to become his closest friend, has broken off his studies of jurisprudence; he "is a master of the art of discussion and complicating things" and frequently gets into arguments with the officers. Their platoon commander, the much-admired Lieutenant Kurtén, also has his plans for the future and spends a lot of time with his books. Their days slip past quietly. There is no fighting going on, though there may be a small explosion now and then. The ground is covered with a fine layer of snow.

---

* The notion of a Greater Finland promoted by certain Finnish nationalists during the early twentieth century was not the usual irredentism in that they talked of including areas that had never counted as part of Finland, neither when Finland had been the eastern part of Sweden nor when it had been a Russian grand duchy. Nor did the Finnish speakers who lived in East Karelia show any great enthusiasm for the idea. For the sake of fairness, it should be pointed out that many of those in government in Helsingfors viewed the occupation of this region as defensible since it could be used as a valuable pawn should there be any negotiations. It is, however, quite reasonable to assume that these regions would have remained in Finnish hands if Germany had won the war.

† It's hardly surprising that the Greater Finland ideas did not appeal to Finland Swedes, since they themselves were victims of a certain amount of pressure from Finnish extremists to use the Finnish language. Over the last year that pressure had, in some cases, come close to harassment.

·   ·   ·

In the darkness of dawn on Monday, November 2, they are driving
into a thunderous void. The only way Keith Douglas can speak to
his two crewmen is by using the internal radio, but the voices in the
headphones sound blaring, metallic and with no sense of closeness, so
he can neither comfort nor calm them. It's even worse with the voices
from the other tanks: they sound thin and wavering, interrupted by
whines, whistles, fragments of Morse code and the strange, organ-like
roar of the enemy radio jammer.

The sense of isolation eases a little—just a little—when it grows
light enough to see and when the dust and smoke of the bombardment
settles slightly. Keith Douglas writes:

> The view from a moving tank is like that in a camera obscura
> or a silent film—in that since the engine drowns all other
> noises except explosions, the whole world moves silently. Men
> shout, vehicles move, aeroplanes fly over, and all soundlessly:
> the noise of the tank being continuous, perhaps for hours on
> end, the effect is of silence. It is the same in an aircraft, but
> unless you are flying low, distance does away with the effect
> of a soundless pageant. I think it may have been the fact that
> for so much of the time I saw it without hearing it, which led
> me to feel that country into which we were now moving as an
> illimitably strange land, quite unrelated to real life, like the
> scenes in *The Cabinet of Doctor Caligari.*

His unit is part of the second wave. The farther forward they go,
the more remains of the first wave they see: scattered materiel, drifting
oily smoke, burning tanks. These were supposed to have driven a hole
through the enemy lines, but they have made a dent at most.

There are bodies everywhere. Some of them shredded, blackened,
covered in flies; others apparently untouched, as if they were just sleeping. From the calls and information over the radio, Douglas understands that the armored brigade that preceded them was more or less
massacred. And now it's their turn.

His unit swings into line, heading north, and begins to exchange
shots through the dust with angular shapes in the distance. He observes
that his new gunner is not a good shot but then, with a shot that appears

to be pure luck, he hits his target. Then plumes of oily black smoke pour from several of the enemy tanks and the remainder trundle off into the haze. Douglas's unit continues to move on westwards. Some-where over there is the target of the attack, a desert road and a small cluster of buildings: Tel el Aqqaqir.

In the heat, Douglas leans out of the turret and looks down into the defense trenches as they sway past them. There might still be enemy infantry in them, but suddenly he finds himself staring down into the face of a hunched New Zealander:

> His expression of agony seemed so acute and urgent, his stare so wild and despairing, that for a moment I thought him alive. He was like a cleverly posed waxwork, for his position sug-gested a paroxysm, an orgasm of pain. He seemed to move and writhe. But he was stiff. The dust which powdered his face like an actor's lay on his wide open eyes, whose stare held my gaze like the Ancient Mariner's.* He had tried to cover his wounds with towels against the flies. His haversack lay open, from which he had taken towels and dressings. His water-bottle lay tilted with the cork out. Towels and haversack were dark with dried blood, darker still with a great concourse of flies. This picture, as they say, told a story. It filled me with useless pity.

His pity quickly finds a subject that is alive. In a nearby pit he sees a badly wounded second lieutenant, weak and close to giving up. Douglas radios his regimental commander and asks—obviously too long-windedly—for permission to take the wounded man back to a dressing station. He is cut off with a brusque reply: "Yes, yes, yes, yes, yes. But for Christ's sake *get off the air*. I'm trying to fight a battle. Off."

The air above the desert sand is shimmering with the heat.

Several hours later the whole unit moves back to refuel and take on ammunition. They are being targeted by heavy artillery fire. Douglas and the others gather in the lee of the squadron commander's tank, instinctively ducking whenever another shell whistles down. Whoever was speaking last would fall silent in the middle of a sentence, wait for the explosion and then immediately start speaking again.

---

* In Samuel Coleridge's poem, where the old seaman's gaze makes the wedding guest stop and listen to his story.

Only long afterwards does Douglas understand that what he was involved in that day was the climax of the battle—what the history books will refer to as the decisive point.

.   .   .

In Leningrad the white nights of summer are long past, as are the golden evenings of early autumn with their high, clear skies. Autumn storms have blown the leaves from the trees in the parks and darkness has returned.

Lidiya Ginzburg realizes they are facing siege winter number two. (No one has even dared think of such a thing before.) This is a depressing recognition for all those like her who survived that indescribable first siege winter. The cold subtracts from all the pleasures, adds to all the pains and multiplies all the difficulties; it becomes an element in its own right, something to exist in and move sluggishly through. Ginzburg is a forty-year-old Jew, born in Odessa, but resident in Leningrad for the last twenty years and working at the university.

But "working" is perhaps not the most accurate word here. The special and uniquely brilliant school of literary studies she once subscribed to and worked within—they were known as the formalists—has been condemned for over ten years now by the Stalinist state and its cohorts of intellectual henchmen: those who haven't retracted or disappeared into the Gulag have, like Ginzburg, fallen silent and are only working in the technical sense of the word. She, who had written earlier about great figures like Pushkin, Tolstoy and Proust, now finds the main outlet for her intellect in private notes that focus on her surroundings and on the city she loves, which has literally been fighting for its existence since the beginning of September last year. Literally. How many people have lost their lives in Leningrad so far? No one knows exactly. As many as a million, perhaps.

Even though the mood in Leningrad is low, it is nothing like the quiet desperation there had been just six months earlier. People had begun to prepare for this winter in a material and in a psychological sense. It surely can't be as bad as last year. Last winter, when things were at their worst, about 100,000 people a month were dying.* What is usually thought of as civilized life came close to breaking down; nothing

---

* The siege was genocide in disguise. Hitler was not interested in taking the city: the primary aim of the operation was to starve the population to death.

functioned any longer; some people murdered for food—to steal ration cards or, in the worst cases, to eat their victims; streets were blocked with ice and garbage; people lay dead and dying on the pavements and passers-by gave them no more than a glance, if that.

Now, however, a kind of normality has arisen in the midst of abnormality. Seven tram lines are running normally and are always crowded; theatres, cinemas, concert halls, public baths and libraries are open; there is electricity for at least part of the day; street traders are back on Bolshoi Prospect and shoe shiners and *kvass* sellers hang around on the street corners; you can get your hair permed at ladies' hairdressers and some women, craving normality, have started to wear makeup again. For all that, Leningrad is still astonishingly quiet for a major city.

Many things have become everyday experiences. Bombing raids and artillery bombardment, for instance. Ginzburg writes:

> In besieged Leningrad we saw everything—but fear least of all. People heard the whistle of shells over their head with indifference. Waiting for a shell you know is coming is considerably harder; but everyone knew that if you heard it, it wasn't going to land on you this time.
>
> The quantification of degrees of jeopardy, or more precisely, the probability of death (the degree of probability) is of decisive psychological importance. Between certain death and almost certain death there is fixed an unbridgeable gulf. In Leningrad the peril was an everyday matter, systematic, and systematically designed to wear out the nerves, but statistically it wasn't very great. Everyday experience showed that the danger from bombing and shelling paled before the enormous toll of death by malnutrition.... In Leningrad there were few who were afraid of bombing—just those with some special physiological predisposition to fear. It soon became impossible to run anywhere. Therefore nobody fled and nobody thought: Why am I staying when everybody's leaving? Composure marked the universal and average behavior, noncompliance with which was harder and more terrible than the actual dangers.... Death can be successfully suppressed for

---

This is why the term "siege" is actually inaccurate—the Russians refer to it more accurately as the "blockade."

the very reason that it is not susceptible to experience. It's an abstraction of nonexistence or the emotion of fear. In the first case it belongs to the category of unimaginable imaginings (like eternity, endlessness).

In the evening of November 2 the air-raid siren goes off yet again. The all-clear sounds at a quarter to midnight. The siege has been going on for 429 days.

· · ·

This is the end of the world. This is the place where our ability to understand fails us. For all those sent here, with the possible exception of a handful, this is not only the point where physical existence ceases, it's also the point at which words and ideas end—where they disappear into something which is utterly unknowable. And its unknowableness is part of the prerequisite for what is happening.

On this Monday, November 2, a train of cattle cars arrives at Treblinka. It contains 4,330 Jews from Siemiatycze, a small town in eastern Poland. They are all murdered before nightfall, apart from a very small number spared to replenish the ever-diminishing gang of workers in the camp Sonderkommando.

One of the people there that day and involved in dealing with the bodies of the Jews from Siemiatycze is Jechiel Rajchman, a twenty-eight-year-old Jew from Ostrów Lubelski, another shtetl in eastern Poland, a small town with a predominantly Jewish population. But Ostrów Lubelski no longer has any Jews: the great majority of them were sent to this place on October 10, just three weeks ago. Among them was Rajchman (usually called Chil) and his nineteen-year-old sister, Rivka; also there was his good friend Wolf Ber Royzman with his wife and two children. Almost all of the roughly 140 people driven brutally into the cattle cars were people he knew, familiar faces from Ostrów Lubelski. And all of them were murdered in just a few hours—all of them with the exception of a number of strong young men, picked out from the mass of naked people. He was one of them.

Rajchman is a quick thinker. When the train disappeared down a siding that ran for a mile or so through scrubby pinewoods before halting at a small station, he became suspicious. (He saw those heaps of clothes. Perhaps he noticed that the clock on the wall of the small station was merely painted on with its hands pointing to an eternal 6:00 a.m. As if this was a place where even time stopped.) So when, after disembarking and undressing, he heard a screaming German voice ask whether any of them were barbers, he immediately claimed he was, even though he was not. He was ordered to get dressed again.

Rajchman then spent three days cutting off women's hair—naked women who had removed their clothes at the far end of the barrack building. In his account of his miraculous escape to the ruins of Warsaw, where he was waiting for the arrival of the Red Army, he wrote: "The murderers are well-mannered in that they do not demand the women to undress outdoors along with the men." Like the other "barbers," Rajchman wore a white coat. The haircuts were rough and ready, mechanical, just four or five passes, after which the hair was pressed down in sacks and the woman pushed out to be replaced by another, who in turn was clipped and pushed out. And so on *ad nauseam.* Quickly they all disappear out through the door, *schnell, schnell, tempo,* between rows of black-uniformed men with whips, towards an opening in a high barbed-wire fence disguised with cuttings of spruce trees. There they queued naked. The opening is the start of what the Germans call Der Schlauch—the hosepipe.

Behind the fence is a wide embankment of sand, and behind the embankment lies the upper camp—a camp within a camp. It's not possible to see in, but at regular intervals a chorus of suffering, wailing, unbelievably distorted voices rises—and then suddenly fades away. And there is happy orchestral music. No one ever returns from the upper camp. After three days, on October 13, Rajchman was moved there, to the *anus mundi,* "[the] ultimate draining site of the German universe," as Primo Levi wrote.

Rajchman is now a Totenjude, a death Jew.

He belongs to the group known as the "ramp column." When the great doors at the back of the gas chambers—they resemble garage doors lined with felt on the inside—swing up and open and the worst fumes have been allowed to disperse, he is one of the thirty or forty men who load the bodies of the murdered victims, one by one, still warm, skin shining with sweat or urine or feces or blood, onto stretchers that look like short ladders. Two men, attached by leather straps, carry each of them. They join a continuous line running at top speed across the sandy ground to a deep pit three hundred yards away. There the corpses are tipped in—after any gold teeth have been extracted. All this is accompanied by shouts and blows from uniformed men. (*Schnell, schnell, schnell, tempo!*)

The pit measures roughly sixty yards by fifty yards. Down in the pit, stepping unsteadily through a muddle of arms and legs and thighs and mouths and penises and tousled hair and the hands of three-year-olds, there are a dozen more death Jews working at packing the bodies neatly "head to toe and toe to head to make room for more." These are no longer dead human beings—the term used for them, even by the prisoners, is "cadavers."

The process has been tried and tested and is exactly the same every day a "transport" arrives. The same on Monday, November 2. There is almost always a jam when the door of one of the gas chambers is opened. Rajchman writes:

> The standing corpses are pressed so tightly together that their hands and feet seem to be intertwined. The ramp column can't get to work until they have managed to drag out the first dozen or so bodies. After that, the piles get looser and the corpses begin to fall out of the gas chamber of their own accord. The crush arises partly because so many people are crammed into the chambers and they all become terrified and struggle to breathe. The terror of death and the jostling causes the bodies to swell up, and so the corpses become a single mass.

This day ends like all such days. At six o'clock there is the sound of the trumpet. Rajchman and the others in the ramp column run to a small storeroom with their stretchers. (They have to do everything at a run.) After cleaning, the stretchers are put away in neat rows. ("Otherwise you get a taste of the whip.") Then it's *appell*—parade, lining up and being counted, accompanied by the sounds of the camp orchestra.* Then they form a column and, in groups of five, they are taken forward

---

* Most camps had their own orchestra. The Treblinka Orchestra was led by Artur Gold, a violinist and orchestra leader well known in Poland. The very talented orchestra performed on a variety of occasions: concerts for the guards, sometimes, and most often for *appell*. A little later they were given specially made clownlike stage costumes made of dark blue material. Gold lost his life in the camp, possibly in connection with the prisoners' uprising on August 2, 1943.

to the window of the barrack kitchen where they receive a piece of bread and a mug of hot, dark liquid that goes by the name of coffee. Finally, they are locked into a couple of linked wooden barrack buildings, close to the main camp fence but surrounded by its own barbed-wire fence—it's the camp within the camp within the camp.

Every evening when Rajchman looks around there are faces missing. The wastage is enormous. The German SS men and the frequently intoxicated Ukrainian guards in their black uniforms shoot people every day, almost in passing, out of boredom, for the smallest infringement of the rules, because someone doesn't look as if they can keep up with the mercilessly fast pace. Or just because they can.* We can assume that it happened on this day, too.

By this stage, Rajchman is familiar with the sight. The individuals to be shot often walk forward themselves and kneel on the edge of the pit, sometimes with a shamefaced willingness that bears witness to how totally broken and lost they are. An individual rarely lasts longer than ten days in the ramp column.[†] The work is so heavy and the guards so brutal. Rajchman has been there for almost three weeks.

·   ·   ·

Dreams are made to be forgotten, but this dream has stuck fast in her memory:

> I thought I stood with the figure in black which, or who,
> has stood beside me in many dreams. We stood on the bank
> of a moving stream, so wide that no banks could be seen,
> so long that no beginning or end could, either. It glistened
> and heaved as it flowed, and was green—all shades of green.

---

* The SS men knew that any gaps could immediately be filled when the next transport arrived. Rajchman states that the most feared job was that of carrying sand to the pit to strew over the bodies. It wasn't just that it was heavy work, but that the SS man in charge of that group was particularly murderous. "He would often turn up alone at *appell*, having shot all his workers, right down to the last man."

[†] Specialists in the camps usually had a chance to survive longer, particularly *kapos* (foremen) and what were called *hoffjuden* (useful craftsmen), but prisoners who ended up in a Sonderkommando were invariably condemned to death: they were always murdered in order to preserve secrecy. In Auschwitz, for instance, twelve Sonderkommandos were executed one after another.

Then I noticed it was leaves that gave it its colour, leaves of all shapes, shades and sizes. Some were spread in beauty and perfection, and sailed tranquilly along, some were cramped for space and their form was not plain, some were withered with curled spoiled edges, some were tender-looking, others spiky and hard. I stared entranced.

This is the first part of the dream. The second part is clearer. But why does she write about this dream in her diary today, in particular, November 2? She doesn't explain. Perhaps it's because it provides her with an important insight just then; perhaps because it reminds her of the woman she once was—because she knows that she's become stronger, more self-confident, more independent.

Here is the second part of the dream:

Then I saw little eddies and, looking closer, I saw they were caused by leaves that were keeping stationary, crossways, hindering the even flow. I saw their edges batter and tear—and yet they couldn't remain still, but were "dragged on" rather than "flowed on." I looked and looked, and suddenly realised that one tired, frayed leaf was me! Turning to my companion I said, "Why, that's me, isn't it?" I felt, rather than heard, the affirmation.

"Tired, frayed." Indeed, that's what she was there and then, often close to a nervous breakdown, overworked, unsure, introverted and downtrodden, a grey and timid housewife ruled by a demanding and dominating husband and trapped in a life of constantly repetitive chores, where the only joy to be found was in her two boys—sometimes scarcely even in them. But everything has changed, and she has changed.

It's not that she is doing less work now. Rather the reverse. She's a member of the Women's Voluntary Service, a branch of the civil defense, and also, with a group of other women, she is running a Red Cross shop, the purpose of which is to provide food parcels to British prisoners of war in Germany. But her work outside the home,* that

---

* A woman of her age was not obliged to make herself available for work, whereas women between sixteen and forty-five were, unless they had children still at home.

neat and almost excessively clean, small house at 9 Ilkley Road—once her great and only pride—has shown both her and others that, when it really matters, she has unexpected talents and unsuspected strength. Her name is Nella Last and she lives in Barrow-in-Furness, the shipyard town in northwestern England on the edge of the Irish Sea. She had her fifty-third birthday last month.

. . .

What sticks in Charles Walker's memory of those three nights of fear and noise on Bloody Ridge? One of his men, who was badly wounded by a bayonet during one of the chaotic battles in the dark, tells of a dreamlike state in which time became elastic and events fragmentary and unreal and impossible to fit together into a logical account.

In Walker's memory, odd episodes rub shoulders with apparently meaningless details. As when he stumbled over Flynn, the first of his men to fall, and he found himself unable to resist the civilian impulse to cover the dead man's face with a handkerchief. Or when Japanese and American soldiers screamed insults and obscenities at each other during pauses and continued doing so during attacks, when the Japanese battle cry "*Banzai*" was responded to by a chorus of American soldiers yelling, "Kill. Kill. Kill. Kill." Or the sight of that Japanese officer, lying about six yards from them after being hit in the backside by a tracer from a heavy machine gun—he caught fire and his body was gradually reduced to something that resembled grey cigarette ash.

. . .

It's a timeless image. A young woman, sitting, waiting and longing. She is well-dressed, but with nothing overdone; her makeup is discreet and her dark hair is nicely coiffed; she probably smells faintly of lavender—she usually does. She's likely to be wearing a cardigan, or something of the sort, as it's cold outside and the chill seeps into the old stone building.

It's almost exactly a year ago that they met here in one of the big lecture rooms, and he knows that she is currently working in the library in the afternoons. She has frequently come to this place simply in the hope that he will appear. And he has done so many times—too many times for it to be a matter of chance or even synchronicity.

A young woman is sitting, waiting and hoping he will pass by. This is what has been dominating her life for the last year: how one love has withered away in pain and confusion, and how another has developed in confusion and joy, or actually simply been discovered and accepted. For love is not something one deserves, but a blessing one has to be open to. They have been a couple for the last half year.

This is a timeless scene, but there is also something timeless about her. We are standing before a young person who views the future with the boundless optimism of her age, reinforced by the expectations that arise from a combination of her own gifts and a happy and protected upbringing.

Her name is Hélène Berr. She is twenty-one years old and the place where she is sitting waiting for her fiancé is the library at the Sorbonne. It's the right place for her. She is good at both Latin and classical Greek, having finished high school with the highest grades. She began studying at the university two years ago, reading English and English literature. She and her family are Anglophiles and she often uses English expressions in her speech and in her writing; and she has also written a highly commended essay on Shakespeare's interpretation of Roman history.

Hélène Berr is an attractive young woman. She has dark, intense eyes and is sensitive, intelligent and has been well brought up, though sometimes, in spite of her age, she can be a touch girlish. Her social talents are considerable and she has many friends. She loves music and she plays the violin. Sometimes she does puzzles, or joins in a game of table tennis, or plays that popular word game Diamino.

But timelessness is always a feeling and never a fact. This is occupied Paris on Monday, November 2, 1942, and Hélène has a piece of cloth with a yellow symbol on her coat: a six-pointed star with the word *Juif*, Jew, in green, pseudo-Hebrew lettering.

Darkness falls and he doesn't come. Hélène sets off home in the cold, past the bare, wintry Luxembourg Gardens (one of her favorite places), across Rue de Sèvres, which used to be so busy, but now she only sees cyclists, even the taxicabs have disappeared. On towards Les Invalides, in the direction of the Eiffel Tower, and on to her family's large flat at Avenue Élisée-Reclus 5, a parallel street to the Champ de Mars.

What is weighing on her mind is not so much the thought of losing love as of losing him. Four days ago in a corridor at the Sorbonne, Jean Morawiecki, the young man she'd been waiting for, told her—not without some concern—that he was considering escaping the occupied zone and even leaving France. His intention was then to find some way to join de Gaulle's Free French Forces. In that case they wouldn't see each other again for some time, perhaps never. Since then she has been waiting for confirmation. And hoping for another meeting.

There is perhaps a concealed element of irony in all this. Her former fiancé, Gérard, for whom, slowly and filled with embarrassment, she lost her feelings, has already disappeared off on the same journey to the Free French Forces that Jean is now proposing. She thinks that Gérard is now somewhere in the mountains of Algeria. She is sometimes ashamed of how little she thinks about him.

. . .

Just over a year later, when Keith Douglas, who had only a couple of months left to live, wrote about his experiences at el-Alamein, the text contained a number of detailed descriptions of the fallen. (Several of his best poems, "Vergissmeinnicht," for instance, build on depictions of the dead.) Was he researching death? Desmond Graham, Douglas's biographer, believes so: "The dead time and again attract Douglas's attempt to comprehend. They represent the ultimate discrepancy of appearance and reality, and in them Douglas seeks a way through the riddles of our perception of the physical world. The intensity of his curiosity about them is such that he seems to be seeking, through this evidence, to comprehend what it is to be dead."

One can also imagine a simpler explanation: that the shock of seeing them becomes etched as images in his mind. Or maybe he is simply curious about the dead, in the sort of way that happens to people not used to the external manifestations of death, but who lose their fear once they stand face-to-face with the phenomenon.

There could certainly be something in Graham's thought that this preoccupation with the fallen—which Douglas was by no means alone in—also has to do with the ambiguousness of the dead: "They compelled attention and gave nothing; they were supremely immune and supremely defeated; above all, they were possessors of a secret that they could not pass on."

. . .

Paolo Caccia Dominioni and Keith Douglas are located in roughly the same sector south of el-Alamein, though they were, of course, on opposite sides. Things are steadily coming to a crescendo. Caccia Dominioni writes: "Just a week earlier the destruction of a battalion had taken half a day; now the whole regiment was wiped out in three-quarters of an hour."

.   .   .

In the morning of Tuesday, November 3, Hélène Berr receives the letter she has been waiting for, and feared. It is short and it confirms what Jean said to her the week before: he is definitely intending to leave occupied France, in order to fight. Love is the most uncertain and fragile part of our existence, but there are certain situations when it can be the most enduring thing, the thing that keeps us alive.

.   .   .

The snow is hard. They march along the badly ploughed and ill-lit streets, but it's difficult to stay in step on the trampled, frozen under-layer. They slither and slide on the steps, and they are freezing cold. This is the second time Leonard Thomas, seaman and engine-room mechanic, has been ashore since their convoy arrived in Archangel. That was the middle of September. He looks all around with a mixture of amazement and distaste, looks at the "depressing acres of dull, dun-coloured concrete structures, box-like, each conforming with its neighbour. No spires or towers to relieve the skyline of so many six-storey boxes, the rain or snow forever permeating this gloomy atmosphere and but few lights hung like lanterns on poles." The windows are usually without curtains, and on virtually every street corner there are poles carrying loudspeakers through which Soviet radio blares out news, martial music, speeches, lectures and yet more news.

Archangel is a city whose whole current existence depends on the war. It sets its mark on the atmosphere, though not perhaps in the way one might expect, with an undertone of sacrifice, communal fate and heroism; the mood is more one of paranoia, cheerlessness and scarcity. On several occasions, twenty-year-old Thomas has seen groups of bent and silent men: slave laborers from the Gulag.*

Despite the endless propaganda proclaiming armed fraternity in the war against Germany, both sides view each other with suspicion. Thomas and his shipmates are only allowed to leave the ship in groups

---

* Arkhangelsky ITL, one of the many camps in the Gulag Archipelago, is located outside Archangel, and in the city there is Arkhperpunkt, a transshipment establishment for prisoners.

that have official invitations, and even then they are closely watched. On this occasion they have received an invitation and several crews have gone ashore to attend a concert—Tchaikovsky—to be played by an orchestra of musicians specially flown in from besieged Leningrad. The date is November 3.

They arrive at the big concert hall, where they are welcomed with many long propaganda speeches in broken English. This sets off a good deal of groaning and sighing and some loud heckling among the bored British and American sailors. Arguments flare up, and there's a really difficult moment when one of the political hacks on the stage gets entangled in the logic of the official party position: pressed by questions, he states that the military aid coming to the Red Army from the Arctic convoys is no more than "a drop in the bucket."* That is not what these seamen needed to hear: they have risked their lives, and will do so again, on this most deadly of all convoy routes. If that were the case, what is the point of their sacrifices?†

So what has stayed in Leonard Thomas's mind from that evening? Possibly the musicians, who undoubtedly played well and drew thunderous applause from the Russian part of the audience; and then the troupe of agile and well-coordinated female folk dancers who came on last and were called back for several encores; then afterwards, while putting on their outdoor clothes in the huge foyer bedecked with red flags, it's likely that a naval officer told them that the Germans were in retreat after a major battle in North Africa; and he certainly remembers his conversation with veterans who'd survived three or four Arctic convoys, during which one of them said, chastened or cynical or fatalistic—or perhaps simply resigned: "It's all over in a flash if you get hit. Have your fun, take your money, but when it does come, don't swim

---

* This wasn't true. As well as much else, the Arctic convoys shipped about five thousand tanks and seven thousand aircraft to the Red Army. The storm of propaganda thrown at these seamen resulted partly from the mistrust felt by the rulers of the Soviet Union after the disaster of convoy PQ17 and the temporary discontinuation of further Arctic convoys following that. They even questioned whether the losses really had been that bad.

† The Arctic convoys were at the most risk by far: given the ice, the weather, U-boats and German bombers based in northern Norway, one in ten ships was lost, whereas Atlantic convoys lost about one ship in a hundred. That statistic refers, however, to the whole war; the 1942 odds were actually much worse than that.

for it. Up here, just put your hands over your head and slide down—
you'll go to sleep in no time."

.   .   .

There are hundreds and millions of people whose highest desire is for
everything to remain as it is, who only long to be left in peace. They
are part of that great uninterested and unwilling mass—the silent,
despairing majority for which history is a remote and incomprehensible enigma which has done, is doing and will continue to do another
of its cruel and unpredictable twists and turns; and as if it were a force
of nature, it has suddenly burst into everyday life and, whether directly
or step-by-step, changed it or destroyed it, in spite of people's hopes
that it won't really be that bad or that it will blow over or that it will
mainly afflict others. She is one of those people. Her name is Elena
Skrjabina, a thirty-six-year-old mother of two, a refugee from Leningrad, currently in Pyatigorsk, a picturesque spa town at the foot of the
Caucasus Mountains.

There is scarcely a single major tremor in modern history that
Skrjabina hasn't seen or experienced close up: the First World War,
when every family and acquaintance in her neighborhood lost someone at the front; the revolution with its pillaging, violence and random arrests; the civil war with its chaos, lawlessness, famine and mass
death; the Stalin period with its terror, surveillance, claustrophobia
and disappearances—even though she herself has taken care to remain
apolitical, she belongs to a family that, for historical reasons, has been
labelled as "class enemies"—Elena Skrjabina's father, a very conservative member of the pre–First World War Duma, joined the Whites
during the civil war and went into exile in Paris, where he died—and
for that reason she could easily have been cut down by the blind
strokes of the scythe; the Second World War and the siege of Leningrad with yet more famine and more mass death—mass death beyond
all imagination and comprehension. (Could there be a worse time
and place to be born than in that city in the first part of the twentieth
century?) She has neither agreed to any of these things nor sought
them out. Rather, they have sought her out and afflicted her. But she
has survived.

There can be no doubt that it's pure chance that has saved Elena
on many occasions. But chance has been aided by her energy, judgment and a keen eye for people. Time after time, chance has been

incarnated in the form of strangers, who have given their support without really needing to. Elena has seen a great deal and knows the brutal and nakedly selfish deeds people are capable of, not least during famine. But she also knows that your life can be saved by a stranger, by a friendly act by an unknown passer-by. Elena Skrjabina is a survivor.

It is Tuesday, November 3, and she writes in her diary: "Again the situation has been improved. The loan saved us. We bought all sorts of foods, enough to last us the winter. Our general mood has also improved."

.   .   .

It's easy to condemn Dorothy Robinson's* happiness as banal. She is carried by a quiet sense of satisfaction at her lot in life, coupled with an open, almost childlike appreciation of little everyday things: the sounds of a sleeping child, a clean and tidy room, cooking smells, puppies, a perfectly made pie, making up a bed for one she loves, her husband, Jim's, voice calling that he is home from work, the sight of well-fed people around her kitchen table, a house full of noise and bustle and happiness and life, sitting down in the evening and reading or listening to the radio.

She is forty years old and finds it hard to imagine any other life than that of a housewife. She lives in one of the small commuter towns on Long Island, just east of New York and a good half hour's drive from Manhattan. She works hard and doggedly to keep her idyll intact. It's Tuesday morning and the weather outside is raw and rainy.

Dorothy's idyll, like all idylls, is structured around contrasts and the need to keep disaster at bay. On one side is the chaos she and her family (and the rest of the U.S.) left behind them a few years before— the Depression, which hovers in the background as a reference point and a bad memory.† On the other side there is the chaos and darkness that is spreading around the world, and she does make some effort to

---

* Her full name is Dorothy Atkinson Robinson (Atkinson was her maiden name) and her diary is published under the pseudonym Dorothy Blake.

† The role played by the Depression in the creation of the American housewife ideal should not be underestimated: unemployment, hardening attitudes and new legislation pushed many women back into the home. Eighty-two percent of the respondents to a 1936 public opinion survey stated that women with a husband in employment should remain at home—a view that was shared by roughly three-quarters of the women in the survey.

understand it, though she is of the firm opinion that it *must* be over-come. And that can only be done by winning this war.

She can remember with unusual clarity that Sunday almost a year ago when, for once, she slept in and woke to the smell of fried bacon, a smell that always lifts her spirits (they couldn't afford bacon during the Depression). And she'd heard the sound of a number of distant church bells all ringing at once and then, later, a voice on the crackling radio interrupting the ordinary program (a report on WOR of a New York Giants baseball game) to announce that "Pearl Harbor was attacked with no warning at 1:05 our time in a surprise attack by a large force of Japanese bombers." She and Jim and their eighteen-year-old son, Art (their daughter, Peggy, had already left home and was at college), stayed there gathered around the radio, and she remembers how, in the shocked silence that ensued, Jim had stroked her hand and, after say-ing nothing for a while, eventually said: "Well, this is it. Here we go."

Up to that moment, she had thought or believed or hoped that the U.S. should or ought or could stay out of the whole conflict. She had lived in a sort of denial, she admits that. She'd read the papers, heard the radio reports, seen the pictures, not to mention all the newsreels that for the last five or six years had mainly been about war or the risk of war, but—like many of her fellow Americans—she somehow managed to prevent that reality from intruding on her world. (A note about the mechanism of suppression: some cinema owners protested by only showing the main film without accompanying newsreels because some of the audience did not want to be reminded of such bothersome things.) That's over there, not here, not us.

What she wants is to avoid this testing time and to keep her nearest and dearest safe. "How utterly selfish as it sounds and is," she writes in her diary with a touch of embarrassment, "and how completely human, until a real test comes to make us bigger than we are, braver than we feel."

Dorothy Robinson's invariable first impulse is not to get involved. That holds true even on this Tuesday at the start of November. There is a congressional election across the whole country and, in New York, they also have to elect the governor. Interest across the country is pretty lukewarm, even though the Republicans have argued vigorously against what they call the president's and the Democrats' mishandling of the war. Their views have met with a significant sympathetic response. Dorothy is one of the lukewarm ones, but she doesn't say so straight out. Instead, as usual, she hides behind a veneer of humorous self-deprecation: those voting machines are far too complicated for little old me. But when the weather clears up and Sally, a relative currently living with them, goes to vote after lunch, Dorothy accompanies her.

So much has changed during the last year. Step by step.

She remembers back to the beginning of the year when, wanting to take the opportunity before the introduction of gasoline rationing, she drove into Manhattan for the first time since the outbreak of war. She noted that everything looked normal, with the noise of traffic and floods of neon lighting. But there was one exception: everywhere you looked you saw men and boys in uniform and many of the dummies in shop windows had been dressed in military clothing.

And that's how it has continued, gradually, step-by-step. For thirty years or more Times Square has been the place where great throngs of people crowd together in something like a communal party to learn the results as they come up on the news tickers.* On this particular evening Times Square is silent, empty and dark. All the enormous neon signs and other strong lights have been switched off so as not to assist the packs of German U-boats that have been hunting with such ferocious success just off the coast. And once the waiting lines outside cinemas and theatres have vanished into the warmth within, the three hundred police officers on duty are left with nothing to do but stand on the empty, wet sidewalks.

·   ·   ·

Back to Elena Skrjabina in Pyatigorsk. The loan she refers to in this Tuesday's diary entry is a short-term loan of 50,000 marks advanced to her by the head of the local economy commando, WiKdo.† She

---

* Not just at election time, of course. New Year celebrations on the square have already become an institution: this year, however, they will change, take on a much more muted form and include a minute's silence and the ringing of a bell for the fallen.

† These economy commandos (WirtschaftsKommando) were an important part of a major organization set in place before the invasion of the Soviet Union in order to exploit the occupied areas in the east. (The German economy had long been running a deficit, so war, conquest and exploitation were not only ideological imperatives but also an economic imperative.) The prime purpose was to favor German economic interests, and that could sometimes include encouraging local initiatives. Thus, for example, the start of the breakup of the collective

intends to use it as security for the small café she and her relatives have opened in the city. The story behind the café and the loan illustrates the resourcefulness and networking ability that has helped her—saved her, in fact—so often before. The story, for instance, of how she and her two boys first of all survived the siege winter in Leningrad and then managed to make the journey all the way down to the Caucasus in one piece has a touch of the miraculous about it.

In the middle of February this year, Elena, her boys, her mother and another woman were lucky enough to be placed in one of the evacuation columns that drove across the alabaster-white ice of Lake Ladoga, defying German bombs and artillery bombardment. The provision of assistance on the other side was, however, badly organized, with the result that the journey drained her mother's last strength and she died in a primitive hospital. In all the chaos Elena lost contact with her eldest boy, who was in a bad way. She herself was on the point of giving up because of the cold when by an even more wondrous stroke of luck she was reunited with her son and she and the two boys were taken safely on board a gleaming new, warm and well-equipped hospital train.

For a while it looked as if Siberia would be their haven of refuge, but in the end Elena Skrjabina decided to risk making the long journey down to the Caucasus, where she thought her sister-in-law Lyalya was. So, at the beginning of May she arrived in Pyatigorsk, at Kotjura 34, a house surrounded by an orchard in bloom. There she found not only her sister-in-law but also her sister-in-law's daughter, Vera, as well as Elena's mother-in-law, who was sitting there taking the sun on the steps.

And that's where they would all have been able to stay if history had not taken yet another unforeseeable turn.

At the beginning of August a column of German tanks rolled past their house just as the sun went down. Pyatigorsk was taken and Elena and her children were now trapped in occupied land behind the German lines. Once again, danger and hunger threatened and their whole support system crashed overnight: Soviet ration cards were no longer valid.

Once again, however, she and her family managed to cobble together

---

farm system in 1942 actually led to increased productivity, and the Germans immediately seized the chance to raise their demands for supplies.

an existence. Just about—thanks this time to timely and unexpected help in the shape of a German soldier who took pity on her and her children and provided them with canned goods and other food from his unit's supplies. Now she and another refugee from Leningrad have started making a living from the simple café they have been given permission to open. She was given this permission by another German.

Skrjabina's capacity for healing is colossal, as is her ability to foster hope; these are probably closely linked talents, but whereas healing is a fact, hope is just a fantasy. Since the front is far away, life has taken on a semblance of normality and she has sometimes been able to put the war out of her mind through the autumn. In just the last month, however, the mood in Pyatigorsk has begun to change and darkness is returning.

Perhaps they won't be left in peace here after all? Rumors abound. People are disappearing. The Jews were first of all ordered to register, and then they were transported. One of them was the skilled seamstress who's been helping Elena with her clothes.

· · ·

Is this a scene being staged for the cameras yet again? Only yesterday did the first Australian patrol reach Kokoda, a small village in New Guinea. The place has already achieved almost mythical status, partly because it has given its name to the sixty-mile-long trail along which thousands of men have toiled, fought and died since July. It's hardly more than a footpath, rarely more than three feet wide, winding its way through rain forest and jungle, up over high mountains and down steep ravines, around swamps and across watercourses. Its recapture has taken on a symbolic significance—it has become the clear and tangible objective used to drive Australian troops onwards, week after week, despite all the privations and foul horrors. "Kokoda or Bust!" That's what they have said to one another time after time, sometimes ironically, but often in deadly earnest.*

As so often in war, it all ended in anti-climax. Not a shot had to be

---

* The Japanese forces broke off their attempts to fight their way through the Kokoda Trail to Port Moresby primarily because of what was happening on Guadalcanal. Peter Williams, in his 2012 book, *The Kokoda Campaign 1942,* has shown that the Japanese plan at this stage was to mount a temporary withdrawal while awaiting reinforcements in the form of troops available after the island had been retaken from the Americans.

fired. The Japanese had disappeared back north the same way they'd come at the end of July. Kokoda turned out to be scarcely more than a cluster of houses on an open plateau squeezed in between a big oblong plantation of straight rows of rubber trees and several streams. But there is also the small airfield, which is what gives the place a value more than the purely symbolic.

It's now about half past three in the afternoon of Tuesday, November 3, and, as usual, it's raining. A ceremony is being held to celebrate the event:

> Australian troops in ragged, mud-stained green uniforms, in charred steel helmets that had been used for cooking many a meal of bully-beef on the Kokoda trail, stood in ranks round the flagpole in front of the administrative building while an Australian flag ... was slowly hoisted in the still air. There was no cheering. There was no band playing. There were merely the packed lines of those hundreds of weary Australians, haggard, half starved, disheveled, many wearing grimy, stained bandages—standing silently at attention in the rain.

One of the men who ought to have been standing there is twenty-two-year-old Bede Thongs, born into a large family in a small town in New South Wales. Before the war he was a carpenter, but now he is a sergeant in one of the militia battalions of the Australian army. These units are part of the image of self-satisfaction bordering on passivity that characterized this country—like others—during the 1930s. When catastrophe came in 1941 many of these units of part-time volunteer soldiers had obsolete equipment, including hastily requisitioned civilian vehicles marked with trade names like Bill Smith's Bakery, and officers past their prime—in both cases, leftovers from the First World War. Men in the regular army often look down on them.

But the sense of comradeship in these locally recruited units is strong. Thongs's battalion, the 3rd, is made up of men who often know one another from before, coming as they do from small tight-knit places like Goulburn, Queanbeyan, Crookwell, Yass, Mittagong, Bowral, Moss Vale, Moruya, Braidwood, Delegate, Dalgety and Adaminaby. (The youngest of them is sixteen, the oldest sixty-one and a veteran of the Boer War.) They have been well-trained, and when the battalion is finally shipped to New Guinea in the middle of May, they have been provided with new combat gear and new weapons, including impressive American Thompson sub-machine guns. This was the first time Thongs had been to sea.

The order to ship them over came as a surprise, but Thongs still had time to get engaged to his nineteen-year-old girlfriend, Joan—she lives in Queanbeyan—and to meet his father, George. His father is a veteran of the last war, wounded at Gallipoli in 1915, and Thongs remembers how calm and collected his dad was when they said goodbye at the Central Station in Sydney. (One of his sons, Thongs's brother Reg, has been reported missing since the fall of Singapore, and he has another son, Alf, also in uniform.) In his down-to-earth way, he urged Thongs to listen and learn—"as that would help me survive."

The 3rd Battalion has been taking part in the campaign along the Kokoda Trail since September 5. At that stage they numbered 560 men. A fortnight ago the number was down to 372, and that was before the drawn-out and costly battles at Eora Creek, which opened the way to Kokoda.*

The Australian attempt to fight their way through was a fairly typical battle for this kind of jungle-covered, extremely hilly terrain: there was complete confusion, hand-to-hand combat and the dread that the enemy is almost always unseen. There were outflanking movements, courageous but suicidal bayonet attacks, and platoons that got split up; there were assaults mounted where the cliffs were steepest, the rain forest densest, the ravines deepest and where men disappear without trace in the labyrinths of lush greenery; there were indecisive officers who misunderstood the situation, argued with each other and issued impossible commands; there was rain and rain and yet more rain; there was your own air support attacking in force but in the wrong place; and there was cowardice, brutality, heroism and death—chance death, as death on the battlefield almost always is.

Bede Thongs was there during the first days. Three of his friends were killed and he himself led an attack after their regular platoon commander was seriously wounded. Eventually the Japanese withdrew.

So this is a staged scene. A soldier from Thongs's battalion actually hoisted the Australian flag over the village yesterday, but the performance is now being repeated for the cameras and so that this new

---

* As in all the earlier battles, the Australians at Eora Creek suffered greater losses than the Japanese: 412 dead and wounded Australians to 244 Japanese.

general, a replacement for their recently dismissed divisional commander, gets an opportunity to shine a little.* (The previous divisional
commander was actually the third commander to be removed as unsat-
isfactory during the operations up and down the Kokoda Trail.)[†] An
American fighter plane dropped them a brand-new nylon flag this
morning.

So Thongs and the rest of the 3rd Battalion should have been present when the flag was raised, but they were left out among the rubber
trees. They feel they have been given the cold shoulder and the mood
among them is surly. (No other infantry battalion spent as long in the
most forward positions on the Kokoda Trail as they did. They are close
to exhaustion and many of them are ill.) And now the brigade commander has given the credit for the Kokoda victory to a regular army
unit instead of them. This will be a sore point for years to come.[‡] Such
is the power of symbols.

There is, nevertheless, a feeling of satisfaction, even though the
flag-raising is a staged ceremony, the men's mood low and the sense
of achievement marred by a degree of bitterness, for they have now
won their first truly significant victory against the Japanese on New
Guinea. Admittedly, it was a dearly bought victory, but it proves that
their opponent is by no means invincible. And the high mountains are
now behind them.

No sooner is this goal achieved than another takes its place. Less
than an hour after the ceremony, the first platoons move on through

* George Alan Vasey, the new commander, is thus linked to a success that was
achieved—with considerable difficulties—under his predecessor, Arthur Allen.
Allen, known as Tubby since he was quite short and fat, had shown great courage
during the First World War, but as with many others of his generation who now
occupied senior command posts, those earlier experiences frequently tempted
him to come up with out-of-date solutions to new problems.

† There was a multitude of problems with intractable and underperforming
commanders even at lower levels. One of the units, the 2nd Battalion of the 25th
Regiment, dismissed two commanders in less than a month, and the third was
a casualty of Japanese shelling on October 15. Yet another officer was removed
from his post three days later as a result of his unwillingness to attack.

‡ The question of what mistakes were made and whether it was right to dismiss
Allen is still a matter for sometimes heated discussion. *The Kokoda Campaign 1942*
gives the clearest account of what happened—and what *didn't* happen.

the rain. In long, well-spaced files they advance north, down from the plateau and into the dark jungle that spreads out below. And Bede Thongs and the sixteen remaining men of the 10th Platoon are already out scouting the virgin forest west of Kokoda. Where have the Japanese gone?

. . .

Anne Somerhausen lives at 6 Rue Vilain XIIII in the center of Brussels. If she turns right when leaving her narrow, three-story house she comes to the autumn-leaved trees that fringe the Ixelles Ponds—a popular outing on weekends. If she turns left, within a few minutes she will come to the wide, straight and fashionable Avenue Louise, which is not only popular with shoppers but also with the Gestapo: they have taken over four of the large buildings and turned them into fortresses surrounded by guards and a dark aura of threat.*

These buildings with their swastika flags detract from the hard-won sense of normality. Brussels is moving into its third wartime winter and, if the past two are anything to go by, it will be a trial.

The city is cold, colorless and a cloudy November grey. It has a great deal to do with the shortage of coal and gas and everything that results from that. Household gas could only be used for two and a half hours a day. But after two full years of occupation and shortages the people are also worn down, both literally and metaphorically. Many of those she meets in the street have lost weight and are wearing old clothes, worn or patched or turned inside out. And the shortage of leather actually makes itself heard in the constant clatter made by the wooden soles used to replace worn-out leather soles.

Brussels is a quieter city. Private cars are a rarity, and those that are seen have usually been converted to some kind of gas system with tubes on the roof or a wood-gas generator on the back. People either walk or cycle. Goods that used to be transported by truck are now taken by

---

* To be terminologically accurate: The SiPo/SD—that is the Security Police and the Security Service, of which the Gestapo formed a part—has taken over the buildings. Two months later, Jean de Selys Longchamps, a Belgian fighter pilot serving in the RAF, made an unauthorized, low-level attack *along* Avenue Louise. He fired on the Gestapo headquarters in the tall Art Deco building at No. 453. With classic British inconsistency, this led to his being both demoted and awarded a medal.

horse and cart. The only things to have stayed the same since before the war are the pale-yellow streetcars which, overcrowded with passengers, rattle along.*

The permanent waiting lines outside food shops have long been a part of the city scene, as have street vendors and the police in their long, dark coats and white, tropical helmet-style hats. (No one ever stops to wonder about this phenomenon.) The Germans in their grey-green uniforms fall into the same category. They are just tourists wandering round in small groups, not usually carrying more than a map and a camera, and for the most part they are careful to be polite. Given that Brussels is an occupied capital city during a war, it's amazing how few armed occupiers are to be seen. A German military band pops up now and again and plays its way along the rust-colored chestnut trees on Avenue Louise. Many people turn their backs on them and pretend to be studying the goods in the shop windows.

Somerhausen knows very well why she comes across so few armed Germans when she is walking on the streets of Brussels. The occupation is largely managed by the Belgians themselves. At the highest level, of course, there is a German governor-general—his proper title is Militärbefehlhaber—whose name is familiar to everyone from posters and proclamations in the newspapers: General von Falkenhausen. Under him there is the usual German array of staffs, special staffs, sub-staffs, groups, sections and offices, but it is the Belgian pre-war administration, left intact, that ensures that decisions are carried out. During the First World War, when the Belgians refused to cooperate, it took about 10,000 German civil servants to administer the occupied parts of Belgium down to the smallest detail. Now, in November 1942, 475 people are all it takes—850 if all the subordinate staffs and special agencies are included. And the area covered is significantly bigger—the two French departments closest to the border are also part of the administered area.

She has seen the statistics and they fill her with suppressed rage and shame. In this, Somerhausen shares a sense of ambivalence common among Belgians, but this arrangement is better than chaos and rule by the SS with a fanatically Nazi Gauleiter like Arthur Seyss-Inquart in neighboring Holland. She writes in her diary: "Their methods are

---

* German specialists have changed the streetcar network. In 1939, there were approximately 150,000 private cars in use; in 1942 that number was 6,520.

such that we actually prefer our Gandhi-like administration that practices passive resistance and whose sluggishness smothers any putatively energetic collaborators that risk entering its sphere of influence."

It is just a temporary arrangement while waiting for peace; that seems to be what she and most other people have thought. But when will peace come? When will this extraordinary existence cease?

With the passing of years, their wait has changed from being a method to being a way of life. They are all waiting for something, impatiently, bored or anxiously—sometimes perhaps without even thinking about it, without really knowing what, something that possibly only exists in their imagination. Somerhausen, too, is waiting—for peace, for good news, for more goods in the shops (many of which are closed before she gets home from work), for the next deal on the black market, for the next letter from her husband in a prisoner-of-war camp in southern Germany.

During her walk through November-grey Brussels, Somerhausen notices two fairly recent phenomena. First, graffiti proclaiming the power of the Allies and promising the defeat of the Germans. Second, signs marking the location of air-raid shelters and stating how many people can be accommodated in each. Ever since last spring, they often hear bombers flying over at night.

· · ·

The Germans and Italians still haven't pulled back. According to the plan, Keith Douglas's unit is to take a particular desert highway and he and the others can see that they are now approaching it since, just beyond a small ridge, the tops of telephone poles are sticking up. But enemy tanks and anti-tank guns are also waiting there and any British tanks that have tried to cross the ridge have been blown to pieces.

Douglas has parked his sand-colored Crusader down in a small hollow, along with several other tanks from the same unit. Every now and again he drives forward a little to scout the situation, but immediately returns to cover. They wait, and wait, and watch. They don't really know what to do. One of them has gearbox problems, another one has problems with his radio. Douglas's big problem is something different. When his own tank developed an oil leak,* he had to borrow another

---

* His tank was a Crusader Mark III, certainly fast and well-armed, but notoriously unreliable mechanically. As a rule, oil leaks developed in the engine block

tank yesterday evening. It was a tank that was mechanically undamaged but two of its crew had just been killed. Everything in the turret
is sticky with blood and bodily fluids: the floor, the walls, the radio, the
ammunition, the machine gun and the breech of the main gun. It stinks
and it's attracting flies.

It's the end of the afternoon of November 3. Smoke projectiles come
hissing over from the far side of the ridge, but nothing happens apart
from the arrival of a cluster of British heavy Grant tanks, presumably
as some sort of reinforcement in case the smoke means they should
expect a counterattack.

But it's an ambush.

Heavy German anti-tank guns such as the hated 88s open fire. They
follow a precise procedure. First, high-explosive shells explode in a
cloud of grey smoke, their detonations creeping ever closer to the
heavy tanks as the gunners on the other side of the ridge work out
the correct range. Then some ear-splitting air bursts to force the tank
crews to close their hatches and thus have a worse view and slower
reaction time. Finally the unpleasant chukkering noises which mean
that armor-piercing shells are coming, followed by the short, sharp
cracks when they strike metal, and then a final *whoosh* that means gasoline has been set alight. Within a few short moments three of the British
Grant tanks have been knocked out and have fire and smoke pouring
out of them. Douglas sees several of the survivors leap clear, supporting
and helping one another to stay upright.

His attention is quickly caught by something else. Down on the hot
sand he sees a stained copy of the American man's magazine *Esquire*
with its familiar, lurid cover depicting a hilariously funny, uniformed
man with a big moustache. Douglas simply has to have it. He is just
jumping out of the turret when another heavy shell whistles overhead.
He snatches up the magazine and, once back inside his turret, he and
his gunner start leafing through the torn and stained magazine.

They all read a lot. When you can't sleep, reading is the best way
of getting time to pass and combating the tedium of the waiting that
now constitutes the greater part of their lives. Douglas, the bookish
ex-Oxford student, has even set up a small library in the turret of his
regular tank. Most of the items are Penguin paperbacks printed on

---

after no more than two or three days bouncing and shaking across the terrain
of the desert.

cheap paper: the green-white-green whodunnits are the most popular, but there are also Westerns, a volume of Shakespeare sonnets and, later, a volume of Nietzsche in German.

This men's magazine, however, represents more than just a way of passing time. It's a hole in the fabric of space and time, a portal into another life. We can assume that they study the smiling, lightly dressed and high-busted *Petty Girl* in this number carefully—drawn, as these fantasy women always are, with disproportionately long legs and disproportionately small heads. These soft pornographic pictures have become the magazine's trademark and an institution for Allied soldiers: they can be seen everywhere, in barrack rooms, in bunkers and trenches, inside tanks, painted on the fuselage of warplanes.* But what fascinates Douglas most of all is a colored photographic spread of some sort of party in Hollywood, where the men are in perfectly fitting dinner jackets and the women in thin, low-cut dresses. For a short moment he seems to be there, in one part of the multiverse that is 1942, a parallel existence of neon lights and soft scents, of dancing, jazz music and misted cocktail glasses, of laughter, carefree white smiles and inviting painted lips.

But in the here and now comes the thunder and roar of the British side returning fire, and the portal closes. Douglas rushes back at lightning speed to his tank with its sticky interior and he hears in his earphones the voice of the colonel of the regiment yelling at what remains of the group of heavy tanks that was now starting to pull back under the lethal fire: "Nobody told you to retire. Get back. Bloody well GET BACK and give the buggers Hell. You're bloody sticky." Douglas sees them cautiously begin to trundle forward again.

The firing from the other side of the ridge eases off and falls silent. Someone says that the Germans have begun to fall back.

---

* In 1944 the American postal service banned the overseas shipment of *Esquire* on the grounds that its illustrations were immoral. The ban resulted in a storm of rage that went all the way up to Congress. A number of similar magazines existed on the British side, but there, above all, was the cartoon character Jane in the *Daily Mirror*, who habitually tended to lose items of her clothing. It was claimed at the time that there was a connection between how undressed Jane was in that day's paper and how well bomber crews performed on their raids. The worse the war news was, the more naked Jane became. But, then, with the invasion of Normandy, the editor saw to it that she even lost her knickers and, for the very first time, appeared as God had created her.

.   .   .

It's the same Tuesday and three trains of cattle cars arrive at Treblinka. In one there are about 1,000 Jews from Gowarczów, in the second some 4,000 from Radoszyce, and in the third about 9,000 from the Końskie ghetto. Apart from the few who are spared to replenish the constantly diminishing band of workers in the camp Sonderkommando, all of them are murdered by the evening—men, women and children.

Taking the lives of 14,000 people in the course of a single day is right at the limit of what the death factory can manage. No doubt the SS men have to use both gas chamber buildings, the old one with three rooms and a maximum capacity of somewhere between 1,350 and 1,500 people, and the new one with ten rooms and a total capacity of 4,000 people.

The real bottleneck, however, does not arise from the numbers murdered, but from the handling of the bodies afterwards. We can be certain that the killers, as always, will have picked out some of the newly arrived young men to assist with the task of moving bodies. But there remains a further problem—how to manage the extraction of gold teeth from the corpses. There are simply too few "dentists."

This creates another respite for Chil Rajchman.

At the morning roll call, SS-Scharführer Heinrich Matthes, commander of the upper camp, orders the expansion of the "dentist commando." Rajchman immediately volunteers, stating that he is a dentist. He is accepted, joins the ranks of the dentists and marches off to their barracks with them.

The wooden building lies close to the older, smaller gas chamber. In it is an oblong table, benches and, in one corner, a locked bureau in which any and all valuables are kept—including items collected from the vaginas of murdered women. Heating is provided by a small stove and light comes from two small windows. When Rajchman looks out, he can see some of the many tall pine trees that grow both inside and outside the camp. (In among the pines there are clumps of withered brown lupins.) And he can see the big gas chamber building, which is quite close. He can, of course, hear the screaming whenever people are being gassed.

Rajchman sits down with the others. They sit close to one another, very close. While waiting for the next transport to be processed, they go through the heaps of extracted teeth and crowns, some of them still bloody or with bits of gum still attached and they clean everything of value. "Two specialists sorted the metals, especially white gold, red gold, platinum and ordinary metal."

Rajchman spends half an hour trying to work out how to go about things and trying the various tools. Then there is a knock on the window—the doors of the first gas chambers are being opened. Six dentists are sent out and he is one of them. He is given two sets of pincers. Firstly they each collect a table from the joinery workshop and set them up in a row. Then each of them fills a bowl with water from the well, runs back and places it on the tables. Now the work can start.

The men of the ramp commando come rushing up, usually two by two, with a still-warm corpse on the ladder-like stretcher. They halt in front of the row of tables and a man at the front quickly inspects the mouth of each corpse. (Could that be Dr. Zimmerman, the squad's *kapo*?) If there is nothing of any value, the bearers are quickly waved on in the direction of the large pit. If there is the glint of anything, the bearers are directed to a dentist and they lift up the body so that the head rests on the table. Rajchman's task then is to yank out any gold teeth and bridges and drop the extracted teeth into the bowl of water. Then the bearers run on with the body. The work isn't easy. Rajchman writes:

> The cadavers from the big gas chambers where death took longer had changed in a horrific way, their faces blackened as though burned, their bodies swollen and blue, their teeth so tightly clenched that it was almost impossible to open their mouths and get at the gold crowns. In that case it was necessary to pull out some of their natural teeth in order to get the mouth open.

And so it continues until work is stopped at six o'clock in the usual way with a bugle call:* tools are collected and the men clean up and march off to form up on the parade ground to the sound of the camp

---

* Stopping work on the stroke of six seems to have been standard procedure even if there were still bodies in the gas chambers and trains waiting at the station. The factory aspects of the killing are emphasized very clearly by the fact that people locked into the gas chambers but not yet gassed are simply left there overnight and only gassed the following morning at the start of the working day.

orchestra. Then comes a head count, supper at the barrack kitchen, and locking up. Thus Tuesday, November 3, in Treblinka, comes to a close.

· · ·

When the sun is at its highest that same Tuesday, a light, all-terrain truck approaches, swerving and bouncing across the desert sand at great speed. That alone doesn't augur well. Has it happened then? The truck brakes and a couple of dust-covered men climb out. They are shaken. Yes, it has happened.

Vittorio Vallicella listens in horror to what they tell him. During Sunday night their artillery battery had moved off south to support the Littorio Armored Division, which, together with German armored units, was to attack the bulge that had formed and cut it off, if possible. But it had been pure slaughter—they actually used the word *macello*. Even before they were close enough for the light guns of their *carri armati* to fire on the enemy, the new British heavy tanks and anti-tank guns knocked them out one by one with worrying ease and they'd had to watch the crewmen leaping out of their blazing vehicles like living torches.

And the artillery battery? Knocked out. The crew? Dead ... or captured. They are the only ones left—they and Vittorio and his companions who'd been ordered to remain here with the baggage truck when the others set off into the night.

What is to happen now? Should they try to get out? *Can* they get out? They are six young men, with no senior officers, no orders, no radio, no reliable information, deserted, alone, shipwrecked in an ocean of sand: Berrà, "the Greek," Baruffi, Doliman, Bellini and Vallicella himself—a twenty-four-year-old truck driver. Berrà has the rank of sergeant and, formally speaking, is in command, but Vallicella suggests that all decisions from now on should be voted on and taken collectively. So that's what they do.

They take stock of their provisions and their possibilities. They have two light trucks that are in working order: one of them is an Italian TL.37, which has enormous wheels and looks as if it were designed from a child's drawing—but it is powerful, reliable and has four-wheel drive; the other, Vallicella's personal favorite, is a light Chevrolet truck, the spoils of war, well-equipped and easy to drive.

They have fifteen full cans of gasoline, which is good, but they only have about sixteen gallons of water, which is less good. (Both they and their vehicles need large quantities of water to keep functioning.) Doliman, their cook, tells them they have plenty of food: a carton of fruit in syrup, a box of Italian tinned meat, a carton of English corned beef, six cartons of German sauerkraut, three boxes of biscuits, and loads of tea and various brands of cigarettes. (A telling detail: Vallicella's diary makes no mention of weapons or ammunition.) The shortage of water is a problem, but it isn't insoluble. They are all veterans of desert warfare, so they know the desert is littered with wrecks in which it's usually possible to find all kinds of things, including water, gas and food.

The night is quiet, apart from a column of vehicles passing close to them in the darkness. They can't see whether it's friend or foe, so they stay hidden. Time after time the horizon to the north is lit up by flashes.

·   ·   ·

That same evening. Dusk at el-Alamein. Keith Douglas and his tank pull back a little to refuel and have a cup of tea and something to eat. They group their tanks together to form a temporary camp for the night and they share a generous issue of rum as a kind of reward for a long and, by all accounts, successful day. Douglas writes:

> the effect of which [the rum] was a little spoiled by one of our twenty-five-pounders, which was off calibration, and dropped shells in the middle of our area at regular intervals of seconds for about an hour. The first shells made a hole in the adjutant's head, and blinded a corporal in B squadron. I spent an uncomfortable night curled up on a bed of tacky blood on the turret floor.

When the sun rises, they will make another attack.

·   ·   ·

On Wednesday, November 4, it becomes clear to Dorothy Robinson on Long Island that the election has led to a landslide victory for the Republicans. The Democrats have lost forty-five seats in the House of Representatives as well as their twenty-year-long control of New York. Dorothy is pleased: she voted for Thomas Dewey, the young, energetic, incorruptible former special prosecutor, and he is now their new governor.

In order to save oil, they've started closing off rooms in the house.

Jim is working more and more and is away more frequently: when he comes home, he is drained and weary. Their son, Art, has volunteered to join the air force and their daughter, Peggy, has moved to the West Coast to be close to her fiancé, who's been called up by the Navy. At night, Dorothy often hears the roar of aircraft engines over the house as the warplanes from the nearby base practice night flying. And these days, in accordance with the regulations, they have several buckets of sand, a spade and a coarse blanket at one end of the house, ready to douse any possible incendiary bombs.

.   .   .

The New Guinea jungle stirs up contradictory emotions in Sergeant Bede Thongs. On the one hand there is the stink, the damp, the decay, the insects, the darkness and the sense of threat that arises from hardly ever being able to see farther than a couple of yards. On the other hand, he can be delighted by the beauty revealed, by the flowers, the wealth of orchids and the big, brightly colored butterflies. He and his platoon—the 10th—are scouting out the country west of Kokoda, in search of the retreating Japanese. No one really knows where they have gone.

Thongs and his platoon have been moving through untouched primeval forest—dark, veiled in moss and, in places, several feet deep in rotting leaves. They are in a world that consists of a thousand shades of green, even in the narrow, insect-filled rays of sunlight that filter through the dense covering of foliage high above their heads. They haven't seen anyone or heard anyone. Long sections of the paths they have been following have been impossible to see. Their maps are crude, with many areas that are blank. This is unknown country in every sense. Thongs and his sixteen men are in all probability the first white men ever to have been here. It's even possible that they are the first people at all to have been here in a very long time. Thongs and the rest of them are bitterly cold at night and drenched with sweat during the day.

It's morning and the patrol has been out for three days. Thongs and the rest of them have just emerged from the dark mossy jungle and they see a small cluster of four huts in the distance. They approach. Silence. No sign of people. They halt, light a fire and make tea, along with which they eat what they've been eating for months now: hard army biscuits and bully beef, cold and straight out of the small, gold-colored, angular tins.* Kokoda is not too far away now. Thongs hears and catches a glimpse of a distant transport plane on its way to the airfield.

Then someone notices the dog. If there is a dog, there must be people here.

The Australian soldiers pick up their weapons and Thongs calls out. No more than twenty-five yards away silent Papuans rise from the dense cotton grass, powerful bows and arrows in hand. There are eighteen of them and they form a semicircle around the Australians. The Australians aim their weapons at them and the Papuans aim at the intruders. This, in a sense, offers part of the definition of a world war, a conflict that is an expanding avalanche that involves and distorts everything, redefines and devastates everything—life, ideas, values, phenomena, fears, expectations and dreams. It sweeps everything in its path, even places and people that have nothing at all to do with it.

Thongs doesn't know what to do. His head is full of conflicting thoughts. He knows he doesn't want to kill them. He knows even if they do kill them, some of his own men are likely to be killed too. He knows how hardy the Papuans are in comparison with the white boys from Goulburn, Queanbeyan, Crookwell, Yass, Mittagong, Bowral and so on. He thinks of those two graves he noticed just outside the village. He thinks the Papuans must have killed the Japanese lying in them. He thinks about how to communicate with these men.

No one moves and nothing happens: time stops while they all just stand there, turned to stone: two different epochs, weapons raised against the other. Then one of Thongs's soldiers begins calling to them, appealing, and the others quickly join in. And he does, too, in improvised pidgin: "Australians, Australians. Not Japanman. We all bilong friends. Bilong Papua New Guinea bois. Not Japanman. Friends. We're your friends."† Later on, Thongs has difficulty remembering how long this went on for, "but it seemed like a long time." (Thongs doesn't mention gestures in his account, but there must have been gestures.)

---

* Bully beef consisted of meat boiled in a salt solution and then ground up. Then, with the addition of a small amount of gelatine, it was preserved in cans.

† Both sides were reliant on native bearers in their campaign along the Kokoda Trail, the Australians with more success than the Japanese since they treated the Papuans far better than the Japanese did. The latter, without giving it much or, indeed, any thought, operated with the same kind of compulsion and violence that they used in China.

In the end, the Papuans lower their weapons and the Australians do the same.

Thongs gives them canned food and biscuits, but what really breaks the ice is when he offers them salt. "I wet the tip of one finger with my tongue and tasted it, and the leadman did the same. He smiled, followed up by a noise like a grunt. The rest of the bowmen gave noises of approval."

The danger is over. Small children and women in grass skirts emerge from the tall cotton grass. When Thongs and his men are eventually departing, they wave cheerfully to the Papuan villagers and the Papuans wave back. Out in front of them there is open country, flat and sunny. Kokoda, not too far now, awaits them—the Papuans have shown them the way. The date is November 4.

.   .   .

In the morning of that same day Vittorio Vallicella and his companions see a number of German tanks trundling past. The tank crews confirm that a general retreat west along the coast road from el-Alamein has begun. Now Vallicella and his fellows have to make their minds up. Some of them, along with Sergeant Berrà, are in favor of getting out, fleeing westwards and finding a way back to their own lines, wherever they may be in this fluid situation, and ultimately getting *home*.

Vallicella comes from a simple farming family in the province of Verona. He is used to working in the fields, used to doing what he is told, used to doing what he has always done. Even though studying has never been in the cards, he likes reading and reads a lot. When his call-up papers came, he obeyed, but his life in the army has been marked by a singular lack of enthusiasm. He is not a fascist and his political views lean more to the left. He is one of the millions who is not interested in the war but who has discovered that the war is interested in him. In so far as he had any illusions, they have gone now, eroded by the better part of twenty months in North Africa. Vallicella is quite short but wiry; he has the dark-blond hair of northern Italy, deep-set eyes, a pronounced mouth and a strong jaw. He is unmilitary in his way of thinking and in his dress; photographs usually show him wearing a white undershirt.

Vallicella has had enough. He wants to stay here, wait for the British and surrender to them. Is it really worth taking the risk of heading off on a long journey into uncertainty? Doliman, the cook, agrees with him. Bellini and the Greek can't decide, but Baruffi and Bassi take Berrà's side. So that settles it. West it is. They start up the trucks and set off on a slippery track through the sand. The sun is blazing down from a clear blue sky.

. . .

Cold rain. Endless grey fields. A landscape devoid of color and of people. A narrow winding road. A cart pulled by a tired horse. Riding on the cart along with the carter are Danuta, a young woman with a little boy in her arms, and her husband, Józek, who is ten years older than her. The parents are dressed in thin clothes, without raincoats or overcoats even, but the child is well wrapped up. This would have been an uncomfortable journey even in peacetime.

Danuta and Józek Fijalkowski are both from Warsaw—she very much so, having grown up in the Polish capital and long been in love with its light, its sounds and its bustle. They have spent the summer in an unfinished house without heating and insulation in Czemierniki, a village near Lublin in eastern Poland. With winter coming Józek has managed to find them a house fit for winter. It's about eighteen miles away, in a small town called Międzyrzec Podlaski, a little north of Lublin. That is where they are going now through this unpleasant autumn weather.

They are in fact fleeing, though Józek won't really admit that. The reason he came up with the idea of their spending the summer in Czemierniki is that it's better for the little boy and that Danuta "needs a holiday." When autumn was approaching and it was time to find a new place, she wanted to return to their small flat in the capital, but her husband refused. "It's too difficult to get hold of food in Warsaw" was his main argument. And that is certainly true. The weekly routine of most Polish city dwellers these days involves using the weekend to go out to the country with empty suitcases, buy or barter black-market foodstuffs from the farmers and smuggle them home, past all the checkpoints and barriers, past the ever-present small groups of German soldiers in their greatcoats with sub-machine guns and dogs.

But Józek doesn't tell her everything. He sometimes nervously disappears off on mysterious journeys and returns, clearly relieved, with some money. But Danuta sees his anxiety and knows he has to keep a low profile. He has been given a conditional release and is supposed to report to the Gestapo at their dreaded headquarters in the posh

neoclassical building at Aleja Szucha 25 in Warsaw. (Which, incidentally, is one of those city streets that is now *Nur für Deutsche*—"Only
for Germans." It has also had a name change: it is now called Police
Street.) But he stopped reporting there last spring. He doesn't want to
go there, he can't, and he won't.

Józek is a marked man. Not primarily in a physical sense, though he
does have a big scar on one of his legs as a result of a dog bite that did
not heal properly, but also mentally. He is afraid, anxious, suffers from
tremors, sweating and palpitations. He has many nightmares.

Józek hasn't done anything wrong—he just happened to get swept
up in one of those random street raids.* Between August 1940 and January of this year, Józek was imprisoned in what before the war had been
an army base with brick barracks southeast of Kraków. The name of the
place was Oświęcim, but like many other places in Poland it has since
been given a German name and is now called Auschwitz.

Danuta does not know exactly what he went through there, nor does
she want him to talk about it since it upsets him so much. What she
has already heard is bad enough: accounts that are hard to understand,
of parades and cold and blue and grey-striped clothing and clogs and
mud and hard labor (the endless number of times he passed under
the cast-iron camp gateway with its slogan *Arbeit macht frei*) and dogs
and SS men who beat prisoners and prisoners who beat prisoners and
hunger and random death sentences and new methods of killing people
en masse (poison gas—surely that can't be more than a rumor, can it?)[†]

* The Germans were mainly looking for men in the age range of twenty-five
to thirty for slave labor in Germany. The only protection accepted were papers
showing that you already worked for them or that you had an important Polish
function. Poles, in practice and irrespective of religion, had no rights, whereas
Germans—particularly the more senior—were notoriously corrupt, made big
money and could commit many excesses, especially those of a sexual variety,
without risk. The General Government, the non-annexed parts of Poland, abbre-
viated as GG, was frequently called the Gangstergau—Gangster District—even
by some Germans.

† Auschwitz, during the time Józek was there, was still a labor/concentra-
tion camp primarily for Polish prisoners (both Christian and Jewish); it was an
extraordinarily brutal camp, but as yet not an extermination camp. Prisoners
could, for instance, receive letters. The first gassing experiments took place in
August and September 1941, when Soviet prisoners of war were murdered with
Zyklon B in the cellar of Block II, one of the brick barrack buildings of the original Auschwitz I, next to the building where Józek was held. The mass gassing

and rules and barbed wire and watchtowers and silence and the black atmosphere of death: death as a threat, death as a spectacle, death as a phenomenon, as a condition of everyday life.

Józek is a man whose soul has been scorched and withered by terror.

A cold grey day. An empty landscape painted in misty colors. They travel on. Mown fields. Drenched autumn woodlands. Villages. They come to a small town. The square opens around them and they are met by a scene that Józek recognizes all too well, and he immediately begins to tremble:

> On one side of the square there are several dozen Jewish women kneel [*sic*] in rows of five with their hands in the air. On the opposite side of the square, Jewish men kneel in the same manner. The SS men walk around and in between the two groups with sub-machine guns and attack dogs at their side, kicking and pushing those who don't hold their hands high enough.

He tells her not to look in that direction. She sees him go pale, tremble and sweat. He tells the driver to take them away from here. Quickly. The cart turns in to a back street and moves on more and more rapidly. He starts explaining, telling her what is happening to the Jews—or what *has* already happened—tells her about the ghettos and transports and camps and death. She places her finger on his lips to silence him. Why talk about it? "I don't want you to relive it."

They come out into the empty autumn landscape. The sky is grey and overcast and it starts raining again. They feel the cold. They'll soon get to Międzyrzec Podlaski.

· · ·

In her diary for Wednesday, November 4, Vera Brittain writes with self-irony that it has been "a thoroughly suburban matron's day." At Marshall and Snelgrove's, the Oxford Street department store, she has found a gold-embroidered collar which she is thinking of using to brighten up her black silk-and-satin evening gown. She and her companion also ate lunch there. Later they walk down Bond Street, past

---

of Jews began in February 1942 and mainly took place in Auschwitz II, the new and much enlarged part of the camp.

more or less refilled craters, houses with boarded-up windows, houses without roofs, houses without façades, façades with nothing behind them, to Truefitt & Hill, where she has her hair permed—she is always very particular about her appearance.*

Vera Brittain, of course, is anything but a suburban housewife, which has nothing to do with her detesting housework and leaving as much as possible to her home help. She is forty-eight years old, an author, a mother of two, a feminist and a pacifist. To the public at large in both Great Britain and the United States, she is known for her best-selling *Testament of Youth*, which came out ten years earlier and deals with her experiences as a volunteer nurse during and after the First World War.

Little more than scattered remnants are left of the peace movement she belonged to during the 1930s—it fell apart under the weight of its failure and internal contradictions. The split was enormous: the movement ranges from pragmatists like Brittain, who can accept doing service such as civil defense, to fundamentalists, who refuse everything and for whom any kind of peace is better than any kind of war, to crypto-fascists who are firmly convinced that Hitler has been treated unjustly and the war is a result of a Jewish conspiracy. But Brittain refuses to recant on her principles.

She has continued to argue for a pacifist perspective, something that demands courage, strength, willfulness and a degree of pighead-edness when enemy bombers are buzzing above your head. She is not, however, one of those intellectuals whose heroic resistance to war and Nazism has led them to seek safety in the United States, even though she toyed with the idea and did send her children there.

Every fortnight Brittain publishes a small pacifist newsletter, *Letter to Peace-Lovers*, which goes out to a thousand or so subscribers around Great Britain. Paper rationing makes things problematic, and the work involved takes much of her time and occasionally some of her money, too. But even though opinions like hers have become more and more unpopular—hated even—Brittain does not give up.† Earlier today she sent a letter with instructions to the woman who acts as

---

* It wasn't just a matter of personal vanity. Since many of Vera Brittain's opinions were considered radical, she made a point of being well turned-out so as to make it difficult to simply write her off as just another bohemian bluestocking.
† She was also seriously committed to the issue of food aid to occupied countries, including Greece.

secretary for the newsletter, and correspondence from other contacts is waiting for her at home. Her latest book, the pacifist tract *Humiliation with Honour*, was published just a week ago and she is interested and impatient to hear how it has been received.

She rounds off the day with afternoon tea at Stewart's. London, with all the sandbagged monuments, bomb-damaged buildings and blacked-out shop windows, is an unusual November grey. But for once there hasn't been any rain.

·   ·   ·

In the morning of that day, Keith Douglas and what remains of his squadron advance up that ridge, past bodies and body parts and the burned-out, blackened wrecks of yesterday's battle. They keep a careful watch as they bump along cautiously, but nothing happens. All that can be heard is the rumble of their own engines and the creaking of their caterpillar tracks. They come to the desert road with its rows of telephone poles. Empty. The Germans and the Italians have pulled back, fled even. They pick up a deserter trudging towards them in the morning light. He confirms things: yes, they've disappeared, withdrawn a long way to the west. Douglas and his men are suspicious: they fear an ambush and don't know whether to believe him. They move on. The landscape opens out before them, flat and wide. Later there are a few clashes, but they are soon over.

·   ·   ·

Weather permitting, Albert Camus is usually to be found sitting on a stone bench outside the small *pension* where he lives. It is run by a distant relation of his wife. He has slowly become accustomed to the landscape here, its colors and forms so unlike his home in Algeria. The sounds are different, too. Back in the open landscape of North Africa, the sound of dogs barking echoes for so much longer than here in the forested hills of the French uplands. He is an outsider here, but at the same time not an outsider.

The *pension* is in Le Panelier, a village in the Massif Central in Vivarais, fifty miles or more southeast of Lyon. On the recommendation of his doctor, Camus has been living here since the end of the summer in an attempt to combat the recurrence of his tuberculosis. Le Panelier lies at an altitude of three thousand feet and the thinner air at that kind of altitude is considered beneficial for TB patients. Every second week he makes the thirty-mile journey to Saint-Étienne, where he undergoes lung collapse therapy.*

The lack of other people makes him less misanthropic, and the absence of women reawakens his old ideas about the blessings of asceticism. He thinks about sex a lot, much of his thinking characterized by an element of sour grapes. (Quotations from his notebook this autumn: "Sex doesn't lead to anything. It isn't immoral, but it is non-productive" and "Unlimited sex leads to a philosophy of the world's lack of meaning. Celibacy, on the other hand, gives the world a meaning.") Paradoxically, the silence, solitude, confinement and limitations on freedom of movement that wartime life brings in its train even in the non-occupied parts of France suits him well, intermittently anyway. He sits in the empty *pension*, concentrating fully on his work on a new novel, an allegory that is to have both "a social meaning and a metaphysical meaning." His plan is to return to Algeria at the end of the month.

Nineteen hundred forty-two has been a productive year for Camus. He has had two books published: *The Stranger* appeared in the middle of June and *The Myth of Sisyphus* was released just a couple of weeks ago. Camus is spending a lot of time sulking about the reception of *The Stranger*. It has had quite a few good reviews, but many have been dismissive, and it's the latter he focuses on. The reviews haven't been anything like what he'd been hoping for. "It takes three years to write a book and only five lines to ridicule it by choosing unrepresentative quotations." (The worst blow is still to come. In September, Jean-Paul Sartre, who returned from being a prisoner of war a year and a half ago, wrote an unusually long review of *The Stranger*; in parts it is appreciative and in others critical. It won't be published for some months.)

The situation is a little strange. Camus's debut brought him to public attention, made him famous even, and *The Stranger* is selling unexpectedly well in spite of the reviews. But Camus himself is sitting in isolation in a little *pension* in the Massif Central. He has applied to the German occupying powers for permission to make a short visit to Paris and, as yet, he hasn't received an answer. So he is carrying on writing his new novel. He occasionally goes out into the damp autumn woods looking for mushrooms. His only company are the three stray dogs he has adopted. He'll soon be twenty-nine.

---

* Both of these therapeutic approaches have since been demonstrated as ineffective.

. . .

Yet another move. Another unknown camp awaits them somewhere. That's bad enough, but what's worse is that the rainy season has started here in Java and that makes moving around a risky business and foot marches a nightmare. Characteristically, he refuses to let it depress him.

He looks at what works, looks at what is good and can be depended on, but he does so soberly, without succumbing to illusions. And he looks for the advantages—in yesterday's diary he wrote: "Will be glad to see the last of these guards as [they are] very sadistic." His name is Ernest Edward "Weary" Dunlop, a thirty-five-year-old doctor in the Australian army, a lieutenant colonel, and a prisoner of war of the Japanese since March.*

In recent weeks there's been a good deal of brutality in this camp, which is situated immediately outside Bandung in the western part of this large island. It's been of the usual sort: blows, smacks, thumps around the head—open-handed or with clenched fist—with canes or other weapons, sometimes with rifle butts. (Always accompanied by yelling and shrieking.) And as always, all this is sparked by trivial things—bowing too casually or too late, smoking in the wrong place, trying to smuggle tobacco. A few days ago a couple of Australian prisoners were caught imitating one of the Japanese guards (most of them are actually Koreans) and it resulted in "an orgy of slapping."

Dunlop has been in the camp long enough to know that every now and then the guards suddenly become more violent for no reason that is apparent to the prisoners. At such times they seize on every excuse to kick or hit, but then the wave subsides just as inexplicably as it started and the guards become correct—polite, even—again. Powerlessness and unpredictability lie at the heart of camp existence, with apathy and physical decline as the usual consequence. (Violence is no more than an instrument.) Dunlop, as the (reluctant) top representative for the Australian and British prisoners in the camp, has done a lot to keep the first two phenomena at bay and, as a doctor, everything possible to defeat their consequences.

The original idea was that he and the other Australian prisoners

* The nickname Weary dates from his time at university. It's a Cockney-style play on words, based on his surname: Dunlop = tire = tired = weary.

would be marched off tomorrow, Thursday, November 5, but there is an unexpected delay. (Unpredictability again.) In today's diary, November 4, he writes: "Spirit in the camp is splendid. I am very busy packing up and going through the files—much appreciate the extra day."

Ever since the day before yesterday, when Dunlop received final confirmation that he and the others were to move on to an unknown fate, he has been untiringly busy. That's his nature. As was the case last spring when, on learning that the Dutch in Java had laid down their weapons, he decided not to flee but to remain with the sick and wounded and wait for the Japanese, even though he knew that after marching into Singapore they had massacred both staff and patients at the military hospital there.* But, at that point, back in March, he'd been "too busy to feel much fear." (His physical and moral courage are inseparable.) And perhaps, even on a day like this in November, working with a variety of tasks, big and small, can provide an antidote to disquiet about the future.

Dunlop's to-do list has been a long one. There is the canned food to be distributed; money to be collected and doled out; final accounts to be drawn up and signed; the camp library to be rescued (each man has to carry one book in his pack); archive papers to be sorted; "carry what we can" (that refers to a host of other things: "Sports equipment"— take little; "Tools"—take a few); the unmarked graves in the camp graveyard have to be marked; three of the eight pigs will have to be slaughtered—and don't forget that half a pig is to go to the Japanese officers, a thank-you and a bribe at the same time; the soldiers' personal equipment must be gone through, checked and gathered, in line with the following list of what they are allowed to take with them: 1 shirt and 1 pair of shorts, 1 water bottle, 1 pair footwear, 1 mosquito net, 1 set of puttees, 1 pack, 1 cap, 2 blankets, 1 sun hat, 1 belt, 1 mess tin and cutlery, 1 sleeping mat. (Remaining equipment is to be handed in to the camp store.)

---

* The victories won by Japan during 1941 and 1942 were all accompanied by massacres, big or small. The atrocities, for the most part, were unplanned and committed almost *en passant:* they were an expression of the general brutality and sense of superiority of the Japanese military. On the other hand, some Japanese atrocities actually were planned: Sook Ching, for instance, the mass murder of ethnic Chinese in Singapore that spring, may have taken between 25,000 and 50,000 lives. There were also the medical experiments on people that were performed by the now-notorious Unit 731.

Everything has now been ticked off. They are ready.

In the breathing space left them, they take the chance to enjoy the fragile bit of everyday life that Dunlop more than anyone has done so much to create. They do it for the joy the day itself brings, but ultimately because it helps them stay sane in the dark, confined and unpredictable world they inhabit.

The camp theatre gave its last performance yesterday evening. It took place in the converted gym hall that they usually use—they call it Radio City and it's always full. It is the place where the prisoners have been able to take part in everything from theatre plays (*Othello, Julius Caesar, Journey's End*) and jazz concerts (the small camp orchestra has drums, a bass, harmonica and violin) to local revues (always entertaining, with many labored and indecent jokes, as well as what is an inescapable element in all camp entertainment—prisoners dressed as women).* In his diary Dunlop writes the following: "Sgt Wynne and P/O Abbot both dressed as whores and looking the part; Berny Weller and his band. Several very pleasant Nip soldiers gave money to players, tried the instruments and eventually came back loaded with cakes." (Once again, that unpredictability.)

But first today they are holding the graduation ceremony for all who've taken part in one of the thirty or so courses offered in the camp: language courses (French and Japanese, for instance), history, mathematics, navigation, technical science, medicine, geography, agronomy. About 140 lectures or seminars are held every week, some of them at a fairly high level. One of the lecturers, for instance, had been doing research in ancient history at Cambridge.

After they had all collected their certificates—probably made by the group of artistically gifted prisoners who produce *Mark Time*, the camp newspaper—Dunlop is forced to get up on the stage and make a short speech, in which he says how "strongly impressed" he was "by the spirit of a university we've built up here." Thereafter comes a football game, a final one between different teams of prisoners—the British and Australians on one side, the Dutch and local people on the other. (A wide range of sports has been practiced behind the wire: boxing, wrestling, basketball, volleyball, athletics, cricket, even a sort of primitive minigolf, but football has been the most popular.) Afterwards

---

* The usually prudish Japanese really appreciated these elements. One of the Japanese officers had even bought expensive makeup for the camp drag queens.

the teams line up and Dunlop harangues them. He makes a point of "how much we've enjoyed the football" and adds—perhaps a touch too generously—that "where we were going, we would stand more chance of winning a match than here." All the men in front of him are thin and sunburned.

And where are they on their way to?

The day is rounded off in the same spirit and Dunlop writes in his diary:

> Nick gave a very charming little farewell dinner party with L and I, John Morris, Frank Burdon, Christmas, Ramsay Rae (administrative staffs). It was the nearest thing to home conditions I have seen, with little table markers and a bare table with a nice center and flowers! We drank much sergeant-brewed beer—peculiar taste like mild ginger beer.

．　．　．

Leningrad has prepared itself for the winter. Arithmetic is on the side of the city. A month earlier, the fourth attempt to break the blockade had failed, but the besiegers had remained fairly quiet since then. After the mass death and the large-scale evacuations, there are now perhaps only 800,000 people left in the city—just over a year ago there were 3.3 million. So there are far fewer mouths to feed. Towards the end of the month the ice begins to form on Ladoga, which will mean that the "Life Road" can be reopened. The cold brings some good in its train.

But fear of another brutal winter remains. Inevitably. The fact that people are now talking about food in such an excited and anxious way is, paradoxically, a good sign. Lidiya Ginzburg writes:

> The food mania, the maniacal conversations about it—all this intensified enormously during the respite. During the days of the great hunger, people mostly kept quiet. Possibilities were cut off completely so there was no space left for psychological adornment of the bare facts or using the eternal human will for the affirmation of values.
>
> Quantity of suffering turns into a different quality of sensation, in the same way that those who are badly wounded experience no pain in the first instant and those frozen to death fall into a pleasant state towards the end. Genuine hunger,

as is well known, is not like the desire to eat. It has its masks. It used to display the face of misery, indifference, an insane urgency, cruelty. It most resembled a chronic disease, and as with any disease, the mind played a most important role. The doomed were not those with the blackest features, or those most emaciated or distended. They were the ones with the strange expressions, looks of weird concentration, the ones who started trembling in front of a plate of soup.

Both the radio and the newspapers report continued fighting in the factory districts of Stalingrad, but it doesn't seem to be anything like as intense as it was a week or so ago. Does that mean that the Germans have been stopped? Today's date is November 5. Preparations are underway for the celebration of the anniversary of the revolution. The siege has lasted 432 days so far.

. . .

He notices that they are getting close. The sounds change, there is less vibration, the destroyer on which they are travelling slows down. Is he also picking up the smell? There are many now who have travelled the same stretch in the same way in the last three days, crowded together in a hotchpotch of men, weapons, equipment, ammunition and stores on the swaying decks of fast-moving destroyers heading southeast under the cover of darkness. And when they arrive and the night breeze strengthens, they can usually smell the island before they see it, or so the story goes. The smell of hot, rotting vegetation drifts over the water. It's a smell that is distinctly uninviting and also strange and new to most men in the regiment, which is made up of conscripts, city boys, students, former factory workers and the like, all just as unused to the jungle as the American boys of roughly the same age and background they are about to encounter.

His name is Tohichi Wakabayashi and he is a thirty-year-old lieutenant from Nagoya commanding the 10th Company of the 228th Infantry Regiment. As the destroyer cuts its speed and it's almost time to go ashore, he feels a not unusual mix of expectancy and concern, to judge from his diary. "I felt my skin tingle," he writes:

The moment has come. The commander said, "If you drink alcohol the night before you head out, strangely enough, the

airplanes won't get you," as he treated us to some beer, and just
as he proclaimed, we began our entry into the landing zone,
miraculously, without any attacks from the sky. As I groped
my way through the narrow dark passage on the deck, I saw
the shadowy black rocky mountains beyond the starboard side
ahead, waiting for me like a demon.

We can assume that the adrenaline flooded through Wakabayashi
in this situation and that all his senses were sharpened in the darkness.
He hears "the grinding and crunching noise" made by the anchor chain
as it runs free. He hears the boom of artillery pieces in the distance.
He watches a flare burst high in the blue-black night sky. He hears
the engines of enemy planes. He hears and sees the anti-aircraft guns
open fire—mainly sees, because the lightning muzzle flash and sudden
bubbles of light slice through the darkness, are reflected by the leaden
sea, die away, flare up again and throb, the sound a little out of sync
because of the distance. The darkness has the same speed as the light.
    The deck of the destroyer is a picture of what is often called chaotic
coherence and, in the melee, the soldiers are trying to get ready to
disembark. (Arms and legs everywhere, bodies, faces, chinstraps being
tightened, rucksacks being put on, belts adjusted, weapons gleaming,
boxes being banged down.) Wakabayashi finds himself on the starboard
side, his eyes fixed on the dark outline of the landforms. And there it
is—a light flashing on and off. The signal. He writes in his diary: "This
is it. Here we go. Without hesitation, I ordered the men to board the
small landing craft." He shouts a word of thanks to the captain of the
destroyer up on the blacked-out bridge. The answer he gets is: "We
pray for your fortune in the battle!"
    The engines of the landing craft are revved up and the vessel thuds
and hammers through waves topped with white foam. Wakabayashi
hears an explosion over to their left. He sees an airplane's blue marker
light coming through the darkness towards them . . . over them . . . past
them. They reach land. Wakabayashi writes:

The boat made it to the beach and we jumped off immediately,
covered by waves from all sides, the current that pulled us
under. I swallowed a few mouthfuls of sea water, as if I was
getting a taste of the bitterness of what we were yet to face
on Guadalcanal.

. . .

All around Charles Walker was another grassy plain. In front of him was more jungle. All this on Guadalcanal. The sea is not far off, maybe not much more than half a mile. The wind, cutting through the dense high barrier of greenery, carries with it a fresh smell of salt. But he doesn't know their exact position and it seems that no one else does either. Walker does not have a map, nor has he seen a map, and what maps exist are full of errors. Some of them are hand-drawn. Nor has anyone told him—except in the vaguest terms—what the point of all this is: Japanese reinforcements have been landed to the east and, presumably, are still there, at a place called Tetere, on the coast. Walker's battalion is to help the Marine Corps stop them. That's the hope, anyway.

It's the early afternoon of November 5. They have been marching for thirty-six hours, through cotton grass ten feet tall, through dense rain forest, down into ravines and up out of ravines, across open ground and back yet again into the half-light of the rain forest. There are swarms of insects, mosquitoes—masses of them—and red ants that are known to gorge on the bodies of the dead, and millipedes, scorpions and spiders. The air is full of the chattering and screeching of hundreds of cockatoos and parakeets. Since they are transporting heavy machine guns, gun carriages, ammunition boxes and all the rest of it, Walker's platoon has had a heavy march—in full battle gear. Their feet ache, their backs ache, and their legs and knees ache. The air is damp and hot. Every so often, as usual on Guadalcanal, heavy showers of warm rain fall from the low cloud cover. A noisy thunderstorm appears from nowhere and disappears just as quickly. They ate their last rations yesterday and now the water, too, is starting to run low.

Walker receives orders to take his platoon and go north towards the coast (or where they assume the coast to be) to reconnoiter things. After less than half a mile his section sergeants turn awkward and argue vehemently that they think it's stupid to go on. (Are they scared? Are they tired? Are they hungry? We don't know. A combination of all three, perhaps?) Possibly because he is scared or tired or hungry himself, Walker acquiesces. They return and by about 4:30 p.m. are back with the battalion, which is camped in a dry flood ravine. *Mission Accomplished. Not!* Using their helmets, the men dig frantically for water and eventually a trickle emerges—brown and stinking. They add iodine drops to it and drink it greedily.

Darkness falls.

But there's to be no sleep for them. An order comes over the radio for the whole battalion to advance the short distance to the sea. (Given the damp conditions, it's a miracle the radio is working. All communications are usually done via field telephone or runners. They've already thrown away those idiotic walkie-talkie sets as unusable.)* They form up and advance across yet more open ground and into another stretch of jungle. That's when it happens. They hear the clatter of machine-gun fire as arcs of tracer bullets cut through one of the columns. Men fall. Many of them. (Ever since the nocturnal battles, they know what it looks like when tracers hit living bodies.) They return the fire and then people begin shouting and hollering. They can tell from the sound that those were American machine guns. The firing ceases. The 2nd Battalion, Walker's unit, has run into the 3rd Battalion of their own regiment. (Weren't they supposed to be somewhere else? What do the maps say? Are there any maps?) Eighteen men have been hit.[†]

Walker feels bad. He knows that he shares some of the responsibility for this. His section sergeants, so sure of themselves earlier, are also ashamed. But the ultimate responsibility lies higher up, on whoever gave the order for this short, nocturnal march in complete darkness. (Walker later learns that one of the Marine Corps battalions received the same order to advance but decided it was foolish and chose to ignore it. They waited until dawn.) At about eleven o'clock that night Walker's platoon reaches the beach and the sea. They dig in there, in the sand. But where are the Japanese?

The following morning the whole battalion moves on eastwards along the sandy beach. They wade across a small river (must be the Nalimbiu, mustn't it?); they wade across a second (Metapona) and come to a third (Gavaga). Walker's platoon with its heavy machine guns is to support G Company, and they follow them when they turn south along the latter creek. Over to one side they can hear the gunfire getting heavier. What is happening—and where is it happening?

---

* As Paul Fussell has pointed out: "You could estimate the lessons that had been learned along a particular piece of road by noting how many of these small, pretentious and expensive strokes of genius lay discarded in the ditch." At about the same time, one of the Marine Corps battalions failed to make contact via their radios and that made the situation even more confused.

† In this context, it should be mentioned that the first death in the 164th had been caused by one of their own men who went out of his mind on his first night at the front.

Walker manages to locate a command post, where he hopes to get information. No sooner has he gotten there than a mortar round lands right in the middle of the group, killing an officer Walker knows and wounding several others. By some miracle, Walker is unhurt. The mortar round turns out to be an American one. Meanwhile an American fighter plane attacks its own side time after time.* There is rampant confusion.

Darkness falls. Their food ran out twenty-four hours ago. Supplies have either broken down or someone simply forgot that detail. Professional soldiers distrust National Guardsmen and National Guardsmen are suspicious of professionals—the Marines look down on all of them. Walker is bitter: "Whoever was in charge of this operation was derelict in all aspects. Famous schools often produce famous fools." Now, he has slowly begun to understand the logic in this crisscrossing of the jungle. Japanese reinforcements have actually landed and the idea is to perform a bold pincer movement, pin them back against the coast and then destroy them.

It's one of those overcomplicated operations that looks good on paper and in the history books; it smacks of a seminar exercise laboriously worked through in a cool classroom at West Point using neat little colored arrows that move across a map with choreographic precision—in utter defiance of reality on the ground.

No wonder then that mistakes and blunders stack up. This is the first attacking operation mounted by the American army since 1918 and it's being carried out by "neophytes and amateurs."[†] As another soldier in Walker's unit said gloomily later: "The Americans learned once again that offensive operations against the Japanese were much more complicated and difficult than was defeating banzai-attacks." The situation, however, is exceedingly difficult to get an overall view of. A map of the north coast of Guadalcanal is, in the words of another eyewitness, "a crazy quilt of red (enemy) and blue (friendly) patches."

---

* Walker's platoon had come close to suffering the same fate a day or so earlier when an American fighter swooped over their heads. If the pilot hadn't noticed them waving their arms and helmets, "we'd have been slaughtered."

† Paul Fussell's phrase. He also says: "Mistakes and blunders are, for the most part, characteristic of the Allies' operations," particularly at the start of the war, we should say, to be fair. Much of it was due to a lack of training and experience, though Fussell believes there was also a cultural factor: the often "individualistic and sometimes anarchic personal backgrounds" of the Americans and the British.

. . .

Hand on heart—isn't it largely for moments like this that they volunteered to serve in U-boats? Coming home; entering the port; the return of the celebrated heroes. It's about lunchtime, one o'clock, Thursday, November 5, and U-604 is entering the safe harbor at Brest.

Their boss, Admiral Dönitz, may be something of a bore in his insistence on U-boat crews being lectured on the misfortunes of venereal disease and the blessings of abstinence (better for young men to devote themselves to sport instead) before disembarking, but he does understand. Which is why there is always a reception committee at the quayside, with a flotilla commander present at least, sometimes an even more senior officer, perhaps even a party bigwig out to bask in the glow of their heroism. There is almost always a band, and usually there are some women—preferably young women.

Women are important, not primarily as a kind of symbolic marker that the crew can now see an end to the abstinence of a U-boat voyage—a matter of some importance to young men whose enthusiasm for sport is usually less than Dönitz hopes—but mainly because the admiring gaze of women is an important element in contexts of this sort. Their presence underlines the meaning of what the young men have just been through and it confirms their role as Victors and Protectors. They are usually Wehrmachtshelferinnen (Armed Forces Women Auxiliaries) in uniform or in mufti, telephone and telegraph operators, secretaries and nurses,* occasionally relatives, perhaps even a troupe of racially pure ballet dancers who happen to be on tour in the vicinity and whose presence has been required by the military entertainment unit.

There are also always uniformed people there from a PK, Propagandakompanie—writers, photographers, filmmakers, people with microphones, sometimes even illustrators and other graphic artists. Heroes are the most important raw material for the regime's

* One should not overemphasize the compulsory aspect of their presence. At this time they were usually volunteers and their service often a natural continuation of their involvement in the female equivalent of the Hitler Youth, Bund deutscher Mädel (BdM—League of German Girls). The acronym BdM was sometimes maliciously interpreted as standing for *Bubi, druck mich* (Give me a cuddle, boy) or even *Bedarfsartikel deutscher Männer* (Essential goods for German men).

incessant propaganda mill. (It's impossible to have too many people of that sort, not just because they are living evidence of German successes, but because they tend to be devoured by the very phenomenon their existence is advertising: the war itself.) And few branches of the armed services offer as many heroic epics as the U-boat service. The successful U-boat captains, "the Aces"—Kretschmer, Hardegen, Schepke, Topp, Liebe, Witte, Endrass, Lüth and others—experience the level of attention that film stars had been given and the sporting elite would be given. (During their free time they are photographed, surrounded by fans and courted—sometimes erotically—in the same way as the most celebrated fighter pilots.) They are proof that the war is not some meaningless slaughter or an anonymous and spiritually dead struggle between mass-produced machines, but an elevated and natural trial of strength in which the individual plays a vital role because victory goes to the most courageous, the most skillful and the most strong-willed. Some of the glory also falls on the crews, of course, who usually act as a kind of joyful stage set when their captain is being lauded on returning from another Feindfahrt (operational patrol).

The time is coming up to two when the grey shape of U-604 followed by two other U-boats approaches the quay in the enormous U-boat pen.* There are photographs of this event. The flotilla emblem, a huge laughing swordfish painted in black, is visible on the sides of the boat's conning tower; on the rear part of the tower a swastika flag flies in the wind; three pennants cut from bed linen flutter from the half-raised periscope, one for every vessel they have sunk and giving the gross tonnage of each of them. The skipper, Horst Höltring, is standing in the conning tower, together with a number of other crewmen. (One of them may well be the detested von Bothmer.) Höltring, unlike most of his men, has taken the trouble to shave. He looks younger than the twenty-nine he actually is. This blond skipper has an attractive appearance, sharp and yet gentle at one and the same time, pleased with himself but nevertheless slightly uncomfortable with the situation.

There seems to be a chill wind from the Atlantic. The sky is overcast, the sun hidden. Most people, including Höltring, are wearing gloves, scarves (of various colors and patterns) and the standard-issue

---

* U-boats usually made their exits from and entries into port in small groups led by a minesweeper.

knee-length, pale-grey leather coats. Höltring's scarf is tied with great precision, and he is saluting.

Once the U-boat has made fast at the quay, the rest of the crewmen quickly emerge and form up on deck. All in all, there are fifty-two men. Many of them haven't seen daylight for three weeks, are pale and look as if they have lost weight. Their expressions are genuinely happy, with none of the forced jollity typical of Nazi propaganda. The photographs reveal how young most of them are, barely out of their teens, their beards thin and downy. We'll have to imagine the music the band is playing.

A pleased Heinrich Lehmann-Willenbrock, commanding officer of the flotilla, goes on board and there are handshakes and many salutes. Lehmann-Willenbrock himself is one of those highly decorated U-boat aces, though only thirty years old. (Behind his back they often call him *der Oberbauernführer* [senior farmers leader] because he insists on wearing his uniform trousers tucked into his high boots and frequently being accompanied by a goat, the flotilla's mascot.) Lehmann-Willenbrock* addresses Höltring while the bystanders, all standing rigidly at attention, listen carefully. Then it becomes more informal, high-spirited even. Höltring is presented with a large bouquet of flowers—chrysanthemums, dahlias and carnations. Several of the young women in civilian clothes slip down from the quay and begin pinning buttonhole bouquets on the crew members' lapels. Kisses are landed "right and left." We can assume beer was distributed, one bottle per man. We can also assume that someone bursts into spontaneous song. Group photographs are taken. Buses are waiting to take them away.

.   .   .

At daybreak Walker is visited by the captain of G Company, who behaves strangely and can't look him in the eye. Out comes the order:

---

* Lehmann-Willenbrock is the model for the U-boat captain (played by Jürgen Prochnow) in the 1981 film *Das Boot*. The film is based on the 1973 novel of the same name by Lothar-Günther Buchheim, which in turn is based on the latter's experiences in autumn 1941 when, as a uniformed propaganda journalist, he accompanied an already famous Lehmann-Willenbrock and U-96 on their seventh patrol. (By March 1942 Lehmann-Willenbrock had sunk twenty-four ships and it's estimated that around 1,200 died as a result.) Lehmann-Willenbrock was the technical adviser for the production. Buchheim didn't like the film as he found the emotional approach exaggerated when compared with reality.

Walker's platoon is to cross the Gavaga Creek and plug the gap in the American lines. It's quite obvious that the captain has been ordered to do this himself with his own company but is shifting responsibility to put himself out of harm's way. There are several thousand well-armed and desperate Japanese between here and the sea and if they gather and attempt to break out at a single point, a solitary company of a hundred men will never be able to stop them—far less an exhausted machine-gun platoon. It's not just an absurd and unreasonable order, it's a death sentence. Walker is furious: "I knew a coward when I saw one." But he has no choice other than to obey: "I was to be the sacrificial lamb."

Heavily laden (with gun carriages, ammunition boxes and full combat gear), they work their way through the tall, thick rain forest. Visibility is no more than five or six yards. They come to the watercourse and start wading across. The water, full of leeches and bugs, comes up to their armpits. Walker is in the lead the whole time and he is afraid for his life. Everything goes slowly. Step by step. They halt, listen, scan ahead, sniff the air. Trouble could start at any moment. He is at the front and if a gunfight starts he will be the first to be hit. Will he even know? Will he end up spending what's left of his life here, like this? Walker is both alive and dead at one and the same time.

They find a way out of the water. Nothing. Jungle to the side of them, jungle above them, jungle in front of them, filled with the usual cries of birds and other strange noises. Then, just a little way into the dense, steamy jungle, Walker comes upon something that halts him in his tracks: a broad trail made by numerous boots running directly north-south cuts through all the greenery. They follow it northwards. They see abandoned enemy equipment all around and they come to the inevitable conclusion that the major Japanese force has slipped out of the encirclement.

On November 12 Walker and his men are ordered back to the defensive positions around the airfield. They are so weak from lack of food that they only manage to move in stages of a hundred to two hundred yards before needing to sit and rest. At one point one of the men refuses to get up until Walker, who is a big man, threatens him with violence. Their uniforms are torn and filthy. In the last week, Walker has had little more to eat than a bar of chocolate and a couple of pieces of pineapple.

. . .

There's a complete change of mood, as fast as it is unexpected. And no wonder: the brigade Keith Douglas's unit is part of has regrouped and is now advancing west and southwest in the dawn light in nose-to-tail columns. It's no longer a matter of breaking through, it's now a case of chasing, cutting off and gathering in. They are moving fast, faster than Douglas has ever experienced at the front, more than thirty miles an hour at times.

In a couple of hours they travel farther than they have in all the earlier days put together and this is where the rapid tanks of his squadron really come into their own:

> The Crusaders, like enough to hounds, raced across the plain, bellies to the ground, and put up small parties of the enemy every few minutes. Gun crews frantically trying to get their guns and vehicles away, infantry surrendering, lorry drivers— all Italians—driving themselves and their comrades to meet us and surrender.

Columns of dust rising everywhere. It's November 5.

This heavy, disciplined advance across the flat desert landscape soon begins to break up as individual tanks disappear, off chasing the fleeing enemy or hunting for loot.

Like every other defeated army, the Africa Corps leaves a wind-blown muddle of discarded and abandoned necessities, clothes, ammunition, weapons, papers and all kinds of bric-a-brac behind them. It hadn't been possible earlier, but now many people stop at motionless vehicles, empty tents or abandoned artillery emplacements, poke about and help themselves. (They do so cautiously, though, as they all know that the Italians in particular have a bad habit of booby-trapping items they have left behind. Quite frequently they even booby-trap corpses.) Douglas is one of these people and he quickly earns a reputation not just as a brave and undisciplined poet but also as someone much given to plunder.

In the course of the day he picks up cameras, binoculars, compasses, pistols (the German Luger P08 is the favorite souvenir, with the compact Italian Beretta M34 coming second, and for a while he has four or five of them), blankets, uniform badges, combs, razors, hair oil, tins of food, camp beds, inflatable mattresses, some German novels, clothes—particularly clothes, and even more particularly, clean new pants.

Later he meets another member of his squadron whose tank is stacked full with boxes of bottled cherries, boxes of Macedonian cigarettes, boxes of cigars and crates of every kind of alcohol: chianti in straw flasks, champagne, liebfraumilch, cognac. Douglas's regimental doctor comes across a couple of Scots infantrymen throwing away a crate of bottles after tasting them and discovering that they contained neither beer nor whisky. The doctor, however, sees from the famous yellow labels that they are vintage Veuve Clicquot champagne. He salvages them for himself.

.   .   .

The operation Charles Walker and his battalion take part in on Guadalcanal is a failure.* He himself refers to it as "a fiasco" and the soldiers call it "the Koli Point Rat Race." (Koli Point was the headland where the Americans had initially hoped to surround the invaders.) And it has consequences. The company captain who sent Walker's platoon to plug the gap in the lines receives a strong reprimand—which Walker considers appropriate; Walker's battalion commander is dismissed from his post—which Walker considers to be wrong, but "someone had to take the blame for the failure of this grandiose plan concocted on high." He thinks he can discern a pattern: in his view close to 75 percent of professional officers are incompetent, particularly those schooled at West Point, but they cover for one another and are quick to award medals to each other.† Later, his regimental commanding officer has a mental breakdown.

.   .   .

Why is he finding it so difficult to sleep? And why does he have such strange dreams? Particularly now, given that he is so far away from

---

* Around 2,500 Japanese slipped out of the trap and were later able to join up with the main Japanese force inland. They had, however, been seriously weakened as a result of attacks by their American pursuers (led by indigenous guides) and a severe shortage of food.

† Much later, when the history of this operation comes to be written, it is turned into a success. All documentation about this operation has disappeared from the collection of regimental papers preserved in the Chester Fritz Library at the University of North Dakota, where, for instance, the important S-2 journals are kept. (These are a sort of logbook that all army units had to keep to record their activities day by day.)

everything and at home in the big former manse with his wife, Gretha, and his two boys, surrounded by familiar things, all his books, his medals, his collections of beetles.

During the night of November 5 he dreams of an ancient cave system on a distant island, but the time is not then but now and the caves are full of soldiers, in great swarms, even though thousands of them have just been killed by a single massive explosion; but they carry on swarming around as if they were ants. On waking it occurs to him that this island—Crete—was the location of the great labyrinth. And what was at the center of the labyrinth? The monster, half human, half animal, that regularly demands its tribute in human flesh.

His name is Ernst Jünger and he's a captain in the German army, currently at home on leave in Kirchhorst, a small village some three miles northeast of Hanover. In less than a week he will be moving on to his next posting: the Eastern Front awaits. This fact alone is enough to make the average person sleep uneasy and dream very strange dreams. But that's not it. And Jünger is anything but average.

This is his second world war, and that is too many. Almost everyone middle-aged, both men and women, in any kind of position of importance or authority, are veterans of or marked by their experiences from 1914–1918. For good or bad, this is what shapes their ideas and thought processes, their frames of reference and expectations. But by this point many people have begun to recognize that things have become twisted: this is not just more of the same, this is something new and unpleasant. What above all makes it incomprehensible is that the old frame of reference no longer suffices.

Jünger's first world war was a triumph. His lust for adventure, his physical courage, his sharp intelligence and controlled, distant nature carried him through the most impossible situations. In spite of being wounded fourteen times, he never lost the barbarian intoxication that comes from charging into battle—an intoxication that many feel the first time around but most people quickly lose when they come to recognize what they are risking and what pain can do to the body both physically and mentally. But Jünger remained untouched by doubt and came out of the war covered in medals.* He quickly became something of a celebrity, mainly because of his own writings about the war,

---

* In September 1918 Jünger became the youngest person to be awarded the highest military honor in Wilhelmine Germany—the famous Pour le Mérite.

where his cool and observant eye went together with a highly elevated aesthetic sense.

That was then.

Jünger's second world war is a sinecure—so far, anyway. He did take part in the invasion of France in 1940 as captain of a company, but he did not see any major battles nor did he look for them. He has been on the headquarters staff of the German army in Paris since last spring, which is located in the deluxe Hôtel Majestic, a short distance south of the Arc de Triomphe. He has his office there, in room 202. In a formal sense Jünger belongs to the Ic/I section, which is partly responsible for the gathering of military information, though he has largely been involved in fairly pedestrian tasks such as censoring soldiers' letters or leafing through French newspapers and magazines looking for breaches of regulations. He and the other staff officers frequently play chess.

He lives in another slightly smaller luxury hotel nearby—Hôtel Raphael on the Avenue des Portugais—and he has plenty of free time. He loves Paris. When Jünger isn't strolling around or searching for rare books among the *bouquinistes* down by the Seine, he visits galleries or attends dinner parties with prominent intellectuals and artists. (Before the war his books had won him a degree of renown in France.) He has gotten to know people like Pablo Picasso, Jean Cocteau, Sacha Guitry and Georges Braque, and he moves in circles of friends of Germany, collaborators* and noisy anti-Semites as well as among groups with very different ideas, some of whom are reputed to be active members of the Resistance.† Jünger is quite short, forty-seven years old but still slim and in good shape, with sharp, distinct features and his hair short-cropped at the sides. He is always elegant, whether dressed in his immaculate, carefully pressed German army uniform with rows of medal ribbons on his chest or in a well-cut suit.

Jünger has an eye for beautiful women, so it's hardly surprising that he has had several affairs. Just now he is simultaneously juggling two different women in Paris, an elegant German Jewish pediatrician and

---

* Usually not overt collaborators so much as people who believe they are building a future for more or less equal French-German cooperation. "Good Germans" like Jünger will have an important part to play in this; Jünger, who is a Francophile, harbors similar illusions.

† This reflects Jünger's stance in 1920s Germany: he flitted with butterfly-like ease between right-wing nationalist groups and left-wing intellectual groups.

an exiled Russian woman writer who has excellent contacts in the cultural circles of the city. (It's not inconceivable that he and Hélène Berr have passed one another on the street at some point since both of them frequent the 5th, 6th and 7th arrondissements. In which case, given how good-looking she is, he may well have given her more than a passing glance and—unprovable speculation—perhaps even felt some shame at his uniform when he saw the yellow star she was wearing?) And he spends all the rest of the time reading, reading and doing more reading, voraciously and thoughtfully, mostly older literature and mainly French and English.

So, in view of this pleasant existence, why does Ernst Jünger have so much trouble sleeping and dream such strange dreams? Why is he losing weight? And why is he afflicted by waves of depression?

In Kirchhorst a misty Thursday morning turns into a misty day. The day's WB—Wehrmachtbericht (Armed Forces Report)—on the radio gives a brief and straightforward report: there is hard fighting in the West Caucasus; mopping-up operations are taking place at Stalingrad; Hungarian troops have prevented an enemy attempt to cross the River Don; German aircraft have destroyed two trains and a freighter at Ladoga; at el-Alamein, German and Italian forces have beaten back "incessant" British attacks in a series of bitter battles; a four-engine enemy bomber has been shot down in northwestern Germany; light German aircraft have attacked "essential targets" in eastern and southeastern England. Things are clearly still going well for the Axis powers.

. . .

November 5. Change of mood, part two! The tone of voices on the radio the soldiers communicate on has changed: they've become self-confident, excited, triumphant. Keith Douglas listens to several soldiers who ended up fighting straggling enemy tanks and he thinks "the voices of the participants seemed like those of boys in a shooting gallery."

The open, fluid situation contributes to the excitement and the excitement, in turn, contributes to the open, fluid situation. Douglas and the rest of the fast squadron continue chasing around, hunting for prisoners, for loot, for dust clouds in the distance. "All the anxiety of the previous days of battle gave way to the exhilarating sensations of sport." Douglas suddenly discovers they are all alone.

They drive up onto a ridge and see the dusty railway track which, according to plan, the brigade was supposed to follow while advancing.

Alongside the line he catches a glimpse of a long column of what he thinks are British trucks driving nose to tail eastwards. Douglas, who is shortsighted, assumes it's the brigade supply trucks and orders his driver to join them. Their tank swings neatly in alongside the moving trucks and slows down to their speed. Douglas glances into the cab of the nearest truck and, to his horror, sees that the driver is wearing a German uniform. And a moment later the truck driver realizes that the tank rolling along beside him is British.

What follows could have been written by Mack Sennett and performed by Buster Keaton. The shocked German truck driver suddenly swerves away up towards the railway embankment and, without braking, he hurls himself out of the cab while the truck is still moving. Soldiers, in a great state of confusion, tumble, fall and jump out of the back of the truck and start running over the embankment in a state of terror. Those aboard trucks number two and three do more or less the same. Douglas is just as disconcerted as the enemy soldiers. He calls them back, berates, swears, insults and threatens them in a mixture of German and English, telling them to give up, but the Germans are in a complete panic. He aims his turret machine gun at the dusty fleeing figures, but it jams and won't fire a shot. He grabs his tommy gun and aims, but there is just a click.

More than anything else, Douglas is relieved. Killing those terrified Germans would be pretty meaningless, he thought. Meanwhile, the trucks farther back in the column have quickly turned and are accelerating away back east, whereas those farther forward have continued trundling steadily on, happily ignorant of the drama that has just played out behind them.

Douglas and his driver, Evan, toss hand grenades at the abandoned trucks to put them out of action, but with little noticeable effect. Then they shoot with their six-pounder gun, but appear to have missed since nothing happens. Frustrated, they climb out of the tank and pepper the trucks' engines with their tommy guns. Finally, they search the wrecks and rescue some blankets and a bulging provisions bag. But then their radio begins to receive messages and the fuel is getting low, so Douglas decides that's enough and they move off back east.

After a short distance they encounter two more German vehicles driving westwards. Douglas chooses to take no notice of them and they do the same to him even though they pass one another at no more than fifty yards. A man suddenly springs up and runs over the embankment and Evan tries to shoot him with his tommy gun, but misses. Douglas thinks that was a "senseless thing to do." He and Evan start arguing.

There is an ambivalence in Keith Douglas that can seem confusing, but is probably quite common. As a rebellious student at Oxford, he had written essays deploring militarism at the same time as taking part with considerable enthusiasm in the voluntary officer training program available at the university. As already mentioned, he managed to trick his way into a combat role at the front and then fought in some of the hardest battles. His tank has knocked out a number of enemy vehicles—at a distance. He has no problem with that kind of abstract killing, but it's obvious he doesn't like the idea of killing close up. A few months later he writes a poem with the title "How to Kill," which contains the following lines:

> *Now in my dial of glass appears*
> *the soldier who is going to die.*
> *He smiles, and moves about in ways*
> *his mother knows, habits of his.*
> *The wires touch his face: I cry*
> *NOW. Death, like a familiar hears*
> *and look, has made a man of dust*
> *of a man of flesh.*

. . .

Later that same day Ernst Jünger is walking around in his garden in Kirchhorst. There is celery, carrots and beetroot. He notices the beauty of the silver bubbles the dew has formed on the leaves of the curly kale.

. . .

Experience helps, but no amount of experience, no systems, can guarantee that you will survive. Death strikes capriciously and ultimately it is the geometry of chance that rules. Fate, is what some people say … afterwards. Luck, say others. Fate or luck and an order from headquarters has today come as a blessing to Major Paolo Caccia Dominioni and his battalion. Initially the instructions told them they should regroup in a new position farther back, where combat was to be taken up again, but they've now received new and surprising orders. Continue on back. Retreat.

Luck is on their side in that they actually *can* get out. They have transport. What remains of Pioneer Battalion 31 is transported west in twelve overladen trucks, with so little space that most of them have to stand. And the whole time they have to guard against stepping on the many wounded men lying on the floor. Clusters of soldiers are clinging to the sides of the trucks and others sitting on the roofs of the cabs. They have abandoned their rucksacks and personal possessions and discarded any heavy weapons. Their water has run out. It's almost exactly twenty-five years to the day since Caccia Dominioni, then a young lieutenant, was part of the massive, chaotic withdrawal from Caporetto, the mother of all retreats. But this is worse.

And their little column is being pursued. A short distance away they can see the dust stirred up by a dozen British armored cars. And then... on the road, three British tanks. They are trapped. Tanks in front of them, armored cars behind and to the right of them, and over to the left a deep offshoot of the Qattara Depression and its saltpans. Caccia Dominioni and the other officers—the captain, adjutant, medic and pastor—hold a quick council of war. There is another amazing stroke of luck—perhaps the most amazing of all. Caccia Dominioni knows this place: Khor el Bayat. He travelled here before the war. It ought to be possible to escape via the depression.

Caccia Dominioni is actually an engineer and architect, but when he was called up into the army in 1940 he quickly ended up sitting at a desk on the third floor of the army information section in Rome. He sat there for fourteen months, growing increasingly frustrated. Then he managed to escape what he called the "sewer" of intrigue, corruption and inefficiency of the capital city by using contacts to get an active service posting as commander of a newly formed battalion of pioneers: 31 Battaglione Guastatori d'Africa del Genio.

It makes sense. For a long period before the war he'd been running a successful firm of architects in Cairo. (His business is still in the Egyptian capital, as is his apartment. Cairo is his home.) He knows the region, he knows the desert, he speaks Arabic. And, amazingly enough, he has been at this spot before.

One by one the trucks sway down the dizzying slope. Dust, smoke, engines roaring, explosions. In all the confusion half the trucks disappear at the same time as six others join them from units he doesn't know.

Later, in a wide sweep, they reach the coast road, which is packed with vehicles, all retreating. Paolo Caccia Dominioni writes in his diary:

5 November 1942. The march continues. Attacked both from the air and by enemy armour. Column surrounded at 14.00 hours. Losses sustained during break-out. Missing: 6 officers; 243 other ranks. Present: 12 officers; 239 other ranks—97 from 1., 138 from 7., 17 from 8. [company]. The engineers under Lieutenant Procacci missing completely. No contact with 24th Engineers under Captain Fasano since 4th November.

When the military records are drawn up much later, it emerges that Caccia Dominioni's battalion is the only unit in the whole of the Xth Italian Army Corps to escape the trap in one piece. He is awarded the silver medal for bravery for this achievement which, incidentally, he doesn't mention in his account of what happened.

.   .   .

November 5. Change of mood, part three! Keith Douglas and his tank are driving eastwards along the railway embankment. He is approaching the small railway station at Galal, where the rest of his unit is supposed to be. They hear excited voices over the radio—the regiment has engaged the enemy. By the time Douglas and his crew have finished refuelling it's all over. Without suffering any losses, the British have knocked out twenty-four Italian tanks. It's a great victory. It will appear in history books as "the Battle of Galal Station."

There is no question about the basic facts. But there are three versions of what actually happened. Version 1: the regiment warded off an enemy counterattack. Version 2: the column of Italian tanks had run out of fuel. Version 3: the column of Italian tanks were coming to surrender. (They had white flags.)

Stanley Christopherson, Douglas's squadron commander, who was present, afterwards inclined towards Version 3. He reports that "we made a horrible mess of them" and when it was all over the regimental doctor and his assistants worked tirelessly to staunch the blood and bandage up smashed limbs. Christopherson writes in his diary for November 5: "It made us think how illogical war was. First of all, we do our best to kill these Germans and Italians, shelling them and machinegunning them, and then afterwards we do all we can to save their lives." The only loss is a tank accidentally shot to pieces by their own anti-tank guns. One of the crewmen is dead and the tank commander has had a nervous breakdown and has to be sent away.

Douglas, on the hunt for more booty, visits the place later. He has managed to have a wash and a shave and all the clothes he is wearing, apart from his boots and beret, are German clothes he has collected in the course of the day. In the far distance, for the first time for a long time, he can see a glittering silver strip of the Mediterranean.

·   ·   ·

It's the morning of Friday, November 6, and Dorothy Robinson and Claudine are deep-cleaning the living room. Robinson washes the curtains and other textiles, polishes the glass and ornaments. Claudine, her Black home help helps her scrub the floor and dust down the walls and moldings. In a sense, Dorothy is doing this for her own sake and to stop things going downhill though she thinks it's tempting "when there are no menfolk around, to let things slide." But that's not her way: she wants to have the house clean and tidy for when "that phone call or letter" comes telling her that one of them is on his way home.

"When there are no menfolk around" is a saying she often falls back on. It's just one of many changes during the last year and it's perhaps the one that has affected her most. Her husband is away on yet another business trip and she knows her son is somewhere in Great Britain along with his air force unit. It's the same all over the neighborhood and among her acquaintances: many husbands and sons are away "for the duration," as another saying runs. And a third saying has started doing the rounds: "When the boys come home"—that is to say, after the war.

Something close to a minor population migration has started, with millions of people leaving their homes to seek a living and a new life in one of the massive centers of war production that have sprung up all around the United States in less than a year.* Industry is crying out for labor and wages are good. So even though Dorothy Robinson sees how slapdash Claudine can be, she is still glad to have her. It used to be cheap and easy to get a Black woman as home help, but now they are being drawn into the war industries where the pay is much better.

Claudine's fiancé, George—Dorothy really appreciates his kind heart and willingness to help—is one of the many who've moved to the factories in spite of suffering constant racism there, mainly from

---

* According to one estimate, when the war ended in 1945 more than fifteen million people were living in a different county than they had been in December 1941.

white workers. A very happy George dropped in less than a month ago to tell them he'd been moved to the night shift, which means a 10 percent increase in his wages. Most of the industries involved in war production are now working a three-shift pattern seven days a week. He showed them the little metal red, white and blue badge on his lapel: "The Army-Navy E," a distinction awarded to factories that achieve very high production quotas. (Dorothy was almost as pleased as Claudine and gave George one of her son's new ties.)

Even in her quiet suburban life, Dorothy can see various signs of the colossal development taking place in American wartime productivity. Jim is working as a kind of travelling troubleshooter in the armaments industry and their daughter, Peggy, is working in a factory on the West Coast. The commuter train is packed with workers in overalls, helmets on head and lunchboxes in hand—people on their way to or from the many factories that are on Long Island. These have either been opened this year or undergone huge expansion: the Republic Aviation factory in Farmingdale, for instance, has quadrupled in size and is now spewing out a steady stream of the powerful new single-engine fighter planes called Thunderbolts. There are big instrument production plants in Lake Success and Garden City.

Three of her son's classmates are now building aircraft at Farming- dale. They dropped by one day to ask how her son was getting on. All the boys were wearing blue overalls and among the many things they told her was that the factory was now so enormous that it took half their lunch break to walk to and from the canteen. Their parting words were, "Tell Art to keep 'em flying, and we'll keep 'em sliding." This is the war fought by the factories.

That evening Dorothy sits by the light of the open fire with Sally, a relative, and looks around with a sense of satisfaction. She sniffs the air and it smells clean. It's been a windy day, but not that cold, and there's been the odd shower.

．　．　．

It's one of the best addresses in Ulm, offering a wonderful view out over the great open square. It stands right by the cathedral-like city church with its dizzyingly tall spire, and close by on the same street there are two of the city's very best shops, the homeware shop WMF and the milliner Berta Kunze. And there, on the fifth floor of Münsterplatz 33, Stair II, lives a solitary young woman, Sophie Scholl. She has a serious face, framed by an artless pageboy hair style, and she is playing the piano, as she does every evening. She is possibly singing too, but we don't know that. The silvery notes flow around the big, beautiful apartment. This, too, is happening on Friday, November 6.

Afterwards she runs a bath, and while the water is filling the tub, she lights candles and burns spruce needles. Then she lies there in thought, comforted by the fragrance, the heat of the water and the gentle half-light of the candles. She is thinking of him, of course: He Who Is Far Away and in Danger.

That is her public life and in that respect she is not unlike countless millions of young women of her generation. In her case the man she is thinking of is Fritz Hartnagel, a professional officer four years older than her and a captain in one of the Luftwaffe ground units, and he is, indeed, far away and in danger: Hartnagel is in Stalingrad.

They can't really be called a pair. They met at a private dance before the war and what has gone on between them since is indeed reminiscent of a sort of dance, in which she leads and he follows cautiously, she withdraws and then approaches once more. She has just broken free from an unhappy love affair with the charming Alexander Schmorell, a close friend of one of her brothers. There is an erotic tension between them, but no evidence that this tension has ever reached physical release. Their meeting place is in conversation, in long, meandering talks about morality and religion and law and art and love and life. And in this, too, she is the one who leads. When faced with this intelligent, well-read young woman, Fritz has to struggle to keep up with her as she flits swiftly from Augustine and the problem of theodicy to current political concepts and the course of the war. What also makes it hard for him is that she is trying to open his eyes to the fundamental error in his career choice (professional officer) and in his world of ideas (his family are convinced Nazis). And she has made some progress in this.

Her arguments are philosophical, moral, ontological and theological—particularly the latter as she is a believer, though in her usual serious and self-critical way. Her parting gift to him when his unit was sent off to the Eastern Front in May was two volumes of sermons by the well-known Anglican theologian John Henry Newman.

And although she won't mention a word about it in the letter she is about to write to Fritz, we can be convinced that she also has other things on her mind. For she has another life, a secret life, to which he is not admitted—mainly out of care for him. In this other life, Sophie and her brother, Hans, belong to a loose circle of students at Munich University who are secret opponents of the regime. They aren't a "resistance group" in the usual sense of the word—that is, a group with a program, leadership, membership and organization. They are a cluster of young people, close friends, who share similar high-culture, bourgeois backgrounds, similar individualistic and intellectual characters, and similar personal histories of small rebellions and especially of disappointment with the desire of the totalitarian Nazis to control everything, to rule everything and to steer everything, even their very thoughts and lives.* Many of them were once members, or almost so. Hans is a former member of the Hitler Youth and even carried the flag at one of those gigantic mass meetings in Nuremberg. Sophie herself used to belong to the BdM (Bund deutscher Mädel—League of German Girls), the young women's equivalent of the Hitler Youth.

With the years, this sense of disappointment has been turned to rage by the knowledge—which reached them bit by bit, directly or indirectly—of what this state is actually capable of: injustice, persecution of those who think differently, the murder of dissidents, genocide even. In many whispered debates behind closed doors or over a bottle of wine in the Englischer Garten, one of the core issues has always been that these crimes are actually being carried out in their name—in the name of the German people. The conclusion has been that they must do something. Something. Otherwise, in moral terms, they will share the responsibility.

Over a two-week period last summer they distributed four laboriously prepared, precisely argued and closely printed flyers condemning the regime for its lack of intellectual substance, its mendacity and appalling crimes; they likened it to a cancerous growth that spreads in the absence of resistance. Among much else, the leaflets contained encouragement to commit sabotage at all levels; they spelled out that the only hope for the cleansing and rebirth of the German people lay in acknowledging their guilt and then behaving accordingly. "We will

* Quite literally. The fact that the regime was so prepared—eager even—to sacrifice young people in the course of its megalomaniac military project was an important source of anger and disappointment. Sophie Scholl knew several of the fallen and this fact clearly played a significant part in her decision to become part of the opposition.

not be silent, we are your bad conscience. The White Rose will not leave you in peace."

The flyers were fine-textured pieces of high culture, with references to Aristotle, Schiller, Goethe, Lao Tzu and the Bible. This partly reflects what the members are: young intellectuals. But it's also a conscious choice: they have given up on the "apathetic masses." They hope to influence other intellectuals and then indirectly, through them, the people. And yet the means available to them are almost sublimely insufficient. The four flyers of the summer were typewritten in a couple of hundred copies and sent out to recipients selected at random from the telephone book, or left lying in locations such as telephone boxes. But at least they felt they were doing *something*.

After her bath, Scholl writes a short letter to Hartnagel and then walks to the railway station to mail it. (It's from that letter that we have the details of her evening.) Scholl knows that Hans will be returning from the Eastern Front any day now, as will several of their mutual friends. Once Hans and the others are back, work on a new wave of flyers will begin—she has been preparing for this by getting hold of a mimeograph machine to duplicate the flyers; she bought it with money borrowed from Hartnagel under false pretenses. (Sophie acts as an informal treasurer for the group.) This was something that Sophie Scholl both wanted to do and had to do. And yet uncertainty gnaws at her.

It's a grey evening but the stars glitter behind the ragged clouds. Scholl is thinking of Hartnagel and that these glimmers of light are shining on both of them, on her here in Ulm and on him far away in Stalingrad.

.   .   .

Early that same Friday the Australian army doctor Edward "Weary" Dunlop and a thousand other Australian prisoners of war leave the labyrinth of low, whitewashed wooden buildings that make up the camp outside Bandung on Java. It's been raining during the night and the morning is cool. The stars are looking down on the scene here, too. There are two versions of what happened. First of all, Dunlop's own account, dry and factual, from his diary:

> Reveille 0315 Fell in 0430 marched out at 0550 reached station 0625. Large crowd up to see us off included Van, Horobin and Nick.

Then the other version, written much later and packed with what was missing at that point—i.e., knowledge of what awaited them. The pen is in the hand of the man Dunlop calls Van:*

> I remember walking between the low barracks and canton-
> ments, under the dripping wet trees towards the prison gates,
> how the stars had just re-emerged from the clouds and in the
> puddles we trod underfoot were reflected the great constella-
> tions like Orion, stars like Sirius and Aldebaran and the great
> planet Jupiter which had newly taken over the role of morning
> star from Venus. And whenever I think back to that walk and
> that moment when Weary, undismayed and even at so gloomy
> an hour, extracting a laugh from his overburdened men, met us
> at the great gate, all the adjectives personified in the Pilgrim's
> Progress made so unfashionable today occur to me as the only
> ones precise enough for the occasion; adjectives like "valiant,"
> "standfast," "tell-true," "great-heart" and so on, but also joined
> to those some not to be found in Bunyan's vocabulary, like
> Weary's unfailing sense of humour and his light and classical
> use of irony as a means of defeating self-pity and reducing the
> intrusions of fate in the life of himself and of those under his
> command to bearable human proportions. It was, we all three
> knew there in the dark at the gate, the end of an era in our
> prison lives, and the beginning of a new one in which we were
> all to be tried and tested in a way we had never been before
> in our lives and for that matter in the lives and memories of
> any men we knew.

Two of the Japanese officers from the camp turn up at the rail-way station to wave him off cheerfully. One of them allows himself a

* Laurens van der Post, the same age as Dunlop, was an unknown and only moderately successful journalist before the war. His main claim to fame at that point was that he'd had a novel published by Leonard and Virginia Woolf's publishing house (Hogarth Press); the novel was severely critical of racialism in his homeland, South Africa. He volunteered for the British army in 1940. After the war he had a major career as author, TV personality and mentor to Prince Charles, Margaret Thatcher and others. A character with his name makes a fringe appearance in the fourth season of *The Crown*.

humorless joke by telling them they are on the way to Surabaya for shipment on to Australia "which was now in Nippon hands!"

The train journey to Batavia—Jakarta after independence in 1949—takes almost eight hours. As a result of Japanese status fixation, Dunlop and the other officers get to travel in a carriage of their own and are spared riding in cattle cars along with the other ranks. He enjoys the slow, winding journey down from the highlands after all those monochrome months behind barbed wire: he sees high, jungle-clad peaks; he sees emerald-green valleys, hazy in the morning mist; he sees village after village with houses of dried brown attap palm; he sees the perfect mosaic of bright green rice paddies. And there and then he suddenly feels calm, his sadness for what has been and his worries about what is to come dispelled at least for the moment. Dunlop writes in his diary: "I feel perfectly cheerful and don't give a tinker's damn what happens."

．　．　．

The Ausland-Presseclub (APC), a club for foreign journalists, is located in central Berlin, on Fasanenstrasse, a side street between Kantstrasse and the fashionable Kurfürstendamm. It is run by the German foreign ministry in a building that used to belong to the German-English Association and consequently its décor is that of a British gentleman's club—comfortable but discreet and well-served by a host of willing and experienced servants. (The association crest can still be seen on the china.) The club has everything a working journalist might need: typewriters, current foreign newspapers and telephone and telegraph lines open twenty-four hours a day. Most of what is needed for relaxation is available too—a bar that serves ridiculously cheap "American cocktails," and a room for table tennis and darts. The APC, or Chez Paul,* as the club is also known, is almost always full of people.

That November evening, among the bustle of foreign journalists, German officials (in or out of uniform), diplomats, businessmen,

---

* "Paul" is Dr. Paul Schmidt, a foreign ministry spokesman, an intelligent, charismatic, pushy and unscrupulous Nazi who holds court in the club most evenings. Some foreign journalists refer to him (behind his back) as Al Capone, partly because he's dangerous but mainly because he's fat.

waiters, young women (frequently blond, flirtatious and usually with no very obvious function) and slightly shady individuals, there is a man of about thirty, well-dressed in a double-breasted suit and tie.

The man is on the short side, and slim—delicate even—with dark, carefully slicked-back hair. His polite, self-confident manner suggests a fairly well-to-do background, as does the superior grin that flits across his thin, elegant face from time to time. There's a slightly fearful look in his eyes. (And he is probably intoxicated—on cognac, his favorite drink, which he frequently drinks pretty well all day long, often taking his first glass in the morning.) He has a pretty, curvaceous French woman at his side—his young, giggly and rather overly made-up mistress. The man's name is John Amery.

Amery is, perhaps, the target of particular attention this evening, being, as he is, new in Berlin. Not only is he that rare creature, an eloquent and opinionated Brit who has openly come out in support of the Nazis, he is also the son of Leo Amery, a member of Churchill's government in London. Rumor has it that John Amery is not only a classic British upper-class eccentric of excellent family and contacts,* but that he is also a film producer, fascist, bisexual, bigamist and fast driver—all in all, a restless soul, a seeker. He is said to have smuggled arms to Franco and diamonds for himself.

The ambience at the press club is strange. The parties, the excellent food, the real coffee—all these are attractive, as is the opportunity to meet other foreigners. Simultaneously, however, the atmosphere has a constant whiff of corruption and suspicion. Corruption, because everyone understands that all this, like the rest of the material privileges— cheap apartments, cheap travel, extra ration cards—are designed to encourage foreign journalists to rank their personal comfort a good deal higher than their passion for truth. Suspicion, because it's impossible to tell the fixed from the fluid in the press club's twilight zone of rumors, uncertainties, disinformation, half-lies and whispered half-truths, where anyone and everyone may be an informer or a provocateur, where one of the most common gestures is what's jokingly called "the German glance"—that is, a quick glance over your shoulder to check whether anyone is listening in. One of the foreign journalists who frequents the club has likened the atmosphere to a detective novel:

---

* Like Lord Sebastian Flyte in *Brideshead Revisited,* he frequently takes his teddy bear around with him, even as an adult.

"You have a feeling the whole time that everyone is deceiving everyone else and that they are all puzzling their heads as to who actually is the big boss, 'the murderer.'"

John Amery is a natural denizen of the uncertain twilight of the club. A vicious, intelligent, spoiled child, much given to outbursts of rage, has developed into a vicious, intelligent and immoral rake accustomed to charming and bluffing his way through the world, a character who has escaped from an early Evelyn Waugh novel but wearing a swastika armband. Amery is a convinced fascist and anti-Semite—though his grandmother on his father's side was Jewish—but at the same time determined to enrich himself in order to finance the luxurious lifestyle his background accustomed him to and that he thinks the world owes him. (He has no shortage of courage and he indeed smuggled arms to Franco during the Spanish Civil War, but he also made a great deal of money in the process. His attempts to become a film producer ended in ruin—as did his other more or less shady business enterprises.) After the fall of France, Amery stayed on in the unoccupied part of the country—Vichy France. His contacts among French right-wing extremists were many and excellent, including Jeanine Barde, his mistress. Unfortunately, he found it impossible to remain within the bounds of the law and earlier this year was arrested for illegal currency transactions.

Somehow or other, the news that Amery was behind bars on the Riviera reached Berlin and Joachim von Ribbentrop, the German foreign minister, recognized immediately that Amery, given his family and his ideological leanings, was a propaganda gift from heaven.* Amery quickly received a German get-out-of-jail card and was taken by train to Berlin accompanied by a foreign ministry fixer. The intention is to use him on the radio.†

Generally, however, Amery isn't allowed to go far unless accompanied by an Auswärtiges Amt, or Foreign Office, official, not so much as a guard as to ensure, first, that he doesn't drink himself incapable

---

* The fact that Ribbentrop, who was notorious for being uninterested in matters of detail, intervened in this case shows the hopes the Nazis had for Amery.

† Amery was happy to go along with this. On the other hand, his own flash of inspiration—that he should be permitted to recruit a band of British volunteers from among the prisoners of war to serve on the Eastern Front—was given a cold and realistic shoulder by more or less everyone.

and, second, to collect the restaurant and brothel bills, along with bills for booze, hotels, rented cars, cleaning and so on that the Englishman leaves in the wake of his unsteady progress.

So, when he's standing there in the APC in a haze of cigarette smoke and jazz music,* what does he actually talk about in his slightly affected upper-class English accent? About his family, perhaps, and certainly about his father. And he probably puts on the old scratched record of words and phrases he has used so often before and which he will return to time and again: that Churchill's alliance with Stalin is a crime; that Englishmen and Germans ought to be fighting together to defeat the barbarism of communism; that the future of Europe lies in the victory of Hitler's New Order; that the war is primarily a Jewish attempt to take control of the world; that the Axis powers are on the way to victory, and so on.

Afterwards, Amery and his mistress are driven back to the Adlon, the most luxurious hotel in Berlin, just a stone's throw from the Brandenburg Gate. It's also the gathering place for a tawdry crowd of foreign fascists, tricksters and opportunists who have flocked to Berlin in the wake of Germany's many successes. His dog, Sammy, is waiting for him at the hotel. In just a couple of days, the Englishman is to make his first radio broadcast.

·   ·   ·

The train carrying Weary Dunlop and the other prisoners of war rolled into Batavia station at 3:20 on the afternoon of November 6. The cool of morning has given way to a thick, heavy heat. The prisoners climb down and form groups of fifty, in columns four abreast, just as they did when leaving the camp. They are not guarded by Japanese soldiers but by native Javanese police armed with pistols and sabres and wearing the blue-grey uniforms of the old colonial power. (Many of the native population have willingly changed sides and are happy to see their former colonial overlords—indeed, all whites—driven out and humiliated.) They set off.

The march is at a rapid pace. After a while the heavens open and

---

* Jazz, especially swing, had been forbidden in Germany since 1935, classified as *negermusik*. But in many different contexts, especially when the musicians were white, the ban was ignored, including at the APC. (Interestingly, it also tended to be ignored on the U-boats.)

a tropical rainstorm pours down. Dunlop is carrying a heavy load, even though as an officer he is permitted to send his luggage on by Japanese truck. But he is carrying the most indispensable things with him: two rucksacks containing among much else a well-concealed and disassembled radio—the possession of such a thing is punishable with death—and a suitcase with various important papers, orders, medical records, accounts and his own diary. Dunlop is tall, well-built and strong. (Before the war he played rugby at an elite level and taught boxing.) But the pace, the weight and the wet affect even him. The troops struggle on, but the going gets harder and harder. Just ahead of him, one of the older sergeants is buckling at the knees. Many of them have poor shoes, some no shoes at all, and the road becomes more and more muddy in the pouring rain. After about four miles men begin to drop: "It was a sorry sight to see some of these emaciated forms and haggard faces as they fell out."

Finally, they arrive at their destination for the day—Camp No. 5, or, more informally, Makasura. He sees the barbed-wire fencing, he sees row upon row of basic barrack huts made of thatched attap, he sees pole latrines, and he sees heavy, sticky red-brown clay . . . everywhere. Standing in the clay, they form up and are counted, then they wait and wait while the rain continues to fall. Those who had fallen by the wayside have been picked up by Japanese trucks and they now arrive. And the waiting continues. (Do the guards need to do a recount? Is it just another means of intentional humiliation?) They are all accustomed to waiting, it's one of the main elements of their existence and they are forever waiting for something; but now they are sodden and exhausted and merely waiting for the waiting to stop.

Eventually the camp commandant shows up, a bearded elderly major. The Japanese major makes the kind of speech always given in situations like this—it's polite in form, threatening in content. Both regulations and etiquette demand that everyone should greet him with a formal bow but, as Dunlop remarks, "of course, some asses saluted in the British fashion."

After that, Dunlop is too tired to change out of his soaked clothes. His ankles have begun to swell up. Their meal consists of rice and tea. Dunlop is already thinking of the things that need improving in this new camp.

.   .   .

It's been an unusually beautiful autumn in Stalingrad. The nights have started turning cold, but the days are still clear and sunny and there hasn't been any snow yet. There's a misty drizzle falling and the weather seems to be changing, so Adelbert Holl has started worrying about winter clothing. The date is November 6.

Holl is a twenty-three-year-old lieutenant in the 2nd Battalion, 276th Infantry Regiment, 94th Infantry Division. He is actually the commanding officer of the battalion's 7th Company, but having been wounded again—this is the seventh time (shell splinters in his right arm this time)—he has been given a temporary posting to the regimental staff. His commanding officer's reasoning is that Holl is one of the few experienced company commanders surviving* and his knowledge will be useful at staff level. It is quite obvious, however, that Holl needs time to recover, not just from his wounds, but from being more or less continuously in combat here in Stalingrad since the end of September. In a moment of, for him, uncharacteristic clarity, he described the place as like Moloch, the monstrous deity with an insatiable appetite for human sacrifice referred to in the Hebrew Bible.

Holl is very experienced and has been decorated eight times, including with the Iron Cross, both First and Second Class. He has been in combat ever since the invasion of Poland, but nothing he was involved in earlier compares with the last six weeks. Right from the start, the 94th Division has taken part in the attempts to conquer the city, all the way from the burned-out suburbs with their forests of blackened chimney breasts and then yard by yard towards the city center and the Volga. (They were the ones who, with a huge effort, captured the notorious big grain silo in the southern part of the city.)

The thought that has motivated men like Holl and his soldiers is that once they have reached the Volga they will have won, certainly the battle but probably the war as well. The river has taken on a virtually mythic status and it has defined the topography of the battlefield in an absolute sense; as the Soviet forces have been pressed into an ever-diminishing area by its broad waters, the fighting has become more and more intense, bloody, bitter, desperate and brutal. (Where do the Russians find their will to resist?)

---

* Almost all the company commanders had been wounded or killed since the start of the battle. Just as in the First World War, the most dangerous position of all was that of infantry officer of the lower ranks. The losses were enormous.

When the battle began, success was defined as capturing a district of the city; that was soon reduced to taking a street, then an individual building, and now a single floor, or a stairwell, or a room. And all this in a city with a name already shrouded in a nimbus of tragic greatness, in a growing confusion of shattered ruins, amid oceans of broken glass, crumbling plaster and dust, fragments of porcelain, remnants of furniture and human remains and the constant stink of cordite, smoke and putrefaction. After the last attack Holl led—it was against a ravine immediately west of the large, hotly contested Barrikady arms factory—his company is left with a head count of seven men. The whole battalion has just twenty-three men.*

When Adelbert Holl learned that they were to prepare for a new push—this was after he had carried out the reconnaissance and sent reports to headquarters "with sketches, by 18.00 at the latest"—he admits that he wept tears of rage and addressed a superior officer with angry words: "So these are to be cannon fodder, too?!" His reaction demonstrates what an extraordinary test this battle had become, for Holl is one of those who had never had any doubts: five years in the Hitler Youth, obedient and dutiful, unwaveringly loyal to the army and to the regime, he is a man who describes the oath he once swore to the Führer as "sacred." It takes a great deal to make a man like that start protesting. It was after this, and after his most recent injuries, that he was given a temporary posting to the staff.

During the fortnight Holl spends on the staff he makes a quick recovery. His sleeping quarters are in a ten-foot by ten-foot earth bunker in a small oak wood. He finds time to go riding on his horse, Mumpitz, and even just sits outside doing nothing but enjoying the autumn sunshine.

Holl is quite short in stature and has a stern appearance. His dress is always correct and accords with the regulations. Things like shaving, formal titles and proper forms of address are important to him. His subordinates are slightly afraid of him and in tight situations he has been known to resort to violence to deal with panic-stricken soldiers. But no one has any doubt that Holl is both physically brave and a competent commander in the field. On this particular day, though, Holl is busy with the less dramatic task of inventorying winter clothing.

The sounds of battle can be heard in the distance. Dense, oily-black clouds of smoke hang over the big and increasingly shattered industrial

---

* The normal strength of a battalion was about eight hundred men.

areas down by the Volga. The Soviet defenders there are still holding out in spite of enormous losses and almost constant bombardment from the air. The trees have lost most of their leaves.

.   .   .

What does it feel like the first time you kill someone? It depends on the circumstances, of course. Doing so in open combat when the choice is between your life and your opponent's is not a moral dilemma. And when the war approaches the kind of destructive, merciless fury it has now reached, when so much is at stake (as is currently the case in the place where Mansur Abdulin finds himself) that the line between life and death, between being and not being, is so thin that it scarcely leaves room for any moral questions at all—what then if you, like Abdulin, have never killed anyone before?

On the same day that Adelbert Holl in Stalingrad is making his inventory, Mansur Abdulin is on duty in a well-camouflaged forward trench some sixty miles northwest of the city. The landscape is empty, flat, silent and still clad in autumn colors. Winter seems in no hurry. The Don, somewhere behind them, is still unfrozen. Does he know that this is a bridgehead?

Abdulin is keeping watch on what he is supposed to keep watch on—the enemy position. And he has seen movement. There are several strange shapes moving in the trenches over there and, when they come closer, they turn out to be three men carrying bales of straw. (Straw is just about the most banal of all the necessities of war: good to sleep on, good for insulation, it can be used to keep the place clean or to clean up and, as a fallback, it can be used to feed the horses.) Mansur is a private soldier in the Red Army (1034th Rifle Regiment, 293rd Rifle Division). He, like about half the men in his division, is a Tatar, born and raised in the Central Asian part of the Soviet Union. He prefers to refer to himself as Siberian. He is small of stature and is just nineteen.

It is interesting to note how Abdulin responds. The moment he sees the men he decides to shoot. It's not that they constitute a threat, just that they are the enemy.

And he takes aim.

But then comes a hint of reservation. Ever since his childhood in Siberia, Abdulin is quite used to shooting: his father, a mining engineer and convinced communist, used to take him out grouse shooting in the forests. But Abdulin has been pondering things, thinking whether, perhaps, it's one thing to shoot grouse, another to shoot people. That, however, was earlier, during the training that turned him into a soldier. But not now: he knows what the enemy is capable of.

Even though all the statistics are strictly classified and even talking about them risks a death sentence, everyone knows that Red Army losses in the seventeen months since the enemy attacked have been utterly appalling.* And they know that the slaughter is still continuing. Away over the horizon, in the ruins of the city engulfed in flames, the men whisper the truth among themselves: from the moment a Soviet infantryman is sent into the line, he has, on average, only ten days left to live.

Odds such as these have given rise to a bitter attitude of mind: your own death may be inevitable, but at least you can take one of them with you. And as the apparently unstoppable German advance continued through the summer and the autumn, the propaganda poured over Abdulin and his comrades becomes more and more harsh, desperate even. There is, for instance, Ilya Ehrenburg's herostratic text "Kill": "The Germans are not human beings. Henceforth, the word German means to us the most terrible curse. From now on the word German will trigger your rifle. We shall not speak anymore. We shall not get excited. We shall kill. If you have not killed at least one German in a day, you have wasted that day...." Or there is the poem "Kill Him!" by the soldier poet Konstantin Simonov:† "If you don't want to give away / To a German, with his black gun, / Your house, your wife, your mother / And everything we call our native land, / Then know your homeland won't be saved / If you yourself do not save it. / And know the enemy will not be killed / If you yourself do not kill him." Why, then, would Abdulin be hesitating?

While Mansur is maneuvering his automatic rifle into the embrasure slot and attempting to line up the front and back sight on the human shape he can see moving over there, his heart begins to beat

---

* Up to February of that year the Red Army had lost over five and a half million men, dead or taken prisoner. Even worse was the statistic that for every German killed, the Soviets lost twenty men, an impossible equation in the long term.

† He is best known for the fine poem "Wait for Me," which was recited many, many times in the Soviet Union during these years. Some of the soldiers in the Red Army carried a folded copy of the poem in their breast pockets as a sort of amulet.

very hard. Sweat runs down from his forehead and his hands start shaking. Something still has to be overcome. The majority of soldiers never fire their weapons: whatever the circumstances may be, they don't want to kill, even when it is a matter of their own life or the enemy's. But Abdulin pulls the trigger, though he suspects he may be a little too early or a little too late.

The rifle cracks, the recoil thuds into Abdulin's shoulder. A miss. Abdulin, humiliated, sinks back into the trench and thinks, If I could kill just one of them. Just to get even for the future. In the death of the other, you are anticipating your own. But Abdulin quickly gathers his thoughts, gets back on his feet and peers along his rifle barrel at the far trench. There they are! The three of them are running in the weak winter sunshine with their bales of straw, but now they're running faster and bending lower. Mansur takes aim … carefully … keeps his sights on the one in the middle, aims just in front to compensate for the man's movement and the speed of the bullet. Abdulin feels calm now, and his hands have stopped shaking.

The rifle cracks, the recoil thuds into Abdulin's shoulder. A hit. The man over there comes to a stop, momentarily straightens up to his full height while, simultaneously, his head jerks back in an unnatural way. A moment later his knees give way and, in a last vain impulse to get away, or perhaps because of the geometry of his joints or whatever else it might be, his body begins a spiral movement, which is cut short and turns into a headlong collapse. The body, no longer a subject, becomes an object ruled by the laws of gravity and nothing else. Death.

And any reservations there had been have now gone. Abdulin is proud.

·   ·   ·

What mainly occupies Adelbert Holl on Friday, November 6, is the business of winter gear. He checks what they have available, both for himself and for his men: two pairs of underpants; two pairs of socks; two pairs of footwraps; one sweater; one pair of trousers; one forage cap; one uniform jacket; one overcoat; one set of fatigues; one camouflaged cape—Zeltbahn—and a pair of calf-length leather boots. That's everything. Holl knows that this won't do when the real cold sets in, but the request for winter clothing seems to have gotten stuck somewhere higher up in the military bureaucracy.

The problem could well be transport. Holl knows that all supplies to the Stalingrad front are using a single road that crosses the Don via a bridge at Kalatj-na-Donu. One result is that food has become pretty poor and many people blame the increased cases of jaundice on the monotonous diet. Something that is also going to be a cause of concern when the cold starts is the shortage of wood—but it's up to them to organize wood and stoves for themselves.

Holl's earlier misgivings, however, seem to be a thing of the past. This battle is going to be won. He has a feeling that morale among the men is still high, and as long as they get reinforcements, they will be able to take those trifling little strips of land by the Volga. "We all had complete confidence in the leadership."*

.   .   .

Autumn darkness. A forest of tall trunks. The train will arrive soon and Nikolai Obrynba and the other partisans are ready. The plan is simple and effective. (Only simple plans are effective for this group.) They have a light anti-tank gun waiting in a thicket of pines close to the winding railway track. (Think about that—they actually have cannon now! The partisan brigade's equipment is getting better and better.) They are intending to knock out the locomotive. And the explosives unit has also buried a hefty charge under the track, just before the location of the anti-tank gun. The rest of the partisans, Obrynba among them, are lying in wait with their weapons on a little knoll overlooking the embankment.

They are waiting for the train.

These are the kinds of operations partisan groups are usually associated with—blowing up trains, dramatic nocturnal ambushes and the like—but, in fact, this is the first one Obrynba has been involved in, apart, that is, from the attack on a small place he took part in just over a month ago. That, to put it mildly, was a chaotic affair in which he came very close to shooting one of his own side in the darkness, and

---

* Holl stands out, both in life and in his written memoirs, as a typical example of what's usually called an authoritarian personality: someone who has absolute confidence in the system and in themselves and has great difficulty in acknowledging that both of these grand things are capable of mistakes.

where the main purpose—to kill the local *starosta** the Germans had put in as headman—was not achieved: they found the man, took him prisoner, read his death sentence to him, but then the man who was to shoot him was either nervous or a bad shot with his tommy gun and the *starosta* survived.

Much of what the partisans have achieved so far involved building up strength, arming, organizing and agitating, accessing provisions and staying alive. The crowds of people who get together and form partisan groups are, to say the very least, a mixture of all sorts. Some are from the Red Army, soldiers who disappeared into the forests when their units were scattered following the large-scale encirclements of last year; some are local members of the Communist Party or Soviet secret police; some are Jews fleeing from mass murder and pogroms; some are adventurers and idealists, heroes and opportunists—including a significant number of young women; a growing number are specially trained volunteers, dropped in by parachute or filtered through the lines; and many, like Obrynba, are escaped prisoners of war.

The train will soon be here.

Nikolai can consider himself very lucky to be alive. When the war broke out, he was working as an artist at the great Museum of the Revolution in central Moscow. His speciality was painting battle scenes, the demand for which never dried up. As he had a higher degree, he was automatically exempt from conscription, but he threw away the documents that protected him and, instead, volunteered for one of the many militia units that was being formed. It was a move that was both courageous and foolhardy.

After being given a very basic training, he and his fellows were rushed off to the front, many of them still in civilian clothes and some of them armed with old weapons from the First World War. They were not much more than cannon fodder, thrown in to delay the apparently unstoppable German armored columns that were heading for the Soviet capital. Obrynba was one of the more than 500,000 Soviet troops taken prisoner in October at the massive encirclement at Vjazma and Brjansk. Exhausted, hungry and bitter—somewhere along the way he lost his faith in Stalin's infallibility.

---

* A village elder. They had an important part to play in the continuing German economic exploitation and in the hunt for partisans and others.

So Obrynba became a tiny drop in the seemingly endless stream of Soviet prisoners of war that flooded the muddy roads in the east in the late autumn of 1941. Most of them soon died of hunger, disease and brutality.* Memories of that time still fill Obrynba with horror:

> Thousands of people, dying of hunger and cold were left at stop-over sites all along our route. The Fritzes finished off those who were still alive: a guard would kick a fallen man and machinegun him on the ground. Before each new march, guards with sticks lined up on both sides of the column and the command "All run!" would be given. The mob ran and blows rained hard upon us. This kind of beating would last for one or two kilometers before the word "Stop!" was announced. Gasping for breath, hot and sweating all over, we would halt— and be kept standing in this condition, in the biting-cold wind, rain and snow, for an hour. The exercise was repeated several times, so only the fittest would survive and march on. But many remained behind and solitary shots would ring out, as the Germans finished them off.

But Obrynba survived, not least because he was lucky enough to encounter Germans who in various simple ways took pity on him at critical points.

It often amounted to little more than gestures, but gestures that were sufficient to allow him to keep hatred at bay and to continue to view his enemies as individuals, among whom some were monsters and others fellow men. (Dangerously, there are times when people can be both. "Compassion and brutality can coexist in the same individual and in the same moment despite all logic," wrote Primo Levi.) Obrynba's real salvation came when the Germans discovered his artistic talents. Obrynba was fortunate that the school of social realism he was trained in lay very close to the kind of kitsch the Nazis enthused about. They took him aside, put him to work painting portraits, decorating offices and the like and rewarded him with food, whereas other prisoners were

* German forces took 3,350,000 Soviet prisoners during 1941. Only 1,100,000 of them were still alive in December 1941; the rest were victims of a brutal and cynical German policy that used hunger as a means of genocide.

starving, eating grass in their desperation or, at worst, each other. During his time as a prisoner, Obrynba focused on three things: survival, escape and remaining human. He summed it up as follows: "It would not be easy to survive in this hell, but it would be a hundred times harder to remain a human being."

. . .

Nothing new on the Svir Front—which, of course, is a blessing in more ways than one for Kurt West and the soldiers of his company. Boredom and monotony were an inescapable result of both sides digging in on opposite shores of the river and neither of them showing any sign of wanting to move. There's been no fighting of any significance since last spring. Of course, random shelling continues here and there; and, of course, Soviet snipers are unpleasantly skillful and constantly on the lookout for targets; of course, too, both sides—particularly the Finnish—mount small raids and patrols. So, men are being killed or wounded all the time, but it could be worse.

Protected by this monotonous stasis, a normal life has been created. Just as when the Western Front was at its most static during the First World War, there is space here for a kind of paradoxical normality. Athletic competitions have been organized; ski races will start as soon as there is enough snow. The regiment has its own male choir, which is currently planning a tour of the district; a little theatre group, temporarily boosted by a number of young female theatre students from Helsingfors, has also been formed and is performing happy comedies of mistaken identity such as Avery Hopwood's *Green Elevator*. Religious services and Bible studies are laid on for believers (and there are many of them). Others use their free time in the bunkers for individual study—in interior photographs of the bunkers we can often see books as well as paraffin lamps, washing hanging to dry, and card games.* At a safe distance behind the front line, the battalions have even built their own small cafés; if you can get to Sjemenski, the regiment has organized a recreation center and a small cinema. Indeed, things could be a lot worse.

---

* With time, studies became better organized. Eventually, for instance, vocational courses were set up and it even became possible to earn a higher school certificate while serving in the field.

Kurt West did not arrive at the front until the middle of September, so neither gloom nor danger has yet become utterly ordinary to him. He is still having to deal with being a newcomer, an innocent, and that's not made any easier by the fact he is quite small and looks younger than his age—nineteen. The first comment he heard when climbing down "freezing and miserably wet" from the truck at the regimental mustering place in Sjemenski was "Have they started sending us children now?" He and the other fresh-faced recruits have to put up with a good deal of ribbing by the officers and men, many of whom are experienced veterans of the Winter War.

It's doubtful if much of the "curiosity and lust for adventure" that bubbled up in West when he was called to the army at the start of the year still remains by this point. During the day his main occupation is digging and reinforcing trenches or hauling timber and scaffold poles with a horse—the latter being particularly filthy work on the small roads, since the autumn rain has turned the soil of East Karelia into an almost bottomless porridge of reddish-brown mud. West has cursed and sworn and sweated.

Much of the time left over is taken up standing guard, wearisome work that some of the veterans consider to be beneath their dignity. He is constantly weary and he often wonders how he will manage when things take a serious turn. Referring to himself in the third person he writes: "Will his nerves hold out or will he just crumble?" He hasn't yet fired his rifle.

·   ·   ·

The waiting is over for Nikolai Obrynba and his fellow partisans. The train is approaching. First, the rails hum quietly, then they hear the puffing of the locomotive and see the plume of smoke from its funnel; then he is able to pick out the long, dark shadow winding its way through the night in a cloud of smoke and sparks. As the train approaches the small pinewood, there is a crack from the anti-tank gun, followed at once by the bang of the shell finding its target. A white cloud of steam spurts out as, stammering and coughing, the locomotive slams on the brakes. Seconds later comes the detonation of the buried explosives and then, lastly, the metallic crashing and grinding noises of the wagons coming off the tracks, overturning and colliding with each other.

Then silence.

Obrynba and the others up on the small hill wait expectantly. Is the train full of German soldiers... or of what? After five minutes a rocket bursts in the dark sky—the signal they have been waiting for. They charge down towards the embankment, hoping for a good haul. Obrynba doesn't see any signs of life, but many of the wagons are loaded with grain. Suddenly, there is the chatter of a heavy machine gun from the end of the train. Another rocket is fired into the night sky—a white rocket this time. It's the signal to withdraw.

Dark figures vanish among the trees. Relieved and excited, they talk about what they've just experienced. Obrynba is especially pleased with a red pocket flashlight one of his companions found by the train and gave him. Behind them, the lights of tracers are ricocheting around in the confusion of derailed train cars.

·   ·   ·

Keith Douglas is sitting by the main coast road, alongside a broken Crusader tank and its crew. They are from a different regiment. He studies the vehicles trundling past. Many of them have come the whole way from bases back at Cairo, as he can tell from the vehicle plates and the expressions on the drivers' faces—they are staring wide-eyed at the devastation all around. There are long rows of abandoned German and Italian vehicles and the road is lined with huge quantities of the debris of war: boxes, paper, empty gasoline cans, clothes, ammunition, empty casings and the occasional corpse. When the crew of the tank offers him lunch and Douglas has nothing to eat with, he just walks down the edge of the road until he finds an Italian mess tin and a knife, fork and spoon to go with it. He is still hard of hearing after the violent explosions of the battle.

The traffic along the road becomes heavier by the hour. At times, the trucks form columns four abreast as they jostle along in the same direction—westwards towards Mersa Matruh. Supplies have to get through and any vehicles attempting to go in the opposite direction are forced off the road. Somewhere in the distance, what's left of the Africa Corps is in full flight.

Every so often, groups of dust-covered German and Italian prisoners pass by, exhausted and dejected, plodding along, heads bent, not even glancing at the vehicles roaring past. The Italians sometimes beg for food, but the Germans never do. They trudge past, shut within themselves "like sleepwalkers." Yesterday it rained for the first time in a long time. Heavily, and the road is muddy.*

Douglas's tank has broken down. Yet again. In the course of this battle—like many of his fellows—he has spent more time mending or salvaging his tank than using it in combat.[†] This time it has gotten stuck in a ditch and shed one of its tracks and so he set off with one of his crew to seek assistance. He is now waiting for it to arrive. It is Saturday, November 7.

Every now and then there is a light shower. Hours pass and when Douglas and his companions get bored, they take out the pistols they've looted and shoot at empty gasoline cans. Some members of the other crew have a completely new type of German pistol and they allow Douglas to try it out. Ammunition is no problem—it's lying all over the place. After a while the new pistol jams and they don't know how to strip it down. A group of four Germans happens to be walking past on the other side of the road and Douglas shouts to them in his halting German. The four Germans are noticeably relieved when they realize the British soldiers by the tank merely want help to strip down the pistol. They deal with it in no time at all.

Douglas speaks to a corporal with medal ribbons who seems to be in command of the little group, which turns out to be the crew of a German tank. Do they have anything to eat? They do, indeed—chocolate! They swap food—tins of British bully beef in exchange for German chocolate, and the mood eases once they are all standing there eating at the roadside. They produce photographs and the corporal shows pictures from France and Greece. Has he been in Russia? No. How long has he been in Africa? Four months. Another of the group is named Willi. He has big ears and resembles Dopey in *Snow White and the Seven Dwarfs* and hasn't been with them more than a couple of weeks. The corporal says he was a student at the University of Cologne before

---

* Some historians think that the unexpected rain of November 6 may be what saved the fleeing Italians and Germans from annihilation. The cloudburst certainly hampered all movement apart from along the main coast road, but it also made it impossible for Allied warplanes to leave their airfields. Air attacks had caused huge losses among the retreating columns.

† This relates to another phenomenon: almost all of them have wounds on their hands. They are small wounds caused by getting their hands jammed or knuckles skinned—the sorts of thing that result from living and working in a tank. In the desert these wounds tend to become infected and more or less chronic.

the war. Ah! Competed against Cambridge in sports. Ah! Douglas asks about the atrocities committed in Poland and Russia. The corporal denies they ever happened. Mmm!

It starts raining again, so both British and German soldiers take shelter in the back of an abandoned Italian truck and sit there drinking tea together. The rain rattles down on the tarpaulin cover while the never-ending stream of vehicles continues roaring by.

.   .   .

The newspapers can't be relied on, being as strictly censored as ever, but the signs have already been there for months. And the rumors are as numerous as they are certain. Everything points to there being a disaster about to hit Henan. Zhang Zhonglou is one of a number of civil servants ordered by the central government in Chongqing to travel around the province, study the situation and also check that the new tax is being collected according to plan. He's one of a new kind of civil servant for China: educated abroad—University of Missouri and Columbia—and more of a technocrat than a phlegmatic and corrupt mandarin of the old sort. His day job is head of the Henan Ministry of Construction.

The front runs through part of the province. It's quiet now and it's not difficult to understand why. For almost a year the Japanese have been concentrating their attention and resources elsewhere: Burma, India, New Guinea and the South and Central Pacific. For the moment, the Japanese seem content to hold on to earlier conquests: Manchuria, of course, which ten years earlier was turned into the vassal state of Manchukuo with its sham emperor, and then in the northeast Hebei Shangxi, Shandong, Jiangsu. In the south they control a number of heavily armed enclaves on the coast, Shanghai and Hong Kong, for instance, from which their troops sometimes sally forth like leaf-cutter ants collecting provisions, particularly at the time of the rice harvest. And then, of course, terror bombing continues, above all of Chongqing,* but this month in Guilin, too. Now and then Japanese planes appear high in the autumn-grey firmament and drop bombs according to some unfathomable logic. They rarely meet any resistance.

---

* From 1939 up to and including 1942, Japanese planes dropped over three thousand tons of bombs on the claustrophobically densely populated city to which the Chinese government had fled after the fall of Nanking in December 1937.

That the situation in Henan in particular is said to be critical doesn't bode well. It is one of China's core provinces and its historical, cultural and particularly economic importance is difficult to overstate. This fertile, populous region immediately south of the Yellow River has long been a granary for the emperor and a recruiting area for his armies, but if even this core zone yields, pretty well any other province could soon give way.

Zhang has been carrying out his investigation for some time now, travelling on appalling roads, moving upstream through streams of refugees—not refugees fleeing the fighting since hardly any fighting is going on, but fleeing an expanding area of famine. Both farmers and state servants have told him that the spring sowing was hit by drought and only produced somewhere between a fifth and a tenth of the expected yield. They'd had hopes for the autumn harvest, but there was scarcely any rain the whole summer, so that was useless too. (And where it did rain, the residents were plagued by swarms of grasshoppers.)

Wherever he goes he encounters people with drawn, sunken features, and everywhere he meets need and desperation. Someone tells him that he will find unusually large numbers of people on the shores of the Luo River. They are collecting and sieving the droppings of wild geese in order to pick out undigested grain which they will then eat. Zhang reports:

> During our trip starving people were digging up grass roots, taking leaves, and stripping bark from trees. Going south from Zhengzou, an unceasing stream of refugees begging for food was so misery-inducing that you couldn't bear to look.

But look at them he must, that is part of his job. In the Fangcheng District Zhang Zhonglou comes to a market where desperate and destitute people are selling their very last possessions—themselves, that is—to avoid starvation. He sees a man who has decided to sell his wife in the hope that both of them will survive. They have just separated when the woman shouts to him: "My trousers are better than yours, take them!" Her husband's response becomes a cry of pain: "I can't sell you—let us die together."

What makes it particularly painful for Zhang is his recognition that this famine is ultimately the work of man. And he himself has a role in it—perhaps even some responsibility.

.   .   .

Seen from a distance—a considerable distance—most of this appears idyllic. When John McEniry first sees Guadalcanal after four and a half hours at the controls of his dive-bomber, he thinks that it's "a beautiful island." The formation of eight pale-blue airplanes is working its way northwards in an arc around the coast. He notes that the island is hilly, that there are both rain forests and grassy meadows, that in most places the jungle runs right down to the beach. The sand looks dark. Close to the shore the water is crystal-clear and you can see down at least forty to fifty feet. (Small boats at anchor down there seem to be floating in the air.) And this close to the equator there is a strange clarity to the air. Indeed, the island seems to be "amazingly peaceful."

And then he catches sight of groups of large, motionless ships and immediately after that he sees the airfield in a big, irregular clearing in the rain forest. Its code name is Cactus. The eight two-seater planes change formation and form up line astern. He knows their approach has to be both quick and tight as the Japanese lines are very close by. The two runways and the surrounding grassy green field are pock-marked with what must be hundreds of craters that have been filled in.

McEniry knows that the situation on the island is critical and that this is an exceptionally dangerous place. They are here to relieve a squadron that has been shattered. Only fourteen pilots remain of the forty-one who came here last month; the rest are dead, missing, wounded or severely ill. And the squadrons that preceded them suffered similar losses. Will they suffer the same fate? McEniry, usually known as "Mac," is a twenty-four-year-old pilot in the Marine Corps.

Less than two years ago he listened to a speech given at the University of Alabama by the governor in which they were urged to be prepared "to sacrifice our lives for our country if it becomes necessary." At the time he thought it was just "ridiculous." The U.S. was at peace and would remain so. *America First.**

There was a war on, but only on the other side of the globe and in cinema newsreels ... and so what? McEniry thought that much of the

---

* That was the slogan of the America First Committee, founded in the autumn of 1940 with the famous airman Charles Lindbergh as its prime spokesman. Its purpose was to keep America out of the war. It met with a strongly favorable response, particularly among young people at various universities.

talk about the dangers and atrocities of the Nazis was exaggerated. It was true that conscription had been introduced in the U.S. and that chance had dictated that his name was the first to be picked out of the list of those liable to be called up in his little town in the South, but since the law guaranteed that you would only have to serve within the borders of the country, the sense of threat hardly increased. An amendment to the law on December 19, 1941, after the attack on Pearl Harbor, changed that.

John McEniry was no star at school, but he was strong, stable and adventurous. After failing an exam disastrously, he recognized he would probably soon be called up, so in the summer of 1941 he enlisted in the Marines, hoping to become a pilot.* This was without any thought that it might mean combat service. But that was then, and now he is here and full of enthusiasm. Guadalcanal. After having circled for a while in a holding pattern above the water, it is his turn to land. McEniry sets down his dive-bomber on the big runway in a cloud of dust. It's about 5:00 p.m. on November 7.

Everything John McEniry sees when he lands that Saturday afternoon reinforces his impression of a place characterized by improvisation—improvisation verging on chaos. Henderson Field has no hangars, no buildings, just sagging tents. There are aircraft parked here and there according to no discernible system, some out in the open, others in among the tall, shattered coconut trees. And here and there he can see the twisted wrecks of aircraft. A number of the carefully filled shell craters are enormous. The long barrels of anti-aircraft guns point to the sky and trucks and jeeps carrying bare-chested men drive around. The mood is nervous.

McEniry and his radio operator climb down from their gleaming machine. The air is close and hot. Together with the rest of the group that has just landed they are directed to the squadron meeting point, which turns out to be a bunker built of logs and sandbags, along with a large tent without walls. There are a couple of benches and a large slate. That's where he learns that the squadron has suffered its first losses. Two pilots he knows are missing.

It doesn't hit him that hard: in the first place he has no real idea how one ought to behave on hearing that kind of news—hang one's head in

---

* Flying was one of his great interests; he could become an officer that way and thus avoid the fate of being trained as an ordinary infantryman.

sorrow or pretend it's of no matter? In the second place he knows intel-
lectually that people are going to lose their lives, people close to him
even. It's inevitable. But for the moment McEniry is sticking firmly to
the illusion that millions of young men currently carry into the darkness and uncertainty. As he writes in his memoirs: "It was always going
to be someone else."

.   .   .

Danuta and Józek Fijalkowski have reached their destination—
Międzyrzec Podlaski. Danuta is disappointed. To her eyes this place
doesn't look like a real town: "no tall buildings, just small houses, cottages, and huts." Jokingly, but with little effect, Józek tries to comfort
her by saying that at least the address is Warsaw Road.

He shows her around, overdoing it somewhat: Look, three large
rooms, a kitchen and a garden of their own out back. They'll be able
to plant their own vegetables there, he says with enthusiasm (which
may be put on), and it gives him warm memories (clearly genuine) of
the house he grew up in in Koło, where there'd been a big garden he'd
loved. It had been full of "aromatic apple trees and wide-spread cherry
trees, blooming flower beds, and delicious tomatoes and crispy cucum-
bers hiding against the fence." But this is not a big, mature, country
garden in the warm light of late summer, it's just an empty, small back
garden in November.

.   .   .

Celebrating the twenty-fifth anniversary of the October Revolution
by attending the premiere of a musical comedy in Leningrad under
siege! Is that possible? Yes, it is. The revolution can and must be celebrated. For reasons that are easy to understand, no parades are being
organized, but the big reception at the Smolny Institute is being held
as usual, under glittering chandeliers in rooms that are all marble, gold
and white. The audience this time, however, consists almost exclusively
of men in uniform.

People are eager to see the first performance of the new comedy *The
Wide, Wide Sea.* They need an opportunity to laugh. There's a stylish
woman in her fifties named Vera Inber in the audience. She is delighted:
"Although from time to time the authors split asunder, as it were, in
the presence of the audience, the piece as a whole is gay and vital." In
the interval she hears two young women talking about where the best

place is to celebrate New Year's: "We have an excellent orchestra," one of them says. "And we have a better shelter," the other one responds.

When they get home, she and her husband sit drinking tea and relax by listening to the radio. The speaker reports that the Germans in North Africa have been retreating for several days. Inber and her husband are unable to catch all the details before the air-raid siren goes off.

She realizes that this is an unusually heavy raid. She can tell from the sound of the engines, by the dull, swelling crash of bombs and the hard cracks of anti-aircraft guns, all of which soon merge into a dense wall of sound that drowns out everything. She hears the splinters of exploding anti-aircraft shells rattle down on the roof. After a while a new flight of bombers flies over, some of them roaring past immediately over their house. Not until 1:30 a.m. does the siren sound the all clear.

· · ·

Back to the little house in Międzyrzec Podlaski. The unspoken but heartrending gap between memory and now, between expectation and reality, is not just about the planned garden. Danuta's husband, Józek, doesn't want to think too much about the fact that he can no longer return to Koło, for Koło is no longer called Koło. It's now called Warthbrücken and is no longer in the voivodeship, or district, of Łódź but in Warthegau, the part of Western Poland annexed by the Germans.* It's currently being "Germanized," which, as everyone knows only too well, means expropriation, exploitation, segregation and massive forced migration.† Danuta and Józek are not only citizens of a country that technically no longer exists, they are also citizens of a country which will not be *permitted* to exist.

For them, as for all other Poles, this is anything but a piece of abstract geopolitics. This is their everyday reality, great and small. All Polish universities and high schools have been closed, which is why Danuta has been unable to take her exams; all Polish libraries, museums and

---

* The other territory annexed is Reichsgau Danzig-Westpreussen, which takes in the region up to the Baltic Sea. In addition to this, certain areas that border the existing German provinces of East Prussia and Upper Silesia are also incorporated.
† There will also be a major influx of German settlers from various German minorities in the east. The population before the war was 85 percent Polish, 8 percent Jewish and 7 percent German.

archives are also closed; the printing, distribution, sale and lending of books in Polish is banned; the teaching of Polish literature, history and geography is forbidden; Polish theatres and cinemas are no longer open (apart from a few that show propaganda or, strangely enough, soft porn); music by Polish composers is forbidden, as is music-making by Poles; trains, trams, cafés, restaurants, hotels, parks, playparks, public baths and bathing beaches either have separate German and Polish areas or they are "*Nur für Deutsche*"; Poles have to give way to Germans on the pavement; Poles are not permitted to drive motor vehicles or to ride in taxis; Poles may not own industries, construction companies or workshops; Poles are not permitted to own radios, make calls from telephone boxes or carry briefcases.

The two of them explore the house. He points out how *big* it is and says it will be their first real home. She notes that, unlike their apartment in Warsaw, there is no central heating, no running water and no toilet. He says they'll be able to bring her mother here and let her open a hairdresser's salon in the room facing the street, right by the square—a perfect location, surely. She takes a close look at the few pieces of furniture: an old bed, a wardrobe that is falling to pieces, and a table and two chairs.

. . .

"Why me? Why me when so many others just the same as me had gone out and not come back?" That's the question still for John Bushby, 83 Squadron, RAF Bomber Command. Perhaps the question remains because it is both impossible to answer and also too early to be asked— the next sortie might easily be the one when, after all the successful sorties and safe landings, the flip of the coin goes against him. Bushby's active service has coincided with the new and more merciless strategy* of concentrating on targets so large that they are impossible to miss at night. He has taken part in bombing many German cities: Bremen (twice), Essen, Cologne, Danzig, Duisburg (three times), Hamburg, Düsseldorf, Osnabrück, Mainz, Nuremberg, Krefeld, Aachen.

---

* Merciless above all for little girls in plaits, old ladies, kittens and the other innocents who would be its victims; but also merciless towards the bomber crews who were exhorted to "get through, whatever it takes," which they frequently did, with a level of bravery that seems incomprehensible these days. There were some raids in which more airmen died than Germans on the ground.

Where Bushby is positioned, high in the cold night sky in a machine-gun turret at the back of the plane, he has an excellent view. Over the months he has watched how the small, vibrant flashes from exploding bombs have begun to form denser patterns, how the fires have grown in size, and how streets and whole districts have been transformed into a shifting network of fire and phosphorus. It's quite obvious that they are getting better and better at doing this, the result both of improved technique and improved tactics.

What began as an archaic dream of a war won by courage, intelligence, precision and a certain level of gentlemanly finesse has transmogrified into a brutal and cynical narrative, governed by the principle of scale: more bombers, more bombs, more victims. It's not a matter of them dropping their bombs without regard for the civilian population; the bombs now *target* the civilian population. "Dehousing" is the euphemism used, in so far as euphemisms are needed at all. The aircrews are not guided by moralistic motives or complex explanations; they are given orders to carry out their missions and these, by their nature, are essentially technical and statistical. So Bushby doesn't have any qualms of conscience, except in one case—Mainz. On that clear, moonlit night in August, he found himself looking down on "a city of pleasant squares and priceless medieval buildings, and we reduced its center to a heap of devastated, smoking rubble in one short half hour."

Uncertainty regarding your own fate and uncertainty about the chances of influencing it have consequences that are both strange and understandable. Few people are as superstitious as bomber crews. At least, that provides a *feeling* of control. Bushby is always careful to pull on his left boot before his right boot when donning his thick, heavy flying suit. He and Wally, the other gunner, always wish one another a polite "good evening" when they climb into their turrets. He always hums the same popular song as the heavily laden bomber begins accelerating more and more quickly past the flickering lights of the runway. Flying with a new crew or in unfamiliar planes is also thought to be bad luck and almost all of them try to avoid that at any cost.

The logic behind these latter points is not insignificant. The members of a crew are in tune with one another and with their machine. It's not just that these machines with four engines—Lancasters in this case—have shown themselves to be so tough and reliable, but that, after a hundred flying hours or more, they have learned all her idiosyncrasies. Bill, the pilot, who always wears the same lucky knitted scarf—six feet long and garishly colored—knows exactly how hard he can push R5673 "L-London" in a dive. Charley knows how the radio might begin to wander on certain frequencies and how to prevent it doing so. Bushby knows that his stream of bullets will be a little high at a range of 220 yards, and so on.

"Why me?" Apart from the inscrutable workings of chance, part of the explanation is to be found here. The 83 Squadron is not only flying the RAF's best and most modern type of bomber, faster than other types and able to fly considerably higher, but the particular plane they have been allotted is an unusually well-functioning one. It's no wonder that Bushby has developed something resembling love for R5673, as if she were a living creature.

Today is November 7 and Bushby and the rest of them are feeling miserable. L-London was loaned out to a different crew yesterday and they failed to return. Last night the bomber collided with another Lancaster from 83 Squadron over Genoa, their target zone. The fourteen missing crewmen are not the first thing on their minds, nor do they think of the grim irony that the other crew could be said to have died instead of them. Their grief is for the machine: "We missed R5673 as one does a household pet, more so in fact, since each of us felt a vague unease that with her passing the chain of fortune had broken."

.   .   .

Night is another country. The landscape changes, taking on new forms and new colors. In the light of the full moon there are times when Willy Peter Reese thinks of the gleaming white shimmer of no-man's-land as "enchanted." Sometimes he looks into the deep black of the starry heavens, ticks off Orion and Vega, Libra and Pisces and Gemini and the strip of light of the Milky Way, but is no longer touched by the beauty. He has become indifferent to it, just as he thinks of the stars as being indifferent to mankind and to the suffering currently filling the earth. The gleam of flares transforms fields and copses, sculpting daylight and shadow into frozen new shapes of golden yellow, light green, cold white and blood red. "And when the flares faded we were thrown back into primeval night." Being the province of fantasy, darkness almost always means fear, terror even. That's when the wind passing through the tall, frozen grass can become one of the Russian patrols they all fear.

But night can also protect them. It's his turn to fetch the food and because of Soviet snipers it has to be done in darkness. The rain-sodden road leading to the ravine where the field kitchen is hidden is a dangerous place. Someone is killed or wounded there almost every day, but it's fairly safe at this hour. The front around Rzhev is still reckoned as being quiet. For once!* Reese and a couple of others stumble on through the darkness. Winter is late in coming.

Things were different a year ago. Then Willy Peter Reese and his division were a small part of the great, sweeping effort to take Moscow. That was his baptism of fire.

The memories of weeping, frostbitten soldiers stay with him; of people going mad, raving mad; of hunger; of diarrhea and exhaustion to the point of hallucination; of hysterical drumhead court-martials and your own soldiers being shot for trivial offenses; of Russian civilians murdered or hurled out into the snow or hanged and swinging woodenly in the cold wind; of Soviet prisoners of war being massacred—not by him but by another soldier who one morning tossed hand grenade after hand grenade in among a hundred or so prisoners and then finished things off by calmly walking around with his sub-machine gun shooting anyone who still showed signs of life; of the rapidly shrinking moral universe of that chaotic retreat. Towards Christmas he and his comrades in arms, those who were still alive, were all "sick and irritated." "Outbursts of bitterness and hatred, envy, fights, scorn and rage destroyed what remained of comradeship."

The experience has changed Reese, hardened him and made him indifferent, sometimes depressed, sometimes filled with an incomprehensible and frightening euphoria. That's why he writes when he gets the chance. He writes to forget, "to get rid of what happened" and thus "to remain a human being." But it doesn't really seem to work. That's also why Reese reads so much, something like fifty books this year alone, everything from Lao Tzu to Ernst Jünger, the great German

* During 1942 the Red Army mounted one attack after another on the well-defended salient at Rzhev, always with the same brutal disregard for their own losses and always with no notable success. Among the Soviet infantry, this sector of the front was known as the Meat Grinder or the Slaughterhouse. The total losses of the Red Army are estimated to have been 2,300,000 men, almost twice as many as at Stalingrad, and to little effect. Soviet historiography concealed this failure.

memoirist of World War I, whom he admires and whose style has influenced him. He reads and writes in order to stay in contact with his old self, the bookish schoolboy, but war, he writes, has made him "a stranger to himself."

They are returning from the ravine carrying steaming hot mess tins. It is probably a moonless night with low, thick cloud cover and they are perhaps a little inattentive or slightly drunk. But all of a sudden Reese doesn't recognize where he is.

They are lost. They feel their way forward in the darkness. They jump over a collapsed trench ... and then open ground. No-man's-land. Not good. They hurry towards what they think are the German lines. They come to barbed wire. And they quickly realize that they are in front of the Soviet position, not their own. Back again. The same dense darkness in which they got lost is now their savior. Silence. No flares go up. No golden-yellow, light-green, cold-white or blood-red flares. No one shoots at them.

When they get back into their own trench, he is surprised by his own reaction, which reveals the distance between the man he once was and the man he has become. No one is trembling with concern and fear. Instead they all snigger and look at "the foolhardy episode as if it were comedy."

． ． ．

The weather in Paris has been growing colder and colder and it's the first day Hélène Berr has put on her fur coat. The cold doesn't bother her to any great extent, no more than the fact that her Jean will set off on his long and dangerous journey in just a week's time, because now they will be able to meet at last. Does she give any thought to that yellowish-green piece of cloth attached to her elegant fur coat? It's quite possible that she even forgets about it. It's Saturday, November 7.

She waits at the railway station and welcomes him when the train arrives. Then they walk together along the Champs-Élysées and turn off down towards Trocadéro. The two of them may be avoiding the tree-lined parts of the Champs-Élysées because they might be considered parkland, and Jews are not permitted to visit parks nowadays. They will probably not take the Métro because she would have to sit in the last car, as people of color must, and the ways back up to the street often have identity checkpoints. They maybe stop and look in a shop window where there is a sign stating that it's an *Entreprise Juive*, a Jewish business. But they certainly won't be going into a restaurant or café; ever since last summer Jews are not permitted to frequent such places. Nor are they allowed to go to cinemas, theatres, concert halls, museums, libraries, camping sites or sports grounds. Hélène can't even use a telephone box anymore—which fits in with an earlier regulation making it illegal for Jews to rent a telephone—or even to own wireless sets.

These and a whole host of other anti-Jewish laws have been introduced by the French authorities—sometimes, but not always, as a result of German pressure. What has made them seem tolerable is probably the fact that the screw has only been tightened gradually. It has happened step-by-step, so the pattern hasn't been obvious.* There has been plenty of room for self-deception and opportunistic thinking, particularly among assimilated and prosperous Jews. They have been able to reason it all away: This doesn't really apply to us; the real target is foreigners/communists/eastern European Jews. Historical experience hasn't offered any sort of guide. In fact, it has tended to encourage passive accommodation: We'll get through all this as long as we keep a low profile/obey the laws/don't stir up trouble.

Most of the people Hélène knows—like the majority of French people—practice *attentisme;* that is, they believe the safest thing to do is to wait and see. They do, of course, obey whenever the new anti-Semitic laws affect them directly, as when her father was made to hand over to "Aryan" managers his share of the major business he had been involved in setting up, or when Jews were forbidden to be teachers, which forced Hélène to change her course of study at the Sorbonne. What else could they do?

The business of wearing the Jewish star was what really put her back up for the first time. Her first impulse had been to refuse to wear it as an act of resistance. She changed her mind quickly when it occurred to her that this might possibly be interpreted as cowardice. And so

---

* We should bear in mind that this is true even when viewed from a Nazi-German perspective. It wasn't until January of this year that the decision was taken to move on from the step-by-step exclusion of Jews from all aspects of society to their complete physical annihilation. It wasn't until this year that deportations from western Europe started—and then primarily from France.

she tries instead to wear it with pride, to hold her head high and look people in the eye. The reaction she gets is, as far as she can see, usually to her advantage.* In spite of that, this star has made her an exile in the city in which she was born, whose topography she knows inside out, whose colors, sounds and smells are a natural part of her inner world. She writes in her diary: "I suddenly felt I was no longer myself, that everything had changed, that I'd become a stranger." And from then on, it was one horror after another.

But the star is shocking, both in its symbolic brutality and because it attempts at one stroke to negate something that has been self-evident to most people and a matter of pride to French Jews ever since the revolution: that it is citizenship that defines one as French, not which God you may or may not worship.† Hélène Berr's family has been assimilated for generations. In culture and in education, in their manner of thinking and living, they are French in every way. Shouldn't that protect them?

Her paternal grandfather had been a military man, her father a decorated veteran of the First World War and a successful businessman. Celebrating the major feast days marks the extent of their religious practices. Not all of her acquaintances even know that the family is Jewish. Jean had no idea. That's why it was a nervous day for her last summer when she let him see her wearing that disgusting little piece of yellow material. How was he going to react? Jean was both depressed and embarrassed—on her behalf.

Hélène and Jean walk on. They cross the Seine by the Pont de l'Alma and arrive at her home at 7 Élisée-Reclus, one of the most expensive addresses in Paris. (There was a time when they thought that would give them some protection, but not after what happened last summer.)

---

* Two examples from June 29. A man comes up to her on the street, holds out his hand and says in a loud voice: "A French Catholic shakes your hand ... and when it's over, we'll have our revenge!" The same day a cleaning woman says that the Russians will avenge her.

† This was actually a significant problem for the Nazis: if an individual's religious affiliation was not considered to be an issue for the state, it implied that it wouldn't be registered anywhere. The solution was to encourage the Jewish population to visit their local police stations and register themselves, which virtually all of them duly did. At this stage in the autumn of 1940 no one could have realized that they were thus contributing to their own downfall, especially as most people believed that the occupation would be short-lived.

Stanley Bay, in Egypt, famous for its waves and the most popular Alexandria beach. In 1942, the beach was full of bathers even when the fighting was no more than sixty miles away.

Bomb damage in Barrow-in-Furness, England. Most of it was from the German raids of 1941, when the bombs missed their intended targets (as usual) and fell here, there and everywhere throughout the town. This is the ruin of the Baptist church on Abbey Road, a place Nella Last often passed on her way home on the bus.

Japanese soldiers in Burma in 1942 firing at a distant target across a river. They are using a Type 92 heavy machine gun, a robust and accurate weapon known to Allied troops as the Woodpecker because of its low firing rate.

Japanese soldiers queueing outside a field brothel in Hankow (now Wuhan) China. Field brothels were often euphemistically referred to as "comfort stations." The Hankow brothel consisted of a cluster of sixty-eight buildings, some of which are visible here. (The photograph was taken by a Japanese soldier named Murase Moriyasu, a keen photographer who also documented the Nanking massacre.)

Finnish troops find driving in the snowdrifts of Soviet East Karelia hard work. A couple of Russian children look on as the car is dug out *(Försvarsmaktens bildarkiv)*.

November 18 on the Svir River front. A Finnish sentry post looks out into no-man's-land over obstructions. The fact that both the soldier and the photographer were so exposed reveals that the location was not particularly dangerous *(Försvarsmaktens bildarkiv)*.

Finnish light artillery firing at night on the Svir front *(Museiverket HK 19810422 35)*.

A Finnish garrison bunker in East Karelia, November 25. Although the photograph is obviously posed, the interior is authentic in every way: the brick stove in the background, the shelf of mess cups, the socks hanging up to dry, the young soldiers' clothing with its mixture of military and civilian items *(Museiverkat HK7744 771)*.

An American aircraft carrier on its way to support the landings in French Morocco. The aircraft on the left are dive-bombers of the same type as John McEniry was flying over Guadalcanal; the aircraft on the right are fighter planes. The American national markings are carefully embellished in yellow in the hope of discouraging French fighter pilots from attacking. It didn't.

It's about 2:00 p.m. on November 5, and U-604 has just come into the Brest U-boat base in Belarus. The commander, clean-shaven Captain Lieutenant Höltring, is saluting the welcoming committee.

One of the victims of the merciless U-boat warfare: Poon Lim on the raft on which he was to spend 133 days as the sole survivor after his ship had been torpedoed. The photo was taken after his rescue.

Amatsukaze, the very modern destroyer commanded by Tameichi Hara during the confused naval battles around Guadalcanal.

There are very few authentic photographs showing Japanese soldiers in combat on Guadalcanal. This is one of them. The soldier on the right is about to throw a hand grenade, which means that his American adversaries are no more than twenty-five to thirty-five yards away, perhaps less.

This is Bloody Ridge on Guadalcanal on the morning of October 26 after that night's attack by the 16th and 29th Japanese Infantry Regiments. Smoke is still rising, both from burning equipment and burning bodies. A Japanese flag is visible among the bodies and rifles are sticking up here and there. The dead are mostly lying at right angles to the hill, which suggests they were shot down as they charged forward to attack. Lying on his side closest to the camera is a dead American soldier. A number of his comrades are standing in the background, looking down; they are keeping their distance and several of them have their weapons at the ready, since the danger is by no means over. There is a Japanese soldier lying on his back with his arm sticking up in the left-hand corner: he is possibly still alive. The attacks continued the following night.

Later, order is restored, the battlefield has been cleared and there is time and energy to pose with souvenirs. Notice how young the American soldiers are, and how thin many of them are.

At the beginning of November, the American forces on Guadalcanal were still having problems with supplies. Very soon, however, the American military began to excel in their strongest suit: logistics. The photo shows equipment being carried ashore on the grey-black sand of the island.

Execution was the fate of many Soviet partisans. This photo was taken in Starij Oskol in 1942. The town was captured by Hungarian forces that summer and they hanged this man, or rather, strangled him. The method was slow and painful.

The Bund, Shanghai, also known as "the Million Dollar Mile," and the promenade down by the Huangpu. The photograph was taken before the war.

They enjoy a pleasant Saturday evening in her flat. One of their friends arrived fairly well-oiled, but he is happy and entertaining and makes everyone laugh. Later they all leave, including Jean. During the night she dreams about him, and when she dreams that he is leaving, she wakes up abruptly.

· · ·

It is Sunday, November 8, and two trains of cattle cars arrive at Treblinka. One of them is carrying about six thousand Jews from the small ghetto in Staszów, which was cleared yesterday in an action carried out by German units along with Ukrainian and Latvian auxiliaries supported by Polish and Jewish collaborators. The other train contains roughly three thousand Jews from the Łuków ghetto. All of them, men, women and children, are murdered before nightfall, apart from a very small number spared to replace the ever-diminishing group of workers in the camp's Sonderkommando.

Chil Rajchman is still working in the camp dental *kommando*.

There are twenty of them and their *kapo*—their foreman—is a prisoner by the name of Dr. Zimmerman. The SS men are not without some degree of psychological insight and many of those they choose as *kapos* are brutalized and amoral. They are armed with whips and given to using their positions in every possible way. The *kapo* Rajchman had over him when he was working in the lower camp as a "barber" was a prisoner named Yurek, known to be lecherous, brutal and quick to aim the vilest abuse as well as blows at the workers and the condemned. Dr. Zimmerman (who really is a doctor) is, however, known to be a decent man, which it is difficult to be and to carry on being. Moreover, he and Rajchman are acquainted somehow, not closely, but nevertheless that provides some small level of protection.

Hardly surprising, no good can be expected from SS-Scharführer Matthes,* the man in charge of the upper camp.† The man is a pedant.

---

* Scharführer was one of the lower ranks, approximately equivalent to sergeant.
† Matthes was a Nazi who before his posting to Treblinka worked in the so-called euthanasia program, Aktion T4, the mass killing of mentally ill and handicapped Germans. Many of those who worked in the camps had a background in T4. Some might perhaps think it to Matthes's credit that he is reported not to have wanted to be in charge of the upper camp. Nevertheless, he agreed to

Apparently, he recently shot two prisoners in the column because at the end of the day they failed to clean the blood off the biers thoroughly. Matthes takes great care that the state of the parade ground is perfect: a prisoner rakes the sand there in exact geometrical patterns every day. When Matthes hits prisoners his face is expressionless, almost apathetic. And like the other SS men, he is utterly corrupt. When he goes on vacation to see his wife and daughter in Germany— and he does so quite often; he returned from his last visit less than a week ago—he always drops into the small barrack building where they sort the victims' valuables and helps himself to jewellery and foreign currency.*

It's starting to turn cold and rainy now, but everything continues according to standard procedure. People stand in line, naked and shivering. There is a big excavator that digs deep new pits. The bowl of water on Rajchman's table slowly fills with teeth.

.   .   .

It is now twelve days since the big convoy left England, twelve days of mounting tension and fear. John Parris has been going around wearing his helmet—that big, obviously new helmet—and has been sleeping fully dressed, even with his boots laced up. In spite of all the anxiety, there have been no U-boat attacks, no air raids, nothing. Yesterday, November 7, after they had passed Gibraltar, what looked like German spotter planes flew over them, small, slow-moving dots very high up in the heavens.

Now it's Sunday, November 8, and they have reached their destination. All the vessels that had been almost impossible to pick out in the nocturnal darkness now begin to emerge as vague shapes. One by one the dull sounds of ships' engines fall silent, to be replaced by the whirring of winches, the thuds and clanging of metal against metal, the shouts and splashes and the pulsing of the V-8 engines of the landing

---

it. It was very rare for SS men to avoid postings to the camps by, for instance, volunteering for the front. Men like Matthes were morally dead: they preferred the camps, where they were out of danger and could also make themselves rich.

* Both the SS men and the Ukrainians stole consistently before regular transports to Germany took away everything else removed from the prisoners, including gold teeth and hair. In a five-day period at the end of November, thirty-five fully loaded trucks departed.

craft. The Algerian coast lies waiting silently; the world consists of nothing but misty grey layers of sea, shores, hills and skies.

John Parris is a twenty-eight-year-old journalist from North Carolina, long based in New York and, in spite of his youth, with a wealth of experience. United Press International posted him to London last year and he is now attached to the 1st Infantry Division of the American army, "the big Red One." Parris is wearing the same uniform as the other troops but has a special cloth badge sewn on one sleeve to identify him as a reporter. He and a group of other journalists have been chosen to cover the American invasion of French North Africa.

For very obvious reasons, the whole operation has been shrouded in a level of secrecy rarely seen, but by this stage Parris has attended a number of briefings aboard ship. He now knows more about their undertaking. It involves a three-pronged attack, aimed at three widely separated geographical points: farthest west at Casablanca in French Morocco; in the center at Oran in western Algeria; and farthest east at Algiers.

Parris is with the force that is to be landed a little east of Oran, in a bay close to a village called Arzew. The mood on board the troopship is good, a mixture of excitement and expectancy. The long and dangerous voyage is behind them. Now comes the landing, but experts on the army staff have judged that the French are unlikely to put up any resistance. They are probably more likely to welcome the American troops as liberators.

·   ·   ·

Sometimes it is difficult not to fraternize. After a cold night spent wrapped in a tarpaulin on the ground, Keith Douglas is back at his bogged-down tank. A breakdown vehicle with repairmen accompany him. His two crewmen are waiting there, along with the five young Italian prisoners they took yesterday morning. (They'd had a slightly amusing way of showing that they wanted to give themselves up: they approached the tank with their hands up, all of them holding up packets of cigarettes and one of them pointing at his wristwatch.) While Douglas was away it has turned out that the Italians aren't ordinary soldiers, but from an entertainment unit. One of them is a tenor from the Milan opera.

The mood is excellent. The Italians sing and help put together breakfast for all of them before performing their morning ablutions.

And when the time comes to fix the tank track, they are happy to help out.

Once the tank is mobile again, Douglas drives them to the coast road where he locates a truck to take the Italians to the prisoner-of-war camp that awaits them farther east. We can probably assume that the Italians give them a happy, smiling wave as the truck drives them off. This happens on November 8.

. . .

At home in Leningrad Vera Inber is tidying up after the anniversary celebration of the revolution. (She doesn't like housework.) She clears things away, dusts and sorts out papers. She drinks a cup of tea. She's feeling low, not so much because of the celebrations as such. She usually feels out of sorts the day after, and she doesn't really understand why. "Is it because I expect too much and they seldom live up to my expectations? Or is it because you lose the habit of work when celebrating?" (When she's writing she forgets herself and her aches and pains, such as her present toothache.) She doesn't know which it is.

There's no doubt Inber is an industrious sort: she spends almost all her time writing. (Today, for instance, she's thinking of maybe starting a play. She's come up with a good idea.) There are similarities between her and Lidiya Ginzburg: both of them are gifted women born in Odessa, both Jewish, both with their roots in the experimental Soviet 1920s—and both of them have lived through the brutal choking off of experiment as the 1930s approached. But that's where similarities end.

Whereas Ginzburg fell silent, Inber maneuvered and adapted. She is celebrated both as a poet and as a journalist, and in both of those functions she necessarily—by no means under duress—follows the party line. She writes articles for *Leningradskaya Pravda*, gives talks on the Leningrad radio, gives public readings to large audiences—all with a heroic edge and aiming to bolster the will of the people to hold out. At the moment, with some difficulty, she is in the process of completing a big, classically structured poetic epic on the city and the siege: *The Pulkovo Meridian*. (The work began in March when things were at their worst and the poem will be some eight hundred lines—she hopes it will be her entry ticket to the Communist Party.) She keeps to herself all her doubts and her anger at stupid decisions, bureaucratic fools and the absence of reliable information.

There is another difference between Vera Inber and Lidiya Ginzburg: Inber is in Leningrad by choice. She arrived in August last year, just before the ring around the city closed. Dressed in a lady's over-coat, elegant hat, high heels and with permed hair, she announced to an astonished functionary at the local writers' union that "as a poet in wartime I should be at the center of events."* And that's exactly where she has ended up.

She has shed her most coquettish and self-assured attitudes. Inber is no longer a young woman and all these months in Leningrad have taken their toll on her body. She has problems with her heart and with her breathing, and there are times when she suffers from indefinable pains and tremors.† Some of them are psychosomatic: sometimes when unusually bad news comes from Stalingrad, Vera Inber has difficulty breathing.

.   .   .

The American war correspondent John Parris is standing on the bridge of the transport ship watching the landings outside Oran through bin-oculars. The report he wrote afterwards is breathless and dramatic:

> The earth trembled and shook and the air churned hot and cold under the convulsion of belching naval guns, heaving coastal artillery, and the muffled crump of bursting explo-sives behind the hills. White geysers erupted about the silently moving invasion craft drifting toward shore. The pulsating roar of motors throbbed above the ear-splitting hell. Div-ing Spitfires, their machine guns chattering death, shrieked in endless procession out of the moonless, star-specked sky, and silver starred-bombers opened up their silvery bellies and vomited upon the land. Tracer bullets splashed the early light with gold and crimson.

This account, unfortunately, has very little to do with reality.

---

* Her husband is a doctor, and in August 1941, when he was given the choice of running a hospital in Archangel or one in Leningrad, the couple—or rather she—chose Leningrad.

† It's worth mentioning that when preparing her diary for publication after the war, she removed the greater part of her doubts and criticisms, as well as her periodic confusion, anxiety and physical difficulties.

The first wave of special troops succeeded in surprising and taking the two coastal artillery fortifications defending the bay—in one case without firing a shot. French resistance after that consisted mainly of scattered fire from field artillery and the occasional sniper. On landing on the pebbled beach, some of the American soldiers in their fresh, unstained uniforms did exactly what civilized people tend to do when told to aim at other human beings for the first time—they either hesitated or didn't shoot at all. Others were so nervous they were ready to shoot at anything that moved. In the darkness one group heard what they thought was an approaching tank and they blasted away only to discover they had killed an old Frenchman on his way to make a morning delivery of wine in his small truck.

The prime difficulty for those landing at Arzew isn't French resistance—that faded away very quickly. The gunfire was sufficient to attract sleepy villagers out of their houses to watch smiling, friendly American troops march up the low but steep shores, in many cases led by a standard-bearer.

The big problem is getting all the men and materiel ashore. Parris uses words like "efficiently," "unfalteringly," and "skill and perfection" in order to describe that process. That is quite far from reality. Darkness and an unexpected westerly current mean that many of the landing craft go off course or are delayed. Added to that, the sea bottom proves to be more treacherous than anticipated.

The plan is for the numerous armored vehicles to be landed from adapted, flat-bottomed oil tankers, but these run aground some distance from the shore. The troops and many of the lighter vehicles are to be landed dry-shod from a completely new type of vessel built of plywood and looking like a long shoebox with a ramp at the front— Higgins boats.* They are designed to be driven right onto the beach, and that works well. Thereafter, and this is the most important detail in their construction, they should be able to back out under their own power to fetch more soldiers; this part has not functioned so well. As

---

* The official designation was LCVP, Landing Craft Vehicle Personnel. There was a touch of genius in their simplicity, and they were churned out by the thousands at an enormous New Orleans factory managed by their inventor, the brilliant Andrew Jackson Higgins. Without the LCVPs, none of the major Allied landings of the war is likely to have succeeded.

a result of delays, the tide has ebbed and the shoreline is now littered with grounded Higgins boats.

When the sun rises over the western Mediterranean it shines down on a chaotic shoreline. But even though the American troops are obviously inexperienced and some of their officers clearly incompetent, and even though the mood among the troops coming ashore is a peculiar mix of overconfidence, amateurism and confusion, it is nevertheless clear that the organization is basically sound. That holds true for the issue that is most important in a military context: logistics. Without that, how would you be able to ship this huge number of personnel, vehicles, supplies and equipment such a great distance, in some cases across the Atlantic, and then precisely synchronize their landing in exactly the right places?

Nor is there a problem with the ability to improvise and come up with solutions. The engineering units build a temporary pier out to the oil tankers in the bay. And bulldozers have begun pushing the stranded Higgins boats out into deeper water, even though the price is many buckled rudders and broken propellers. In spite of the problems, troops and vehicles continue streaming ashore.

Parris writes: "On this golden Sabbath morning of November eight, the war seems to have moved on from the beaches here in Arzu [*sic*] to the hills and beyond." He leaves the bridge. "The wireless room is whistles and chatters in rattling cipher, bringing news of the landings, the progress of our lightning offensive." The reports are promising. The landing west of Oran also seems to have gone more or less according to plan, and the paratroops have managed to take control of one of the airfields outside the city.* But the coup that was to be carried out by special forces in the port of Oran doesn't seem to have gone well, and piecemeal reports say that "fighting is heavy" and tell of "stiff resistance." When Parris goes back up on deck, he can hear the dull, rolling thunder of heavy naval guns from the direction of Oran. "When

---

* The effort of the parachute troops was an almost complete fiasco, not least from the navigational perspective. One of the transport planes landed in Gibraltar, three others in Spanish Morocco, where those on board were immediately interned, and one landed just outside Oran: those on board that plane had been told not to expect any resistance and they allowed themselves to be arrested by the French police.

the wind freshens from the southwest it carries an acrid smell of gun powder."* It's November 8.

Parris is in no hurry to go ashore. That can wait until tomorrow.

. . .

The weather has changed in Paris. Hélène Berr writes in her diary: "I walked in the direction of Rue Vauquelin in glorious weather, a sharp golden sun, a bright blue sky and crystal-clear air." Yesterday's meeting with Jean had been wonderful, the whole day had been wonderful and she'd dreamed of him all night. She is in an excellent mood. It's quite noticeably warm for November.

Hélène is on her way to a hostel for orphaned Jewish girls in the 5th arrondissement, at the entrance to a small side street off Rue Claude Bernard, a couple of blocks southwest of the Jardin des Plantes. The address is Rue Vauquelin 5, a five-story building with many balconies.

The hostel is run by UGIF, Union Générale des Israélites de France, an umbrella organization in which a range of different Jewish groups and communities cooperate to support Jews in need, which includes providing food and clothing for those incarcerated, reuniting families and looking after orphaned children. After that awful business in the middle of July, hundreds of children, including many little ones, had been left to their own devices on the street, but people from the UGIF had sought them out immediately and brought them together in a number of improvised hostels like the one on Rue Vauquelin.

After that event last summer Hélène volunteered to work for UGIF. She devotes a great deal of time to the orphaned children, playing with them and taking them on outings. Given her protected and privileged upbringing, she has never encountered this kind of bottomless poverty before and it has been a shattering experience for her. And a formative one. Trying to help and ameliorate the situation has become a

---

* The Oran attack was planned by the British naval command and carried out despite American protests. (One of them referred to the plan as "suicidal and unhealthy.") To sail two small vessels packed to the gunwales with special forces into a harbor full of French warships could only end in a massacre. All the more so as French naval personnel remembered all too clearly the July 1940 attack by the British fleet at the same location, when many French vessels were sunk or severely damaged and almost 1,300 Frenchmen killed. For further information on this event, I recommend Rick Atkinson's *An Army at Dawn*, which also provides the best account of the whole invasion of French North Africa.

categorical imperative for her. It doesn't bother her when some people maintain that organizations like this—and the notorious Jewish councils in the ghettos in the east—are ultimately doing the occupying power's job and helping administer their own oppression. Nor is she concerned that quite a few people volunteer for the UGIF in order to be given the special identity papers that give them the status of "official Jews," which is supposed to protect them from arrest.*

Working with these children is Hélène Berr's contribution to the as yet weak French resistance to the occupying Germans. UGIF actually has a sixth, secret section that smuggles orphaned children from hostels like this out to protected homes in the countryside, usually with Christian families who conceal and care for them.† This is risky when people are being deported for such trivial things as not sitting in the last car on the Métro or wearing the Jewish star in a slovenly manner. Today, however, the duties waiting for her at Rue Vauquelin are just everyday ones. Nevertheless, this is still a special day, and not just because of the sudden sun and warmth. Everyone is taken up with the great news of the day: the Americans have landed in Algeria and Morocco.

The landing is more than news, it's *huge* news, particularly in Paris. The American army is now on French soil. Hélène writes in her diary: "Everyone seems to be bubbling over with expectation. Mummy and Daddy are so excited. I *ought* to be, too, but I don't seem able to manage it just now."

She tries to work out why she can't be as excited as everyone else. Like everyone else, she's been living for years in a twilight world in which news is twisted by censorship and by transparent propaganda, both of which make it uninteresting. And if not that, it contains truthful

---

* Is this true of Hélène Berr, too? Certainly not as her only motivation: her outlook on the world and of her own self is too strictly moralistic for that. But it may have been a contributory factor, since both in the West and the East, survival in the ghettos was very much a question of class—having money to buy extra food (often at exorbitant prices), being able to bribe the ghetto police, the German guards and high-ranking SS men.

† The efforts to save Jewish children is a bright spot in the otherwise dark history of France during the occupation. One-third of all the adult Jews living in France were deported and murdered, whereas nine out of ten Jewish children survived. One of them was a boy who would grow up to become the peerless Georges Perec, who would give a brilliant account of his experiences in his book *W, ou, Le souvenir d'enfance.*

reports of yet more triumphs for the Axis powers: this is unwelcome
to the great majority, to the few active resisters, and not least to those
who live in denial. Turning your back on the news may perhaps have
felt like an act of resistance similar to turning your back on soldiers out
sightseeing. Or like leaving a museum when a party of grey uniforms
come in, or like folding Métro tickets into a V before throwing them
away.

She thinks her own lack of enthusiasm has to do with being out of
practice, with "an inability to adapt to this sudden fanfare of news,"
as she puts it in her diary. But she recognizes the significance of the
event and adds: "In spite of everything, this is perhaps the beginning
of the end." A scorching sun is shining on Paris that whole Sunday,
November 8.

.   .   .

Anne Somerhausen has been waiting for this for a long time, perhaps
without really daring to hope. (The landing at Dieppe that summer
had clearly been a disaster, though as she commented at the time, it was
still perhaps "a ray of hope.") For this will change her life, her world
and the world as they all know it. In Brussels Anne writes in her diary
and her eagerness is such that the words almost trip over one another:

> What joy, what a triumph! The Allies are strong, they will be
> victorious! The English started a major offensive at el-Alamein
> and Rommel is on the retreat. The Russians have checked
> the Germans at Stalingrad. Invincible Germany is no longer
> invincible. And news has reached us today that there's been a
> surprise American landing in North Africa.

There's no mistaking the sincerity of her joy—though there may be a
downside to the news.

Anne Somerhausen is a forty-one-year-old mother of three children. She is dark-haired, lively and intelligent. Her children are Jean,
age fifteen and very much his mother's son—dark hair, dark eyes, alert
and loquacious; Mathieu, age twelve, slim and fair-haired, "sensitive,
taciturn and whimsical"; Luc, age six, fair-haired and blue-eyed, loves
"picture books, dogs, cats, rabbits, birds and mice." Husband and wife
are the same age and they met after the last war in the U.S., where Marc
had gone on a scholarship after he'd taken his law exams. That's also

where Anne had landed up after a wandering life—a rather unusual one for those days. She was born a von Stoffregen in Riga, which was in Russia at that time, and towards the end of the war she moved to Germany; she then lived in Holland for a year and a half, then in France for a while, and then in Cuba before attending the University of Wisconsin, where she studied journalism. That's where she met Marc, a Belgian lawyer. Somerhausen then fit in ten years as a journalist, freelancing for the *New York Herald Tribune* among other papers, before having a family slowed her freelance work. Then the German occupation put a stop to it.

She hasn't seen Marc for two and a half years. While commanding an anti-aircraft battery on a hill outside Brussels in May 1940, he was taken prisoner and is now imprisoned in a camp in Germany.

When the Belgian army laid down its arms in May 1940 after eighteen days of fighting, the overwhelming majority of the Belgian population welcomed the fact. It wasn't that they welcomed the invading Germans with any degree of warmth. But the great majority of people, in a country that had witnessed foreign armies coming and going through the centuries and which had only just dragged itself out of the destruction left by the last war, hoped that the occupation would be short-lived and that negotiations would lead to some kind of settlement so everything could go back to being normal. In this situation, the attitude towards war is significantly ambivalent.

The majority of people favor the Allies and their cause, but the approach is watchful, passive and quiet. And while waiting for the war to suddenly stop and for peace to fall from the heavens, the Belgians bite their lips and give—or pretend to give—the Germans what they want. This is made easier by the occupiers making an effort to behave correctly and with quite a considerable degree of restraint.*

But there is cooperation and cooperation. And the politics are not exactly crystal-clear, not even among the most obvious collaborators on the populist, semi—or semi-demi—fascistic extreme right such as

---

* This policy of restraint proved successful for the Germans and, for instance, provided a much better result in economic terms than the more draconian occupation of the Netherlands. To quote the historian Werner Warmbrunn: "By doing their best to respect the fundamental agreement of 1940, to work within the framework of the basic structures, feed the Belgian people and refrain from deporting the Belgian workforce, the German military regime retained the willingness of the Belgian elite to cooperate right to the end."

the Rexists in their dark-blue Nazi look-alike uniforms. The shadings are many: Is the aim simply to protect Belgium or is it a part of something greater still?

Anne Somerhausen, too, finds herself in the grey area that is characteristic of the Belgian situation. She works as a clerk in a textile factory producing Zellwolle, a German variant on rayon which, among much else, is used in uniforms for the Wehrmacht. Or to be more accurate, their factory *will* produce it to order once the process is fully set up. Somerhausen's position is more important than her title suggests: she is the one most fluent in German and consequently the one who looks after many of the most important contacts with authorities and potential customers. She does all this, but not without a degree of concern. She writes:

> I would never have believed that Zellwolle would give rise to a serious issue of conscience for me. But it has. Within one or two years the production of rayon by the business in which I work will not only be based on a German patent but will also to a certain extent serve German ambitions.

What to do, then? She has struggled hard with this:

> All work plays into the hands of the Germans, but the alternative is starvation. That's the dilemma we're faced with and there is only one solution—work combined with sabotage. That has to be the daily solution, more and more.

And what has she done about it herself? Last month instructions were given that working in Germany would no longer be voluntary* and that henceforth Belgians could be ordered to take on any duties required of them—the penalty for refusal would be six months' imprisonment.

The feelings of shock, anger and desperation this caused in Belgium still hang in the air like dark clouds.† Somerhausen calls it what it is:

---

* Given that there was high unemployment in Belgium, that conditions were good and there was a relatively friendly attitude towards Germany, the voluntary system had initially functioned well.

† Bad memories of mass deportations in the First World War were still very

deportation and slave labor. One way of protecting yourself against this is to have an occupation designated as vital to the war effort. By using a contact she has in the German economic administration, a certain Herr Gminder, whom she suspects of being anti-Nazi, she has tried to help people achieve this status, most recently thirty workers at a firm in Dolhain, who manufacture the drying ovens necessary to the production of Zellwolle.

News of the landing in North Africa brings pure, unalloyed joy— jubilation even. But what Somerhausen is holding on to this Sunday is still the dream of a quick, bloodless, negotiated peace. She writes in her diary:

> What is it that is preventing the Germans suggesting an armi-
> stice? Clearly they are no longer in a strong position. They are
> on the defensive. They are doomed. All of us are betting on
> when the war will end—I put my money on Easter next year.
> It's worth a bottle of Bordeaux, and if I lose the bet, I'll help
> my colleagues drink the bottle.

·   ·   ·

In Berlin another rainy day is coming to an end. Jürgen, Ursula von Kardorff's little brother, has to return to his unit tomorrow. They might perhaps have gone to the cinema, but Jürgen is clearly not enthusiastic about the light films that are on show everywhere. It may be that they are simply not in the mood given his imminent departure. Family and sibling solidarity is still strong even though the differences in their views are becoming more and more marked. It may be that feelings and family are more important than politics—after all, the von Kardorffs are an old Prussian aristocratic family.

Her father, Konrad, the well-known artist and portraitist, is an out-spoken critic of Hitler and the party and, like many of the old aristocracy, considers their doctrines to be empty, false and vulgar. He lost his teaching post at the Gruneberger Art School as a result. Her younger brother, Jürgen, given his firm Christian faith and high-culture outlook, shares Konrad's skepticism. On the other hand, her mother,

---

much alive. Even the Nazi-influenced Rexists attempted to get the decision reversed.

Ina, is a convinced Nazi and her older brother, Klaus, has a past in the SA (Sturmabteilung). As for herself, she finds herself in a grey zone somewhere between the two.

The contradictions meet in her.

Ursula was one of those who welcomed Hitler's assumption of power in 1933, not with enthusiasm but without any great reflection, hoping, as she says, that he would "clean things up." Moreover, she started her career in 1937 as a journalist on a Nazi paper and has been through official indoctrination and the background checks and selection process everyone in the press has to submit to in order to find work. She was passed, though there were reservations.*

Even though von Kardorff mainly works on politically innocuous topics, for the most part writing cheerful pieces on travel, culture, film and fashion aimed particularly at female readers, she has also produced articles in which Nazism is presented as a blessing for women, something that provides them with meaning and strength. Off the record her attitudes towards the party swing between goodwill and sarcasm. Her disposition is clearly nationalistic, which is true of all the family irrespective of their political leanings. Fighting the war is seen above all as fighting for Germany, not for Hitler.

She isn't an anti-Semite. The family has, and has had, many Jewish friends and acquaintances, most of whom emigrated some years ago. And they've had neighbors who have disappeared to an uncertain fate. (Frau Libermann, an old Jewish woman, is still living in their house.) And even though she ought not to have been shocked by the violence and vulgarity of the anti-Semitic campaigns of the 1930s, she definitely was. It's as if she'd chosen up to that point to think of Nazi anti-Semitism as something staged, as just a political pose.[†]

---

* Her "appraisal to be employed as editor" (Schriftleiteraufnahmeprüfung—a term typical of the Nazi 1930s) states that she has passed but that she should be used "only for non-political [items]." She was the only woman who applied and the only person not a member of the NSDAP.

[†] The things that von Kardorff does *not* call shocking are in themselves quite telling: there is nothing about book burnings, the banning of trade unions and political parties, the police state, concentration camps and Gleichschaltung (the synchronization of German institutions). All of that kind of thing was part of the "cleaning up" process she desired. And her shock wasn't great enough to prevent her from starting her career as a journalist with *Der Angriff,* the party organ known for its virulent anti-Semitism.

The contradictions can be seen in her in a purely physical sense. She has Jürgen's happy and bright eyes, but her older brother's thin, bloodless lips and firm jaw.

Ursula von Kardorff emerges as a not unusual type in 1930s Germany. We are talking about someone with only a fleeting interest in politics, someone whose support for Nazism does not arise from high ideals or strong feelings but principally from a profound desire for order, normality, welfare and, it has to be said, comfort. Simultaneously, however, she has never really put the happy 1920s behind her: she is sociable, energetic, vain, self-assured and full of life. She has a sharp mind, but a superficial one.

For Ursula personally, even the 1930s was in every sense a happy time—a waking dream of travel and pleasure, flirting and parties, balls, beautiful clothes and sailing on the Wannsee. Nazism did not entail any limitations on her life. Even though the party never tires of hammering home its message that the role of a woman is to be Mother and Housewife, at the age of thirty-one von Kardorff is still a career woman, pleasure-seeking, well-coiffed and unmarried.* She is also a smoker.[†]

A life of double standards and denial has become second nature to von Kardorff. She is one of those people who are "integrated but who do not identify fully with this state," in the words of German author Peter Hartl.

It is Sunday evening now and she and her younger brother are hunched over the radio, interestingly enough not listening to the most important event of the day—the broadcast of Adolf Hitler's traditional Munich speech—but listening on shortwave to the BBC news. (That, of course, is forbidden, but it's yet another contradiction she seems to have no problem with.) That's where they hear the news of the American invasion of French North Africa.

---

* The contradiction between dogma and reality wasn't something that even ideologically convinced women found difficult. Ursula's mother, profoundly infected by Nazism as she was, was also a successful career woman. She ran a workshop specializing in interior design and the wives of many highly placed Nazi bigwigs were among her regular customers.

[†] There were campaigns against women smoking: pregnant women and women under twenty-five could not get tobacco on their ration cards, and certain organizations excluded women who smoked in public.

The atmosphere in the room changes. "At that moment it became clear to me that neither of my brothers any longer believed in victory. I became clearly aware of it…. Distressing feelings." Does this imply that the war has turned?* When she and Jürgen are on their own, they talk about what defeat might mean for them, that they might have to leave their home and become refugees. She writes: "We outbid one another in cynicism. Remarkably, once the two of them are back at the front, they do whatever is demanded of them."

·   ·   ·

That same day Vittorio Vallicella wakes to the roar of a sandstorm. The noise tells him that this is an unusually powerful one, so he crawls into his hole and pulls the blanket across the opening. Their adventure has gone unexpectedly well so far—it's been a journey out into emptiness and they have met no one and seen nothing. They have stumbled across signs pointing to headquarters and bases and the like, but when they reach them, they found nothing more than deserted bunkers, empty supply depots and paper blowing in the wind.

Yesterday evening they halted within sight of Mersa Matruh. As far as possible they want to avoid the main coast road, not just because the British air force is hunting there day and night, but worse still in Vallicella's eyes is the probability they'd be swept up by the army and possibly subordinated to some new boy from Italy, his head full of grand, fine-sounding words—a commander who suddenly gets the idea that it's time to stop the enemy and win some medals. As long as they are on their own, they are free and happy orphans.

The wind is so strong that he can't poke his head out. Round about midday the storm increases in fury and the only thing he can do is lift his blanket with a stick at regular intervals to prevent the sand from burying him. He is becoming more and more hungry, but there's nothing to be done about it. Fortunately, like other desert veterans, he always carries a canteen around his neck, though as the hours pass and the storm still rages, his water begins to run low. It's nine o'clock

---

* This is one of the places where her contemporary diary entries differ from the published version. In the latter, she writes that she both hopes and fears it will lead to a quicker end to the war. In the sections dealing with her, when the two versions conflict, I have consistently chosen what she wrote at the time.

in the evening before the wind dies down. Everything is in darkness. Exhausted, he and the others fall asleep in their small holes, under a starry African sky which, as Vallicella writes in his diary, is "exquisitely beautiful and indifferent to human tragedy."

When they wake the following morning, Monday, November 9, he finds it hard to believe his eyes. "It's as if we had suddenly been thrown down on the moon," he writes. The landscape he sees now bears no resemblance to the landscape they stopped in. Where there had been bushes, there is nothing but the crests of huge sand dunes. Their trucks have disappeared beneath tons of shifting sand. Vallicella and his companions haven't had anything to eat for over a day now, so they begin digging where they remember last seeing their vehicles. At first they dig with nothing but their bare hands. And they dig and dig.

NOVEMBER 9–15

ENCOURAGING NEWS

"The houses and rows of houses radiate a sombre but palatial grandeur in their ruin. You glide past them as if viewing an alien, colder world where death resides."

"The continued experience of tragedy gradually atrophies the senses and creates a defense mechanism of callousness without which the normal person could not endure."

"Oh, these lazy thinkers! With their sentimental 'die and become.' Life only arises from life—have they ever seen a dead mother give birth to a child?"

His cabin is cramped, barely seven feet by ten. It contains a bed, a chair, a small table and a small sofa. There is also a wardrobe and a sink with his toiletries. It's a stern and impersonal environment, apart from one thing: on the table he has a photograph of a serious-looking woman in a kimono, two ten-year-old girls and a small boy. His family. When he looks out of the porthole, what he sees is turquoise water, the jungle-covered peaks of volcanic islands and distant breakers that mark the line of the coral reef. And grey vessels, riding at anchor—many grey vessels. This is Truk, a large atoll, and it is Monday, November 9. The man's name is Tameichi Hara.

Hara has just reached the age of forty-two and he's a captain in the Imperial Japanese Navy. He is commander of *Amatsukaze* (Heavenly Wind), a new, state-of-the-art, 2,500-ton destroyer, 390 feet long and low, slim and fast. The ship is heavily armed with gun turrets and torpedo tubes. She is in the process of warming up her engines and the vibrations can be felt through the decks. They will soon be weighing anchor. Hara is proud of his ship, pleased with his crew, sure of his role and devoted to his task. All the same, he feels a certain sense of disquiet, an ambivalence he often manages to suppress but that always seems to be just beneath the surface.

Ever since he was a child Hara has wanted to be a warrior, a samurai like his grandfather, not least because it's a way of coming up in the world given that his family are poor small farmers. The day he was accepted into the navy was one of the happiest days of his life. He loves the white naval uniform, its "wonder and honor," and he loves the enormous status it brings in militarist Japan—the looks, the bows, the respect.

Hara also enjoys the special happiness that comes from having achieved virtually complete mastery of his profession: the Japanese navy's new guidelines on torpedo warfare are based on his calculations and practical experiences. If it hadn't been for his ability to turn his skills into the form of manuals, he would probably never have been given command of a vessel. Hara has a weakness for alcohol, and the revelation in the mid-1920s that he was cohabiting with a geisha very nearly cost him his career. What's more, he is a member of the suspect Christian minority. There are, however, aspects of the navy he finds difficult to accept: the bullying, the rigidity, the contemptuous attitude towards conscripts (they are often referred to as "cattle"), the reluctance to accept new ideas, the blind obedience and—almost as much of a problem—the blinkered self-assurance.

Dressed in his white uniform, Tameichi Hara takes his place on the bridge. If his own writings and photographs are to be relied on, he is strict, reserved and determined. He is quite short but well-built. He is probably wearing white gloves with his all-white uniform and, even though he isn't superstitious, he is likely to be wearing a *senninbari* belt around his waist under his clothes.* And it's likely that the sweat-soaked clothing the crew hangs out to dry overnight has been taken in. Order and discipline!

Curt commands given in harsh forced voices. Short responses. Salutes. Whistles, shouts in the speaking tube. The sounds of signal horns. *Amatsukaze*, accompanied by eight other destroyers and a cruiser, slips out from among the many ships in the wide lagoon at Truk and navigates out to the open sea through one of the channels through the coral reef. They form up line astern and steer south-southeast.

Their destination is Guadalcanal in the Solomon Islands.

·   ·   ·

That same day Vera Inber is attending an official meeting in the Red Army House. Inber is on tenterhooks since she knows that a speech

---

* A *senninbari* is a cloth girdle decorated with a thousand stitches, each of which is done by a different woman. It is traditionally claimed to make the wearer invulnerable to gunfire. Hara's *senninbari* was made by his sister-in-law in Osaka, who, following tradition, stood on the street in her hometown and got passing women to add one stitch each.

Stalin gave in connection with the anniversary of the revolution is currently being rebroadcast. As soon as the meeting is over, she and several others rush to the manager's office, where the wireless is on. (Of course.) She is surprised by the quality of the reception. Very little crackling and interference. It's as if Joseph Vissarionovich was actually in the adjoining room. But it isn't the clarity of the sound that grips her, it's something else. The voice.

The voice embraces her and makes all her anxiety evaporate. Inber writes: "There is something irresistible about Stalin's voice. You can feel from the sound of it that its owner knows everything, and that he will never be a hypocrite. In this speech he spoke calmly and confidently about our relations with our allies, about victory, that is indisputable. Nobody doubts it, the only question is when it will happen. But after this speech even the 'when' has become somehow nearer."

The mood of euphoria occasioned by the voice lasts until the evening, but then the sirens sound again. She writes in her diary: "Last year the raids continued until December. The same thing seems likely to happen this year, too, and today is only November 9. We still have a long way to go."

·   ·   ·

Dorothy Robinson's muscles are aching. She has spent several hours digging in the garden—what used to be part of the lawn. Like many other people, she's following the exhortation to supplement the family diet with vegetables she grows herself in her "Victory Garden." (You can see them everywhere—not only in people's backyards, but also in parks, on vacant lots and even up on roofs.) Jim, as usual, is away travelling and George, her Black maid's ever-helpful fiancé, probably has too much to do in the factory, so she is having to do the picking and shovelling herself in order to turn the heavy, wet autumn soil.

Shortages of fresh vegetables have become quite frequent, so the little garden has actually fulfilled its purpose and they'll carry on sowing right through to spring. But it's not only fresh vegetables that run out now and again. More and more often she finds herself staring at empty shelves in the supermarket. Everyday items such as sugar and coffee are rationed—the rationing of coffee in particular has caused a lot of moaning*—and fresh meat has gone up in price and become more difficult to get hold of.

A semi-voluntary program has been started, urging each family not to eat more than about two pounds of meat a week. In today's paper, however, the omnipresent OWI—Office of War Information—reassures them that this doesn't include turkey, so there is no threat to the traditional Thanksgiving Dinner. (Families are, however, being encouraged to share a bird, and they will be much more expensive this year.) Another article says that overweight women "[are] digging unnecessarily into the country's food supplies" and they should start dieting, which would also benefit their health. It mentions that in a number of the countries with minor food shortages, the occurrence of some diseases—diabetes, for instance—has actually diminished. There is no evil that doesn't bring some good in its train.

As a result of the meat shortage, Dorothy has started experimenting with various kinds of offal—the sort of thing she wouldn't normally have touched. Today they are having oven-baked calf brain for dinner. It has been coated with a thick layer of bread crumbs and served with a highly spiced tomato sauce. This isn't Dorothy's proudest culinary moment. The date is November 9, her muscles are aching and she spends a lot of time thinking about her son, Art, and wondering how things are going for him.

·   ·   ·

The electrifying news of the American landings in Morocco and Algeria has spread around the world and even sent brain waves into the Warner Bros. boardroom in New York. "*Casablanca* had sold the need for engagement on the side of the Allies against fascism. Now the war sold the movie," wrote Aljean Harmetz years later. The moguls are both excited and united: this has to be milked for everything it's worth. They contact Jack Warner in Los Angeles. They want to make a new ending for *Casablanca,* an ending that shows how the bitter bar owner Rick (Humphrey Bogart) and his newfound ally, the corrupt but elegant chief of police Renault (Claude Rains), return with the American forces to free the city.

---

* Some commentators argue that the anger against coffee rationing, at least in the Midwest, led to a protest vote that favored the Republicans in the November 3 Senate elections.

. . .

It's almost nine in the evening of that same Monday and it's raining outside. John Amery is sitting in a radio studio in the huge Haus des Rundfunks on Masurenallee in Charlottenburg in Berlin. He is wait-ing for the green light to come on. We can assume that he is leafing through his manuscript, making sure that it's all there, and we can also assume he is nervous. What Amery is about to do is, to say the least, remarkable. He is about to broadcast on the German radio, on short-wave, direct to the British public, exhorting them to rise against their own government.

There's little doubt that radio is the most powerful medium, the one that reaches the most people and has the most influence. Film is impor-tant and undoubtedly has a great emotional impact, but it needs halls and screens and all the other infrastructure. The strength of radio is its relative technical simplicity. And it reaches out to millions, directly into their homes.* The majority of people receive their information via that little box with its little illuminated window. It's the first place people go to get their news, and also their music, lectures, entertain-ment, talks, diversions, distortions, shameless lies and words that kill. All around Europe, all around the world, there is a bottomless hunger for information, which is why it has now become a fixed routine for people to put aside whatever they are doing to listen to the daily news broadcasts.

Nowhere else in the world is listening to the radio anything like as widespread as it is in Germany, where it has virtually become a ritual. The law states that factory and office work must come to a halt to allow everyone to listen as a group when there are particularly important broadcasts such as speeches by Adolf Hitler. For the same reason, all restaurants and cafés have radios, and in some places loudspeakers have been put up on special poles at street corners.

The Nazis were quick to recognize the importance of radio, initially

---

* The Nazis have shown they recognize this: they've introduced the cheap and simple Volksempfänger, a wireless set that can only receive German broadcasts. (Later they introduced an even smaller and cheaper version, the DKE.) This year, 1942, the number of German households with a radio has almost quadru-pled since 1933. At this point, listening to foreign radio is a criminal offense that can lead to a concentration camp. In some of the occupied countries—Poland, for instance—the population is not even permitted to own a radio.

as a weapon for internal politics: Goebbels, the propaganda minister, called radio "the eighth great power," and said that they'd never have succeeded in coming to power without this wonderful new medium. And then, they also pioneered its use in foreign politics.

By the middle of the 1930s the Nazis have already constructed a network of powerful shortwave stations designed to broadcast beyond Germany. The foreign sections of German radio employ about five hundred staff broadcasting in fifty-three languages. The English-language section is perhaps the most important of these and employs some thirty personnel of British or American background, the best known in Great Britain being a certain William Joyce, known as Lord Haw-Haw because of his nasal, upper-class voice.*

Now it's time for Amery to make his debut. His script has been approved[†] and there is an employee sitting in the control room ready to follow it word for word and ensure there are no impermissible deviations.

The introduction is finished: it has carefully emphasized that Amery's father is a minister in Churchill's government. The green light comes on and Amery begins to speak:

> Listeners will wonder what an Englishman is doing on German radio tonight. You can imagine that before taking this step I hoped that someone better qualified than me would come forward. I dared to believe that some ray of common sense, some appreciation of our priceless civilization would guide the counsels of Mr. Churchill's government. Unfortunately, this has not been the case!

Amery has a very pleasing radio voice, slightly high-pitched perhaps, though that might well be nervousness. It's clear he has often heard his father speak and he copies that statesmanlike style. Amery avoids

---

* Amery will come to know most of them, in particular Joyce and his wife, Margaret, both of whom are well on the way to complete collapse into cynicism and alcoholism.

† All scripts are checked in advance, unlike reports sent home by foreign correspondents. The Nazis made a great point of not practicing advance censorship, but they would then go through all published material with a fine-tooth comb and were quick to apply heavy sanctions when they found content they disapproved of.

coming over as rabble-rousing, hyperbolic and extreme—unlike other defectors such as his notorious colleague Joyce, who makes vain attempts to imitate the coarse and brashly rhetorical style that is a central feature of *lingua Tertii Imperii,* the language of the Third Reich. Amery, on the other hand, makes a clear effort to present himself as a cross between cool English gentleman and dispassionate, unbiased commentator.

But Amery soon moves up a gear, in content if not in tone, and there are no surprises. Everything. Is. The. Fault. Of. The. Jews. They are the people behind the war and they are sacrificing Englishmen in an unnecessary conflict which is already lost. In conclusion he exhorts his listeners—all ordinary British people—to come together and overthrow the London government and to do so for the sake of PEACE. Then his final point: "Between you and peace stands only the Jew and his tool, namely the Bolshevik and American Governments. I am saying this not as a defeatist but as a patriot whose primary concern is the preservation of the British Empire."

The green light goes off.

·   ·   ·

That same day, also in Berlin, Ursula von Kardorff writes:

> Jürgen has gone! We pretended to have a pleasant family breakfast, with the kind of tense jollity that always accompanies farewells. Talked about completely trivial things. Avoided sentiment. Klaus and I accompanied him to the station. It was raining. When Jürgen walked ahead of us with his baggage, and his figure, clad in a gleaming raincoat, disappeared into the crowd, Klaus said: "This is the decent Germany, it won't go down." How I hate these farewells! These railway stations! They are the expression of this hopeless time. Places of busy desolation, exiting the stage—which so often means exiting for ever.

Her brother Klaus's comments show that they are still feeling yesterday evening's mood of doom, which is perhaps inevitable. But Ursula von Kardorff's anxiety is not abstract, nor about the future. She knows that this is quite likely to be the last time she will see Jürgen. The fact that he survived his first winter on the Eastern Front is itself something of a miracle—he was the *only* survivor among the young officers in his regiment. And tomorrow Klaus will be leaving, too. For her, that's what this war is really about: not abstract principles, victory and flags on a map, but the ever-present fear of losing someone she loves. And that's the case for the great majority of people.

Since it's Monday, von Kardorff goes in to her job at the editorial office of *Deutsche Allgemeine Zeitung* at Ritterstrasse 50 in Kreuzberg. She is coming apart, struggling hard not to cry. The boss's secretary sees she is in a bad way and comforts her with a cup of tea.

· · ·

Meanwhile in Los Angeles: news of the North Africa landings sparked an idea in the Warner Bros. New York boardroom that has now bounced across the continent and landed on Jack Warner's desk. Warner, sitting there with his small moustache at his enormous desk in his enormous office with its enormous, gold-plated telephone and its backdrop of enormous prize statuettes and portraits, is aghast at the directors' suggestion to film a new ending for *Casablanca*, and not only because of the extra costs and delays involved.

By this point the rumor has begun spreading through the Hollywood studio that this film, which began life as a B movie with a fairly low budget, skeptical stars* and a chaotic series of script changes and last-minute additions, looks—against all odds—to be turning out to be a really, truly fine film. As early as the end of August that was the talk among the film cutters, who eat together at a long table in the staff canteen. The man responsible for making the trailer—a hardened veteran, sparing with praise and some would even say cynical—was one of the first to see the film and he gave it top marks: "We have beauty."

Jack Warner thinks likewise and he sends a telegram to New York. (We can probably imagine him excitedly pacing the room while dictating it to a secretary he has summoned.) He takes the following position:

---

* Humphrey Bogart and Ingrid Bergman met at a lunch before the start of filming and mostly talked about how they could get out of the project. Their primary objection was the script: they did not like the dialogue and thought the action was—in part, anyway—incomprehensible. Bogart had fears of his own: the dance scene terrified him as he couldn't dance, and he discovered that Bergman was half a head taller than him. (They overcame this in the film by standing him on blocks or sitting him on cushions.)

It's impossible to change this picture and make sense with story we told originally. Story we want to tell of landing and everything would have to be a complete new picture and would not fit in the present film. It's such a great picture as it is, would be a misrepresentation if we were to come in now with a small tag scene about American troops landing etcetera, which as I have already said is a complete new story in itself.... Entire industry envies us with picture having title "Casablanca" ready to release, and feel we should take advantage of this great scoop. Naturally the longer we wait to release it the less important title will be.

The answer from the directors in New York hasn't been preserved, but it must have been quite forceful, as Warner gives way. Hal Wallis, the producer, is ordered to film a new ending that includes the landing.

Practical arrangements are started. Michael Curtiz, the director, is called in and a studio is booked for Wednesday, November 11. The set designers begin building something representing a boat. Humphrey Bogart and Claude Rains are summoned, along with some fifty male extras.

· · ·

Early in the morning of November 9 Ernst Jünger is lying dreaming anxiously in his bed at Steller Strasse 15 in Kirchhorst. This time he's dreaming of some sort of futuristic bombing warfare:

In the fire, a composite machine the size of the Eiffel Tower flew over a residential area and alongside it was a construction resembling a radio mast with a platform on which an observer in a long coat was standing. Every now and then he made notes and threw them down in smoke canisters.

The dream is transparent. So far, Jünger's war hasn't been a war at all. The only things he's experienced have been distant bombing raids—no more than sensations of sound and light—and the execution by firing squad of a deserter—a German soldier who deserted to live with a French woman, who informed on him when he started beating her. It was an event Jünger witnessed with a mixture of unease and morbid curiosity.

At the same time Jünger knows from letters from his wife, Grethe, that she and the children are in much greater danger at home than he is in Paris. Hanover is not far away and the RAF is attacking the city regularly, usually dropping their loads without any great precision. (John Bushby, 83 Squadron, RAF Bomber Command, has never taken part in a raid on Hanover, though he has in all probability flown over the city.) In June nine bombs were dropped over Kirchhorst* and they exploded on the meadow behind the village bakery. No one was killed, however, apart from some cows that were out to graze. But it could be more serious next time.[†]

In Jünger's eyes this is yet another example of how this war represents something new—monstrously new—compared with older wars. Targeting women and children violates his ideas of the chivalry, transcendence and primordial force of war. After receiving a letter from home with details of yet another raid on Hanover, Jünger dreamed he was back in the trenches of the First World War and his children were there with him—a transparent and logical dream.

Through the windows of the restaurant car of the train on his way from Paris to Kirchhorst he could see the ruins of Cologne, which had been the target of the very first RAF "1,000 bomber raid." For once in his life, Jünger, usually so cool and collected, was shaken: "Houses and rows of houses radiate a sombre but palatial grandeur in their ruin. You glide past them as if viewing an alien, colder world where death resides."

Düsseldorf offered a vision just as depressing after the firestorm unleashed by British airmen just six weeks earlier. At that point Jünger thought he could see the future. Or the futures. Either one could expect "Americanized" cityscapes of technocratic creations with neither history nor soul, or, as Jünger thinks, "there will be flocks of sheep grazing among the ruins as in the old images of the Forum Romanum."

---

* Clearly dropped blindly or in an emergency. Nine 500-pound bombs was pretty well the standard payload for a Wellington, the most common RAF bomber at this time.

[†] Hanover was a regular target for the RAF partly because of its industries and the fact it was a railway hub, but also because the flying distance was relatively short. The city was also unusually easy to locate from the air thanks to two large lakes—Steinhuder and Maschsee—and a very large baroque garden, Grosser Garten. The RAF didn't only bomb what they had to, they bombed what they could. By 1945, 90 percent of Hanover was destroyed.

. . .

A new ending for *Casablanca*? Why not? There are few films that have had so many changes made, literally right to the very last minute. Most of the things had to do with problems with the script. At the beginning of the year, a gifted set of twins, Julius and Philip Epstein, had been entrusted with the job of turning a fairly mediocre theatre play using the war as background into a romantic film with box-office potential. One of them referred to the job as "Slick shit"—a polished piece of trivia.

Complications soon arose. One of them was that the producer, Hal Wallis, wanted to give the female lead to a relatively unknown Swedish actress, Ingrid Bergman, whose career was showing signs of stalling. That meant that the character would have to be changed from an American, Lois, to a Scandinavian named Ilsa. In addition, Bergman's English was still weak.*

The Epstein brothers were masters of sharp, amusing dialogue and witty retorts. Their script is full of them, but Wallis believed the film needed weight and brought in a third scriptwriter, Howard Koch, who introduced more seriousness and background, particularly in the male lead. Koch rewrote the brothers' script and they rewrote his. (They never actually met, each side pounding their typewriters separately.) Two further script doctors were also brought in, which only added to the confusion.

The filming had started before there was a final script and some scenes were rewritten just hours before they were to be filmed. Newly written material was sent to the studio on different-colored paper— pale blue, pale pink, pale green—so that the various versions could be identified.

The ending, in particular, proved to be a headache. The motor that drives the narrative is a love triangle. Rick is in love with Ilsa from earlier, but Ilsa is married to the resistance man Victor, and the couple need help to get away from the Nazis. The ending was left up in the

---

* The year before her debut in the United States, Ingrid Bergman had acted in a film in Nazi Germany, *Die vier Gesellen* (The Four Journeymen). It was by no means a worthless film and it had an unexpected crypto-feminist theme. She had a contract for two more films, the intention being to make her a star, but she went to Hollywood instead. A good career move, one might say.

air for a long time. Should Ilsa join Rick? Should Ilsa choose Victor? Should Victor escape alone? As a solution to the dilemma, there was even some discussion of allowing Ilsa to get shot and die. Quite soon, however, producer and authors decided to go for what they called "the Sacrifice Ending": Rick gives up the woman he loves and helps her escape with her husband. This was the ending that best suited the central narrative of the film: the metamorphosis of Rick from a cynical and self-centered onlooker to an unselfish warrior for what is right. It was also an image of the conversion of the United States.

Like the rest of the film, the final airport scene was filmed in the studio with the airport backdrop bathed in a misty chiaroscuro that the public would later consider extremely romantic, but which was designed primarily to hide the fact that the aircraft was a fairly unconvincing half-scale model made of wood and paper.* The idea of the corrupt police chief eventually helping Rick had been decided by the time the final filming started, but having him accompany Rick as an ally in the future struggle against Nazism was one of the changes made at the very last moment. And as if that wasn't enough, Bogart was called back two more times, first to make a new version of the scene in which he shoots the Nazi Strasser,† and then later in August when the whole film was being finalized to dub in a new concluding line: "Louis, I think this is the beginning of a beautiful friendship."

As the directors in New York presumably saw it, a film that had undergone so many changes and labored with so many different endings should be able to take yet another new ending—an ending that set the story right at the heart of its time and signalled a feeling that this war had at last reached a turning point.

· · ·

Monday, November 9. Repeat of a timeless scene: a young woman is sitting, waiting and hoping. Hélène Berr is in the Sorbonne library again, hoping that Jean will happen to come by. He still hasn't set off.

---

* In an attempt to make the half-scale plane slightly more convincing, someone came up with the idea of "employing a group of dwarfs to play at being mechanics." This was actually done.

† In the original version it is made to look as if Strasser pulls his gun after Rick in self-defense, but moral purity demanded that it was the German who drew his weapon first.

The hours slip by and when the library is due to close, she gives up. But that's when he shows up, "as in a dream." Is it her waiting that has made him materialize, or is it vice versa?

They go down into the street and start walking. They leave the small, crooked streets of the Latin Quarter behind them and walk along the tree-lined Boulevard Saint-Michel down to the river. The weak November sun is setting.

Paris is no longer the City of Light, neither visually nor metaphorically. The shortage of gas and electricity means that houses and streets are poorly lit, the gleaming play of light from shop windows and neon signs has been switched off, as have the illuminated façades of the grand buildings. They cross the Seine and reach the large, open space of the Place du Carrousel. In the twilight she thinks the Louvre stands out "like a big, dark ship against the clear grey of the sky."

They cross Rue de Rivoli and turn into the wide Avenue de l'Opéra. Paris has been occupied for just under a year and a half now. The town the two lovers are walking through is, in a sense, unchanged: there are no ruins or damaged buildings;* street life is normal; cinemas, theatres, restaurants, coffee shops and pavement cafés are as full as during peacetime. There are people who think that the city, paradoxically, is now actually more like itself than it was before the war. The absence of heavy traffic and glaring lights make it possible to see the city as it was actually meant to look in terms of views and proportions after the major, radical redesign of the city that began a little less than a century ago. With most of the traffic on the streets now consisting of bicycles and carts, Paris is a much quieter city, and there are few people who don't appreciate that.† Sounds that had become inaudible have returned, so when the two of them cross the Seine, they can hear the lapping of the river water.

But there are also plenty of signs that the city, despite its paradoxically

---

* There had, however, been sporadic bombing of the outskirts of Paris, most recently in May, when the Gnome et Rhône aircraft engine factory in Gennevilliers was attacked by British bombers: this raid demonstrated once again that Bomber Command had a problem with hitting specific targets at night. The factory survived unscathed, but 87 neighboring residential properties were hit and 34 people killed and 167 injured. Incidents of this kind fed the existing French bitterness against Britain.

† This made it a much safer city, particularly for pedestrians. Traffic accidents were radically fewer.

normal external appearance, is not living its normal life: there are the
ever-present waiting lines outside various shops; there are German soldiers everywhere in their field-grey uniforms, rarely armed with anything more than cameras and street maps—they are tourists, soldiers
on leave, often in large groups wherever there are places of interest or
brothels or strip joints; there are the empty plinths of statues removed
by the occupation power and melted down to make ammunition; there
are the big black stains on the plane trees where the authorities have
tarred over the Crosses of Lorraine people had carved into the bark;
there are posters and portraits of a grim and staring Pétain everywhere,
or signs in Gothic script that is difficult to read; and pedestrians walk
past well-guarded roadblocks around various tall buildings or districts
where enormous swastika flags hang loose in the November wind. New
borders, impossible to cross, have shot up here and there, borders surrounded by ignorance and an unpleasant silence. "The city was like a
submarine, with major sections closed off by watertight doors," in the
words of author Ronald Rosbottom.

Hélène Berr and her Jean certainly see all this when they walk down
the Avenue de l'Opéra, but whether they pay it any mind is another
matter. It's too ordinary and too everyday for that, and they are probably far too taken up with one another. Hélène thinks the walk is "as
in a dream." They part at the Gare Saint-Lazare.

· · ·

In the night between November 9 and 10 Kurt West is wakened by a
noise he has never heard before: the rolling thunder of heavy, concentrated artillery fire in the distance. Still half-asleep, he and his comrades
climb out of the bunker and notice that the noise is coming from the
west, from the sector defended by the 2nd Battalion. They hear later
that the Russians have made major inroads and an emergency force is
to be sent there to push them back. West's platoon is to contribute a
non-commissioned officer and five men. The section NCO organizes a
lottery, though he has some hesitation when he sees that Kurt West is
among those chosen. West, however, wanted this, though his stomach
tells him how afraid he is. The connection between fantasy and reality
is being prised apart. Departure is at 7:00 a.m.

· · ·

On Monday evening Ernst Jünger and his wife and child visit one of their neighbors. They've hardly had time to sit down and start talking when they hear the sirens from Hanover. Another air raid. They all go down to the basement, all of them wearing their outdoor clothes, and the host couple take several packed suitcases—"as if we were on board a ship in distress." He notices how people's behavior has changed—it's serious now. "It shows how close to catastrophe we are."

Through the window Jünger sees a necklace of red tracers ascending from the distant city and vanishing into the cloud cover; he sees the sudden flashes of explosions; he sees the glowing reflections of burning houses; he can clearly feel the house rock even though the bombs are exploding so far away. But what really disturbs him is that the children are witnessing all this. Their presence makes the experience even more stressful and depressing. Jünger started the day dreaming about an air raid. He is finishing the day by witnessing one. For once, the world is complete. More's the pity.

· · ·

It's dawn on Tuesday, November 10, and Kurt West and the rest of the group chosen are hurriedly packing their gear. They are to keep it as basic as possible. They'll be taking ration packs, of course—canned meat and crispbread. Ammunition is distributed—plenty of it—and weapons. To West's surprise, he and the law student Hans Finne are the ones given the group's sub-machine guns, whereas the others have ordinary rifles. He doesn't really know why, but he is pleased anyway:

> One of the older ones might have been a more suitable choice, I thought, but I felt proud of the confidence the others had in me. We all felt pretty nervous as we still didn't know much about the task we were about to undertake. Judging by the equipment we were taking with us, we suspected it would involve tough going.

One of the other young men comes up to West and "cautiously" offers to take his place. West considers it for a moment before saying no.

In the grey of dawn they set off, shouting "Bye" and "Back soon" to the comrades who are watching them go. They exchange the usual jokes and banter, but without much conviction—there is a noticeably serious undertone instead. "It was highly likely that not all of us would be coming back."

The emergency force—seventy-eight heavily armed men from different companies—gathers at battalion HQ. Most of the faces are unfamiliar to West. The force is led by a lieutenant named Hardy Herrgård, who makes a speech, informing them that the Russians attacked and took two important strongpoints, Teeri and Kako, during the night. These must now be taken back. Herrgård finishes his talk with, as West himself puts it, "various high-flown words."

So they set off and march for quite some time. As the path deteriorates and gets narrower, the column spreads out. The blue of dawn breaks in the dense young forest of birches, and the morning is cold and windy. Soon, however, a warm sun shines from a blue sky. Gradually the distant noise of shell bursts grows ever stronger and sharper. Now and again, the sound of aircraft engines can be heard. Soon they will be there.

·   ·   ·

On this same Tuesday Hélène Berr gets together with Jean. They meet at her home, Avenue Élisée-Reclus 5. Her parents are away and the apartment is empty apart from her big sister—who seems to know to stay out of the way. Jean brings some records with him: Beethoven's Violin Concerto in D Major and Mozart's Sinfonia Concertante. They put the gramophone on and, as the apartment fills with the warm comforting tones of the violin—"and that for someone those notes are / more real than everything else," wrote the Swedish poet Tomas Tranströmer—they drink tea on the bed in her room. (That's all she says in her diary.) Outdoors it is sunny but cold. Jean's journey has been postponed for a while.

·   ·   ·

A scene, repeated millions of times: the bomb falls and a house is smashed to pieces. The less familiar scene, repeated almost as many times: people return and walk around in the dust discussing repairs. Vera Brittain is back in the old family house in Chelsea doing just that. She is accompanied by a man from Gregg's, the construction firm.

Five or so years ago the family moved into 2 Cheyne Walk, a narrow, Georgian, five-story, red-brick house with a view over the Thames. Like everyone else, she followed the regulations and prepared the house for war. She took down all the pictures on the walls, taped the windows, filled the bathtub with water, and like many other people (not just the pacifists) she formed a mental picture of the expected apocalypse from the air—bombs raining down and clouds of poison gas. In spite of that, she was taken by surprise by the sheer force of the blitz that hit London.

It took a while for it all to become routine: the sirens, the drone of aircraft, the crack of anti-aircraft guns, the beams of light, the dull rumble of distant bombs (felt before heard, since a pressure wave travels faster through the ground than sound travels through the air), the rushing down into the chilly coal cellar that is used as an improvised air-raid shelter. And every dawn reveals new bomb damage, more rubble in the gutter, constant smoke and the stench of burning.

Were the statistics on her side? She was in the bathroom one day at the end of August when she heard a bomb whistle past and land a short distance away. A week later, when she was visiting her mother, a bomb exploded so close that the blast hurled her and her mother down into the cellar; they came to to the clink of falling glass and Vera Brittain had mild burns on her face. She was close to a mental breakdown at that stage, mainly as a result of lack of sleep; when things were at their worst she would lie face down in the air-raid shelter with a cushion over her head.

When a bomb damaged their house—it fell in the garden—Vera Brittain wasn't at home. She decided then that the house should be closed up, their home help's husband dealing with the heaviest tasks. She went to the house herself and picked out the most important things: two of their best paintings, her diary from the 1914–1918 war, some manuscripts and some warm clothing. Everything was covered in dust from the explosion. She had lugged all this onto the bus herself, "overwhelmed with misery of [the] present world."

But today is November 10 and she is back at 2 Cheyne Walk. The sun is shining.

By this point it is fairly safe to return. London hasn't suffered any serious air raids since May of last year.* Vera Brittain and the man from the construction firm walk through the empty rooms. There is dust everywhere, and the crunch of broken glass and plaster from the ceiling.

* In 1940, 13,596 civilians were killed in London; in 1941 the number was 6,487; in 1942, 27.

And rain has come in through the shattered windows. In spite of all that and a hole in the roof made by an incendiary bomb, the house is in surprisingly good condition. The builder looks around and makes notes.

Brittain writes in her diary: "Despite dirt and falling plaster, the house seemed so bright & sunny that I longed to get back to it—even though it is surrounded on all sides by big areas of ruins." Scarcely two weeks later she received the construction firm's offer: the bomb damage was going to cost £32 to fix; on top of that there were general repairs, painting, plasterwork and so on, which will add up to £78. It could be far worse.

. . .

On Slipway 2 at the Southeastern Shipbuilding Corporation in Savannah, Georgia, work is continuing on what is to be the first Liberty ship launched at that yard. The estimate is that this will happen within a fortnight. At this point, the vessel appears to have been classed as "a hot ship," which means that extra workers were moved over from neighboring slipways in order to speed up completion.

Given the present circumstances, it's a uniquely motley mixture of people who are climbing over and working on and inside the 440-foot-long and 56-foot-wide hull. There is work for everyone now, even for those who, before the war, were considered unemployable or just unsuitable. "Women, African-Americans, southern white migrants, ex-convicts, teenagers, the elderly, and the physically handicapped all found jobs at the shipyard," wrote American author Tony Cope.

The great number of women is perhaps the most striking aspect. There has been resistance, predictably enough mainly from the male shipyard workers, but it is gradually being broken down. Women, for instance, have frequently proved to be better welders than men—the usual explanation being that they are more patient. And the special wartime contracts guarantee them the same pay as male welders.

But the women still have to deal with the usual downsides: whistles, comments, suggestions and groping. And married women can find themselves holding down two jobs at once—many of them can't handle that and stop work.* Simultaneously, however, there is a kind of twilight

---

* Married mothers leaving their children unattended or in the hands of others to go to work was a matter of concern, even by the state. The ideal female worker was unmarried.

zone created by the rapid growth of this mixed milieu and previously fixed moral boundaries show signs of breaking down. There is sexual activity, especially during the night shift, in the many hidden corners and passages of the shipyard and it is not unusual for used condoms to turn up in the many dark crannies of the hull.

The atmosphere is good, though. One of the young shipyard workers writes: "As bad as war is in its ultimate sense, it can bring out the best qualities in people—sacrifice, devotion. I saw all of this at the shipyard." And someone else says: "Everyone worked, the pay was good, the job was good, the people were treated good, and they worked well." There is a dining room at the yard that can feed a thousand or more at the same time. Many of the employees are Black. They can work there, they can buy food there, but they aren't allowed to sit and eat there.

.   .   .

In Brussels, it's another day at the office for Anne Somerhausen. We can assume that, as usual, the working tempo is consciously low. Wasting time, going slow, spinning things out, bungling things—these are all more or less routine, intentional, when, like her, you are working for the Germans. She allows herself time to read a German daily paper— *Frankfurter Zeitung.**

Somerhausen reads a lot. All those in the office read a lot. The reasons may differ. It may just be a way of passing the time and the endless waiting that characterizes so much of life in occupied Belgium. Even though everything published has to be approved by the German censor, even though rationing leads to everything being printed on thin, depressingly grey paper, many new books do appear.

Detective stories are especially popular: they are easy to read and easy to forget. This year, for instance, Georges Simenon's famous

---

* Her choice of German newspaper is by no means an accident. The *FZ* was for many years an organ for the educated German public, liberal, democratically inclined, known for its brilliant writers such as Stefan Zweig, Heinrich and Thomas Mann, Walter Benjamin, Sigfried Kracauer and Alfred Döblin. By this point, it was also the only seemingly independent paper in the Third Reich—it was quite consciously and cunningly tolerated by Goebbels, who saw it as a channel to influence the overseas image of Germany. It was, however, shut down in 1943 on the direct orders of Hitler. (What led to this was a "criminally" positive portrait of Eleanor Roosevelt.)

Detective Inspector Maigret has returned in a volume of three long
short stories (*Maigret revient*) and none of them makes any reference
at all to the war. Nor is it possible to find a mention of the war in any
of the other novels written by Simenon during this period. He is not
alone in this. To give another example from another popular genre:
when Somerhausen reads today's edition of the major Brussels paper
Le Soir, she will follow Tintin, the young reporter with the refractory
forelock and golfing plus fours, who is now well on the way to solving
the mystery of the *Secret of the Unicorn.* The story makes no mention
of the occupation nor of anything else unpleasant.*

Both of these Belgians, Simenon and Hergé, are talented opportunists, willing (as are many others) to work within the framework of the
occupation system and thus carefully avoiding anything the censors
object to and the wider public does not welcome. Cultural life, lively
as it may be, offers plenty of opportunities to escape reality.

Theatres attract large audiences, the repertoire consisting mainly
of classics: Molière, Musset, Racine, Corneille, Shakespeare—risk-free
and unimpeachable as far as the authorities are concerned. The opera
puts on superb performances, operettas are popular, and all kinds of
variety shows are even more popular: *artistes* such as Charles Trenet,
Maurice Chevalier, Edith Piaf, Tino Rossi and Django Reinhardt fill
the theatres. (You can even listen to jazz in spite of the Germans having banned it—the titles of the tunes have sometimes been slightly
changed.) Just as everywhere else, however, movies are the most
popular entertainment and a sort of unholy alliance between censors
and audiences ensures that cinemas remain temples of forgetfulness:
French entertainment films are the best draw[†] and in so far as the Belgians bother with German films at all, they abhor heavily propagandist
productions and favor the musicals and light comedies the German
film industry continued to churn out at an astonishing rate.[‡]

---

[*] In Tintin's previous adventure, *The Shooting Star,* there are hints of the age,
especially in the clearly anti-Semitic portrait of the rogue banker Blumenstein.
After the war, Hergé, Tintin's creator, took care to modify both his nose and his
name.

[†] German goodwill and German capital ensured that the French film industry
continued to flourish during the war years. In 1942 alone, twenty-one French
feature films had their premieres and we can assume that pretty well all of them
will have found their way to Belgium.

[‡] For obvious reasons, more recent American films are not shown, though some

So culture can mean escapism and that is exactly what it is for many people. But what Anne Somerhausen is reading in her office this Tuesday has nothing to do with a flight from reality—it's an attempt to make contact with it.

She is carefully reading a long and ambitious article surveying a number of new books of reportage published in North America. The bias of the survey is clear, more than clear—these books give a false and distorted picture of Germany and they are, to quote the title of the article, "The Bestsellers That Brought the USA into the War." But Somerhausen is trying to read through the bias, to dig under the surface of the survey. She is absorbed in the article because it gives her a glimpse of a world that is currently beyond her reach. She writes in her diary: "I have never longed so much for foreign literature, for things from the nine-tenths of the globe from which we are cut off. Radio is not sufficient to quench our thirst for contact with the greater world."

. . .

Barrow-in-Furness, Nella Last's hometown, is an industrial town, a steel town and above all a shipbuilding town. What dominates the town skyline is no longer the tower of St. Mary's church or the clock tower of the neo-Gothic sandstone town hall, but the cranes down at the Vickers shipyard. Warships were being built there twenty years before the last war and it is now building more than ever—of every kind and every size, from submarines and destroyers to enormous aircraft carriers.* Just as in Savannah, the life of the town is tied to the shipyard.

And Barrow-in-Furness is a working-class town. Many of the workers at Vickers live in the many long, narrow streets of small, redbrick terraced houses that have been built within walking distance of the shipyards. In April and May last year, when German bombers made repeated attempts over a number of nights to knock out the shipyard,

---

cinemas still show worn copies of non-dangerous pre-war productions such as Laurel and Hardy's *A Chump at Oxford.*

* Prime Minister Winston Churchill made his only visit to the town for the launching of the aircraft carrier HMS *Indomitable* in May 1940. "His direct manner had appealed to all," Nella Last writes in her diary and she was reluctantly impressed, even though Neville Chamberlain had always been to her taste. Of Churchill she writes: "He has a funny face, like a bulldog living on our street."

almost all the bombs missed their targets—as usual—and many of them hit these residential areas.*

All in all, eleven thousand or so houses in the town were damaged (about one in four) and six hundred were completely destroyed. Many of them have been repaired or patched up, but when Nella Last walks through the town now, it is still a depressing sight. There are gaping grey ruins and many shops are closed: "mainly little sweet and tobacco shops and fruiterers." Even some of the larger shops are empty and boarded up, and those that are still open have replaced their display windows with boards and plywood, perhaps leaving just one small pane of glass to let in the light.

Nella Last is in a hurry this afternoon as she wants to get the bus home before the shift changes at the shipyard and thousands of men come flooding out with dirty faces, dirty overalls and lunchboxes. They make it difficult even to find standing room. Nella lives a little distance away, on Ilkley Road, and as the bus trundles along the wide main street, Abbey Road, she sees several collapsed houses, just heaps of rubble in which sodden autumn weeds have taken root. One of these piles of rubble is all that remains of the town's main hotel, the Waverley. The autumnal trees lining the street show old scars made by bomb splinters. The date is November 10.

.   .   .

It's an existence of uncertainty, rumors and silences. Elena Skrjabina writes in her diary that day:

> We are living in complete ignorance of what is happening around us; whether the Germans have gone far into the Caucasus, what is happening on other fronts, on whose side fortune is at the present—all of this is shrouded in mystery. We feed on rumors from the girls, from the secretaries, and from Russian visitors to the café, who are inclined to speak about such topics. We are in no way able to judge what is true and what is not.

---

* Barely a single day's work was lost at the yard. The same lack of precision that was characteristic of the RAF bombing of Germany was also visible here and led to neighboring towns being attacked in the belief that they were Barrow-in-Furness.

There are occasional air raids by Soviet aircraft, but the effect is more psychological than physically damaging. And it has been a long time since anyone heard artillery fire. Elena Skrjabina belongs to the section of the townspeople that has chosen to accept the German occupation.*

It's not hard to understand why. She and those closest to her make quite a good living from the simple café with its four tables and twenty chairs. They charge sky-high prices for items such as fresh boiled pierogis and other baked goods. And they have also moved into an apartment that used to belong to a member of the Communist Party who fled when the Germans marched in at the beginning of August. Dima, their fourteen-year-old, is a voracious reader and she has been able to buy loads of books at the local market—people are selling their possessions cheap in order to buy food.

Pyatigorsk has returned to a kind of temporary normality. Small shops and kiosks have opened up here and there. Many people earn their daily bread by providing services for the Germans in apparently innocent activities such as interpreting, clerical work, kitchen work, carrying or laboring: this is understandable in these exceptional situations when all support systems have collapsed. In some occupied areas and towns—Stalino, for instance—more than one in ten male inhabitants work for the Germans. But where does the borderline run between working to keep body and soul together and becoming a collaborator?

Ignorance is to some extent a fact—what is truth and what is a lie? What are facts and what is just propaganda? But it's not just about the usual balancing act between the uncertainty of knowing and the force of the emotions. Ignorance is in fact an attitude for people like Elena Skrjabina, is a case of not *wanting* to know. In her diary she writes of living in "*complete* ignorance [my italics]." That, at best, is a form of denial, since no such thing exists, not even here in this little town at the foot of the Caucasus. The Jews have disappeared—but will it stop there? On this day Elena Skrjabina writes in her diary:

* An element of this is that the German occupation of the Caucasus was not quite as harsh as in other parts of the Soviet Union. This was partly for pragmatic reasons—they needed the population to cooperate—partly for ideological reasons: many of the ethnic groups there were considered to be racially "superior" to, for instance, Russians, White Russians and Ukrainians.

The most disturbing question for all the inhabitants of Pyatigorsk, and us too, is the question about mixed marriages. We
finally asked the Germans. They either really don't know or
don't wish to say.*

Elena's sister-in-law Lyalya, who lives with them in Pyatigorsk, has
been married to a Jew and her daughter Vera is therefore half Jewish.
In the occupied parts of the Soviet Union, the children of mixed marriages were usually murdered.

.   .   .

Nella Last gets off the bus and walks the last bit to her neat house at
No. 9. She gives a sigh of relief: "I felt thankful to shut the door on all
the day's worries." Her little dog, Sol, meets her and "frolicked round
my feet, as if glad I'd come at last," but then he suddenly coughs and
collapses. Nella writes in her diary:

> As I knelt and gently stroked him, it came to me with a pain-
> ful shock that soon my little friend and I must part. He is
> turned thirteen, and showing signs of ageing quickly. To me,
> he is more than an animal: he has kindness, understanding and
> intelligence, and not only knows all that is said, but often reads
> my mind to an uncanny degree.

She also has a cat, Mr. Murphy. She is a real animal lover. During the
dreadful air raids last year, she used to mix an aspirin into the cat and
dog food to try to calm their terror. At the time, the dog had been so
frightened she had seriously considered having him put down. She
herself frequently takes an aspirin as a sort of sleeping pill. And when
her own house was so badly damaged, Nella still found time to pick
up a sparrow, one of several killed by the blast, and look at it sadly: "It
looked as if they had bent their little heads in prayer."

---

* They did know. During these months Pyatigorsk was the base for Einsatz-
kommando 12; in addition, Walther Bierkamp, head of the superordinate Einsatzgruppe D, had his headquarters there. The majority of the town's Jews were
murdered in an action on September 10, 1942. Smaller massacres in the area
continued with the help of local volunteers right through the autumn. They
sometimes took the form of mass shooting, sometimes gassings in specially constructed buses.

What it actually comes down to is Nella Last's capacity for sympathy. Animals do not take the place of people, their sufferings do not displace human suffering, but they offer an image of the inevitability of suffering. And it's an image that eats its way into your soul.

She often weeps, but does so mainly when alone. Outwardly she takes care to appear happy, cheerful and controlled, not just for the sake of others but for herself and as a way of keeping it together. Her external reaction to bad news of any sort is brief and restrained, with a touch of fatalism. But inside herself, she is unsure whether she is actually getting harder, or whether it's all no more than a façade. She has always loved the sea, loved the sound of the waves breaking on the shore. No longer: "They make me think too much of shipwrecks and horrors." The seashore is no longer what it was. You can never be sure now what you might come across. Every now and again an unidentifiable corpse is washed in from the Irish Sea.

She talks to little Sol and strokes him. He wags his tail, and she takes her coat off and becomes her efficient self again. Then she goes and feeds the hens, puts up the blackouts on the windows—no light to be visible after 6:00 p.m.—pokes the fire and prepares the table for supper. But then her energy runs out. Supper this Tuesday will have to be canned salmon. She knows that the dog loves salmon, so he will get half of it.

·   ·   ·

Today is Armistice Day and Dorothy Richardson is at home in her house on Long Island with Sally, a relation of hers. It's a special day in solemn remembrance of those who fell in the last world war. They celebrate it with church services, speeches, meetings, the laying of wreaths and two minutes' silence and a halt to all traffic at 11:00 a.m. That war was to be the end of all wars, yet most words and thoughts today are concerned with what is happening in this new war. Dorothy Robinson and her companion are listening to the radio, which allows them to participate in several ceremonies, one of which is the president speaking at a ceremony at Arlington Cemetery: he emphasizes how essential it is for the nation to dedicate itself once more to "winning this war and building a just peace."

Radio is an extraordinarily important source of information for Dorothy and Sally. There are news reports on the hour every hour from eight in the morning to eleven at night. When they aren't listening to the radio, they are reading the newspaper. On November 11, *The New York Times* has sixteen pages devoted almost exclusively to news of the war—from all fronts, major and minor. That is more or less the norm. The headlines on the front page deal mainly with the continued advance of American forces in Morocco and Algeria, but for some days now Robinson's attention has been on reports of British successes in Libya: afraid, as she is, of "over-confidence," she cautiously describes them as being "encouraging."

There is a lot in the paper that has nothing at all to do with the war.

So, for instance, 8,559 spectators in Madison Square Garden yesterday watched the New York Rangers beat the Chicago Black Hawks 5–3; the deer hunting season opened in the state and the heaviest animal of the day weighed in at more than two hundred pounds, and was shot by a hunter from Brooklyn by the name of Rufus Hill; there were nine fires in Brooklyn and Queens yesterday, none of them especially serious; the play *Without Love,* with Katharine Hepburn in the leading role, opened on Broadway to lukewarm reviews; a twenty-five-year-old male patient died after a bizarre accident with laughing gas at a sanatorium in Glen Gardner, New Jersey; Milton H. Myers, one of the last veterans of the American Civil War—he was still riding his bicycle at the age of ninety—has passed away at the age of 101; the town council of the small town of French Lick Springs, Indiana, has decided that all black cats must from now on wear bells whenever it is Friday the thirteenth.

Dorothy Robinson herself shares something of this obvious and peculiar duality. The war is constantly present in her thoughts, while her life is simultaneously dominated by something else. Some of the really major events do figure in her diary, events that were deemed worthy of the kind of headlines and attention that made them virtually impossible to avoid. They stay in the memory, both the individual memory and the official memory: the Battle of Bataan, the Doolittle air raid on Japan, the naval battle of Midway, the ongoing battle for Guadalcanal. These are mentioned in the diary, but only in passing and with a minimum of detail. That should not necessarily be seen as a lack of sensitivity—it could equally well be the opposite.

The contrast between her life and what is happening out in the world is obvious even to her. On one occasion after she had carefully redecorated and cheered up her kitchen with new curtains, new dish towels, the mugs arranged on hooks so that the red, yellow and turquoise colors showed to best effect, she was suddenly brought up short by the thought of "men dying and suffering and struggling and I was hanging cups on hooks and thinking about breakfast cereal. And Artie going to heaven knows where or what. I have no right to be so happy over simple, homey things." Her thought continues, however: "Yet what is it all about if those small things don't endure and homes go on being homes and havens of peace and love and understanding?"

·   ·   ·

"Trapped like rats!" The words are those of Albert Camus, writing in his notebook. The exclamation mark is unlike him, as is the fact that he has included the date: November 11. Like millions of others he has been lying low, hoping that things will change, had some thoughts of "doing something" (his own words), and even—like many other people—had moments of weakness when he had paid no attention to the war in the slightly absurd hope that the war would pay no attention to him.

But now he knows better.

That is precisely what he is writing about, as he sits there in the little hotel in Le Panelier, for the war has been creeping closer, even if only slightly. The French authorities have started rounding up men of his age to pack them off to forced labor in Germany, and this process is now even reaching into areas as remote from the centers of power as where Camus is. His tuberculosis will, however, protect him from that fate. Unusual guests have started to pop up at the hotel, people Camus avoids, not just because he wants to protect his working time, but because they probably aren't the people they claim to be. Everybody knows that there are Jewish refugees hidden here in Vivarais, but no one knows where and no one knows who is hiding them.*

Camus's predicament was both impossible to predict and simultaneously completely logical. In response to the American landings in the French parts of North Africa, German troops have moved quickly into the non-occupied southern regions of France—into the overblown

---

* Almost all the farmers in the region are Huguenots, with memories of being persecuted and with traditions of helping those fleeing persecution. Their concealment of Jews occurred spontaneously, with no organizational structure, and this made it very difficult for the French authorities to track anyone down. This made it a very different situation from various underground networks of refugee smugglers, which were closed down with some regularity.

nationalistic fiction called Vichy. The relative and insecure freedoms permitted in those parts of the country are now over. And Camus's road home to Algeria is blocked from both directions.

Camus goes out for a walk. It has been a cold night and the rime frost is coating everything. Only slowly does the sun begin to warm the frozen earth. The fragile layer of ice crystals begins to melt away, tinkling almost inaudibly as they go. On his walk Camus comes to a place where two watercourses flow together. He writes:

> Freed from the frost by the first rays of the sun, this becomes the only thing alive in this landscape, which is as white as eternity.... Sitting high in the prow, I continue this unmoving voyage in the land of indifference. No less than the whole of nature and this white peace that winter presents the over-heated heart—in order to calm this heart that is being consumed by a bitter love. I see how this burgeoning light that negates the portent of death is spreading across the sky. At last a sign from the future, above me, for whom everything now speaks of the past.

Indeed, he is trapped, like a rat. What now?

.   .   .

At the same time in New Guinea—a new battle. It might well be a carbon copy of what happened a couple of weeks ago at Eora Creek. In front of them lie jungle-covered hills, where the Japanese have dug in, with great care—as always: foxholes, trenches, bunkers built of logs, assault barriers of plaited lianas and other climbing plants. There are machine guns, direct-fire mountain guns, snipers high up in the trees. And everything is camouflaged with amazing skill. In such dense rain forest it is impossible to pick out your enemy until firing starts. The Japanese heavy machine guns are called "woodpeckers" by the Australian troops because their firing tempo is quite slow and they usually fire in short bursts. *Tack-tack-tack-tack* is the sound they make—and someone falls to the ground.

Just as at Eora Creek, this has been going on day after day for almost a week now. And just as there, the Australian attack is tentative but definite, through thickets, through the dampness, but the Japanese defense is firm and stubborn. What is happening may have some logic when seen as blue and red arrows drawn on a plan: there's the Kokoda Trail leading to the coast, there's a river swollen by the rains, there are two small villages—Oivi in the west and Gorari in the east (the battle will be named after them afterwards), there are the breakthrough attacks, the reconnoitering attacks, the covering fire, the counterattacks, encirclement, regroupings, feints.

For the Australian troops like Sergeant Bede Thongs and his men in 10th Platoon, 3rd Battalion, what happens scarcely amounts to more than the sighting of plumes of dirty smoke rising through the dense green undergrowth and the usual cacophony of noises and echoes: explosions, cracks, roars; shouts and screams—often incomprehensible; the buzz, swish and whine of shell splinters, bullets and projectiles; the rustle and creak as severed leaves and branches rain down. The Australians are frequently so close to their unseen opponents that they can hear them talking, hear the clicks as they pull the pins from their grenades, hear the rattle as they reload their rifles.

Bede Thongs and 3rd Battalion have been fighting close to Oivi, the western village. Attacks on this spot haven't had any great success and things have been fairly quiet since November 7—apart, that is, from Australian grenade launchers constantly bombarding the Japanese lines,* and the occasional American plane dropping bombs and then flying off. The noises of war are very much louder to the east, in the direction of Gorari village.

Yesterday, Tuesday, November 10, Thongs was called to Lieutenant Colonel Cameron, the commander of the battalion. Cameron is the only one of the battalion officers that Thongs has confidence in. Thongs actively dislikes many of the officers he has had to deal with since arriving in New Guinea: he finds them weak (physically or morally or both), theoretically rigid, stuck in dated experiences, unreliable, self-centered, even cowardly. He particularly scorns that last category: "They never have the stomach for a fight." Leadership is informal and is mainly in the hands of non-commissioned officers like Thongs. He

---

* The continuous bombardment signified a very important change after the capture of Kokoda: it was now possible for supplies to be regularly flown in to the small airfield outside the village. Now, for the first time, the Australians had plenty of ammunition, especially for the heavier guns. And their sick and wounded could be flown out, which gave them a much-enhanced chance of survival.

refuses to carry out orders that are crazy or impossible, or he'll sabotage them.

Lieutenant Colonel Cameron wanted Thongs to go out reconnoitering yet again. Where is the flank of the Japanese line of defense? Several patrols had been out looking for it and returned without any results. It took Thongs and 10th Platoon three hours of slogging through vegetation and damp before they could return with the requested information—and with one man wounded.

Today, Wednesday, the battalion is going to make another attempt on Oivi and Thongs and his platoon will be under fire yet again. A thought occurs to him: today is the anniversary of the end of the last war and it's also the day on which his father was wounded at Gallipoli in 1915, "and here was I, myself on this Armistice Day 42 leading this attack." It turns out to be easy this time, though, unexpectedly easy. The Japanese have already begun to withdraw.

For the time being, the Australian troops can take a breather. They can count their dead. During one week of fighting, 121 of them have been killed and 225 wounded. One of them may possibly have been the man Bede Thongs wrote a poem about much, much later: "What Do You Say to a Dying Man?"

> *What do you say to a dying man?*
> *Do you call him Bob, digger or mate*
> *as you look at the face you have known so well*
> *and the look in his eyes says: "It's late."*
> *You recall the first handshake on a troop train,*
> *with many men going to war.*
> *Training in various military camps,*
> *Wallgrove, Greta, Bathurst, Ingleburn and more.*
> *To go hungry, have tired muscles and thirst,*
> *The pub Duke of York where we had our last drinks*
> *before leaving Australia's fair shores.*
> *A fleeting last thought of his loved ones*
> *you knew from being his friend.*
> *If you happen to live through this onslaught,*
> *they'll ask you about his life's end.*
> *Just three minutes ago he was so full of life,*
> *firing bursts from a Bren at his hip.*
> *The Platoon attacking as it had many times before,*

when all of a sudden he's hit.
A Japanese sniper, so deadly,
had fired from a dark weapon pit.
The sniper was caught by the last burst from the Bren,
and my best friend fell close to my feet.
"Tell them I tried" were the last words he said.
My words of goodbye froze on my lips.

Something has happened, however: for the very first time they can count many more Japanese dead than Australian. In one place their dead enemies are lying in heaps—the result of what they call "the Death Valley Massacre," where a Japanese unit was taken by surprise. And for the first time, the normally very disciplined Japanese soldiers seem to have been panic-stricken. They didn't withdraw, they fled. The only men left were three hundred terrified native bearers.

. . .

Meanwhile, Lieutenant Tohichi Wakabayashi on Guadalcanal finds time at last to write something in his diary. His first entry since they landed on November 5—his time has obviously been fully taken up getting his company into position.

They are located on a hill a short way from the shore. They spend their nights under almost constant bombardment by American mortars and they can't move around during the day because of the many enemy aircraft. The latter circle above them like huge raptors hunting for prey, often swooping so low that their noisy tailwind causes the branches of the trees to move. "This is what it means to be in a straitjacket," he writes. He composes a *tanka*, a short poem:*

Jungle leaves quiver
As my hatred
For the dominating
White starred planes
Begins to grow

. . .

* The *tanka* is a Japanese form of short, concentrated poem, similar to the *haiku* except that it has five lines whereas the *haiku* has three.

That same Wednesday, just after nine in the morning, a messenger knocks on the door of the small house at 6 Central Road, Portsmouth, UK. The woman who answers the door is the mother of Leonard Thomas, seaman. Telegrams are bad news, especially just now: notifications of death usually arrive in this impersonal way. This is a moment of profound, dizzying horror, even for a woman from a family in which several generations of men have gone to sea, where the threat of death or of going missing has always been present, though suppressed or sublimated.

How much does she know about what her son does or where he is? Probably very little. The feeling of uncertainty is nothing new to her—her boy was only seventeen when he went to sea for the first time. (Leonard Thomas was a bright boy, no doubt about that, but the family was too poor to permit further studies.) But this is different. Just like everyone else back at home, she exists in a cloud of unknowing created by the censoring not just of the news but also of letters—letters which frequently arrive after long delays or sometimes not at all.

She possibly knows that Leonard is serving as a diesel mechanic on HMS *Ulster Queen,* a passenger ferry that sailed between Ireland and the northwest of England in the 1930s that has now been requisitioned by a slightly desperate Royal Navy and converted into an air defense vessel, painted in a somewhat Cubist grey-white and dark blue camouflage and sent into service to protect the hard-pressed Arctic convoys. Formally speaking, Leonard remains a civilian, but is under Royal Navy regulations.

But Mrs. Thomas is not likely to know that he set off at the start of September with PQ18, a convoy destined for Archangel: that information is top secret. And she certainly won't know that this is the first Arctic convoy to sail since the start of July, when its predecessor, PQ17, was virtually annihilated, only eleven of its thirty-five ships reaching their destination: this fact is top secret, highest category. Leonard Thomas himself knows what happened, but only in vague terms, and when the ship's command refers to the catastrophe, they do so only indirectly and evasively. At one point on their way to Archangel he himself sees both wreckage and old, disintegrating corpses drifting in the waves. And here he was, having volunteered for this to avoid conscription into the army!

Mrs. Thomas opens the telegram. The sender's address is simply "Soviet Union." She reads: HOPE YOU ARE ALL WELL EVERYTHING ALRIGHT HERE FONDEST LOVE = LEONARD THOMAS +

·   ·   ·

An unusually cold November 11 is coming to its close on Long Island.
It's evening and Dorothy Robinson is writing in her diary:

> I believe all of us have, at last, realized that there is a long,
> hard road ahead through darkness and difficulty and each one,
> in his own way, must help. The whole pattern of our lives is
> changing and we have gradually learned to accept it from day
> to day and hour to hour until it is sometimes strange to try to
> think back to nine short months ago.

When she looks out into the darkness, she can see the dark shape of the
commuter train crossing the high bridge some distance away. All the
windows are carefully covered in accordance with the new regulations
and it occurs to her that she hasn't seen a chink of light in a single one
of them. That is promising.

·   ·   ·

A parcel arrives at a Stalingrad medical station on that day. It's addressed
to Captain Fritz Hartnagel, the sender being Sophie Scholl in Ulm.
Hartnagel opens it. The parcel contains several books, hazelnut cakes,
chocolate—a real rarity!—and a long letter from her, dated October 28.
    In his letters Hartnagel has told her of the frequent discussions
he's had with his fellow officers in the battalion. He has had difficulty
defending himself when they spout various half-digested Nazi doctrines, such as the uncompromising law of nature claiming that the
strong will be victorious and the weak must go under, or the primacy
and sacrifice of death, or the notion that the campaign in the east is
ultimately a struggle for self-preservation, a defense of Germany and
European civilization against the threat of the hordes from the east.
    Sophie Scholl writes that she wants to help him with arguments and
we can see her rage and impatience with the ideas that have mesmer-
ized so many of her countrymen:

> The dominion of brutal power will always mean that the spirit
> goes under or, at least, becomes invisible—is that what you
> want, you who are fighting for me? Oh, these lazy thinkers!
> With their sentimental "die and become." Life only arises

from life—have they ever seen a dead mother give birth to a child? Have they ever seen a stone—which has an appearance of life that cannot be denied since it exists and has a fate—reproduce itself? They haven't yet got around to considering the absurdity of the statement: It is only from death that life arises. And their urge for self-preservation will mean that they are forever moving towards self-annihilation. They know nothing of the world of the spirit, in which the law of sin and death is overcome.

Sophie Scholl's letters are important to Hartnagel, important for his intellectual and spiritual survival in a context where things like that are set to the side. For a while now Hartnagel and the others have been digging bunkers and embankments—a tedious business made all the more necessary and tiring by the arrival of the winter cold in Stalingrad. This Wednesday they had to interrupt that work to hastily construct a potato cellar. They've had a delivery of almost five tons of potatoes that need to be covered over quickly so they don't freeze.

Fritz Hartnagel is particularly delighted with the chocolate she sent. In his answering letter he writes: "When I consider how gladly you would have eaten it yourself, I would almost rather pack it back up and give it to you. But my temptation is not small and gradually everything that has to do with food plays a much greater role here in Russia." Hartnagel fantasizes about escaping the winter in Stalingrad by being unexpectedly moved to, say, Morocco instead.

.   .   .

"Indefatigable" may possibly be the best word to characterize Weary Dunlop. "Tireless" is too weak. They have been located in the mud of Camp No. 5 outside Batavia for less than a week, but there is already a good deal he has managed to organize. He has, for instance, appointed a group whose job is to improve the primitive latrines—a high priority—and started reorganizing the way their communal finances are dealt with, written a letter of complaint about a variety of shortages to the Japanese officials responsible, and gotten the education program going.

On top of all this is the fact that Dunlop is also the medical doctor for 1,400 prisoners of war in the camp. This Wednesday—November 11—he and his staff hold the usual sick parade in the primitive sick room.

Three seriously ill prisoners are sent off to a school outside Batavia where the Dutch have set up a hospital for prisoners of war of all nationalities. (When an operation is needed, the prisoners are sent on to a Japanese military hospital, where Japanese surgeons take over.) One case, in particular, concerns Dunlop this morning, and he writes in his diary: "Case of Sergeant Page: complete collapses; weakness in legs and arms; would seem to be definitely a neurosis or hysteria. Treatment: massage and understanding."

They have been prisoners since March, but cases of mental breakdown are few. In fact, Dunlop can see that surprisingly many of the prisoners, particularly among the other ranks, seem more or less at ease with their lot, some of them happy even, in spite of shortages, unpredictability and threats. It really seems absurd, and when Dunlop tries to understand why, he comes to the conclusion that "their lives are completely ordered ... and there is no possibility of any advancement, hence no place for jealousy or competition." The atmosphere is notably good.*

God knows, it hasn't always been like this. After the capitulation at the beginning of March, these men were demoralized, depressed and even rebellious. They greeted their officers with boos and whistles. Many of them had been sent long distances with little warning—in Dunlop's case all the way from the Middle East—to be part of a muddled, badly planned and pretty hopeless attempt to prevent the Japanese invasion. Most of the men didn't fire a shot, or even hear a shot being fired, before the order came from the top Allied commander on Java for them to lay down their weapons. The pointlessness of their sacrifice is as obvious as it is heartrending.

The reason so many people, even among the Allies, thought that the Axis powers were well on their way to winning the war was, of course, that they were continuing to win victory after victory, continuing to take unimagined and unimaginable amounts of territory, not least in Southeast Asia. What was happening seems to confirm the idea preached so emphatically by the expanding regimes: the primacy of will. The battle is decided not by materiel alone. More important than the tools is the will with which they are wielded—the will to fight, the

---

* The Japanese guards found this incomprehensible and even provocative. How can anyone live and actually thrive in a state of defeat?

will to win, the will to sacrifice, the will to power. And doesn't what has happened so far offer utterly convincing proof that the democracies are decadent, split, corrupt and weak? And that it is impossible for them to measure up to the vital, united, disciplined, youthful and strong Axis powers? What does it matter how many guns and ships a country can produce if it lacks the ability and will to use them well?

It is this, rather than the statistics of shipping tonnage, tank production and aircraft performance, that leads so many people to fear or hope that the Axis powers are on their way to victory. The Allies appear to be irredeemably incompetent. And up until now, the war on their part has been an unbroken series of fiascos, misjudgments and mistakes. Not to mention carelessness. The prisoners of war in Camp No. 5 outside Batavia are stuck where they are precisely because of a series of clearly wrongheaded decisions.

Dunlop has managed to address the demoralization, partly by re-establishing discipline—parades and inspections, rules and punishments, good order and neat appearance—but mainly by re-creating that paradoxical and fragile sense of everyday normality: that is what all of these activities are aiming to do—volleyball tournaments, lectures in ancient history, courses in marine navigation, jazz concerts with drums, bass, harmonicas and violins, drag shows and performances of Shakespeare. The men have not just stayed sane, they have started to hope.*

Dunlop, like everyone else, has lost a great deal of weight, but he feels strong, both physically and mentally. Since the march, however, he continues to suffer edema in his ankles. One of the medical orderlies gives him an injection of "500 units of Vitamin B1," after which he just gets on with things.

.   .   .

It is Wednesday, November 11, and at Warner Bros.' sixty-two-acre studio complex in Los Angeles they are all set to shoot the new ending for *Casablanca*. Michael Curtiz, the film's director, is intending to film two short scenes aboard a naval vessel, showing Rick and Renault's return with the American troops. Scene one takes place in the ship's

---

* Interestingly, it emerged after the war that the prisoners who had been most involved in educational activities frequently fared better even in a purely physical sense.

radio room and Bogart and Rains's characters (in full combat gear) are seen listening to the actual radio speech in which Roosevelt announced the landings and appealed to the French in Morocco and Algeria not to obstruct them. ("Help us where you are able, my friends, and we shall see again the glorious day when liberty and peace shall reign again on earth.") Scene two is to be played up on deck where Bogart and Rains, together with fifty or so extras representing soldiers of the Free French Forces, are on their way to Casablanca under cover of darkness and mist. To disguise the fact it's being shot in a studio, we should imagine a thick mist, just as in the original closing scene at the airfield.

Everything's prepared. The two sets are ready and waiting, as are the cameramen, sound technicians, lighting technicians, dressers, props people, makeup artists, at least one smoke-machine operator and all kinds of assistants. The uniformed extras are all ready, as is Humphrey Bogart. And there is Michael Curtiz—we can assume he is wearing his usual riding breeches and high boots. But where is Claude Rains? It turns out that Rains has retreated to his farm in Pennsylvania—as is his habit—and because of the new wartime travel regulations it has proved impossible to obtain an air ticket for him at such short notice.

The filming is postponed to await the arrival of Rains.

.   .   .

Camp No. 5 outside Batavia on Java: Weary Dunlop is getting on with another of his many tasks—bookkeeping, and particularly the camp accounts book. He keeps the books for rations, medical supplies and for the extra ration officers are allowed: "Cigarettes 10, Tea 30g, Butter 20g, Coffee 70g, Sugar 100g, Bananas 150g three times a week."

Few things cause so many meetings and so much dissension, particularly among his officer colleagues, as the business of distributing their meagre financial means. They need money mainly to buy provisions from the civilian population, especially the eggs and carbohydrate- and vitamin-rich mung beans needed to supplement the scant and monotonous camp diet. But money is also needed for many other purposes, both large and small, whether it be leather to mend boots or amalgam for primitive dental surgery or makeup for the theatre group.

Many of the men, officers in particular, were carrying cash at the time of the capitulation, and the officers—and only the officers—receive pay from the Japanese: this is a random and thoroughly uncharacter-istic adherence to international rules on their part. The money is paid in gulden, the Dutch currency.* But what is the best way of dealing with these scanty economic resources? Right from the start, Dunlop's approach has been clear and sensible, though unpopular with the more well-heeled prisoners in the camp: all resources should be collected into a common pot and then redistributed proportionally, depending on need. From each according to ability, to each according to need.

One of the most remarkable things about the abnormal existence they experience as prisoners of war is that a kind of practical social-ism develops in the camps. That, along with the fact that many of them are still highly critical of the way their generals managed the war, probably lies at the root of something that Dunlop himself notes: "a marked swing to the left amongst our lads and socialist ideas are always heartily supported in a debate." And authority among them is actually to some extent democratic. Dunlop has instituted a council to which the whole camp sends elected representatives to discuss and decide important questions, and their long and rambling discussions are carefully recorded on toilet paper.

Dunlop, who doesn't have any radical tendencies himself—but he was an outspoken anti-fascist before the war and a critic of Chamberlain—is nevertheless disappointed and disillusioned by all the selfishness he encounters. But he sticks to his guns: the only sensible thing to do is to share out their meagre resources fairly. Which is why he insists on careful bookkeeping and recording the sums involved. Fair is fair, and he goes on to write:

> Monthly expenditure on the whole camp is to be 2232 gulden approx.; medical supplies and hospital fund extra. I have also collected 100 gulden from the CCS [casualty clearing station] officers and Fred Smedley for the Theatrical Company, this to be distributed over 91 men. My contribution 30 gulden.

· · ·

* In the bureaucratic ethos that is typical of all armies, "food and accommoda-tion" costs were deducted from pay. Other ranks who did certain jobs outside the camp were also paid, but only minor sums.

It's over. Kurt West is utterly exhausted. Drained. Empty. He looks at the rest of them, those who are still on their feet, and he thinks they look "like ghosts." From the way they look at him, he can see that they are thinking more or less the same about him. "I felt it was an eternity since we set off that morning," he writes. And in a way it certainly was an eternity—an eternity of six and a half hours, on one side of which he'd been a young and naïve nineteen-year-old and, on the other side, changed forever, though still the same age in calendar terms.

How many has he killed? He doesn't say, and for the rest of his life it is something he never wants to talk about. But there must have been a good few. It's about noon on Wednesday, November 11, and the battle for the strongpoint Kako on the Svir Front in East Karelia is over. For the moment.

At 5:30 a.m., after an opening artillery barrage of four thousand shells, he and the others in the first wave stormed out into the November darkness, up the slope, through a hail of Soviet fragmentation shells and Stalin organ rockets, through choking gunpowder gas, to the linking trench that led towards the top of the high ground where Kako is located.[*]

No one knew at that stage how many Soviet troops were in the trenches and bunkers up there—at least a battalion, perhaps five hundred men. The attack took the form of a classic exercise in trench clearance: in practical terms that means that most of the fighting was performed by just three men as there is no space for more: the first has a sub-machine gun, the second throws hand grenades, and the third supplies fresh ammunition and grenades to the first two. Number Two tosses a hand grenade around a bend in the trench and, as soon as the grenade explodes, Number One throws himself around the bend and opens fire on anything and everything that moves. The group then moves on to the next bend and follows the same procedure.[†]

---

[*] The intended target was the strongpoint Teeri, but the situation at Kako was considered more vital.

[†] This method was explained to me by Harry Järv, a legend in his own lifetime and a veteran of the 61st Infantry Regiment. After the war Järv became head of the Royal Library in Stockholm, a translator and a Kafka expert. This mild and modest man told me that there were only three things he was really good at: "photography, punctuation and clearing trenches."

This first close-combat trio was followed by two similar groups, ready to take over when the preceding group was knocked out—West was a member of the third group. By about 9:00 a.m. they had successfully retaken most of the two hundred yards of trenches up on Kako, but it had cost them. And then the enemy mounted the first counterattacks.

It is broad daylight by this stage and Kurt West's uniform is coated in soil, mud and blood. His face is all sooty. The soil is the result of the virtually incessant detonation of Finnish and Soviet shells, the noise of which makes it impossible to communicate except by shouting. The mud comes from having to drag fresh boxes of grenades to the forward group—two boxes at a time and at great risk to himself: West may be short, but he is strong. Since the walls of the trenches have collapsed in places, he often has to move doubled over or on all fours. The blood comes from crawling over corpses, some of them half-naked and shattered, or of being alongside wounded or dying men. In some places, there are so many of them that progress becomes difficult. (Erik Jakas, the leader of West's small group, is taken out by a shell only seconds after the two of them passed one another down in the trench—not a trace of his body could be found. At one point West helps his friend Lars Åberg withdraw from the front line with a shell splinter in his back, and when they reach the aid station they find it full of the wounded, dying and dead and with two men sitting outside, suffering mental breakdowns.) The soot stains derive from the TNT and gunpowder gases that color the dawn light pale yellow.

It was when the Soviet troops mounted their counterattack that West really began shooting, at first with his sub-machine gun, then with a Soviet automatic rifle he took from a dead Russian, and then with a Finnish machine gun he found in the trench. They came in wave after wave. "The number of attacking Russians seemed never-ending," West writes. "The most forward of them no more than 50–60 yards from our trench." The battle was for the top of the hill, smaller than a football pitch and, given the small area, the horrors were all the more concentrated. The ground was churned up, the snow blackened, the trees all swept away. In the distance was hillock after hillock, open fields, fences and the ruins of houses. When, as an old man much later, he looked back on that day and what he came to call the hell of Kako, he states that neither before nor after did he see such numbers of corpses. Most of the fallen are wearing new white furs and new felt boots. Asians. Probably an elite unit.* They certainly fought like one.

But now the attacks seem to be over. All the collected energy has been used up. Now comes the reaction.

Before that day Kurt West had thought a great deal about how he would perform in a test like this. Now he knows. He writes: "It came to me that I hadn't actually really been frightened during the attack. Everything felt so unreal. I didn't really understand myself." But he understands it better now: "I had in fact been dreadfully afraid but had somehow managed to suppress my fear when it was necessary to do so." He is filled with a remarkable, almost euphoric sense of relief. "All I wanted was just to be able to lie down in the bottom of the trench, shut my eyes and not bother about any of it."

At Kako a long, long day is followed by a long night, with both sides firing flares and tossing hand grenades at each other. In the darkness, one of West's comrades throws a grenade that bounces back and blows him up. At eight o'clock in the morning of November 12 they are relieved by a battalion from another regiment. About half of the group of seventy-eight men who set off on November 9 remain: sixteen have been killed, nineteen have been wounded. The mood is low.

·   ·   ·

Zhang Zhonglou continues his journey of inspection in Henan. Things just get worse and worse. He writes:

> Wherever I went, there were refugees fleeing south, begging for food and those who couldn't move any more just dropped dead by the side of the road. You could exchange a child for a few steamed rolls. When I went to Luoyang, all around the station there were refugees, groaning and crying—hearing them was unbearable. If a train came, they would fight to get on it, hanging from the roof—they didn't care how dangerous it was. Those who couldn't get on the train ... wept and sold their children—no matter what the price, they just handed them over. When the train went west, when it entered a tunnel, because the people on the roof were piled up, countless

---

* The Red Army rifle regiment that carried out the attack at Kako was the 326th Infantry Regiment. It was almost wiped out in the fighting.

numbers of them were crushed against the roof of the tunnel, and fell down dead.

How could things have gotten into this state? Drought and grasshoppers are not the whole story. In one sense, the coalescence of the original Chinese-Japanese war with the new global trial of strength between the Allies and the Axis powers has actually gone the way people hoped: the Japanese invaders now have their hands full in other areas. At the same time, however, it has led to other serious and unforeseen consequences. One by one, the supply routes from Burma into China have been cut off and the Chinese army can no longer be supplied with grain from India. So Chiang Kai-shek's central government in Chongqing has decided that the farmers are to hand over part of their harvests as a tax in kind. It is an absolute necessity if they are to stop the poorly fed Chinese armies from fading away.

The problem is the unfeeling and brutal way in which the decision about taxes in kind has been introduced. (Individuals like Zhang Zhonglou are a cog in the machinery of state.) What happens in reality is nothing short of confiscation. Farmers* have to hand over a certain stated amount regardless of how much or little they have left after the drought and the grasshoppers. The system is cruel, badly managed and corrupt.

Zhang arrives in the Zheng region and finds Lu Yan, the governor of the region, in tears. It is proving impossible to collect the quantity of grain the government is demanding. Lu tells Zhang about the Li family. They obeyed and handed over the last of their grain to the tax collectors—and then the whole family committed suicide by drowning themselves in the river. Including the children.

The governor goes down on his knees to Zhang. He weeps, beats his head on the ground and pleads to be exempted from the order to collect more grain.

.   .   .

The 3rd Battalion is one of the units ordered to pursue and harry the Japanese as they retreat towards the north coast of New Guinea. As

---

* Henan is already hard-pressed because of the numbers of people conscripted into the army and, as a result of its proximity to the front, by the numbers pressed into forced labor for the Chinese military.

they advance through dense, damp undergrowth, Bede Thongs and the others come across discarded equipment and weapons and the bodies of wounded Japanese who have committed suicide. When the Australians reach the green and brisk Kumusi River, they find that all the rain has caused it to burst its banks and flood. The Japanese have gone, but upturned boats and drowned men in uniform reveal their desperate efforts to get across the wide, fast-flowing watercourse.* And the fleeing Japanese have been forced to leave behind all those mountain guns the Australians have learned to hate.

.   .   .

Vera Inber is completing her preparations for her second winter in besieged Leningrad. It is easier to keep one room warm than two, so she moves the sofa, the dining table and the bookcase holding her china into the room where she sits and works at her typewriter. She had a small stove installed in the room a short time ago. The worst of the draft is kept out by a curtain she had nailed up. The electricity shuts off in the latter part of the evening, but she and her husband have a small paraffin lamp they use to read by. A combination of worry, gunfire and air raids means she has trouble sleeping at night and she feels tired almost all the time. She does have sleeping pills, but she is often afraid to take them—what if she were to sleep through the air-raid siren?

.   .   .

Hélène Berr is sitting in the warm and overcrowded Lecture Room 1 at the Sorbonne. (Heat is a constant topic of conversation, given the shortage of coal, gas and warmth indoors.) She is there for a lecture on English literature by her old professor Louis Cazamian, who is perhaps France's leading scholar in the field. Being back in these familiar corridors and lecture halls feels slightly bewildering and unreal after all that has happened to her and Jean. She is sweating.

Hélène is in the lecture hall without really belonging there. The anti-Semitic laws introduced by the Vichy regime mean that she is not permitted to work towards what is called the *agrégation*, which would give her the right to teach. (Jews are not permitted to work as teachers.)

---

* One of the men drowned while attempting to cross the river was Major General Horii, commander-in-chief of the successful Japanese corps that had earlier threatened Port Moresby but was now being driven back.

So she is there as a private student. She has just started working on a doctoral thesis on John Keats and Hellenism.

Her studies and the Sorbonne feel like a refuge in time for her, a place where everything is almost as before. But she knows, of course, that even this refuge is illusionary. And studies don't necessarily have to be seen only as an expression of escapism—they can also be interpreted as an act of resistance, an expression of her unwillingness to bow to circumstances. (Since last summer, paradoxically, the attitude towards Jews at the Sorbonne has become more welcoming.) At two that afternoon another professor, the poet and Virginia Woolf expert Floris Delattre, will be giving a lecture and once again Hélène manages to squeeze into a crowded lecture room. All of this is on Thursday, November 12.

. . .

In Culver City, in western Los Angeles, is the office of David O. Selznick, the energetic and temperamental producer, the wunderkind known for such mega-successes as *Gone with the Wind* and, most recently, *Rebecca*.* He was the man who invited Ingrid Bergman to come to Hollywood in 1939 and make an English version of her Swedish success *Intermezzo*. Since then, he has continued to promote her career onwards and upwards.†

That is probably why Selznick met Jack Warner yesterday evening and was given a private showing of *Casablanca*. Selznick thinks the film is brilliant and he recognizes that it can make his protégée Ingrid Bergman a major star. He sends a telegram to Hal Wallis, the producer of the film, and gets straight to the point: THINK IT IS A SWELL MOVIE AND AN ALL-AROUND JOB OF PICTURE MAKING. TOLD JACK AS FORCIBLY AS I COULD THAT I THOUGHT IT WOULD BE A TERRIBLE MISTAKE TO CHANGE THE ENDING. AND ALSO THAT I THOUGHT THE PICTURE OUGHT TO BE RUSHED OUT.

This telegram is sent on November 12. Selznick's words—words

---

* The fact that his wife, Irene, was the daughter of the film mogul Louis B. Mayer did him no harm, of course. Selznick's colossal energy was fuelled to a great extent by amphetamines, which could legally be bought across the counter in pharmacies at that time.

† Given Bergman's height, thick eyebrows and bad English, he had suffered moments of doubt.

from on high!—cause the directors over on the East Coast to recon-
sider, and they drop the idea of a new ending. They follow Warner and
Selznick's advice about taking advantage of the events of the war and
releasing the film as soon as possible. The date for its premiere is set
for November 26, just two weeks away.

.   .   .

A desert gazelle! It's the first sign of animal life Vittorio Vallicella has
seen for a long time on his travels through the empty grandeur of the
desert. It's a small-horned animal with a beautiful light-brown hide and
white belly, and stands less than two feet at the shoulder.* Vallicella and
his companions are yet again searching through a load of old wreckage
to see if there is any water, fuel or food. What's there looks as if it is a
year old as it's half-buried in windblown sand and showing signs of rust.
Their journey has been getting more and more difficult and dangerous,
and only a couple of days ago they were attacked by two British fighter
planes. One of their trucks—the TL.37, with its huge wheels—went
up in flames, along with much of their fuel. Bellini has dysentery and
his temperature is rising.

They take out their weapons—not something they do often—and
spread out. But the shy beast vanishes, so they carry on poking about
in the rusting wreckage. One of them finds two cans of water and two
bottles of whisky in a British tank. There's always something! Then
Vallicella hears Bassi shouting: "The gazelle! The gazelle!" Baruffi raises
his rifle and fires a shot. The little animal leaps in the air, then drops
down dead. They all yell, cheer and laugh. Fresh meat! This also is on
November 12.

Later, under the dark and starry vault of the sky, they enjoy the best
and sweetest meal they've had for ages: grilled gazelle with pasta and
sauce, followed by a dessert of canned fruit and rounded off by coffee
or tea. (And presumably a little whisky too.) Vallicella is happy.

Alone out in the desert they lead a strange, out-of-the-ordinary sort
of life, free of structures, order, rumors and news. They don't have the
least idea what is happening out in the world, and the world knows
nothing about them. Does the world even care? Their names may

---

* I assume that this was a Dorcas gazelle, an animal fully adapted to desert existence. It can go through a whole lifetime without drinking water as the moisture
in the plants it eats is sufficient.

possibly be on some list of the "missing." The emptiness of the desert becomes an image of the safe limbo in which they find themselves. "These," Vittorio Vallicella writes in his diary, "were the best days we'd had since arriving in Africa." He noted a couple of days ago—not without some surprise—that all of them had started laughing again.

.   .   .

At that moment, Ernst Jünger is sitting on the train to Berlin, on the first stage of his journey to the Eastern Front. His thoughts are drifting: "I have never before started a journey with so little idea of where it might lead and what the result might be. I'm like a fisherman casting his net into murky waters on a winter's day."

So what is his journey actually in aid of? It is not service at the front that awaits him. General Carl-Heinrich von Stülpnagel,* Jünger's superior officer in Paris, has given him the task of sounding out the mood and attitudes of German officers in the east, primarily those in the Caucasus. Mood and attitudes about what? It's not possible to say exactly,† but it's obvious that this mysterious journey is a small part of the underground resistance to the Nazi regime that has put out tentative shoots in the staff headquarters in Paris, with the conservative von Stülpnagel at its head.

This is where all the contradictions that make up Ernst Jünger come together.

Early in the 1920s, Jünger became something of a cult author among nationalists, right-wing extremists and anti-democratic veterans of the war. And that was by no means pure chance: they were drawn to his highly strung writings about war as an elemental force that allows man to make contact with the inner nature of existence. They were drawn, too, by his unambiguous rejection of democracy, coupled with his invocation of new man—a man of polished steel, dedicated to total

* Von Stülpnagel, too, was a complicated character. Even before the war he had been active in the anti-Nazi resistance and yet, with growing qualms of conscience, he sanctioned repressive actions against innocent civilians both in France and on the Eastern Front. He was one of the most active and successful participants in the July 20 coup against Hitler, for which he was hanged with a piano wire on August 30, 1944.

† After the attempt on Hitler's life, Jünger burned all his papers in the Paris headquarters, thus destroying most of the background to his journey east.

mobilization. And yet, from early on, Jünger resisted all overtures from the Nazis.*

To an aristocrat of the intelligentsia, an individualist and aesthete such as Jünger, the Nazis are vulgar rabble, stirred up by vacuous and banal slogans. Nor does he have any time for their anti-Semitism, which he finds crazy and incomprehensible. Jünger's status as war hero and popular author has shielded him, though he has gradually been marginalized and, since 1939, he has no longer been permitted to publish in Germany.

Silence is not just a matter of coercion, it can also be choice. Taking an aloof, distanced view of things is second nature to him and he has come to see life in uniform as an elevated form of inner exile. And he is not alone in that. As chance would have it, a surprisingly high number of officers with scornful and skeptical views of Hitler and his henchmen have ended up clustered around the staff headquarters in Paris. Jünger has both inspired and been inspired by the milieu in a place where Hitler salutes and various Nazi organizations are avoided as far as possible and where many subversive or semi-subversive discussions take place under a cloak of cognac sipping and cigar smoke. Up to now, the Paris resistance has been more of an attitude than a program, but Jünger's journey may be seen as a sign that even in these circles there is now a sense of seriousness, a hope of forging contacts and a desire to grow. But it is not his contacts with anti-Nazis on the staff that is weighing on his mind; it is something else. Ultimately, this journey has to be seen as a kind of penance.

Jünger uses some of his time on the train to study his fellow travellers and allow his imagination to work. He focuses in particular on one young woman—hardly more than a girl—and thinks that the corners of her mouth reveal almost imperceptible signs of sexual experience. "That is how lust, like a diamond, makes its mark on a face."

On arrival in Berlin he stays with a friend, the lawyer, philosopher and Nazi Carl Schmitt. He spends several comfortable days there. The

---

* One of Jünger's admirers was Joseph Goebbels, who wooed him constantly, to little effect. (Jünger met Goebbels privately and noted with astonishment that he used the same platitudes in conversation as in his public speeches.) Hitler, too, was one of Jünger's readers and there are some hints that he was prepared to turn a blind eye to Jünger's indiscretions.

first snow falls and he and Schmitt take walks through the blacked-out streets while conversing about the Moravian Brethren, Nostradamus, the prophet Isaiah and prophecies in general. Perhaps it's possible to foresee the future, not so much in terms of actual events as in the form of abiding by certain laws.

.   .   .

An elderly man turns up that winter in the small village of Duanzhang in Henan. He is yet another refugee from the famine. The old man moves into a tumbledown and deserted house at the east end of the village. There isn't very much to eat in Duanzhang either. How should the famine in Henan be tackled? In so far as the central government reacts, it does so too late; in so far as relief supplies are organized by other provinces, they have difficulty getting through because of the almost impassable roads; in so far as there are reserve stores set aside for exactly this kind of eventuality, it becomes apparent that corrupt civil servants have left them half full or, even worse, empty.

So there is very little help available and the famine moves slowly, heavily, glacially, towards its conclusion. One eyewitness tells of "dogs eating human bodies by the roads, peasants seeking dead human flesh under the cover of darkness, endless deserted villages, beggars swarming at every city gate, babies abandoned to cry and die on every highway." And yet the restaurants are still open in the cities of Henan.

One of the starving villagers in Duanzhang, Wang Jiu, a short man with bulging eyes, gangs up with two other men and they murder a beggar. They cook and eat various parts of the corpse. Over time, they turn this into a system: they lure famine victims to them, murder them and eat them.

One day a forty-year-old woman arrives in Duanzhang accompanied by a seven- or eight-year-old girl. Wang invites the two of them to live with him. When they can't get hold of any other refugees, the three men quickly come to a decision: Wang's two friends strangle the woman and eat her. The girl is Wang's share.

.   .   .

Night is the province of confusion and uncertainty. Tentatively, fearfully, blindly, the two sides sail their darkened ships into the broad sound off Guadalcanal. There are very many vessels—including big, heavy ships—and they feint and thrust blindly at one another like two herds of cattle that don't really know where the other is or what is supposed to happen. That's the situation Captain Tameichi Hara, commander of the Japanese destroyer *Amatsukaze,* finds himself in.

Amatsukaze, ten other destroyers and a light cruiser are there as escorts for two heavy battleships which, under cover of darkness and at close range, are meant to bombard and destroy the airfield the Americans are still occupying. The aim is to open the way for a major landing of Japanese troops planned for tomorrow. It's very dark. The moon is waning and the sky is covered with dense, low clouds. Hara is wondering why the Japanese squadron is remaining so rigidly in such a complicated formation. The battleship *Hiei* suddenly starts sending its communications via medium wave radio. Hara thinks it's madness; could it be because the squadron commander is missing a ship in the pitch-black night? Everyone is wondering where the Americans are. The command for them all is to make a 180-degree turn; the dark shadow they can make out over there is land. The group of destroyers splits up to avoid landfall. The destroyer *Yūdachi* has sighted the enemy, but no one knows where *Yūdachi* is, so the report isn't much help.

Then a number of searchlights come on a short distance away.

All hell breaks out.

The darkness is broken up by a disconnected muddle of flashes, lights and muzzle flames from vessels opening fire and being fired on, firing torpedoes and being torpedoed, sinking and being sunk. *Amatsukaze* is close to being hit by fire actually aimed at the battleship *Hiei* (fire so intense "that for many moments I stood blinded on the bridge for a long time," Hara says). Then someone fires flares and the shapes of five or six enemy ships are revealed as if on photographic paper ("I gulped. My heart bubbled with excitement," Hara says) and his ship fires eight torpedoes. A Japanese destroyer is about to collide with an American destroyer and the same American destroyer almost collides with another American destroyer, and the latter destroyer is hit by the *Amatsukaze*'s torpedoes and explodes and sinks; no, it doesn't sink, it just disappears ("That was a spectacular kill and there was a roaring ovation from the crew, I didn't hear it. It was all too easy," Hara says). One by one, the wavering lights of the flares die away and darkness closes over the still surface of the sound as though the photographic paper has been overexposed and gone black. The *Amatsukaze* turns back and its crew sees flashes, they see lights, they see a big, slim shape just a little way off and fire torpedoes at it. ("A huge, reddish flame rose from our target," Hara reports.)* Then he steams northwest, away from the battle and towards the burning battleship *Hiei,* the only vessel they are able to identify. ("The scene was strangely quiet. Dim distant gunfire appeared like fireworks. It was impossible to tell who was fighting," Hara reports. And, true enough, in all the chaos there were times when ships were firing on vessels of their own side.) Then all of a sudden, so suddenly that Hara gives a loud scream of surprise, a big, unlit ship appears like a black wall right in front of their bow and their helmsman throws himself at the wheel. ("There was nothing that the rest of us on the bridge could do but watch helplessly as the ships drew swiftly closer.") They avoid a collision, but the two vessels pass so close that Hara finds it impossible to recognize the other vessel's shape.

In this situation Tameichi Hara makes four fatal mistakes.

Mistake number one: since the unknown vessel doesn't appear to have gun turrets, Hara thinks it may possibly be one of their own supply ships, the *Jingei* perhaps, so he hesitates about opening fire. Then, "in desperation," he gives the order to switch on the searchlights and sees that, far from being a Japanese supply ship, it is a large American cruiser. In what must have been even greater desperation, Hara then gives the order "to open fire with everything we've got," including the last four of their deadly torpedoes.[†]

Mistake number two: in what is usually called the heat of battle, Hara doesn't recognize that the distance is so short (under 550 yards) that the range security mechanisms in the torpedoes are still on and so the torpedoes simply thump harmlessly against the hull of the great cruiser. "Meanwhile, my gun crew continued firing as though shell-drunk. Every shot was hitting home. The phantom ship wobbled on, spewing fire and smoke throughout its length."

Mistake number three: in all the excitement, Hara forgets to give orders to switch off the searchlights. So, when shells begin to rain

* The *Amatsukaze* had torpedoed the American light cruiser USS *Juneau,* with five brothers from Iowa in the crew—Joe, Frank, Al, Matt and George Sullivan. Three of them were killed, but Al and George were among the hundred or so who survived the sinking. In the general confusion, however, the survivors were forgotten about and when a rescue action was eventually mounted a week later, only ten survivors remained. The rest, Al and George included, had died of hunger, thirst, madness or shark attacks.

[†] The torpedoes used by the Japanese navy were superior in every way—speed, range, explosives and reliability—to those of their opponents.

down around the *Amatsukaze* he thinks the "phantom ship had revived and was offering a last-ditch fight." He orders his gunners to carry on firing—"Finish it off!" he yells.

This is his fourth mistake: the shells are coming not from the silent "phantom ship" but from a different American cruiser that has obviously seen the searchlights, crept up unseen on the port side and is now shelling the *Amatsukaze*.

By the time Hara realizes this, it's too late.

There are two huge explosions, both literally deafening, and initially he can't hear a thing. He rises to his feet very slowly, unable to think, his head empty for some seconds. He feels his body and can't find any wounds. He looks around and sees several men getting to their feet, but he also sees one of his officers hanging lifeless across the rangefinder. He sees that the man's head is smeared with blood. He screams the man's name—"Iwata, Iwata!" No response. He leans forward to the speaking tube and calls to the fire control turret—no response. He calls to the radio room—no response. He smells burning and sees flames. He knows that if the enemy ship lands any more hits on them, it will be all over. He gives orders to make smoke.

It takes a little while before Hara discovers that the *Amatsukaze* is going around in a circle. She seems to be impossible to steer. Is the rudder jammed? The hydraulics have been knocked out, as has much else. While his crew struggles to bring the fires, themselves and the vessel under control, at least the shelling ceases. They slink away into the night, "the ship moved like a drunken man, skidding wildly from side to side." The *Amatsukaze* leaves the Guadalcanal straits behind her. Hara is hoarse from all his yelling, soaked with sweat and depressed by the mistakes he has made. Dawn is beginning to light the sky in the east. It's the morning of Friday, November 13.

Sea battles at night are always tales of confusion, but this one sets the record. Confusion ruled long afterwards, reinforced by censorship and propaganda on both sides. It would be many years, in some cases a decade or more, before historians managed to come up with a more or less coherent picture of what happened during the forty minutes the engagement raged. Some of the issues are unlikely ever to be explained. Over the years, Tameichi Hara would spend a lot of time and energy attempting to understand what he and his destroyer crew had actually been involved in.

When the sun rises on the morning of November 13, one thing

becomes clear to all those involved: Henderson Field has not been bombarded and, in the dawn light, American aircraft, loaded with bombs, are taking off as usual.

.   .   .

Charles Walker has been following the naval battle from the shore—in so far as "follow" is the right word. For him, more or less as for Tameichi Hara, the whole thing has been a muddled jumble of light and sparks, fragmentary images, glimpses of geometrical shapes, beams of light suddenly scissoring across the gleaming water and dying out just as suddenly, projectiles that paint low, fiery streaks on the darkness before disappearing in sudden flashes a mile away.

Everything is silent in that ash-grey Friday dawn. Just a mile or so away Walker catches a glimpse of the overturned hull of a large vessel lying there like the huge carcass of a dying whale. He thinks it is an American ship. Walker writes:

> Crews in small boats were picking up survivors, American and Japanese, and bringing them to the beach. I watched as they walked to the dispensary about three hundred yards inland. These men were covered with a thick, viscous tar. As they unloaded from the landing craft and walked to medical aid, there was no fight left in them, they were just glad to be alive. Many were blinded by the tar-like substance and needed to be led. The several Japanese sailors seemed despondent, harmless, their part in the war over. Strange to say, they were walking unguarded among the casualties, even helping them.

Walker and his comrades in arms look at their Japanese adversaries with a mixture of fear, reluctant respect and instinctive, crystallized hatred. In the eyes of many people, they are little more than animals and should be treated as such. (It is quite common, for instance, for soldiers to take body parts from fallen Japanese soldiers as souvenirs.)* It's doubtful whether he has seen a single living Japanese close up during

---

* The Americans were by no means alone in disrespecting the enemy dead in this way: Japanese soldiers frequently cut souvenirs from dead Americans they came across.

his weeks on the island, so seeing that they can behave like ordinary human beings comes as a surprise to him.

.   .   .

Winter in Archangel. More snow from a steely grey sky. The ships are lined up, waiting silently at the harbor entrance for the next convoy, if there is to be one: rumor says that PQ18 was the last. Existence aboard HMS *Ulster Queen*, cold and at anchor, is numbingly monotonous in every way—life, thought, feelings, work and food. Leonard Thomas can't go ashore, nor does he want to, as there is very little to attract him in the snow-covered, blacked-out city. There is no point writing letters, as any letters will accompany the ship and arrive at the same time as him. He has read all the books, some of them several times, and he is now reading them again. He has washed all his clothes—thoroughly— and he washes them again at the least excuse. He has listened to all the gramophone records time after time, those that aren't broken, anyway: those that are left are mostly Bing Crosby recordings and the sailors have started composing their own obscene variations of the texts.*

The shrapnel damage to the superstructure, the result of German bombs or possibly trigger-happy anti-aircraft gunners on other ships, has long since been patched up and everything that can be repainted has been repainted. They now move on to cleaning up the areas that are difficult to access—the tanks and the bilges—something that was usually left to be done until they returned to Belfast, their home port. "Somehow it was the air of the place which drove us to do with great thoroughness the everyday tasks, the menial jobs."

Thomas wants to get the time to pass. He wants to get away from there.

Their diet is one of miserable monotony. Almost everything contains corned beef—diced or fried or boiled or stewed or roasted or thinly sliced on dry, crumbly bread for breakfast. He and his fellows frequently avoid meals, making do instead with a bar of chocolate and a cigarette. Thomas has lost weight. "Sometimes we got into that listless

---

* He doesn't say which, but in all probability they would have been *Song Hits from Holiday Inn*, released in July 1942 and extremely popular. It contained the song "White Christmas," which, with just a month left to Christmas, was climbing to the top of all the charts.

mood that even the hunger we suffered from could not be assuaged by the untantalising food we were expected to live on." Sometimes they organize talent competitions, sometimes simple games or sports events. A small boxing group has been formed, and card games are played all the time. And they do a lot of singing.

They want to get the time to pass. They want to get away from there.

The nights are worst. They give them far too much time, Thomas says, "to think, not to dream, of much unattainable, some remote and hopeless."

.　　.　　.

There is something about the younger generation that amazes Dorothy Robinson at the same time she admires it. She herself has had to struggle not to resign herself to her fate but to become one with it, to embrace it even. Some aspects of her forceful promotion of housewifely idealism and the sharp comments she can make about other women suggest perhaps that she is still struggling with it.* Dorothy Robinson remembers what an effort it was for her to do what was expected of her when she was their age.

But young people, not least her own two children—particularly Art—are now being faced with a test far greater than any that faced her generation, a test that is only indirectly hers. She is more than a little frightened by the speed at which they seem to grow up, and she is amazed how they "step out and mature and meet life with the casual acceptance I have never attained."

She remembers when Art took his exams last June. He was one of those whose name was marked with a star in the program, the star meaning "Left school to join the armed forces of the United States." How happy they all were, or seemed to be, even her and her husband, at the same time as both of them were feeling a level of sublimated anxiety: "On the surface smiles, waves of the hand, seemingly wrapt attention, and, underneath, a sense of strangeness as though we were living through a dream of something that never happened."

It's Friday the thirteenth, but it is not an unlucky day for Dorothy.

---

* Dorothy Robinson could have been something other than a housewife. Her wide reading and not inconsiderable educational level spans everything from William Turner and Antoine de Saint-Exupéry to Marcus Aurelius. Her mother was a fairly successful writer of children's books.

The postman, a figure they always await with a mixture of expectation and dread these days, has brought a letter from Peg, their daughter, and one from Art. Peg is writing from the West Coast:

> Phil [Peg's husband, who has been recently recalled by the U.S. Navy] had three days' leave and that was wonderful then, bing, he vanished into thin air without a word. He said it would be that way and I thought I could take it in my stride and go on making ham sandwiches and coffee for the swing shift boys at the plant. But, when I realized he was actually gone I didn't know whether I was making cheese on rye or ham on white.... The only thing that bothers me about the mountains of food that pile in every day is the smell of mayonnaise in the morning—that gets me.

And Art writes from somewhere in Great Britain:

> The R.A.F. men are O.K. and one of them sure made me think of Mom coasting down our hill when he told about a crash landing and called it "a bellyflop"—made me sort of homesick. I'm not really, but coming back will be O.K. by me when we finish up the job. Only now I know, what I always kind of thought, that I belong in a plane and nowhere else.

The temperature falls during the afternoon and a wind whips in from the Atlantic. That night there is the first frost on the grass.

·   ·   ·

Yesterday, Thursday, it was raining in western Algeria; today, November 13, it's sunny again. Yesterday, the American war correspondent John Parris attended the funerals of six dead Americans, buried with full military honors—trumpeters and the lot. All in a grove of palm trees by an airfield. Today he's been given permission to accompany a couple of officers to Oran in their jeep. The French forces in the city have capitulated now.

The jeep arrives at around nine in the morning and they quickly leave Arzew behind them. The small harbor is packed with transport vessels unloading. The amount of materiel, ammunition and other provisions being brought ashore is astonishing.

They drive through a landscape of small green hills and olive trees, where solitary Arab shepherds in long white robes tend flocks of grazing sheep and goats. After a little while, this pastoral image is shattered and the road is lined with small burned-out French tanks and abandoned trucks. A number of uniformed Frenchmen are going through the wrecks to salvage what can be salvaged. The Frenchmen salute when the jeep drives past. Parris writes in his diary: "It's hard to believe that just twenty-four hours ago they were trying to kill us and we were trying to kill them."

At 2:40 in the afternoon they drive through the village of St.-Cloud, with its light-brown houses and streets lined with palm trees. Parris writes in his diary:

> The folks here appear none too friendly. A lot of people were killed here. Buildings along the main street are shell-pocked. Half the church steeple is gone—one of our shells wiped out a machine-gun nest there. Resistance was stiffest here—there was a pro-German mayor who ordered the visitors to take up arms.[*]

Outside the village they come across another group of small knocked-out French tanks and on the field by them a dozen or so dead horses, legs spread in the air: "The smell of decaying flesh is horrible." They pass a French funeral procession and spontaneously bare their heads. Parris thinks how hard and confusing things must now be for the French. When they eventually drive into the confusion of tall white buildings of Oran, he notes that their reception is chilly here too. The jeep sweeps up into the palm-shaded square outside the big and picturesque Grand Hotel, which has been requisitioned by the American army. The stores are full of American troops out shopping.

.   .   .

Cleaning up. The seriously damaged Japanese destroyer *Amatsukaze* is now some forty miles north of Guadalcanal and the crew are preparing

---

[*] Most of those who put up resistance at St.-Cloud were not villagers, but a battalion of tough French Foreign Legionnaires who not only beat back repeated American attacks, but also mounted a heroic (but quickly defeated) counterattack with the help of tanks dating back to the First World War.

to consign their dead to the sea. The bodies have been gathered, all forty-three of them, and carried to the bow of the ship. That means that about one in six of the men aboard the vessel lost their lives, most of them within the course of just a few seconds.

Tameichi Hara is standing on the bridge in the Friday sunset watching as the bodies (or what remains of them) are first washed with hot water and then sewn into weighted sailcloth. The destroyer has already received several telegrams of congratulations for her efforts in the night battle, but Hara feels no joy at all—instead, he is overwhelmed by an almost paralysing sense of guilt. Had it not been for his mistakes, all these men might still be alive. One by one the shrouded bodies are sent down into the sea. The procedure is precise. The trumpeter sounds his trumpet; the body is released; there is a splash and the assembled crew all salute. Many of them weep.

The first of the dead is Lieutenant Shimizu, the ship's gunnery officer. The only part of him recovered was one of his legs, so his sailcloth shroud is small. The ceremony continues for the rest of the day. Darkness has fallen by the time the *Amatsukaze* steams north towards Truk again.

. . .

In all proper Boys' Own adventures, other people represent a threat rather than a promise, something to be avoided rather than turned to on the homeward journey. That also holds true for Vittorio Vallicella and his companions as their truck trundles across the desert. In the slow, reluctant light of the grey dawn of November 13, however, they discover all too late that they are no longer alone.

They begin to catch glimpses of groups of people: one, two, several, many. Hundreds of men in German and Italian uniforms—the shattered remnants of defeat. Vallicella and his men have stumbled upon a gathering point for fleeing soldiers. Warning shots force them to get out of their truck, hands in the air. A German lieutenant comes up to them and asks brusquely who they are and where they have come from. The military hierarchy is quickly reestablished: Sergeant Berrà steps forward and explains (presumably with salutes and clicked heels) that they are what's left of the "VI Battery of the III Group of the Trento Division." They take the opportunity of drawing the German lieutenant's attention to Bellini, whose dysentery has gotten worse—he is lying in the back of the truck and has a high temperature. The German examines him and says they should take him to Derna, where there is a field hospital. Aha, here's their chance of escape. Freedom. They jump back into the truck and prepare to drive off, but the lieutenant shouts for them to stop. They swear. Is this the end of their freedom?

But no, the German simply wants to tell them that his unit has an ambulance, which will be leaving for Derna within half an hour and he offers to take Bellini with them. They accept. The lieutenant then tells them that all Italian units and scattered remnants should head for a place outside Derna, where they will be reorganized. The German hands them a sheet of paper and then adds that the British are closing in: Tobruk will be surrendered tonight. He turns on his heel and leaves them reading the paper with growing unease and anxiety:

High Command of the Motorized Division Trieste
(General Staff)
doc. n. 41

Order of the day:

The Trieste Division has been ordered to fill out its troop numbers with the surviving units of the following divisions: Brescia, Bologna, Pavia, Trento, Folgore, Ariete, Littorio and the mortar battalions from Sardinia. Loyal and warm greetings from me and all my soldiers to those officers, non-commissioned officers and troops who join us. Given this addition of brave hearts, of ancient and new honor and of noble traditions, "Trieste" will go forward as always and succeed in the tasks it has been called upon to perform. At this decisive hour every man must make a keen and impassioned contribution. All strength, all efforts and all sacrifices will lead to fruitful and successful results for our Fatherland.
    Long live Italy, Long live "Trieste."
    P.M. 56 12 November 1942 XXI

All those words again (honor, sacrifice, venerable traditions, decisive hour, greatness of the mother country), all those words, images and fantasies they have been living on for decades; their logic has been less important than the emotions they stir up. According to his own account, they make Vallicella feel like throwing up.

The fact that many Italian soldiers are reluctant to fight says nothing about defects in the national character. It is above all a result of the fascist system that has made its mark on Italy for almost twenty years and has led to levels of corruption, nepotism and incompetence that the war has brought to a head and the defeat revealed.* Vallicella is bitter. While the ordinary soldiers go hungry, the fascists and senior officers evoke the fatherland and live well and then send "thousands of poorly armed, badly equipped and badly nourished young men to the slaughter." Then they have the gall to blame the utterly predictable catastrophe on "bad luck."

They drive on. Vallicella has no desire to go to Derna and be reorganized. Perhaps there's a way of avoiding that trap, too. After driving twelve miles they come to a desert road they recognize and know it will take them to the coast. There it is! The sound of breakers, the glistening waves and an unending lapis-lazuli horizon. The sea! The sea! They throw off their clothes, tumble naked into the waves and arise reborn from the foam. The word Vallicella uses in his diary is "*rinascere.*"

Vallicella finds the place so beautiful that he manages to convince his companions to stay here until tomorrow. During the afternoon he and some of the others explore the sandy shoreline and quickly discover that for all its beauty it is full of the debris of war: rusty oil drums, boxes of food, scattered clothing, both military and civilian, and washed-up corpses, unrecognizable, faceless, hardly more than skeletons gnawed clean. They turn back. Their meal that evening is pasta and meatballs.

.   .   .

The dive-bomber pilot John McEniry and his comrades at Guadalcanal are also living in a distorted, slightly bizarre world in which everything they hear may be untrue, censored or just rumor, and consequently nothing is truly real. They are allowed to know what they need to know and sometimes not even that. Which means that, at best, the picture they are given of what has happened or is happening or about to happen is an edited and cosmeticized one. This is a core aspect of the

---

* The historian Amedeo Osti Guerrazzi thinks that the significant difference was that the Germans and the British still trusted their own national and military leadership and their own officers and so "they closed ranks in this time of danger and gathered behind their institutions." This trust was largely absent among the Italian soldiery.

constant uncertainty they live in and it serves to increase their sense of being trapped—trapped in something immense and amorphous in which their lives are gambled for incomprehensible or arbitrary reasons. The idea of hope is left up to the individual.

McEniry has experienced all this. They get their orders and "our function was to say 'Yes, Sir' and only that," as he writes in his memoirs. There is no need for them to know how their mission fits in with the overall context—if an overall context even exists. But something unusual is happening this evening; the veil of silence and guessing is being lifted.

It's the evening of Friday, November 13, and McEniry and several other pilots are on call. They are sitting in darkness in the big open tent that serves as the squadron communications center when a general walks in. He is the new commander of the military air forces at Guadalcanal. The general walks over to the map that covers the whole of this part of the Pacific Ocean and then gives to this small group what is quite clearly an improvised talk and, as a result of that, unusually openhearted. McEniry reports:

> He said something to the effect that there were twelve transports at the Shortlands* with 30,000 troops[†] . . . of the division which had taken Singapore and that by tomorrow morning they would be about 150 miles away on the way to Guadalcanal. He said that the Navy had done everything that it could do, that there was nothing between these troops and Guadalcanal except our dive-bombers, and that if we were unable to stop them the only question was whether an evacuation was possible. He ended by saying, "We lay the fate of Guadalcanal in your hands and know that each of you will do his best." For a second lieutenant who really thought that there was no question of winning, it was a very dramatic moment.

---

* Islands close to Bougainville.

[†] This was an overestimate. There were about seven thousand men of the 38th Infantry Division on the way and they had not been at Singapore; they had, however, taken Hong Kong in 1941, where the troops had been guilty of war crimes. Even just seven thousand men, however, would give the Japanese a clear and probably decisive numerical superiority on the island.

McEniry wasn't alone in being pessimistic. Depending on how much you know, you are either gloomy or desperate. Many of them feared that the battle for Guadalcanal would end up being one more American defeat. Military morale is not at its best.

Later that night the airfield comes under heavy shelling by Japanese cruisers and destroyers out in the straits. (This is a general rule: night belongs to the Japanese.) It's a new sound to him—the swish of shells "sounds like a freight train going overhead." McEniry stumbles to take shelter in an overcrowded bunker while the trains continue thundering down and the ground shudders and shakes.

An hour and a half and 1,300 shells later he and the others leave the shelter and pick their way through fires and choking cordite smoke. The airfield and its surroundings have always been a messy place, littered with military debris, but now it's worse than ever. When he eventually gets to where the squadron's dive-bombers are lined up, to his amazement he discovers that almost all are undamaged. As soon as the sun begins to rise on November 14 the first of them takes off. Now they know what is at stake.

.   .   .

At Slipway No. 2 at the Southeastern Shipbuilding Corporation in Savannah, work is continuing twenty-four hours a day on the yard's first Liberty ship. Thousands of workers, Black and white, women and men, pour in and out of the huge shipyard three times a day. Those arriving for their shift come from the gigantic parking lot or the place where the buses drop them: those leaving work form a counterflow heading for the same spots on their way home. The weather is still dry and warm for the time of year. That makes everything easier.

After twelve long years of Depression, Savannah has suddenly been transmogrified into a boom town, a rapidly expanding town with a steadily growing population and economy. One of the problems for everyone who has found work at the shipyard is how to get there and get home again. Many people share lifts—the yard encourages that—and others take the bus on the route that's been set up specially for the yard. Some people come by ferry. But commuting times are long and a lot of people only manage to get home, eat, sleep, wake up and leave for work.

Nevertheless, the transportation works surprisingly well, and the same applies to accommodation. Everything that seemed virtually impossible before the war has suddenly turned out to be ridiculously easy once there is the political will and the state is prepared to open its wallet.

It's not just the shipyard which, like so many other industries all over the U.S., has shot up quickly; so have cheap and good houses for the workers.* Thanks to the national housing program, numerous new houses have been built—and are still being built—around Savannah in new, well-planned districts with schools, parks, shops and community centers where the residents have a voice via district councils and where welfare and child health are given priority. Most of the housing consists of small terraced houses with garden plots. The only thing that really catches the eye is that, given the importance of saving metal, they all lack gutters and drainpipes—these will be fitted when peace returns.

There's only one week left to the launching.

.   .   .

It's an ordinary day in Mandalay. Monsoon rains have been unusually heavy this year, but they have passed now. The weather is hot but not stifling, the nights have started to grow cool, and lush, fresh-green foliage can be seen everywhere. Everything is also as usual for Mun Okchu at Taegu Inn, a field brothel.† That means she will have sex with between twenty and thirty Japanese troops before the day is over.‡ The timetable is fixed: ordinary soldiers between nine in the morning and four in the afternoon; officers from four until ten at night. Officers can stay all night if they pay extra. The oldest of the girls is twenty-one, the youngest fifteen. Mun Okchu is eighteen.

Mun Okchu and the seventeen other young Korean women are

---

* Black workers have been ignored in this, as in much else: the new residential areas close to the shipyard are reserved for whites.

† The couple who run the brothel, as well as all the young women in it, come from Taegu in southern Korea.

‡ There are times when they are forced to service sixty men and more in a single day. When that occurs, they are usually allowed a couple of days' rest. In addition to the evidence given by Mun Okchu in connection with the lawsuit against the Japanese state in the early 1990s, I have based my descriptions of these routines on records about field brothels in Burma, drawn primarily from Allied interrogations at the end of the war. Some regulations pertaining to field brothels have been preserved.

expected to be available for service virtually every day, even when they are menstruating: in that case, they have to put balls of cloth or cotton into their vagina to soak up the blood. There are times when Mun Okchu has tried to refuse intercourse during her periods, but it has led to her life being threatened. The soldiers are often drunk or violent, though that is not looked on kindly by the couple who run the establishment, nor by the officers in charge. Really troublesome customers are thrown out.

Neither Mun Okchu nor the other comfort women are here voluntarily: in practice, they are prisoners in this two-story building and only allowed to leave it once a month. But Mun Okchu is by no means helpless. Just as the troops lining up outside all behave differently and treat the girls differently, the comfort women also have different ways of dealing with their situation. Mun Okchu has spirit and not infrequently says no: there are soldiers who try to avoid the clearly stated rule that condoms must be used for intercourse—the condoms are coarse and thick and can, when money is tight, be washed out and reused—but Mun Okchu simply rejects those men and threatens to report them to the military police.*

Mun speaks good Japanese, has learned popular songs, has adopted a Japanese name (Fumihara Yoshiko) and is the only one of the Koreans who attends the parties organized by Japanese officers, usually when they are about to set off for the not-too-distant front on the Indian border. Things are quiet there just now. They give her tips and offers of cigarettes and drinks, all of which she is careful to exchange for ready cash afterwards. Mun misses her family very much and suffers from deep troughs of depression, but she has clearly made the decision to save as much money as she possibly can.

Once the day is over and darkness has fallen, she gathers up all the brown cards that act as tickets and takes them down to the office where Mr. Matsumoto counts them up. Ordinary soldiers pay 1.50 yen, non-commissioned officers 2 yen, officers 2.50 yen and senior officers 3 yen. Once a month the young women are given half of what the soldiers have paid, minus deductions for expenses Mr. Matsumoto considers he has had for such things as clothes, cosmetics, tobacco, alcohol and

---

* Soldiers are punished for breaches of the regulations, as well as catching a venereal disease.

medicine. Deductions are also made for the "advance payment" made
by the Japanese army to buy the girls from traffickers or relations.*
And sometimes deductions are also made for a virtually random item
called "contributions to national defense." The result of all this is that
many girls earn nothing or even find themselves in debt. Mun Okchu
is not one of them. Thanks to the status of "paramilitary functionary"
that the Japanese military bureaucracy has invented for them, she has
found a way of using the local field post office to send money home to
her mother or to put it in a bank account.

She isn't beautiful but she's considered to be quite pretty. She often
wears Western clothing such as a blouse and skirt.

.   .   .

In Shanghai it looks as if it's going to be a grim winter for twelve-year-
old Ursula Blomberg, her family and the other European refugees, as
well as for the ordinary inhabitants of the city and, above all, for the
Chinese poor and refugees who have fled to the city from the countryside. Both famine and disease are widespread. The reasonably effective
health-care system put in place by the old colonial powers has collapsed since Japanese troops occupied the city: those who previously
manned the system have either fled or been put in camps. There is a
great deal of typhus at present.

The contrasts are brutal: between the exquisitely beautiful Art
Deco buildings in the city center and the abyss of poverty down below;
between those who have time, money and deluded arrogance (horse
racing continues, as do fashion shows) and those who have nothing;
between the luxurious and celebrated Shanghai that existed just a few
years ago—the pleasure center of Asia, a must for tourists and the
rich and famous of the world, a city of many millions known for its
restaurants, dance halls, jazz clubs, shopping streets and night life, its
bordellos, casinos and drug dens—and the cold, grey, joyless shell that
remains today.

It is not unusual to see dead bodies in the streets. Most of them are
beggars and other homeless Chinese who died on the spot, others have
been laid out by people in the houses: dead family members rolled up

---

* In many of the contracts that were drawn up, it stipulated that the women
could return home once the "advance payment" was fully paid off, something
that did happen.

in rice mats. They will all be picked up and loaded onto the trucks
that make daily rounds of the district to pick up new bodies. One of
the Jewish residents living not far from Ursula and her family at this
time writes: "Human life in Shanghai had always been rather cheap,
but today it appears to be totally worthless."

.   .   .

Two days have passed since the great battle for the Kako strongpoint
on the Svir River in East Karelia. Kurt West is now back at Orren, his
strongpoint. He reports:

> The talk and the card games got going as usual. That was
> the only way of suppressing all the dreadful things we'd been
> involved in. For my part this baptism of fire was something
> utterly different to anything I had ever imagined in my wildest
> fantasies. I think I aged a whole year in just a few days.

When West attempts to understand why he survived uninjured when
so many others were killed or wounded, the only conclusion he can
come to is that it was some sort of divine protection. (He comes from
a religious family and his father, in particular, is a very firm believer.)

After breakfast the soldiers get together for a briefing. They hear
that they are to return to Kako. "That order caused considerable dis-
pleasure among the men—swearing and other improper words could
be heard," West reports. "We were to be sent into the line again! Wasn't
there any other unit?" They march off without any enthusiasm. The
sounds of artillery are in the air. By this stage West knows the way
through birchwoods and bogs, past the long narrow lake—Kakojärvi—
after which the strongpoint is named.

But it could be worse. It is not a counterattack that awaits them—
they are going instead to help build a new strongpoint close to a bog
a little north of Kako.* So West and his companions begin digging

---

* West and the others are, of course, unaware that the situation at Kako has
been discussed at the highest level. Kako was the most critical point since it
overlooked a road leading north all the way to Petrozavodsk (or Äänislinna, as
the town had then been named). West's regimental commander, Alpo Marttinen,
had talked on the telephone to Mannerheim, the commander-in-chief, and said
that any attempt to retake all of Kako would need "massive air and armored
support" and that he "could not allow his young Finland-Swedish soldiers to

a trench and erecting barbed-wire barricades. Every so often a shell comes over, but West has learned how to interpret the sound. And interpreting it is something that happens in a flash, physically and almost subconsciously, rather than via thought processes.

It takes a soldier one or two months to learn these things: how to judge not only the approximate calibre of the shell but its approximate landing place; and how best to read the terrain and recognize, for instance, that a barely noticeable depression of six inches or so in the ground can be sufficient to save your life. But until you have learned these things, you are living dangerously. That's why many new arrivals are killed so soon.

And experience also brings something else: strong self-control, a coolness that is often accompanied by black humor, which, taken together, mean that veterans are usually able to keep a calm head even when under great pressure—everything only gets worse when you let fear take over. Unfortunate newcomers are at a dreadful disadvantage in this respect, too: they become panic-stricken in difficult situations and consequently do idiotic things. Many greenhorns show that they are afraid even before being faced with danger. The mere thought of what is to come gives them palpitations and nightmares. For the majority of those afflicted by mental breakdown, it happens in connection with their very first combat experience or on their way to it. If you get through that first full month in the line, as Kurt West has done now, your chances of survival rise substantially.*

There are, however, no systems, no level of experience that will guarantee survival. It is the geometry of chance that will decide in the long run. There is a chance of ducking those heavy shells that announce their arrival with a whooshing, droning, pulsating sound, but the Russians also use light, direct-firing anti-tank guns that fire shells at the speed of sound or faster. Particularly when the lines are as close together as they are here, the sound of firing followed immediately by the sound of the hit. There is no advance warning, just the single crack.

---

die in an undertaking that was doomed to failure before it started." Instead, they convinced Mannerheim to construct new positions north of the strongpoint.

* Up to a certain point. Coolness can gradually turn into a jaded casualness. Not far behind that comes fatalism, and after that apathy is lurking. That's usually the end of it.

West and his companions are digging. (It's likely to have been relatively light work as the ground frost won't have penetrated especially
deep yet.) And that is when it happens. A sharp crack. Small black
lumps of soil and snow spray around. One of the diggers is down. They
rush over. West knows the man lying there. Alf Nordberg. They are
the same age and were in the same company during basic training
in Nykarleby. Nordberg is beyond help, his body sliced through the
middle. This occurs on Friday, November 13.

What do the people back home know about what has been happening on the Svir Front this week? Initially little more than a short,
telegrammatic sentence: "Localized fighting in central Aunus Isthmus."
In terms of space, this was trumped by the report of a young female
shop assistant killed in a tram accident on Runebergsvägen and another
about a ten-year-old drowned by falling through the ice on Likolampi
Lake. A day or so later, there is a report that the enemy attacked and
suffered significant losses. And then, at last, on November 13, the action
pops up almost casually at the bottom right of the front page of *Hufvud-
stadsbladet,* under the headline "Renewed Russian Attack in Aunus—
the Enemy Suffered 400 Dead." At the same time, the death notices
began to appear one by one, each embellished with the characteristic
military cross. Some of the fallen are named in a couple of lines under
the heading "For the Motherland," tucked in between short notices
about football pools and new regulations for the use of hot water in
apartment houses.

·   ·   ·

An ordinary day in besieged Leningrad. Much mental energy, time and
emotion are focused on one thing, food, and in this case the opposite
pole to food—hunger.

Lidiya Ginzburg:

> Why was hunger, as the Germans realized, the most power-
> ful underminer of resistance? Because hunger is a permanent
> state, it can't be switched off. It was constantly present and
> always made its presence felt (not invariably in a desire to
> eat); the most desperate and tormenting thing of all during
> the process of eating was when the food drew to an end with
> awful rapidity without bringing satiety.

Also Lidiya Ginzburg:

> Sometimes there were lucid intervals. Then you felt like gorging yourself to bursting point, till you were sick of the sight of food, to vomiting point—just so as to put an end to the shame, just to free your brain. But fear took hold of the malnourished brain—what on earth would happen if it disappeared? If this complex of desires and goals were to resolve itself away? What was it so sickeningly like? Something from the previous life? Ah, yes—being unhappily in love, when she was slowly releasing the bonds and you feared to lose along with her, not hope by now, not the emotion, but the guaranteed, accustomed filling of the vacuum.

Vera Inber:

> A story told by Z. V. Oglobina. A patient in a ward says to her: "Doctor, I look upon you as God"—"Or as a kilo of bread," another corrected.

· · ·

His appearance is anything but imposing. He looks like a bookkeeper who's been forced into uniform: plumpish, slightly clumsy and notably shortsighted. He wears round spectacles and his bent back bears witness to many hours, years even, at different desks. His name is Vasily Semenovich Grossman and he's a reporter for *Krasnaja Zvezda*, the Red Army newspaper. He will be thirty-seven in one month's time, if he lives that long.

In fact, he should already be dead.

What hasn't he seen? What hasn't he lived through? Grossman has been in Stalingrad ever since the battle for the city began towards the end of August. By that stage he was already experienced and hardened. He has been reporting on the war ever since the preceding August, when—after learning to shoot a pistol and going down in weight from 200 pounds to 165—he was sent to the front for the first time and became a shaken witness to one chaotic Soviet defeat after another. Then he was struck, as he described it later, by "the penetrating, sharp foreboding of imminent losses and the tragic realization that the destiny of a mother, a wife and a child had become inseparable from the destiny of the encircled regiments and retreating armies. How can one forget the front in those days—[the cities of] Gomel and Chernigov dying in flames, doomed Kiev, carts retreating and poisonous-green rockets over silent forests and rivers?"

The shock of last year's catastrophes is still with him, as an emotion and as an insight. It becomes confused with the pain of a deep, personal guilt and is thus burned in.

Grossman was born into a Jewish family in northern Ukraine, in Berdychiv, a town with a large Jewish population statistically speaking, but where many of them have become secularized and assimilated and, just like his well-educated parents, have Russified their names. His youthful dreams were of becoming a researcher in the field of natural science, but History interposed in the form of world war, revolution and civil war. His home areas became a playground for repeated, violent clashes between whites and reds, greens (Ukrainian nationalists) and blacks (anarchists), with the constant threat of pogroms, famine as a weapon and widespread lawlessness. Robbery, rape and murder were aspects of everyday life.

From his earliest teenage years, he learned the cruelty that human beings are capable of. The remarkable thing is, though, that this experience did not make him hardened or cruel himself, rather—by some sort of psychological alchemy—it sharpened his sensitivity and understanding. He owes much of that to his mother. His father disappeared from his life early on, became a grand but absent figure, a correspondence parent, and so Vasily and his mother, Jekaterina, became that much closer to one another.

His mother, a teacher of French, protected him both physically and psychologically, and she gave him unconditional love. It's from her that he gained his self-discipline, intellectual strength and multifaceted cultural interests. He became a chemist and then worked for a time as an engineer at a mine in the Donbass, but his literary interests took over. He wrote short stories, was noticed by the great Russian writer Mikhail Bulgakov and, even more importantly, by Maxim Gorky, the godfather of Soviet social realism, and since the mid-1930s Grossman has been a full-time writer.

Yes, he really should be dead already. It's not unusual for physical and moral courage to refuse to come together within one and the same human being. Maybe there is some kind of compensatory principle that will only allow the one to grow at the expense of the other. But in Grossman's case, the courage is both physical and moral.

He wouldn't have survived the last months in Stalingrad without physical courage and, admittedly, a good bit of luck. The war is into its second year and nowhere has destruction and bloodletting been so extreme as in this shattered city, where the number of dead per square yard is in the same class as on the worst battlefields of the First World War, though the fanaticism and brutality here exceeds all of them. Grossman has been at many of the very worst places—the northern front at Rynok, Mamajev Kurgan, the Barrikady armaments factory; he has crossed the 1,500 yards of the Volga countless times ("frightening as a scaffold," he writes in his notes) into the smoky maze of ruins where there are "the usual smells of the front, a mixture somewhere between a smithy and a morgue."

And at the same time, given his moral courage he ought not have survived the random purges of 1937–1938, when no one was safe and many disappeared for the most absurd reasons—acquaintanceship, relationship, rumor, a couple of lines in an old dossier, envy or just because the local NKVD had its quota of shootings and prisoners to fill. Grossman had taken a colossal risk by contacting the highest commander of the secret police, the feared Nikolaj Jezjov, and argued for the freeing of his recently arrested wife. And he succeeded—against all odds. Having watched the apparatus of oppression become hyperlogical and lay waste to itself and society, Grossman no longer has any illusions about the Stalinist system.

Fighting is still continuing around the narrow strips of ruin-filled ground along the Volga that Soviet troops are clinging on to, but German attacks are on a smaller scale now. Both sides are exhausted, expecting snow and the winter. For the moment, Grossman has left the city and today, November 13, he finds time to write a letter to his father:

> I work a lot, the work is stressful, and I am pretty tired. I have never been to such a hot spot as this one. Letters don't reach me here, only once they brought me a whole bundle of letters, among them was a letter and a postcard from you. . . . It is quite frosty here now, and windy.

Grossman is weary, you can tell that from his mood: he is snappy and easily irritated. The hair at one of his temples has gone white. Does a single day pass without him thinking of his mother and his responsibility for her death?

·   ·   ·

For a long time Nella Last's life moved between two poles: her children and the house at 9 Ilkley Road, Barrow-in-Furness, England. The two poles defined her life and gave a direction to her existence. Not her husband—no, never Will. (Will, though, works at Vickers shipyard. One routine in their lives is that she ensures his slippers are warmed just right by the time he comes home from his shift.) He was, of course, a necessary precondition for life and its security, but he was never its center.

The boys are grown up and have flown the nest. Arthur will be thirty next year and works as a tax inspector in Northern Ireland—a safe occupation in a safe place. Clifford, never called anything but Cliff, will be twenty-four next month and is located in an unknown place in an unknown part of the world. His army unit was shipped out in the greatest secrecy in the middle of July and his mother hopes her boy has ended up somewhere fairly safe, somewhere like India.*

And what about their house? Over the years Nella has seen how pride in a beautiful, orderly and clean home is what has provided the meaning for many women's lives, especially after their children have grown up: pride, yes, but it has also kept women trapped in a narrow and limited life. (Cliff has warned her about becoming excessively "houseproud.") But, in a sense, the bomb that fell that night in May last year took the house from her.

It is still perfectly habitable—the roof held up—but as Nella wrote at the time, it "will never be the same again." The worst of the damage has been repaired, the tears in the curtains and cushion covers patched, and the horrid dust that worked its way into every crack and cranny has finally been gotten rid of. But the signs can still be seen everywhere:

---

* This guess is not completely unfounded. She and Cliff agreed on certain codes he would use in his letters, and the code in his last letter said India. At this point he was actually in North Africa. Nella Last's greatest fear was that Cliff was likely to be sent in on "that second front," some sort of major landing on the Continent, which was being talked about more and more. The totally failed landing at Dieppe was a scary thing to consider.

the façade spoiled by cracks made by bomb splinters, the little garage has moved six inches or so, cracks are visible in places in the cream-colored walls. She has aways loved doing the spring cleaning, but "this year, I had no pride in cleaning, none at all." She wrote in her diary:

> Rather, it was the careful "make do" care and attention that one would give a hurt or sick child: no hard rubbing that would loosen slack and damaged plaster or ceilings, and the tiles in the bathroom and kitchenette had to be held flat while wiping over them, for so many are loose. A feeling of "There, that's over," rather than lingering to admire the polish and sheen on freshly cleaned furniture, brass and floors. Something died in me that night—and perhaps something was born. Perhaps a balance was struck.

It's November now and the "perhaps" in the next-to-last sentence can be deleted. Her whole life has changed. No longer is her focus house, children and husband—the two of them quarrel more and more often, and it's almost always her who puts Will in his place—unlike earlier. Her focus now is the world outside, serving in the civil defense, working on Red Cross parcels for prisoners.

Her husband has aged noticeably since the outbreak of war. There's no doubt that Nella may feel weary and low at times, but she actually has more energy than before. She's known for almost always being in a good mood. No longer the pale neurasthenic who needs to fill herself with aspirin and rest behind closed doors several times a day, she is now the active one, the one who organizes, helps, supports, comforts, cheers and explains. She pays more attention to her appearance than she used to and she rarely goes outside the door without putting on her lipstick.*

. . .

Life has gone back to normal for Sophie Scholl. That is, to a double life. On the surface, it doesn't look any different from the life she and her brother and their friends have had for a long time: lectures, walks, music making, reading books, concerts, a glass of wine or two. One of the young men in her circle has returned to his fencing lessons.

---

* Lipstick had a rather symbolic significance for Nella Last: when she got married, she was forbidden by her mother to wear any makeup at all.

Several of them sing in a choir and are rehearsing Bach's version of *Messiah*. Sophie Scholl is still writing letters to her fiancé (*in spe*), Fritz Hartnagel. He is in Stalingrad and she is becoming more and more concerned that he hasn't written back for a long time. (Has he been killed?) But then, behind carefully closed doors, in rooms heavy with pipe smoke and suppressed concern, the six core members of her group hold low-voiced discussions about what is to happen next. They are all frustrated that the four leaflets they distributed last summer haven't had any noticeable effect.* They decide their next action must be on a larger scale: more leaflets, in more places.

When you find yourself in danger, it is so easy, isn't it, just to save yourself and those close to you and to flee the burning house, ignoring all moral calls? It's asking a great deal of someone safely outside to actually follow the ethical imperative and voluntarily go into the smoke and the fire.

.   .   .

The slumbering giant has wakened. Up to now, the American operation on Guadalcanal has been characterized by improvisations and stopgap solutions, particularly in the field of military logistics—the field in which the U.S. has the reputation for absolute superiority, an extension of that country's massive economic and industrial weight. It is Saturday, November 14, and Charles Walker is down on the shore once again. Something big is happening as, behind them, formation after formation of planes is taking off from the airfield and disappearing into the distance. But Walker and his men have a different job. They have been ordered here to fish out the drums full of fuel that American freighters released out in the sound, calculating that the current and winds would carry them ashore.

It's another piece of improvisation, whether cunning or just desperate is hard to say. At the same time, however, there are more and more signs that the American armed forces are starting to get their organization of supplies in order. (That massive industrial weight is

---

* Over half of those who received the leaflets in the mail immediately took them to the police. A special unit within the Munich Gestapo, with a variety of experts attached, has been working hard since the summer to locate those responsible. We need to remember that the Gestapo was a small and undermanned organization, heavily reliant on informers—of which there was no shortage.

beginning to seriously make itself felt in practice and not just in terms of statistics.) While Walker and his squad are manhandling heavy fuel drums out of the water and onto the trucks waiting in the shade of the coconut palms, he can see large landing craft coming into the beach, laden with all kinds of provisions including carton upon carton of oranges and stacks of frost-coated boxes of frozen boneless meat. But he quickly learns that these goodies belong to the Marine Corps. The rivalry continues to be razor-sharp, as does the petty-mindedness.

That afternoon Walker borrows a truck and steals loads of oranges and frozen meat, all for his own battalion. (Everyone steals from everyone else.) After dark, however, he pulls off his really big coup: at the start of yet another Japanese air raid, the guards take shelter in trenches and bunkers and Walker is able to smuggle a cask of medical alcohol out of the gated store; "before daylight the split had been made, all the way up to the battalion commander."

Alcohol is one of the items most desired among the soldiers on the island here, and everywhere else. If there is none to be gotten hold of, which is usually the case on distant places in the Pacific like this,* the soldiers brew up all sorts of mash themselves and call it swipe or raisin jack. It was made of a mixture of sugar, tinned fruit, raisins, potato peelings and anything else, all put to ferment in a closed container.† Some of the most desperate on Guadalcanal even drink aftershave lotion mixed with grapefruit juice or filtered through bread. They drink from habit, because that's something a man does; they drink as a way of escape; they drink to anesthetize themselves; they drink in order to get by.

Everyone Walker encounters the following morning is to some degree intoxicated,‡ even the new battalion commander and Walker's new company commander. There's one man lying on the ground, screaming and shouting, so drunk that he can't stand. The sergeant in

---

* The first consignment of beer reaches the island in December.

† Seabees, the non-combatant units that build and maintain the airfields—a hugely important function and a good example of the superiority of the American logistical setup—are well-known for their excellence at producing moonshine, which they sell to the soldiers or swap for souvenirs.

‡ Apart from the battalion medical officer, who is afraid the intoxicant might be wood alcohol. His skepticism about drinking is not unjustified: there were periods during the war when more American soldiers died of alcohol poisoning than disease.

charge of supplies is carried out speechless on a stretcher. The drinking continues into the following day.

.   .   .

November is always a monotone, chiaroscuro month, but the question is whether the city of Shanghai has ever been this cheerless. The neon signs in the great shopping streets are turned off. There are few cars to be seen on the streets apart from the khaki vehicles of the Japanese military. Fuel is especially hard to get hold of and anyone caught hoarding gasoline is threatened with severe punishment. So, when Ursula Blomberg and the rest of them at Place de Fleurs intend to go anywhere far away, they have to go by bicycle. But possession of a bicycle requires a license.* Even if you have both a bicycle and a license, you still can't move freely through the city and its stream of pedestrians, bearers and rickshaws. The moment you leave the French district, you encounter Japanese guards, barbed wire and roadblocks.

But it's not all that, not the typhus epidemic nor the question of food for the day that concern Ursula most. Her life is shielded from the worst sights, protected by her parents in their walled house, and by the strange normality that operates under the plane trees in their particular district of the city, while danger, death and misery rule no more than a couple of zones away: this city has always been difficult to understand, with all its zones, its boundaries and its parallel lives.† Her family is managing pretty well and if things get critical there are welfare charities to assist the Jewish refugees in the city.

What troubles Ursula Blomberg most is the uncertainty. She writes:

> Living in the French concession gave us the illusion of immunity from the Japanese, simply because none of their troops cluttered the streets as they did in occupied Hongkew. We sort of blended in with the Russians, Portuguese, Germans and members of other "friendly" nations who made their homes in the quiet streets of this pleasant part of the city. But would it last?

---

* Since 1941, sixteen thousand new licenses have been issued in Shanghai. Hundreds of bicycle workshops have opened all over the city.

† Since Vichy France was regarded as a friendly state, the Japanese had to a considerable extent left the French quarter alone.

Apparently not. The Japanese troops who have behaved so properly up to now have started to get aggressive. There are occasions when they gang up in small groups and break into houses, pulling things apart in a hunt for radios, American dollars and gold. Apart from that, rumors have continued to come from Europe, rumors "that disturbed and frightened us to the very core of our being" about Jews being transported to camps in the east, about "unspeakable brutalities." But that's not all, she writes:

> More rumors made their way through Hongkew. We heard that a high-ranking member of the Gestapo, a Colonel Josef Meisinger,* had visited Tokyo to discuss the Jewish refugee situation there. He was now in Shanghai conferring with Japanese government officials about all of us. That was not good news.

The rumor is that Meisinger's mission is to annihilate all the Jews in Shanghai, possibly by initiating a pogrom. Another rumor has it that a ship with a cargo of poison gas has arrived in the harbor. Have they travelled halfway around the world only to suffer the same fate that has already consumed so many of their kin back in Europe? Guesses and ominous talk are spreading. And suicide has become increasingly common among the refugees.

Yesterday was a day of heavy rain. Today, Saturday, November 14, it is just drizzling. The wind is coming from the west-northwest, from inland China. The temperature is upwards of sixty-one degrees and quite pleasant for late autumn. Everyone knows that the cold will soon arrive.

·   ·   ·

Yet another foggy day in London and Vera Brittain is staying at home to answer letters. (Her correspondence is considerable—she receives

---

* Meisinger was an unusually brutal and vile sort, even by SS standards. He was also corrupt to the core. His posting to Asia seems to have been a move by his superiors to get him out of the way without having an embarrassing trial. Shanghai also seems to have been a convenient dumping ground for a variety of incompetent and unpleasant Nazis who, when they weren't frequenting nightclubs and brothels, used much of their time spying on other Germans and slandering one another.

many letters from readers and she also has many, many contacts with people in the scattered peace movement.) She concentrates and works her way through the stack of envelopes. What gives her the most pleasure are letters from two acquaintances who heap praise on her recently published *Humiliation with Honour*. She has been feeling low for a while, but the words of praise lift her spirits.

Vera Brittain's usual publisher had his doubts about the book because of its pacifist message, so it has been published by a small, one-man press in Hertfordshire. Thus far, the big newspapers have killed it by silence, or given it a disparaging reception, so the praise she receives from friends and acquaintances is important to her.

It's interesting to ask whom she wrote *Humiliation with Honour* for. The form she chose—letters to her fifteen-year-old son in the United States—was the result of a change of approach halfway through the writing, and it works pretty well. But it's hard to get away from the feeling that the book, despite its proselytizing tone, is ultimately an attempt to convince other pacifists (herself included) that they had, and have, right on their side whatever misjudgments and failures they are guilty of.

Brittain's world view was formed by her tragic experiences in the First World War. It's almost as though she is trapped in an unending loop in which everything leads back to 1914, as if her imagination simply cannot escape the snare of extrapolation that history often sets. Since the grand, glorious words about the struggle to save civilization from barbarism turned out to be manifest lies then, they must also be lies now; if concocted or exaggerated stories of atrocity were used to whip the populace into a warlike fever then, such stories are likely to be just as concocted and exaggerated now; since victory over Germany and her allies was pointless then and did nothing but create the preconditions for another war, victory now will be just as pointless.

Consequently, although she condemns Hitler and Nazism, she considers much of what is happening to be Great Britain's own fault and believes the country should not have gone to war over Poland.* The only way out is an immediate cease-fire and peace negotiations, along

* In her diary entry for May 26, 1940, she is a little more specific. She blames Great Britain's being dragged into the war on three groups: the communists and their fellow travellers who had whipped up feelings against Germany; irresponsible liberals who had offered "to guarantee small powers all over Europe without

with a generous sharing of the natural resources that Germany and Japan have currently felt compelled to take by force.

But even though Vera Brittain is struggling, picking facts and hopes that accord with her old experiences and self-righteous pathos and thus being fatally wrong about the situation, she and her text reveal a moral passion drawn from the same experience—a passion that allows her to perceive something fundamental. She writes:

> The continued experience of tragedy gradually atrophies the senses and creates a defense mechanism of callousness without which the normal person could not endure. With the less than normally sensitive, this process soon degenerates into barbarity. With all of us, actions once unimaginable come to be accepted as normal, or, at worst, unavoidable.

This section of her text concludes with sharp criticism of the bombing of German civilians. During 1942, RAF Bomber Command, under its new commander-in-chief, Arthur Harris (whom she quotes with distaste), has introduced a new kind of operation: big firebombing raids concentrating on German cities with the explicit aim of breaking the civilian population's will to resist. The attacks, with growing success, have targeted a number of major cities, most recently Hamburg, five days before. These raids prey increasingly on her mind. The date is November 14.

By Saturday evening Vera Brittain has finished all her letter-writing and can, with a mixture of pleasure and relief, return to her novel—she hasn't done anything with it for a month and it will be a while before she finishes it. Her next big project is a book openly questioning the bombing of German civilians. It will make her even more unpopular.

·   ·   ·

Dusk on Guadalcanal. John McEniry is standing looking at the dive-bomber he's just climbed out of. That he managed to land it is an achievement as the machine is a wreck. The engine cut out as a result of a couple of oil lines being shot away; the fuel pump is shot to pieces, as are many of the instruments on the instrument panel, the radio,

---

knowing whether we could"; and nostalgic Francophiles who tied the fate of the country to that of France.

large parts of the cockpit cover, and the triggers and one of the shields on the radio operator's machine guns. There are several machine-gun bullets and parts of an exploded 20mm shell lodged in the armored plate behind the pilot's seat. There are bullet holes visible all over the wings and the fuselage. The heel of one of his boots is missing after being hit by a bullet fired by one of the Japanese fighter planes that had swarmed around, above and behind his dive-bomber while trying to shoot it down. Some of the holes were probably caused by shells fired by the Japanese ships they had been attacking, which had fired back with everything they had, including heavy cannon.

Attacking enemy ships as the light is starting to fade is a very special experience. The swinging, elliptical lines of tracer bullets are clearly visible, whereas the bright tropical sunlight of the middle of the day normally obscures them. And it suddenly becomes possible to see what a huge quantity of projectiles is filling the air as the spots of light rise slowly up towards them before suddenly whipping past.

The machine is a wreck, which is bad news.

Planes are in short supply here on the island. It's the rule rather than the exception for these hardy dive-bombers to return peppered with bullet holes that the mechanics simply cover by riveting on aluminium patches which they give a quick coat of green, rustproof paint. Some of the planes have so many green patches on their pale-blue surface that they end up looking like rugs made of rags. The work of keeping so many aircraft airworthy and flyable goes on all day and all night. The number of combat-ready aircraft is the statistic watched most nervously; there is no shortage of pilots.

This is a war of machines and people are no more than the servants of the machines. That's how it can be interpreted and that's what the cliché suggests, though under all the clichés there lies the varied human experience, so huge, fragmented and contradictory that it is impossible to summarize—which is why formulae like "this is a war of machines" are needed.

But, even in an abstract sense, there is something in the statement: the organizations that are fighting this war—armies, navies, air forces— may be seen as immense machines composed of a pretty well endless number of mobile and interlocking parts of which the smallest, most anonymous and most frequently replaced component is the human one. Individuals are subordinate to the blind, impersonal power of the great machine the whole time. They are nothing outside it and, given that they can be replaced, they are virtually nothing within it as well. That demoralizing insight strikes them all at some point.

Mechanics push McEniry's plane away from the runway while he and his radio operator go to the mess hall to get something to eat. They aren't likely to have had much to eat all day. It's the evening of November 14 and darkness is falling.

John McEniry finds it hard to understand what he's been involved in. He writes: "The number of attacks and hits and by whom they were made will never be known with precision. The day was one of takeoff, attack, return, reload and repeat. No one knew for sure who went on what attack."

Much later, when he tries to put together an account of what happened, his memories and those of the others don't really agree with what the logbooks—the squadron's diaries—state, and they, in turn, do not really agree with the various official reports. The basic facts, however, are simple. From early morning on, there were rolling air attacks on the big Japanese convoy of troopships on its way to Guadalcanal, the convoy the general had told them about the night before: "Take off, attack, return, reload and repeat." Aircraft from every imaginable unit and of every possible type took part.

McEniry had flown four sorties. The first, at 6:30 a.m., which took slightly less than three hours from start to finish, was an attack on two cruisers. The logbook states that his 500-pound bomb hit the stern of one of them, but he recalls it as being a near miss. His sharpest memory, perhaps, was the relief he felt getting away from the heavy anti-aircraft fire and being able to have a cigarette. The second sortie took all of two hours and the target this time was the transport convoy. This time, too, his bomb missed. His sharpest memory, perhaps, was his first sighting of the convoy, the biggest he had ever seen. The third sortie took about two hours and once again targeted the convoy, which was now becoming more and more dispersed. This time he hit the target. His sharpest memory, perhaps, was that after landing, Major John Sailer, the fair-haired squadron leader, a professional officer more than ten years older than McEniry and a man they all admire for his fearlessness while being a little nervous of his temper, comes over to him and says: "You got a beautiful hit, Mac. Now that we know how, let's go again." And that's what they did.

When McEniry looked in the squadron diary later, there is no trace of this fourth sortie, but it's actually the one that "will always remain in my memory." It's not clear whether McEniry hit any of the transports—he probably did; the air force doctor's report of February 22, 1943, states "4 hits on ships"—because he was so preoccupied taking evasive maneuvers and surviving the anti-aircraft fire and the dense swarms of Japanese fighter planes that, on occasion, his eyes were temporarily blinded and his body forced this way and that by the g-forces. And there were those familiar, stinging smells the whole time—oil, exhaust fumes, cordite, aircraft fuel, hot metal. His sharpest memory, perhaps, is flying low, low over the deep-blue waters; tracer bullets dancing around, over, under and in front of his dive-bomber's nose; then the crack and screech of projectiles striking his plane's fuselage and spouts of water spurting up. One of the fighter planes flies so close that he can see clearly the face of the man trying to kill him. But it's the Japanese pilot who dies instead.

Just a week ago, when he arrived on Guadalcanal eager for combat, he was certain he would survive the battle and the war, that it "was always going to be someone else." But lying in his small tent trying to get to sleep later this Saturday evening, the thought that comes to him is: "If there were many more days like this, I might not make it." Something within him has shifted.

.   .   .

At the same time on the same island, Lieutenant Tohichi Wakabayashi is trying to understand what actually is happening of all the things that seem to be happening. Through his telescope from his position on the jungle-clad hill, he can see and count the aircraft taking off and landing on the enemy airfield, but they don't have the weapons or the ammunition to do anything about it. Wakabayashi has also seen and heard the great nocturnal sea battle, which has inspired him to write another poem. In free form this time:

> *Rumble rumble boom boom boom*
> *Like hundreds of thunderbolts striking at once*
> *My dream of a trench is gone*
> *From the peak of Guadalcanal*
> *I look north to the waters of Tulagi*
> *The red flame blaze scorches the sea*
> *No way to tell who is friend or foe*
> *Hot masses of shells rip through the air*

Flares drop from aircraft overhead
They light up our ship. Lights come together, quivering.
The silver scales that graze the wheel of light and death.
My destroyer is no longer anywhere in sight.
Oh, a shadowy shape of a ship in the light. It's an enemy battleship.
A thunderous roar shakes the earth.
One, two . . . Towering pillars of fire.
All gone. Splintering and fragmenting into nothing.

He knows that the convoy of transport ships is supposed to arrive today. "I pray for their success," he writes in his diary. He knows, too, that they need them, the thousands of soldiers and heavy weapons they are carrying, but also the provisions which make up a good deal of the convoy's cargo. They are suffering a shortage of food. Their rations are worryingly small. He notes: "Ever since I landed, I have been craving vegetables. Today, I ate the stem of a palm sprout."

During the night of November 14–15 Wakabayashi can still hear the rumble of guns out at sea. In the morning, the news that the convoy has arrived spreads around and he notes: "I cheered with joy when I heard of their success. *Banzai!*" A few hours later his company is sent off through the jungle to a position nearer the north coast. "Enemy planes swarmed above." Since dusk was falling, accounts of what actually happened become more and more confusing.

·   ·   ·

Mansur Abdulin and some fellow soldiers are moving forward through the connecting trenches in the darkness to take up their position. It is the evening of Saturday, November 14, and there is silence. The only sound to be heard is the crackle as their boots step on the thin ice covering the puddles. There was light, freezing rain earlier, but the clouds have dispersed and the temperature is falling.

Abdulin stops and gazes out into the darkness of no-man's-land, towards the enemy lines some 350 yards away. A beautiful full moon slowly rises in the sky and its clear, sharp light picks out shapes, details, images from the previously flat and featureless surface. The attack ended a few hours ago and the scene is an appalling one.

Earlier today, Abdulin's regiment, the 1034th, was ordered to storm the enemy trenches opposite "and take control of their defensive installations." This is their first attack, their first real combat. They have a couple of veterans among them, survivors of the massacres of last year,* but most of them are new recruits with three months' rudimentary basic training behind them at most. In the majority of cases, the soldiers and their officers have only known one another since October: the regiment, indeed the whole division, was staffed and equipped with gear at a depot in Buzuluk on the other side of the Urals. That's why there is a large contingent of Central Asians.†

Over the spring and summer, the unit was involved in one long, humiliating retreat after another: at one point, the morale of the section of the Red Army that was fighting on the southern front looked as if it might collapse completely. Panic and resignation became everyday occurrences and desertions rocketed.‡ But something has happened since then.

It's partly a mixture of shame and vision. The constant withdrawals have begun to seem insupportable, in a number of ways. They are morally indefensible: they involve surrendering ever larger numbers of your own population to an occupier who, by this stage, you know to be capable of every sort of atrocity. They are geographically indefensible: if things go on like this, the country's most important and resource-rich areas will be gone and the empty steppes of Asia will be all that is left.

But it also has to do with changes to the kind of thinking and behavior that the Stalinist dictatorship had imposed on the people (thoroughly, causing great sacrifices). Out went wishful thinking, the search for scapegoats, rictus optimism, the denial of unpleasant facts, reflexive obedience and the equally reflexive reluctance to take real

---

* Several times during 1941 and 1942, the 293rd Rifle Division, of which the 1034th is a part, has avoided—mainly by chance—the fate that has befallen so many other units of the Red Army: getting encircled, isolated, hammered and wiped out.

† The fact that by this point ever more national minorities—not least Central Asians—could be seen in the Red Army has a mainly demographic explanation: many of the annihilated armies consisted largely of Russians and many of the areas currently occupied by the Germans had a Russian population. In spite of this, or perhaps because of it, there was prejudice and bias against Central Asians specifically.

‡ At no point was the Soviet Union closer to losing the war than during the catastrophic summer of 1942, when nothing seemed to be going the Red Army's way and the country's massive industrial base had not yet made its full weight apparent.

responsibility. That kind of thinking had been a factor behind the defeats, and the shock of the defeats finally led to change: a start has been made on clearing out old party hacks left over from civil war days, along with any other incompetent bosses, and the right of party commissars to interfere in military decisions has been withdrawn.

And there are also changes that are more than symbolic, but where symbolism has a role to play. New regulations regarding the award of medals were introduced only three days ago and, henceforth, the Red Army is to be quick and generous with its awards. In many cases medals meant direct material advantages, such as increased remuneration for a soldier's family, free travel, lower rents, a small annuity and so on. Now, in the middle of November, news has come through that epaulettes are to be reintroduced for officers. This is one more sign that the only things that matter now are rank and military competence. Since epaulettes, in particular, are linked with the Tsarist army and the old order, and since many churches have been reopened and anti-religious campaigns put on hold—there is even a rumor that the detested collective farm system may be abolished—many of the men in the Red Army see a new and more hopeful dawn on the horizon: "For the first time, soldiers could really think that the pre-war order—bosses, prison camps and all—was coming to an end. They could believe they were fighting to create the promised, longed-for better world," as British historian Catherine Merridale wrote.

But even though the majority has recognized by this stage that they are literally fighting for their own and their country's survival and that there is more to fight for than to flee from, and even though ideological idealism and self-sacrifice are developing strongly in the Red Army, the system still retains a cold and brutal weapon to fall back on: coercion. Shirkers or those who refuse to obey orders run a great risk of being shot out of hand, and by this stage of the war there can't be many who haven't witnessed or at least heard of summary executions of that kind.* Immediately behind the lines there were always NKVD squads with orders to pick up all shirkers and deserters (they have the right to shoot them on the spot) and with the authority to open fire on any of their own units that are beginning to flee or give up. A human life counted for little in the Red Army.

---

* Even regimental commanders and higher officers risked being shot in such circumstances, and from time to time it did happen.

Mansur Abdulin is standing in the trench looking towards no-man's-land, out across the 350 yards that his battalion tried to cross a couple of hours ago (strangely, with no more than symbolic support from the artillery). The objects that appeared in the darkness to be geometric shapes or tree stumps or just tussocks of frozen grass now, in the light of the full moon, turn out to be dead people, many of them personally known to him or people he knew by name. The falling rain has frozen and formed a shimmering veil over their faces and uniforms, giving the corpses the illusion of being made of ice. Abdulin remembers:

> Some were lying flat on their backs, others twisted and con-torted. Some were sitting lopsided with raised hands, as if urg-ing comrades to continue the attack. Petrified faces with wide open eyes and screaming mouths. Piles of bodies were heaped on the barbed wire, hauling it to the ground with their weight, clearing a way to the Nazi trenches [filled with Romanians, not Germans]. One's mind could not grasp the scene, failing to accept the frozen composition as a fact of life. It seemed as if someone might suddenly switch the camera back on, the freeze-frame would start moving.

During that night the first snow falls.

When morning comes, the flat terrain is silent and still, virginal in its purity, all traces of the events covered by a soft, white blanket. It was as if the terrible scenes of yesterday had never happened.

Much later Mansur Abdulin learns that his battalion was never expected "to take control of the enemy's defensive installations." The purpose of the attack was to discover where the enemy had its heavy weaponry, strongpoints and minefields. This was standard procedure in the Red Army before a major attack.* The 1034th Rifle Regiment was just the bait—it was an expendable item.

---

* So much so that the German army came to regard this kind of attack as a clear indication that a major assault was to be expected within twenty-four hours. The Red Army had now begun making changes in this respect too: the generals still considered that cynical and bloody operations of this kind were a necessary pre-liminary to a major assault, but had started to recognize that the risk of warning the enemy diminished if the major operations did not follow immediately after the smaller attacks. The attack of November 14 was part of the preparation for Operation Uranus.

. . .

The following day in Stalingrad, Adelbert Holl receives a pleasing
piece of news. Some time ago he was told he was to be sent to the infantry combat school outside Berlin-Döberitz on a month's posting,
which includes permission to visit his family for Christmas. It could
hardly be better. Like many soldiers at the front, he has become a convinced fatalist: God or fate or luck will decide where and how he dies
and there is no point in complaining about it—which is why there is
no point in dwelling on death or fallen comrades.

He knows the many manifestations death takes, and he has no hesitation about killing. Rather the reverse. There have been occasions
when he's gone out of his own accord on private sniping expeditions
in the muddle of ruins simply to pick off enemy soldiers—hardly a
proper thing for a company commander to do. Perhaps he is one of
those people who find it easy to kill, are attracted by it even. Pretty
well everyone has killed someone in battle, so it's not something that
gets talked about.

Holl's attitude is simple: you obey orders and refrain from too much
thinking. But of course he wants to go home—he and his wife, Ilse,
haven't seen one another since the summer, and he loves her very
much. The commanding officer of the regiment informs Holl that he'll
be allowed to leave Stalingrad on November 25, which is just ten days
away.

He scarcely registers the news that the Americans have landed in
North Africa—"I did not have time to muse over these wider questions." A letter he receives that same day has more of an impact in that
it tells him that several old friends he grew up with in Duisburg are
dead, gone down on the same U-boat.

. . .

That Sunday, the church bells are ringing all over London in celebration of the victory at el-Alamein. That's new; the last time something
like this was done was at the end of the First World War. It makes Vera
Brittain frown. Brittain does, of course, follow the detailed reports in
the papers and on the wireless about what is happening in North Africa
and she has to admit, a touch reluctantly, that something big is going on
there, something decisive even. But she finds the whole business with
the church bells "childish" and wrong, not just because it is Churchill's

idea (she has an instinctive dislike of Churchill), but because she cannot separate the victory from the price that has been paid, both there and here at home. No, the only thing worth celebrating will be the end of the war.

In the afternoon she attends a meeting in Muswell Hill in north London. Brittain is an experienced public speaker and she has made hundreds of appearances over the years, both in Great Britain and in the United States. She gives a reading of several things at the meeting, including from *Humiliation with Honour.* It all goes well, but she feels a cold coming on.

During the night Brittain is so congested she could hardly breathe, and she's plagued by peculiar nightmares all night. She stays in bed in the morning until Amy, her home help, comes in and makes her breakfast. There's a letter in the morning mail from her U.S. publisher. He explains at length that he, too, has decided *not* to publish *Humiliation with Honour.* The date is Monday, November 16.

·   ·   ·

Late autumn in Międzyrzec Podlaski. Danuta and Józek Fijalkowski are in the process of setting up home in the house on Warszawska Road. She does the unpacking, arranging and organizing while he does bits of repair work and looks after their little boy, Jędruś. She talks to the neighbors, but he mostly stays indoors. Something has changed in their relationships and in their roles.

He is ten years older, stable, experienced, serious and intelligent, with his round glasses and slicked-back hair; she is girlishly naïve, small, pretty and vain. Her mother with her beauty salon had always been quick to encourage this and she really is good-looking with her blond hair, clean, open features, high cheekbones and almost perfect profile. Could this in some way have contributed to his salvation? Józek and others may have thought of her earlier as a bit "childish," but, then, she was the one who against all probability, the system and logic managed to get him freed from Auschwitz.

Danuta refused to accept Józek's being locked up and carted off to a camp, so, in the firm belief that he had done nothing wrong and therefore shouldn't be imprisoned, she started working to get him freed. It hadn't dawned on her at this point that this wasn't the normal way of going about things and this wasn't a normal war; in fact, a certain level of naivety probably helped her in this. So she spent a lot of her time—tirelessly, fearlessly and well-coiffed—petitioning amid the labyrinth of corridors, offices and Gothic-script acronyms of the occupying power. And she wrote letter after letter to every imaginable individual and authority: all of them, including Adolf Hitler.

What then happened may be summarized as follows: In one of her letters to Józek (Prisoner No. 3088, Block 12, KL Auschwitz), Danuta writes that she'd like to send him a photo of the newborn child. In his answer of August 31, 1941, he writes that she "may not send any photographs directly to me...." Danuta fixes on the word "directly." She composes a request to be permitted to send photos, attaches two of them, and sends everything to the commandant of the camp, SS-Sturmbannführer Rudolf Höss. Józek is called to interrogation. Höss questions him about why he was arrested and Józek answers in his perfect German. Höss drums his fingers on his desk. (It's the same desk, incidentally, at which he is dutifully, pedantically and with techno-cratic coolness drawing up plans to convert his camp into an industrial killing machine.) Höss allows Józek to look at but not touch the two photos. There is a pause. Höss orders Józek to be sent into "quarantine." Józek has an idea what that means and, surprised, raises his eyes from the floor where they had previously been fixed out of fear and subservi-ence. Höss stares back, with deep-set, expressionless eyes. During the following time, Józek is put through both medical tests and a kind of political checkup to ensure that he will continue to be "a loyal servant of the Third Reich." On January 19 Józek is signed out of Auschwitz with forty-five Reichsmarks in his pocket and an Entlassungsschein, a release certificate, covered in stamps, in his hand.

Why? Could it have anything to do with the letter? Danuta has a neighbor, Mrs. Sowínska, who is a German speaker and is one of those who had herself registered as Volksdeutsche, with all the privileges that brings. Mrs. Sowínska helped Danuta write the letter, which is phrased in an almost literary High German. In addition to that, Józek himself speaks German like a native. Furthermore, both Danuta and Józek are blond and have blue eyes. Furthermore again, Danuta is particularly good-looking. In Jósek, did Höss see a racially pure German in the making?*

---

* The "Germanization" of the annexed areas was not always practiced with the kind of pseudoscientific precision the fanatical ideologists of race proposed. In the Reichsgau Danzig-Westpreussen, skulls weren't measured and noses and eye

Or was it, perhaps, just a sentimental whim? Prompted by the photo of the young and beautiful mother with her small child? Quite a few functionaries like Höss can sometimes show sudden signs of sentimentality when faced with children, animals, nature, art and, most of all, music. This isn't an anomaly; it's an important part of their psychopathology.

Their sentimentality is self-centered. It proves to themselves and to others that in spite of the inhuman actions they perform or cause to be performed, they remain, at heart, feeling human beings. In their own eyes, this—along with the absence of explicitly hate-filled attitudes towards their victims—absolves them of moral responsibility. We can imagine that Höss felt pleased with himself when he went home to his wife and three children later that day.

Without Danuta's indefatigable efforts, Józek would probably have been a dead man by this point. She was made by the same unforeseen circumstances that broke him. He has remained the passive party and she is now the active one. In the village they lived in over the summer, her courage and newly acquired ability to navigate through the impenetrable German bureaucracy has made "the lady from Warsaw," as she is respectfully known, a popular person, particularly among the farmers of the district.

German economic exploitation was draconian even in the Polish rural areas. There were exact quotas of agricultural products that had to be handed over to the German authorities without payment, and, in the worst scenarios, those unable to deliver were threatened with the death sentence. When people ran into problems, they would turn to Danuta to speak for them. "She manages to release one farmer from the milk quota, another farmer from the potato quota; she arranges for permission to buy building materials for one family and fertilizers for another." And her reward for this came *in rerum natura*. There are times when she is the one who, in practical terms, supports them, while he has learned how to do the cooking and washing.

In Warsaw, they had sometimes danced the tango in their small apartment to the sound of their portable gramophone. Do they do the same here in these dark November days in the Warszawska Road house, or do they wait until Jędruś has gone to sleep?

———

color weren't registered, and there was no checking of ancestry; anyone who felt they were German in that area was considered to be German, irrespective of hair color or name.

•   •   •

Elena Skrjabina is still in occupied Pyatigorsk at this point and the
mood is still a strange one. On one hand there is a muted fear about
what might happen, on the other an almost desperate longing for normality. On Sunday, November 15, she writes in her diary:

> The theatre is open, always full. One has to order tickets two
> weeks in advance. We don't have this last problem, since the
> entire Radlovsky Theater is at our place almost every day and
> we get so many complimentary tickets that we can even give
> them to our friends.

A small theatre with musical comedies, and, at the same time, fear of
what might happen if Soviet partisans should turn up and take it into
their heads to kill a German, even an insignificant German. She has
heard rumors of the unparalleled brutality the Germans resort to in
those cases—most recently in a town in the Ukraine, where they even
shot children. In Elena Skrjabina's eyes, the partisans are "terrorists"
who endanger her children's lives.

•   •   •

John McEniry is woken as usual at half past three, on the morning of
Sunday, November 15. He crawls out of his sleeping bag and walks
in the darkness with his fellow airmen across the big runway to the
squadron mess. There they are given their orders for the day's operations and served a simple breakfast—"powdered eggs, which none
of us could eat, one slice of bread, jelly, and coffee with no sugar or
cream."

As soon as it starts getting light, they take off from Guadalcanal
once more, John McEniry in a new, heavily laden dive-bomber. Their
target is the four Japanese transport vessels which are all that's left of
the large convoy, and which have been run aground farther up the coast
in a quite clearly desperate attempt to get the troops and stores ashore.

One of McEniry's colleagues thinks their attacks on these freighters
in the last couple of days have been a bit unpleasant, as the decks are
packed with soldiers and the dive-bomber pilots are able to see through
their telescopic sights exactly how much damage their heavy machine

guns inflict on the tightly packed crowds of people. If McEniry feels the same way, it is not something he mentions.

He gets an excellent hit on one of the ships that is still unloading its cargo. When a 550-pound bomb hits a ship, "stuff"—as one of the pilots in the unit puts it—are thrown 500 feet into the air. Then they use their machine guns to spray the soldiers on the shore or among the coconut palms. Afterwards, McEniry makes a note in his diary: "Must have killed hundreds." Once again, exact details escape them, but they all recognize they have taken part in something big, possibly decisive.*

. . .

That same Sunday, which had dawned with so much joy and hope for Tohichi Wakabayashi on Guadalcanal, ends in stoic sorrow. He has received news that two of his friends have just been killed there. One of them, Arioka from Kagoshima, fell during a counterattack— Wakabayashi hears that he had charged into a hail of bullets from American automatic weapons with his samurai sword drawn "saying he hates every one of the damned enemy"—a hero's death in every minute, theatrical detail. The second death was an old acquaintance and drinking companion from his years at the cadet school, a second lieutenant, Kojima, whom he hasn't seen since the war in southern China in 1940.

Wakabayashi is no ordinary career officer. Born as the second son to a family of modest resources in a beautiful but not very affluent part of Honshu, and with a restless youth behind him, he joined the army in 1933 as a simple private. The military academy was not open to him as he had earlier been convicted of a number of petty crimes. Wakabayashi has, nevertheless, worked his way up step-by-step and achieved top grades.

He is described as an intelligent man, not without an artistic temperament, charming, courageous, a little restless. He's in good shape

---

* In practical terms, the interception of the great convoy of reinforcements meant that the Japanese lost the battle for Guadalcanal; had it gotten through in one piece, they would probably have been victorious. Almost everyone understood that. The progress of the convoy over those days was consequently being followed with close attention—even in the White House. James Vincent Forrestal, FDR's secretary of the navy, reported later that the only time they suffered the same degree of trepidation was the night prior to D-day in 1944.

physically and is a talented sportsman. He has a reputation for being especially good at dealing with difficult recruits—so much so that such cases are often passed on to him.*

He has belonged to the 228th Infantry Regiment since 1940, a well-equipped, well-trained and experienced body of men.† He has been with them from the deadlock in China in 1940 and then during the successful attack on Hong Kong in December 1941: his regiment stormed burning Kowloon, not without problems and losses, and played a key role in the fall of the city. Most recently, he took part in the successful operations in the Dutch East Indies.

So what has Wakabayashi seen or done during these years, and what effect have these experiences had on him? He makes no mention of the massacres of prisoners of war and civilians his division had undoubtedly been involved in—time after time—during the last year. It is, of course, impossible to tell whether the silence signifies disapproval or acceptance or even something worse. He believes in the greatness of Japan and he believes in Japan's cause and in this war—and he believes all the grand talk of the creation of a new East Asia, freed from white colonialism and corrupt liberalism: a new multiethnic coalition of Asian nations and races united under the firm hand of Japan.‡

A solid foundation of emotions underlies this ideological superstructure. (One of the most unavoidable and even attractive effects of living in a war situation is that it both sharpens and simplifies one's emotions.) What Wakabayashi was brimming with when he landed on Guadalcanal ten days before was the self-confidence, the aggressiveness and the lack of doubt that the repeated experience of great

---

* We shouldn't be in any doubt that Wakabayashi, just like other Japanese officers, beat his subordinates, abused them even, but that's not the whole story. His own checkered background gave him insights and a psychological finesse the other officers lacked; this showed itself in genuine care for those under him.

† They were part of the 38th Division, which was categorized by the Japanese army as Category B, which meant it was equipped for combat in difficult terrain but nevertheless equipped with extra artillery and light—very light—tanks.

‡ The concept of the "Greater East Asia Co-Prosperity Sphere" met with a not inconsiderable response here and there, though gradually the majority came to see that it was nothing but a Trojan horse for Japanese imperialism, and that Japanese racism could be at least as unpleasant as the white version.

victories nourishes. Up to this point, the Japanese army has conquered all and everything it has met. Why should that not continue?

At the same time, though, Wakabayashi is sensitive enough to notice details and pick up a sense of atmosphere. The fact that both Arioka and Kojima have fallen shows, in a symbolic sense if in no other, that this is not going to be as easy as many have assumed. For at the same time as he is vowing to avenge Arioka, he and his soldiers are spending most of their time staying low in the jungle so as not to attract the attention of the enemy aircraft he has come to hate with such vehemence.

When Wakabayashi comes closer to the coast, he can see two of the transport vessels in the distance. Both have been run ashore and both are on fire: thick black smoke is rising from them. He writes in his diary: "It's sad, but I guess it is inevitable."

. . .

That same Sunday, Paolo Caccia Dominioni and the rest of his battalion reach Sirte. El-Alamein lies far behind them, as do Mersa Matruh, Sidi Barrani, Sollum, Bardia, Tobruk, Gazala, Benghazi and el-Agheila. It's a damp, grey dawn by the seashore and the soldiers are lighting a fire to cook breakfast. Caccia Dominioni is shivering. He looks out over the leaden sea. The sky and the water look the same color; the only patches of light are the columns of white foam that rise when heavy waves break against the rocks or on the wreck of a ship lying there, twisted and shattered. There's a cold wind coming from the northwest.

An old Bedouin approaches them. The man doesn't speak any Italian so Caccia Dominioni greets him in Arabic and asks him what he wants. He's just another beggar, begging for bread and cigarettes, of course, but Caccia Dominioni is curious about him because there is something proud in the old man's bearing and something intriguing about his words. "Even when we occupied Libya thirty-one years ago, he was already too old to learn the language of the invaders. But he is a wise man—a Socrates of the desert." And the two of them talk.

Caccia Dominioni asks him what he thinks of everything going on around him. A short way down the coast road, in the milky dawn light, a British Hurricane roars low overhead spraying machine-gun bullets as it goes. The old man says nothing for some time, his gaze wandering

over the Italian's head and away over the dark sea. Then he answers
with a single word: *Takfir.*

Takfir may be translated as "penance," paying for one's sins.* Caccia
Dominioni writes in his diary:

> This harsh and monstrous word seems to fill everything
> around me when the old man goes off. There is *takfir* in the
> low clouds, in the column of black smoke rising after the Hur-
> ricane has swept past, in the reddened body of a soldier lying
> face down in the dirt by his burned-out truck. Everything is
> *takfir* now—all the innumerable, innocent people who have
> been sacrificed for the will, ambition and hunger for power
> of a handful of men—like a curse, in this war and every other
> war.

---

* Nowadays, the term has been hijacked by Islamists, who have turned it into a
concept justifying the murder of Muslims not considered to be living according
to the word of the Koran.

area wur

It is the night between November 15 and 16 and British Bomber Command is once more bombing Genoa. Their Lancaster bomber is ED311 "K-King," the replacement for R5673 "L-London," the shattered remnants of which currently lie somewhere down there in the city far below them. The crew consists of the machine-gunner John Bushby and the rest of the seven-man crew: Bill, the pilot with the big, waxed moustache and the long, knitted scarf, sociable but controlled and gifted with natural authority; Wally, the other gunner, a thin Londoner, "cool and competent" in his work, but something of an outsider in this otherwise tight-knit group; Charley, the wireless operator, a taciturn young man from Liverpool; Davey, the best navigator in the squadron, sociable, easy to get on with, "unflurried and unruffled under fire"; Bish, the bombardier, with a sardonic but warm sense of humor, competent, "entirely unflappable," which is not the easiest thing to be, given that few people are ever in such an exposed position, both physically and psychologically, as bombardiers when they are flying in a straight line across the target area, through an illuminated curtain of searchlights and exploding shells while lying on their bellies and adjusting their sights in the small, Perspex acrylic bubble right at the front of the plane; Tommy, the flight engineer, "a gentle soul, originating from up in Northumberland," the youngest of them, popular, but the only one who shows signs that the mental stress is beginning to bite.

They drop their blindingly bright target indicators and their bombs, and then they turn away from a city so cloaked in smoke and explosions that it's difficult to make a precise estimate of the damage. The port of Genoa has been hit, but so have many of the residential areas

(which are targeted quite consciously) and the historic center of the
city, with its churches, cathedrals, palace and monument. Including
tonight's raid, 936 tons of bombs have been dropped on Genoa in less
than a month.*

We can assume that the mood on board is one of relief, cheerful
even. For once, it has been a "milk run" for them, rather than the usual
getting through one more difficult mission—an experience that often
leaves them feeling relieved but with a bitter aftertaste. This time, however, they have had the rare experience of a mission with minimal risks
and similarly minimal losses. For the last three weeks, Bomber Command has been attacking various cities in the north of Italy and, compared with Germany, these are easy targets, almost defenseless. The
blackout on the ground is sloppy, there is no radar, few night fighters,
no great number of searchlights and meagre anti-aircraft defenses—
and by the time the bombers are dropping their loads, the anti-aircraft
guns have stopped firing.

Bushby and the crew have to withstand the cold and possibly some
tedium, since the flight there and back takes eight hours. The plane
does, however, have a portable chemical toilet—an Elsan, painted
green, located at the rear of the plane: the fact that many of them are
scarcely more than overgrown schoolboys means that they never tire
of jokes about "the Elsan."

When they reach England, their airfield is covered by a thick blanket
of low autumn clouds and they are redirected to a different airfield,
where they come close to crashing as a result of too high a landing
speed. Tommy, whether from tiredness or distracted by something,
forgot to lower the flaps. They circle and prepare for a second attempt,
only to miss by a hair's breadth colliding in the darkness with another
bomber that has flown in below them on their approach. Their third
attempt, however, is successful.

* The material damage was enormous: 1,996 buildings were completely or
almost completely destroyed; 1,249 were only partially habitable; 4,438 suffered
light damage but were still habitable. About one-third of Genoa was destroyed
in a short time. The harbor, perhaps the most important military target, was
struck, too, but it quickly returned to full use. The numbers killed were relatively
small, about 500, mainly because there were various tunnel systems under the
city which provided good shelter. The shock was great, however. King Victor
Emmanuel III visited the city, which, at this date, was the hardest hit in the whole
of Italy.

NOVEMBER 16–22

It Can Be Called the Turning Point

"Anything can happen at any given moment. No decision is ever final: it may be sharpened, changed, replaced by a later decree. The worst thing about dictatorship is its arbitrariness."

"It is the war of the people, of all the people. And it must be fought not only on the battlefield but in the towns and villages, in the factories and on the farms, in the home and in the heart of every man, woman and child who loves freedom."

"It would not be easy to survive in this hell, but it would be a hundred times harder to remain a human being."

It is the night between November 15 and 16 and British Bomber Command is once more bombing Genoa. Their Lancaster bomber is ED311 "K-King," the replacement for R5673 "L-London," the shattered remnants of which currently lie somewhere down there in the city far below them. The crew consists of the machine-gunner John Bushby and the rest of the seven-man crew: Bill, the pilot with the big, waxed moustache and the long, knitted scarf, sociable but controlled and gifted with natural authority; Wally, the other gunner, a thin Londoner, "cool and competent" in his work, but something of an outsider in this otherwise tight-knit group; Charley, the wireless operator, a taciturn young man from Liverpool; Davey, the best navigator in the squadron, sociable, easy to get on with, "unflurried and unruffled under fire"; Bish, the bombardier, with a sardonic but warm sense of humor, competent, "entirely unflappable," which is not the easiest thing to be, given that few people are ever in such an exposed position, both physically and psychologically, as bombardiers when they are flying in a straight line across the target area, through an illuminated curtain of searchlights and exploding shells while lying on their bellies and adjusting their sights in the small, Perspex acrylic bubble right at the front of the plane; Tommy, the flight engineer, "a gentle soul, originating from up in Northumberland," the youngest of them, popular, but the only one who shows signs that the mental stress is beginning to bite.

They drop their blindingly bright target indicators and their bombs, and then they turn away from a city so cloaked in smoke and explosions that it's difficult to make a precise estimate of the damage. The port of Genoa has been hit, but so have many of the residential areas (which are targeted quite consciously) and the historic center of the city, with its churches, cathedrals, palace and monument. Including tonight's raid, 936 tons of bombs have been dropped on Genoa in less than a month.*

We can assume that the mood on board is one of relief, cheerful even. For once, it has been a "milk run" for them, rather than the usual getting through one more difficult mission—an experience that often leaves them feeling relieved but with a bitter aftertaste. This time, however, they have had the rare experience of a mission with minimal risks and similarly minimal losses. For the last three weeks, Bomber Command has been attacking various cities in the north of Italy and, compared with Germany, these are easy targets, almost defenseless. The blackout on the ground is sloppy, there is no radar, few night fighters, no great number of searchlights and meagre anti-aircraft defenses— and by the time the bombers are dropping their loads, the anti-aircraft guns have stopped firing.

Bushby and the crew have to withstand the cold and possibly some tedium, since the flight there and back takes eight hours. The plane does, however, have a portable chemical toilet—an Elsan, painted green, located at the rear of the plane: the fact that many of them are scarcely more than overgrown schoolboys means that they never tire of jokes about "the Elsan."

When they reach England, their airfield is covered by a thick blanket of low autumn clouds and they are redirected to a different airfield, where they come close to crashing as a result of too high a landing speed. Tommy, whether from tiredness or distracted by something, forgot to lower the flaps. They circle and prepare for a second attempt, only to miss by a hair's breadth colliding in the darkness with another bomber that has flown in below them on their approach. Their third attempt, however, is successful.

---

* The material damage was enormous: 1,996 buildings were completely or almost completely destroyed; 1,249 were only partially habitable; 4,438 suffered light damage but were still habitable. About one-third of Genoa was destroyed in a short time. The harbor, perhaps the most important military target, was struck, too, but it quickly returned to full use. The numbers killed were relatively small, about 500, mainly because there were various tunnel systems under the city which provided good shelter. The shock was great, however. King Victor Emmanuel III visited the city, which, at this date, was the hardest hit in the whole of Italy.

Stiff and weary, Bushby, Bill, Wally, Charley, Davey, Bish and Tommy can return to Wyton and go to bed in the small wooden barracks hut with its seven beds. Maybe they'll go to the pub that evening once they have all woken up. Maybe Bill will plonk himself down again at the old mess-hall piano that is sticky with beer while Bushby and the rest of them, "with full lung power and red faces," join in and sing the songs, "some cleverly obscene, some obscene for obscenity's sake."

Then, later, they go to the chief of the ground crew and take back the farewell letters they routinely give him before every mission. On this particular Monday, none of the letters needs mailing, neither from their unit nor from any of the others: for the second night in succession, not a single one of their planes has been shot down. A small bomb is always painted on the plane to signify a completed mission, but these raids are considered so easy that a stylized ice-cream cone is painted on instead.*

. . .

The men of U-604 call the grand mansion Schloss Chateauneuf, though its proper name is Château de Trévarez. It was requisitioned last year and is now a place where naval personnel can rest and recuperate. With its pinnacles, its towers and its battlements, as well as an enormous garden, it looks like a Renaissance castle straight out of a fairy tale. In fact, it is actually a redbrick, romantic, historical fake and barely forty years old.

It's no accident that this is where U-boat crews are sent to rest: it's in an out-of-the-way location, a good hour southeast of Brest. Letting them remain in Brest would involve some risks: the British have been bombing the city since March last year, targeting the big U-boat pens in particular. They have not had much success but, to avoid unnecessary losses, the U-boat crews are bussed out of Brest as quickly as possible.

There are other risks, however. Brest, being an old seaport, can offer

* "The Italian Blitz," the bombing of Italy, was coordinated with the Allied counteroffensive in North Africa. The aim was to weaken the resolve of the Italian civilian population to continue the war—and that was achieved. It is, in fact, the only example we have of strategic bombing functioning according to plan; the main reason, however, was that it clearly revealed the incompetence of the fascist regime and its inability to protect its own citizens.

a rich range of temptations for young seamen—cafés, bars, dance halls and, not least, brothels. There are, of course, the strictly controlled field brothels run by the military authorities* (including one housed in what until recently was a synagogue), and the standard fee is three marks for fifteen minutes. The U-boat crews, like all Germans in uniform, are forbidden to have sex with any French women other than those employed in these establishments, and there are harsh punishments for anyone who gets infected with a venereal disease. Now it is considered to be "cowardice in the face of the enemy" and can lead to ten years' hard labor. But cases of venereal diseases and general dissolute living have continued in spite of that, and there is the problem that U-boat crews, once ashore, want to live like pirates—having a riotous time drinking, brawling and smashing things up. That is why the grand isolation of places like the Château de Trévarez has been set up.

So the idea is that the forty or so young men from U-604 should spend ten days there, resting quietly and occupying themselves with sporting and cultural activities. The food is superb—men in the U-boat service are always particularly well-fed in comparison with everyone else.† And there is also a well-stocked wine cellar—and women: the crews have "unlimited access" to both.

It is now the middle of November.

Towards the end of the month, U-604 will put to sea again.

. . .

Camp No. 5, outside Batavia on Java. It is Sunday, November 15, and a church service is being held in the shade of the coconut palms. But Weary Dunlop's mind is elsewhere—he is thinking of Helen Ferguson, his girlfriend. They met during their time at the University of Melbourne and finally got engaged two years ago. Like many others at that time and of their generation, the war forced them apart. There have

---

* There are about a hundred official field brothels in France this year.
† That was one of Admiral Karl Dönitz's ways of boosting the combat morale of his men. Another way was to present them with valuable secondhand watches of dubious provenance—they probably came from gassed Jews. Also, when at sea, the men wore soft, warm, felt-like stockings made of woven animal hair—few people knew that human hair from the gas chambers was also used. The hair was packed in fifty-five-pound bales and sold to interested businesses for twenty-five pfennigs a kilo. This grotesque material was made by the German car-parts company Schaeffler, which had a special factory three hours from Auschwitz.

been lengthy periods when they have kept their relationship alive by constant letter-writing, but even that is impossible now. Does she even know that he is still alive?

It is the little things that remind Dunlop of her: a beautiful sunrise, a song, a date in the calendar. He writes in his diary:

> Poor darling, I don't know how she can stand these long dreary years of waiting at home. If she packs up and marries an American or something I suppose it would be best for her, but I don't know what I would do with my life then. She is the only stable thing left in life—the only thing which enables me to see anything to look forward to in peace. Somehow, peace has been spoiled for me.

.   .   .

It's the middle of November and Keith Douglas's regiment is still located outside Mersa Matruh. They need to rest and to be given reinforcements, both in terms of new tanks and of men. (Sixteen of the twenty-two officers in the regiment have been killed or wounded.)

Rumors are flying and, as usual, many of them are merely wishful thinking interpreted as fact. Perhaps they will take part in the advance on Tunisia. Maybe they'll be sent to Syria or India. Or back to Great Britain. Or take part in a major landing in the south of France. Or perhaps it will be just as the colonel told them in his speech before the big attack on November 2: others would be left to chase the defeated Germans and Italians, whereas they would be sent back to Cairo to bathe, go to bars, enjoy themselves and sleep in proper beds. (Incidentally, the colonel had only escaped death by the skin of his teeth during the battle for Mersa the week before: a shell hit his tank, killing his driver, his gunner and his loader, leaving him as the sole survivor. Some people reckoned you could see his nerves were on edge. In spite of that, he's just as popular as he was before.) But there's great excitement. What if...? What if...?

While waiting to get news, they play football, bathe in the sea, do gymnastics, listen to uplifting speeches, attend religious services, service their tanks, go off to do some casual looting, quarrel, laugh, sleep, eat and drink. The whole regiment suffers from severe stomachaches. Douglas's squadron has set up an improvised officers' mess on the back of a three-ton truck, where they gorge themselves on wine, cigars,

cigarettes, chocolate, cherries, canned fruit, sliced meat, cocoa and
ersatz German coffee, which Douglas thinks is excellent. They have
also seized a load of white flour, so cherry tarts are on the menu morning, noon and night.

Down in the harbor one day, Douglas meets a friend and rival from
Alexandria. Douglas finds the encounter painful. The friend is wearing *her* necklace around his neck. When they were last in Alexandria,
both of them courted the same young woman, Milena—warm, dark,
striking, and as polyglot and cosmopolitan as her amazing city with
its "five races, five languages and a dozen religions." (She speaks fluent
Arabic, French and Italian, and English with an accent Douglas calls
"absurd.") She also looks good in a swimsuit.

He had fallen hopelessly in love and for a while it looked as if his
love was reciprocated. They went to bathing beaches and cafés, had a
good time at dance restaurants and cocktail bars, and she introduced
him to her parents; he wrote love poems for her and sketched her in a
state of undress.

But her love for him cooled and, even worse, this friend has taken
his place in Milena's bed. It's a disaster that Douglas cannot forget and,
as the poet he is, he tries to work his failure and, above all, his sexual
jealousy into a poem—"I Listen to the Desert Wind," which includes
the following lines:

> *Like a bird my sleepless eye*
> *Skims the cold sands who now deny*
> *the violent heat they have by day*
> *as she denies her former way*
> *all the elements agree*
> *with her, to have no sympathy*
> *for my impertinent misery*
> *as wonderful and hard as she.*
> *O turn in the dark bed again*
> *and give to him what once was mine*
> *and I'll turn as you turn*
> *and kiss my swarthy mistress Pain.*

How real is the war, in fact, in comparison with such unhappiness—a
distraction, just a backdrop? Even before the relationship crashed, he
had threatened—in a fit of male self-pity—to seek his death at the

front if she ever left him. It was, perhaps, with those thoughts at the back of his mind that he'd left his post on divisional staff before the battle in order to rejoin the regiment. Perhaps that was why he found it so easy to risk his life. Was his mood actually one of sublimated depression?

At this moment Douglas recalls with crushing exactness the scene in the restaurant when Milena broke up with him. He recalls her bored expression, her look of increasing indifference to him and his words, her gaze drifting off down the street; and he remembers her whispering, "Don't make a scene, please, Keith; people are looking at us."

His friend offers him cigars and grog, made of gin and orange juice. Douglas drinks, copiously, and the sorrow and pain and thoughts and memories of Milena gradually fade. When he returns to the regiment, he is blind drunk.

.   .   .

Food is the usual topic of conversation when people meet on the street. Anne Somerhausen in Brussels frequently greets people with a cheerful, "And have you eaten your daily herring?" Food. That is probably what occupies her mind much of her time. She tries counting her three children's calories. How many are they getting? How many do they need? The two older ones don't seem to be growing as they should and she assumes that to be a result of deficiencies in their diet. (It's a known fact that puberty is delayed for many children and it's thought that this has to do with their nourishment.)* For a long time, her seven-year-old grew thinner and thinner and more and more unhealthy, with strange boils on his body, but after staying with a well-off family in Lessines for a month he has regained the weight he lost and feels much better.

They are now on their way into the third winter of the war and the food situation actually looks better than it did both in 1940, when things were really dreadful, and 1941.† She has plenty of potatoes in

---

* There is a steep rise in certain diseases, including TB. At the same time, diseases arising from an affluent lifestyle (being overweight, for instance) have diminished radically.

† The supply problem was particularly acute in Belgium since 50 percent or more of foodstuffs were imported before the war. In defense of the German occupying administration, it has to be said that they genuinely did work to improve

the cellar and, like many other people, she has converted her backyard into a vegetable garden, where she grows white cabbage, red cabbage, green cabbage and Brussels sprouts. And her pantry is full of unusual quantities of herring.

The war has led to many remarkable and unexpected results. In the same way as the absence of private cars means that Brussels's air is much healthier than it has been for years, the elimination of many factories means that many Belgian rivers are cleaner. Fish have started to return to them. And since much of the commercial fishing fleet was knocked out in the previous years, herring numbers have recovered and they are shoaling in amazing quantities: boats prepared to face the dangers and risk sailing out along the coast have harvested record catches.

So they end up eating herring every day, both lunch and dinner. "Salted, in vinegar, fried, cooked in white wine, pickled, coated in pseudo-mayonnaise, rollmops [a variety of pickled herring], mashed," she writes in her diary, "herring, herring, herring." After dinner, she and the boys clean the herring, cook the fillets or place them in a barrel, "layer upon layer of slippery, gleaming silvery fish, covered in sparkling white salt." Their favorite dish, however, is bread pudding. Somerhausen's recipe: 1. Crumble the sad, greyish brown, rationed bread. 2. Soak it in a mixture of milk and egg. 3. Stir in dried orange peel. 4. Bake in the oven for about half an hour. 5. Sprinkle with sugar and eat.

Somerhausen is getting by. Her pay as an office worker won't stretch far enough, especially since, like everyone else, she has to buy much of what she needs—butter, milk, eggs—on the black market.* She finds herself selling off things she owns, most recently a couple of paintings, a vacuum cleaner, her husband's portable Corona typewriter,† and she rents out rooms. Currently, she has two ladies from Iraq and a young German couple. The husband is an electrician and away during the week: he is one of the growing number of workmen building bunkers

---

the supply situation by, for instance, promoting a large-scale change from meat production to vegetable production.

* "Everyone else" is not an exaggeration. Few countries had such a widespread (and tolerated) black market as Belgium. Even the German armed forces made major transactions on the black market and attempts to charge individual marketeers often failed because they were under German protection.

† Vacuum cleaners and typewriters could command high secondhand prices in Germany since the factories that had produced such goods were now producing war materiel instead.

and fortifications all along the coast, and he is obviously well-paid. In addition, he has been issued with almost double food rations.

The German couple have moved into the room that Somerhausen used to let to a Jewish woman, a desperately anxious refugee from Austria (Anne's diary refers to her cryptically as "Mlle. V"), but she disappeared last August, as did many other Jews—the elderly woman who used to make her blouses, for instance. It's becoming much less common now to see anyone on the street wearing a yellow star.

So the problem of food is not the worst thing. It's the uncertainty. She writes in her diary: "Anything can happen at any given moment. No German decision is ever final: it may be sharpened, changed, replaced by a later decree. The worst thing about dictatorship is its arbitrariness."

Brussels is grey, dark and cold. The pavement is stained with wet leaves. There is a new and unusual feeling of threat in the air. There has been an assassination.

·   ·   ·

It's an ordinary squash court located in the basement of the empty west stands of the University of Chicago football stadium at Stagg Field. She knows the building well, with its crenelated façade and neo-Gothic windows, because she used to play there. The entrance faces Ellis Avenue, but access is now forbidden: deep inside the labyrinth of corridors there are now armed guards who check that only those with a special pass are allowed in. She is one of them. Her name is Leona Woods and she is a twenty-three-year-old research student in physics.

Over the course of the last year, she has become an ever more solitary figure in the department. Many of her male doctoral students have either been called up or disappeared to do various kinds of essential war work in industry. Things might well have stayed like that if Leona Woods hadn't had the summer habit of swimming in Lake Michigan at five o'clock every afternoon. She is intelligent, modest and tall, athletic in disposition and in physique.

During her swimming sessions, she has gotten to know Herbert Anderson, another physicist of the same research generation as her. (There is also a quiet Italian among the swimmers: his name is Enrico Fermi, a man in early middle age, whom she immediately recognized as the famous Nobel Prize winner who was forced to flee the dictatorship in Italy, his homeland, a few years earlier.) Anderson discovered that Leona Woods had some special insights into vacuum technology and, consequently, he has recruited her to a top secret project he and Fermi are leading at the university—it has been given the nondescript name Metallurgical Laboratory. (That, in turn, was part of a larger organization with an equally nondescript title: Manhattan Engineer District.) Her principal duty is to build and manage a measurement instrument of a hitherto unknown kind capable of measuring neutron activity. She was also tasked with keeping the minutes during Fermi's briefings to the research group.

November 16 is an ordinary winter's day in Chicago. It starts off mild but the temperature drops quickly during the afternoon. The squash court is unheated and the change in the weather makes itself felt among the people gathered down there, who are either wearing laboratory coats or overalls. Fermi is directing the work from a position up on the small spectator stand on one of the long walls. Using a rope and tackle, they hoist a strange, light grey cube made of balloon fabric, a cube that almost fills the area. The bottom lies flat on the floor, the upper part is fastened to the roof, three of the sides are attached to the walls, and the fourth—the one pointing to the stand—is rolled up.

Someone draws a circle on the bottom and then men in overalls* start pushing oblong, polished black blocks into the small hall on slides. The blocks are carefully fitted tightly together under the bright electric light. Once the circle has been filled, another layer of blocks is placed on top of the first—a layer that is slightly larger than the previous one. The work is time-consuming as the layers are held in place by a framework of precisely matched pieces of wood that lead out to the hanging balloon fabric. There are no detailed drawings, but there is a carpenter measuring things on the spot and then going to the adjoining room where he cuts the pieces with a circular saw. (Another of Leona Wood's responsibilities is to obtain large quantities of wood of a standardized diameter. She finds it at Sterling's Timberyard, where her orders have been met with some surprise, not because her purchases are strange in themselves, but because she produces an official document stating that these orders are of the "highest priority" and should be dealt with before everything else. Timber?)

---

* Most of the manual work was done by thirty or so young "high school dropouts" who had taken this as temporary work while waiting for call-up.

The work continues until the cold of evening, when the night shift takes over. Leona Woods has probably gone home by that point. She shares an apartment with her sister in a nearby building.

Her sister has no idea what Leona is working on, and most of the people down there in the basement in the stadium don't know what they are working on. Leona Woods is one of the very select group who knows what the purpose of this peculiar construction is. They are building a machine of a kind that has never existed before, and which some of them think cannot possibly be built. Up to now, it doesn't have a name, though it does have a designation: CP-1.*

The purpose is to test whether it is possible to set off a controlled chain reaction in fissile radioactive material, a reaction which, if it functions as intended, should be able to produce a new substance, an element that doesn't exist on earth, but does exist among the stars—plutonium. Purely theoretically, it should be possible to use this material to build a bomb so powerful that one single device would be sufficient to annihilate a whole city.

Tonight's news summary at 11:30 on WGN Chicago reports fighting off Guadalcanal, fighting in Tunisia, fighting on New Guinea, fighting at Stalingrad. It is followed by Harry James and his orchestra playing cool and easy-listening jazz (as a guess, pieces like "You Made Me Love You," "Sleepy Lagoon," "Easter Parade"). Leona gets to sleep, silent and still as the great city around her, while down in the subterranean squash court work continues untiringly. There's no time to waste: CP-1 is to be finished in two weeks.

. . .

Prison Camp No. 5, outside Batavia on Java. Today, Weary Dunlop's Monday, November 16, is pretty well the same as other days, though for some reason he writes down a kind of simple program of what he usually does:

---

* We, of course, call it a nuclear reactor. The designation used at the time was an abbreviation of Chicago Pile 1. "Pile" was the word Fermi himself chose for the arrangement and the others went along with him. Some people guessed wrongly that it had to do with the Italian word *pila*, "battery," but it is simply the English word "pile," i.e., to stack or heap.

07:00 Reveille. 07:30 Parade. Shave then breakfast by 08:00. Clean up my bed space, smoke and read until 09:30. Then see my sick in hospital. 10:00 P.T. Led by Sergeant Aldag. 11:00 French lesson or conversation. [He has given up his attempts to learn Dutch.] Perhaps a little more hospital work and various administrative tasks. 14:00 Exercise such as volleyball. 18:00 Chess or reading. 19:00 Chess or reading. 22:00 Lights out.

. . .

At nine o'clock in the evening of the same Monday, Ernst Jünger sets off again on his mysterious journey eastwards. His wife, Gretha, waves him off from the platform at the Berlin Ostbahnhof. The next stop is Lötzen, in East Prussia, and the intention is that he will fly from there to Kiev on a transport plane.

. . .

Vittorio Vallicella and his companions are still managing to support themselves by looting, theft and trading. Particularly the first of those. In their efforts to lie low during this time of collapse, they fall back on the methods that kept soldiers alive a thousand years ago.

Looting is perhaps too strong a word. They don't threaten anyone—in fact, as far as possible, they avoid people. They might, perhaps, be seen as scavengers living on the detritus of war. They search through wrecks, stranded vehicles and abandoned camps with the experienced eyes of veterans, hunting for anything usable such as water, fuel or food. (Usually in that order, and often with only an hour or two left before their fuel runs out.)

Like this Monday, for instance, November 16. They have searched a deserted airstrip outside Derna and among the things they found were twenty rucksacks containing all kinds of exciting things, no more than slightly smoke-damaged. They have managed to top up their water from a well in the desert just outside the town no more than half an hour before it gets blown up. In the little harbor town they come across a couple of shops in the process of being destroyed and in one case already on fire; there they harvest cheese, five sacks of corn, two boxes of sardines and sixty-five pounds of spaghetti. They barter fresh eggs off an Arab—then they bump into a German NCO, a blond paratrooper, who speaks Italian and agrees to give them gasoline in exchange for cigarettes.

They have dinner ready just before sunset and they invite the German paratrooper to eat with them. The menu is irresistible—as so often, it's the sum of their latest acquisitions: spaghetti with sardines, corned beef and eggs, and the blond German contributes freshly baked whole-wheat bread and a bottle of mineral water. They round the evening off by sitting in their foxholes under the starry sky and smoking, drinking tea and talking. The German comes from Nuremberg. He speaks good Italian because the summers of his childhood were spent with his maternal grandfather in Florence. Vallicella finds him a likeable fellow.

Then the German begins talking about the state of the war. Vallicella and his companions, who haven't heard any news for two weeks, sit there open-mouthed and listen. The German is very calm and seems to be well-informed. Then it begins to dawn on Vallicella that they are dealing with a convinced Nazi here. Just before they leave, Vallicella asks the German what he thinks will happen with the war. "The war," the German answers confidently, "will end next year with the defeat of the Anglo-Americans." And he adds: "Just this evening there was a radio report that the German army has now taken the whole of Stalingrad."

.   .   .

The days are getting ever shorter in the White Russian forests. Nikolai Obrynba finds life as a partisan anything but simple. During the short time he was in the Red Army he found it extraordinarily difficult to kill. "To kill, even to save your life, means turning upside-down all the thoughts and feelings in your mind and heart," he writes. And he adds: "At the start of the war, getting people ready to kill—hardening them to it—was a reconstruction of the whole human mentality. And it was a long and painful process."

Has Obrynba reached the end point of this process? In a sense, yes. Today, for the first time, he will execute someone. In a different sense, no. The anguish hasn't gone away and he would rather not do it.

What has happened is that a deserter from the other side has appeared—a White Russian, what is known as a *Polizei*—that is, a member of one of the armed militia units that the Germans have set up in most larger villages.* Such units vary in size and in effectiveness,

* It is a shortened version of the original German title Hilfspolizei (auxiliary police). For ideological reasons that term was replaced with Schutzmannschaft,

but there is no doubt that they are an extended arm of the occupying power. (Among other things, they have played a significant role in the mass shootings, both small and large, of Jews that took place this year across virtually the whole of White Russia.) Clashes between them and the partisans are both common and merciless. Neither side is given to taking prisoners.

The partisan commander suspects that the Polizei deserter may be an infiltrator, and in order to be on the safe side, he has decided that the man should be executed without further ado. Obrynba is the one to do the deed and he has been given precise instructions. The man has been informed that he is to be escorted to the village of Antunovo. On the way there, he is to be killed. Obrynba and a second partisan are to walk behind the unsuspecting deserter and Obrynba will shoot him from behind.

But will Obrynba be able to pull this off?

He knows they talk about him behind his back and say that he is soft—after all, he's an artist, for heaven's sake, a sensitive soul. Obrynba already suffers feelings of guilt for having survived prisoner-of-war camp when so many others died. And he recently learned that a Polish woman he'd sketched when the partisan unit stayed at her and her husband's house has been killed by the Germans. Along with her husband. The reason was that the Germans found the drawing, for which the cheerful and somewhat unruly woman had posed wearing a Soviet army uniform cap with a red star. That detail was sufficient for her execution.

.   .   .

That same Monday a train of cattle cars arrives at Treblinka carrying about a thousand Jews from the village of Gniewoszów in Poland, where the temporary ghetto set up in August was liquidated yesterday.*

Chil Rajchman is still working in the camp dental squad. He and the other death Jews in the upper camp have a week of intense work

---

but the original title stuck. At this point in 1942 there were almost 300,000 Schutzmannschaften in Ukraine and Ostland (the German term for the Baltic states and Belarus).

* The transport documents for Treblinka state the date as being November 15, the same day the ghetto was liquidated, but bearing in mind the procedures and the distance, the train is unlikely to have arrived before the following day.

behind them as a number of temporary camps and small ghettos around Bialystok in northeastern Poland have been emptied, step-by-step, transport-by-transport.

Rajchman, being a specialist, is to some extent protected, though even the twenty or so men in the dental squad can get into trouble. The biggest mistake is to miss a gold tooth in a body going past them. There is usually an SS man standing over by the pit checking. Rajchman reports:

> I was there on one occasion when the German saw the glint of a gold tooth in a corpse's mouth. Since I was standing last in the line of dentists, the sin was laid on my shoulders. I was immediately forced to jump down into the pit, where I immediately did several somersaults. I quickly extracted the tooth and as soon as I climbed back out, the SS man commanded me to lie down on the ground and stretch out my hands. I counted up to twenty-five lashes with the whip.

The same thing happened again yesterday.* "This time I was given seventy lashes in all" and it resulted in blood poisoning. To get anything like that in the upper camp amounts to a death sentence. The Germans shoot all the sick and the weak.† But his *kapo*, Dr. Zimmermann, saved him. Rajchman reports again:

> My good fortune was that it happened on a Sunday, when we were free of work. Dr. Zimmermann brought his implements with him and carried out the operation in the barrack hut. He even managed to give me a painkiller, and opened and cleaned the wound, thus saving my life.

---

* The date is an assumption as this episode is not dated in Rajchman's account. It must, however, have been November 15 as that appears to be the only Sunday in November when no transports arrived at Treblinka.

† There was no hospital in the camp at this time. There was, however, something called the Lazarett in a corner of the reception and sorting zone of the lower camp—a fenced-off area with a large red cross marking the entrance. Behind it lay a long pit in which the weak and injured from the transports were executed by being shot in the back of the neck with small-calibre weapons: it was done this way so as not to alarm new arrivals unnecessarily.

Monday follows the usual pattern. Apart from a very small number of the thousand Jews from Gniewoszów who are spared to refill the constantly diminishing gang of workers in the camp Sonderkommando, all of the rest are murdered by the evening: men, women and children.

.   .   .

The guerrilla war in the White Russian forests is more than brutal; much of it is played out in a moral grey zone, a borderland in which heroic acts and crimes shade together. Up to now, it's quite likely that partisan groups like Obrynba's have killed more of their fellow countrymen than Germans.

In White Russia, just as in other parts of the occupied Soviet Union, more than a few people have chosen to collaborate with the Germans, in spite of the fact that the Nazis view Slavs as subhuman and despite the unscrupulous, unstable and contradictory policy *vis-à-vis* the civilian population this leads to.

For some of those who collaborate, it is a way of ingratiating themselves with the new masters, with accessing power themselves, enriching themselves, avenging themselves and being able to kill without consequences. Many of them are people who in one way or another fell foul of Soviet rule and whose resulting lack of any real loyalty to Stalin and his party made them open to Nazi inducements and blind to the full consequences. For the majority, however, collaboration is just a way of getting by in a situation of famine, violence and extreme uncertainty: service with the Germans means a wage, food and other advantages, sometimes even the difference between life and death. Entering German service meant, for instance, that your family was exempted from forced labor and would receive a pension if you were killed by partisans. And for many people, collaboration was a way out of a prisoner-of-war camp or even a concentration camp.

It's impossible to say why this particular Polizei deserter joined up and, in any case, it is now irrelevant as he is going to be shot and it is Obrynba's job to do it. The man walking in front of Obrynba does not know he is going to die. Presumably Obrynba is carrying his own revolver, a Nagant. Obrynba draws it and takes aim. Presumably at the back of the neck, that being the usual place. He fires. The man crumples and falls. Blood.

This is probably the first person Obrynba has killed, at such close quarters, anyway. In the account he wrote after the war, he says that later he "behaved quite boastfully" to the others. He has proved he can do it. Within himself, however, he is troubled.

He has problems sleeping after this and the scene comes back to him time after time, waking him. He sees it again. Blood. What was it he had thought back in the prison camp? "It would not be easy to survive in this hell, but it would be a hundred times harder to remain a human being."

.   .   .

What Vittorio Vallicella is witnessing in North Africa is not just a military collapse but also a colonial one. Ever since Libya was taken over by Italy thirty years earlier, the area—divided into the three provinces of Cyrenaica, Tripolitania and Fezzan by using a ruler and a pen—has been the object of the customary colonial process: invasion, war, the brutal suppression of any local resistance,* population transfer, frontier changes, guerrilla warfare, assimilation, the influx of white colonists, the exploitation of raw materials, the building of roads, railways, factories, hotels and monuments.

As with so many colonial projects, the material gains have been less than expected, but essentially the subjugation of Libya has not been about economics. Libya is a symbol, a mirage and a dream. The region is often referred to as Quarta Sponda (the Fourth Shore), because without this piece of land all the hectoring of Mussolini at the assembled masses from the balcony of Palazzo Venezia in Rome, claiming the Mediterranean to be Mare Nostrum (Our Sea), would be no more than empty verbiage. But Libya has given the words geographical and geometric reality.

This is the end of all that. It is not only Italian troops who are getting out of Libya at breakneck speed, it is also Italian officials, civilians and colonists—many of whom were ordinary farmers attracted here during the Depression. Vallicella and his companions have driven through towns and villages emptied of their white population. And the men on the truck are quite often at least as afraid of the increasingly aggressive Arabs as of the British.

The farther west they go, the more alive the landscape becomes.

---

* In this case, particularly brutal: the methods included mustard gas, mass executions, starvation and concentration camps. It is estimated that one-quarter of the indigenous population of Cyrenaica was killed by the Italians.

There are houses, whole villages even, confusingly like those back in
Italy. Vallicella, a farmer's son, enjoys the greenery and is pleased to see
fields blue and pink with alfalfa. They stop for a while in Beda Littoria,
one of those model colonial villages founded less than ten years before.
It has a futurist-inspired center as a symbol of the grand future that
awaited it. Now it is empty and deserted. Even the priest has taken off.
It is Tuesday, November 17.

That night, Vallicella and the others break into one of the larg-
est boarded-up houses. In the flickering light of a lamp, the darkened
house becomes a series of impressions. There is an enormous dining
table and cupboards full of china, cutlery and crystal glass; soft beds
with clean white sheets; a photograph of a prosperous man with a
moustache; a group photograph with a familiar man with a goatee
at the front—Marshal Balbo, airman, governor and fascist; there are
several pretty young women posing on the beach in bathing costumes.
The photos, like the house, are redolent of power, affluence, far-off
happiness.

The only really useful things they take from there are clean sheets,
some pillows and a sack of rice. They find two dead cats in the garage.

·   ·   ·

Yesterday at last, someone whispered to Leonard Thomas that HMS
Ulster Queen and the other vessels would be allowed to leave the harbor
of Archangel very soon. He is full of contradictory emotions. At last,
at last, but still.... He walks back and forth almost manically, back and
forth across the clattering plates of the engine room floor, thinking,
fantasizing, rejoicing, worrying. On the one hand, he will be getting
away from the monotonous, monochrome, virtually prisonlike existence that has been his lot since September and going home, perhaps
just in time for Christmas. On the other hand, he is full of trepidation
about what awaits them and everything that might happen as they run
the gauntlet of the Arctic Ocean.

His voyage here with convoy PQ18 was, without any doubt, the
worst experience of his life.

Not only were they about to follow in the tracks of Arctic Convoy
PQ17 that had been virtually annihilated, but they recognized that the
Germans had had plenty of time to prepare and would now be waiting,
determined to repeat their triumph. As an engineer, Thomas was stuck

down in the engine room, trapped behind tightly closed watertight doors and bulkheads. The critical days when he, like the rest of the crew, had been dumbstruck with terror had been little more than noise to him: the rhythmic bark of the anti-aircraft guns, the rattle of empty shell cases on the deck above, the mournful wail of the sirens, the drone of the engines which every now and then rose to a roar—always a bad sign as it meant the vessel was having to make a rapid, sharp turn. Then there were the explosions of depth charges, sometimes no more than a vague hum in the distance, sometimes worryingly strong; whichever it was, it was a welcome sound, a safe sound, especially when compared to the most horrifying sound of all—the thin but unmistakeable whirring of a torpedo speeding by.

After several days of this, Thomas had lost all concept of time. This was partly due to sleeping so little, not just because of all the noise, especially that made by constant depth charges. He couldn't sleep because he was so frightened and, at the same time, actually frightened to fall asleep. For a while, he avoided scanning the sea, afraid he would catch sight of one of those torpedoes. PQ18, his convoy, was stated to be a great success, even though by the time they arrived they had lost thirteen of the convoy's forty freight vessels. Thomas has had moments of doubt. Given the odds, why run the convoys at all? "Sometimes agreement and bits of paper were our death warrants."

It's a cold, dark night when HMS *Ulster Queen* works her way out of Archangel harbor. Thomas can see the dark shapes of the transport ships waiting in a line outside the entrance. This is QP15 and the date is Tuesday, November 17. The wind freshens. They move slowly north-northwest. Heavy, grey-black clouds stretch in front of them. A deep depression is sweeping in from the Arctic Ocean.

·   ·   ·

On that day yet another German attack is fought out at Stalingrad. The last one? The snow still hasn't settled on the city, but the ground is frosty and ice floes can be seen drifting gently downstream on the black waters of the Volga.

The other regiments in the division Adelbert Holl belongs to have moved off to other positions on the steppes north of the city, the intention being that they will spend the approaching winter there. Holl's regiment—if it can still be called a regiment given that there are barely

ninety men left*—will take part in an attempt to wipe out the last
pockets of Soviet resistance. In their case, what they have to do is to
take the last of the two small suburban areas, Rynok and Spartanovka,
on the northern edge of the city, districts like so many others in Stalingrad that have been ground to dust as the dance of death of attack
and counterattack rages back and forth.

Few of the people there actually believe in this planned attack: not
the regimental commander, not the battalion commanders Holl later
talks to, not Holl himself—though he doesn't raise any objections. "I
was just a small cog in a very big machine." Nor do many of the officers
in the armored division, which is also to be part of the attack, see the
point of the operation. The commander of the corps is indignant.[†] But
since the order for the attack came from the Führer himself, there is
no choice in the matter.

A short directive signed by Hitler has been passed down step-by-
step through the military hierarchy, right down to the decimated and
exhausted units that will have to carry out the operation. And Friedrich
Paulus, the commander of the 6th Army, who like many of Hitler's generals is chronically spineless when it comes to the dictator, has added
a sentence: "I am convinced that this order will give new strength to
our brave soldiers."

Think about it! This is something the Führer wants! (The dictator's
mastery of detail is at a level that enables him to point to which individual building complexes are to be taken.) A devotee like Holl must
have heard the radio speech a couple of days earlier in which Hitler
forecast the fall of the city. Holl writes: "In the last resort, we were soldiers who had to obey and carry out orders. The combat effectiveness
of our army stands and falls on its obedience and the trust it has in its
commander." So no one says anything. Hierarchy, following orders,
marionette games. *Befehl ist Befehl.*

It is unusual for Holl not to be in the first line, but merely to *hear*

---

* This regiment even had a number of Russian "volunteers" in its ranks: these
were Hiwis (*Hilfswillige;* those willing to help), deserters or former prisoners of
war, who did not have to fight, but who, in exchange for food, assisted in practical
duties such as transporting ammunition or the wounded or doing manual work.
The 6th Army had about sixty thousand Hiwis.

[†] Walter von Seydlitz, the commander of the corps that the 94th Infantry Division belongs to, commented: "After all our efforts, I took this order to be a slap
in the face."

the noise of combat. The visibility is poor. There are crashes and explosions. Around lunchtime the first reports come in. The attack has ground to a halt after no more than two hundred yards. The Soviet artillery fire is too strong. (Where are the Russians getting all their shells?)

·   ·   ·

Bede Thongs and the rest of the Australian 3rd Battalion are held up at the Kumusi River for three days, while the engineers build primitive rope bridges across the waters with considerable difficulty. Not until Wednesday, November 18, have they all managed to get across. On that day, the battalion commander sends Thongs and his platoon out on patrol. They are to go upstream along the river and hunt out any "stray Japanese," not so much in order to bring them in as to kill them. (One can assume.)

Killing enemy soldiers does not bother Thongs. Any doubts he had earlier disappeared after seeing the remains of a decapitated Australian. That was when he and his men decided: "No quarter!" Thongs had probably been personally acquainted with the two men of the 3rd Battalion whose bodies they had found during the confused battles at Eora Creek: the bodies had no arms, and large pieces of flesh had been cut from their thighs and legs and were discovered wrapped in leaves close by. This confirmed the rumors that the Japanese were starving and were resorting to cannibalism in desperation.

The 10th Platoon finds itself yet again struggling through the tangle of dense, humid jungle. Bede Thongs doesn't feel at all well. Like everyone else, he has lost a lot of weight since the beginning of September when their road to Calvary along the Kokoda Trail began.

As far as can be judged, he has a temperature and a headache.

·   ·   ·

Looking out through the ventilation shaft, Tameichi Hara can catch a glimpse of turquoise waters, peaky, jungle-clad volcanic islands and distant breakers that mark the line of the coral reef. And grey-painted vessels at anchor. The destroyer *Amatsukaze* is back at Truk—or, to be more accurate, what remains of the destroyer. Hara goes out on deck. An engineer from the repair ship *Akashi* is coming aboard. Salute. Pleasantries. Hara says he wants the destroyer back in service "in a week to ten days."

In a sense, it is a surprising statement. It is clear that Hara is still in some sort of shock after the sea battle off Guadalcanal during the night of the twelfth. People think he looks ill.

There can be no question that Hara is an experienced naval captain. His baptism of fire took place in the port of Shanghai in 1937 and he has taken part in several naval battles since—the invasion of the Philippines, three sea battles, the big and decisive battle off Java in February, and the Midway operation (though that was as an onlooker), but he has *never* experienced anything like Guadalcanal in terms of scale, intensity and consequences.

The feeling of failure and of guilt that has seized him is genuine. The fact that he has already been praised for torpedoing two enemy ships counts for little compared with the memory of the forty-three men who died as a result of his mistake. The events of the last few days have also served to reawaken his old mistrust of elements in the leadership of the navy, and, it seems likely, his old doubts about the war itself.

Prior to December 1941, the mood within the Japanese navy might be characterized as an almost hysterical desire for war. Tameichi Hara was one of the few who questioned the wisdom of taking on the United States, not from any moral scruples, but because it was doubtful whether Japan really had the resources necessary to achieve victory. And Hara had visited the United States as a young cadet.*

Many people, however, and not just high command, don't let facts and statistics affect them to any great extent. Almost as a matter of course, they look down on their opponents, dismiss them as decadent, vulnerable and weak,† while promoting an image of themselves as invincible. (And, as always in authoritarian regimes, unwelcome information and disagreement tend to be weeded out rapidly.)

Hara does, however, wonder whether what is asserted almost as a mantra really is the case: that "the invincible Japanese could shatter outnumbering enemy forces by their aggressive spirit." The improbably great successes of the last eleven months have, however, led him to doubt his doubts. And this despite knowing that some of the

---

* His long career had left him with memories of the strong Western influences on the Japan of the 1920s; these were thoroughly purged during the 1930s.

† In this they reflect attitudes among the Western great powers, who had consistently underestimated the Japanese threat, frequently on the basis of racist attitudes.

communiqués of victory have been "adjusted" and some are false. So Hara has chosen to withdraw into the comfortable role of samurai—an apolitical soldier, a technician with tunnel vision: "I could not allow myself to dwell on overall problems of war, but must fight to the best of my ability in my limited role."

We know from the last war that great loss of life does not automatically lead to criticism and rethinking. Up to a certain point, it can have the opposite result and strengthen the will to fight on even harder and to invest even more. After all, we don't want the fallen to have made their sacrifice in vain, do we?

Tameichi Hara and the engineer carry out a thorough inspection that lasts all day. The destroyer really is in a wretched state. In the hull, they count thirty-two holes of more than a yard in diameter, plus five smaller holes where unexploded shells penetrated. They start counting damage caused by shell splinters, but give up after reaching forty. And there are so many small holes made by machine-gun bullets that counting them all becomes pointless.

Come the afternoon, the engineer announces that the *Amatsukaze* will have to return to the yard in Japan if she is ever to return to active service and that the work there is likely to take a month. In order to be able to undertake that journey, the destroyer will, however, need provisional repairs to be done here in Truk. And that will also take a month. That news sends Hara into an even deeper state of depression and he sinks down into a chair in his cabin with the engineer standing in front of him. He wants to *fight*. He comes up with a lame protest:

> "But," I stammered, "there is evidence that the enemy can affect major repairs in much less than sixty days. Why can't we?" I knew that the answer lay in the enemy's tremendous industrial capacity, so far superior to Japan's, and realized how embarrassing my question was. An awkward silence followed.

The repairs begin the next morning and in the following period Hara will be politely showing groups of visitors around—staff officers and other bigwigs who want to take a closer look at this destroyer that has survived such incredible damage. One thing strikes him: they are interested in the *Amatsukaze*, smoke-stained and bullet-ridden, as a curiosity, but they don't ask any questions about the battle itself. Hara writes:

When this lack of curiosity continued throughout the week,
I began to wonder about the ability of these men. It was dis-
quieting to think that they, who were helping to form plans
and strategy, were not interested in learning from recent battle
experiences. Perhaps they were not as well qualified for their
jobs as they should be.

.   .   .

On Wednesday, November 18, Adelbert Holl's regiment mounts yet
another attack in northern Stalingrad and yet again he follows the
attack from the rear lines. Judging from the reports, the attackers do
not get much farther forward this time under the storm of steel thrown
by the Soviet artillery on the other side of the Volga.

It is questionable how wholehearted the performance of this operation was. As said earlier, no one from the commander of the corps down
through the ranks believes in the mission. They have perhaps done as
much as was demanded of them in order to be able to report—all the
way up, step-by-step along the proper route, from regiment to division, division to corps, corps to army, army to OKH, OKH to OKW,*
and finally from OKW to that enclosed and slightly moldy-smelling
bunker in the East Prussian forest where the Leader himself is standing bent over a 1:10,000-scale map with a huge magnifying glass in his
hand—that, well, the order has been carried out but unfortunately...
Holl spends a lot of time thinking about the men in his old company
and what they must be going through now:

> What the men in the forward line had to perform almost bor-
> dered on the superhuman. Most of them still lacked winter
> clothing. In other words, they had to make do with their nor-
> mal kit. They squatted in fox-holes in front of the enemy with
> only their Zeltbahne as protection against the damp and cold.
> There, the hours were an eternity.

.   .   .

* OKH = Oberkommando des Heeres (Supreme Command of the Army);
OKW = Oberkommando des Wehrmachts (Supreme Command of the Armed
Forces).

One evening in Thuringia eleven days earlier, a hospital train carrying wounded soldiers from the Eastern Front had been moved into a siding while waiting to be given the green light. (The reason for the delay was damage caused by British bombing, though it's unlikely that the wounded men lying there in pain and in the smell of blood and carbolic acid ever knew this.) Then another train was shunted into the siding and came to a halt. No more than a couple of yards separated the two trains and the astonished soldiers in their hanging stretchers could look across into a luxurious, brightly lit dining car in which a uniformed party was eating dinner served on elegant china. The diners' attention was focused on a gesticulating speaker they all recognized immediately. It was Him. The Führer. "Suddenly he looked up, at the awed faces staring in at him. In great anger he ordered the curtains drawn, plunging his wounded warriors back into the darkness of their own bleak world."*

·   ·   ·

Things have been fairly calm in the last few days at Guadalcanal. It will soon be a fortnight since John McEniry last took off his flying overalls. They are torn and filthy, and he himself is thoroughly dirty. It's two months since he had a haircut. "It rained almost every day, and all of the foxholes had mud or water in them. The area outside of them was either muddy or dusty." When they are issued with new underpants and stockings, McEniry and some of the other pilots decide to go and take a bath. This happens on November 17, or possibly the next day.

There is a small river, the Lunga, surrounded by trees near the southwestern end of the main runway. Many of them go there to bathe, even their much-admired squadron leader, Major Joseph Sailer Jr. On their way there they encounter "a patrol of ground Marines, with their rifles at ready, creeping along the trail" and the pilots ask what they are doing. One of the Marines tells them that a Japanese sniper has slipped

---

* According to author and historian William Craig. Hitler was on his way to Munich to give his traditional speech to the party faithful in the Löwenbräukeller to mark the anniversary of the failed putsch in 1923. The speech he gave is memorable for two reasons (apart from the fact it is one of the few speeches where the dictator uses both irony and his ordinary voice). Firstly, Hitler forecast—for the *fourth* time that year—the extermination of the Jews; secondly, he promised that Stalingrad would soon be taken—which made Stalingrad a matter of personal prestige for him.

through the American lines* and was trying to shoot people by the
river. McEniry and his companions offer to act as "bait" and, without
hesitation, continue on down to the river.

McEniry thinks the river is looking "wonderful." (They still haven't
lost their sense of humor.) They undress on the bushy banks and it
becomes evident that they are all losing weight. Food on the island
is both limited and fairly unappetizing, consisting mainly of corned
beef or some other sort of canned meat, or soup made thereof, fried
onion on bread, coffee, dried potato and egg powder and monotonous
quantities of rice that is more or less "off."† Almost all of them are suffering from occasional diarrhea and cases of malaria and yellow fever
are becoming common.

Naked, they go down into the shallow, clear, fast-flowing water. The
bottom is stony. They don't know it yet, but life is so cruel and memory so elastic that those that survive this month and these years will,
when they become old men, dwell on this time and perhaps even long
to return to it, not least to moments like these, almost archetypically
carefree and playful in their youthful immortality under a blue sky and
eternal, constantly changing clouds.

·   ·   ·

The road to Alexandria is like a film in which the narrative of the battle
is played backwards. Initially, the muddy road Keith Douglas and his
two companions follow is as empty as the flat desert that surrounds
them—the final stage of the retreat. But soon they see more and more
debris, things thrown away, abandoned vehicles, paper spinning in the
air at every puff of wind—the start of the retreat. Then more and more
burned-out trucks, often in long rows, and hastily dug graves. The
collapse. Then came clusters of blackened, burned armored vehicles,
blown-up tow trucks, abandoned artillery pieces with their barrels
pointing blindly, vultures—the breakthrough. And then, last of all,
the barbed-wire entanglements, fluttering with rags, and then craters,
loads of craters—the artillery barrage. They bounce and sway over and

---

* Japanese snipers filtering in through the lines was a constantly recurring problem at Henderson Field at this time. It was never completely safe there.
† The rice came from Japanese stores captured in August and the first wave of
troops to land would probably have gone hungry without it. Japanese mint sweets
were far more popular items to capture.

around the last of the refilled shellholes, switch into the highest gear and, under a clearing sky, their fifteen-hundredweight truck speeds towards the great city.

Few places exercise the same pull on soldiers in the British army as Alexandria, frequently just known as Alex. The contrast between the emptiness of the desert sands and the green parks and popular life of Alexandria is total. The city has everything—bars, cafés, restaurants, cinemas, golf courses, private clubs, shopping streets, fashionable hotels, wide bathing beaches—absolutely everything: it also has thieves, muggers, con artists, smugglers, British-hating conspirators, spies, beggars, drug sellers and hosts of prostitutes of both sexes—no other Egyptian city can boast of as many brothels as Alexandria. And all this no more than two hours' drive away.

Keith Douglas's journey has two purposes. First, he has been given £50 and a horrendously long shopping list of things he is supposed to buy for the regiment—this includes two thousand eggs and three thousand *petits pains*. Second, he needs new spectacles; Douglas is very nearsighted, something that photographs don't reveal as he is sufficiently vain as to remove his glasses at the first sign of a camera. He has lost one pair of glasses and the second pair was broken during the battle. It is now the second half of November.

The palm trees tell them they are approaching the city. He sees green fields, he sees more and more buildings, he sees the sea. They drive into Alexandria.

They have to stop and wait by a small bridge as a long column of dusty prisoners of war trudge past. They drive on, crawling through the hot, narrow streets between pedestrians, donkey carts and trams. Some people point and wave at the filthy, picturesque army truck, pitted with splinter holes. By the time they reach the center of the city and Muhammad Ali Square, the only thing on his mind is how he might swallow his shame and humiliation and visit Milena.

They drive along the seafront and the palm-fringed Grande Corniche, past "bathers and sunbathers, a blaze of coloured costumes as bright as a garden; at Stanley Bay troops on leave and the huge indolent population of smart women hid the sand and dotted the blue half-circle of sea." The contrasts of the scene are almost archetypical, but Douglas doesn't seem to be particularly concerned that while thousands are being killed or wounded or trapped in their tanks and burned alive no more than sixty miles away, others are lying here eating ice cream under colorful parasols or playing in Stanley Bay's phenomenal waves. Maybe this is because he would have been doing exactly the same thing if he had been on leave.* After all, what happens when you die? Nothing, everything just goes on as usual.

Quite right: a couple of evenings later, Keith Douglas himself is sitting rather unconcerned in one of the many cafés on La Grande Corniche. He is accompanied by a female acquaintance. Not Milena. This meeting, however, turns out to be an embarrassing mistake and he soon gets rid of her. He plucks up courage (or swallows his pride) and rushes off to invite Milena to the cinema.† She accepts. He tries to put his arms around her in the taxi on the way home. Nothing doing. He feels as if there was a "sheet of metal" between them. It really has finished. He has lost her.

.   .   .

It's Wednesday, November 18, and Ernst Jünger is stuck in Lötzen in East Prussia. Even though he has received his travel documents and been given a ticket, the number of flights has temporarily been cut back because of bad weather. One of the big three-engine transport planes crashed three days ago as a result of ice forming on the wings, so there is nothing to do but wait patiently.

Rather than just stay in his room in the rundown hotel, Jünger goes out and looks around the little town, which is situated on a large lake. He spends the morning visiting the big cemetery for the fallen of the 1914 battles and in the afternoon he takes a look around the small museum set up after and about the last war. Jünger is in low spirits after the visit: all the objects he sees displayed in cases or mounted on the walls are too close, too familiar. They become images of the world of

---

* It was a different matter when it came to Cairo, which swarmed with officers who had used the old boys' network to access a comfortable posting on one of the overstaffed and inefficient staffs and who thus lived a life of leisure and luxury in bars, brothels and polo fields, well away from any danger. Such officers were hated by soldiers at the front with an intensity as strong if not stronger than had been evident during the First World War.

† He doesn't say which film they watched. It is difficult to imagine Douglas in that situation wanting to see any of the numerous war films making the rounds, so it's likely to have been something more entertaining. We can only guess. *The Magnificent Ambersons* by Orson Welles? *Miss Annie Rooney* with Shirley Temple? *My Favorite Blonde* with Bob Hope? *The Ghost of Frankenstein* with Bela Lugosi?

the fallen, the world on the other side, and they make him remember things he clearly doesn't want to remember. Nor does the war cemetery raise his spirits. Hardly surprising, as it is too desolate, harsh and empty—a place for ghosts.

.   .   .

The following morning, when Keith Douglas and his helper climb into the truck to return to the regiment, he is in a surprisingly good mood in spite of the fiasco with Milena. The job is done: the truck is full to the gunnels with cigarettes, cigars, gin, spirits, eggs, canned meat and God knows what else. And there's a heavenly smell coming from the sacks of freshly baked *petits pains* they have just loaded. Just one job left now—to drive to the big NAAFI (Navy, Army and Air Force Institutes) at Borg el-Arab just west of the city and buy beer and bars of chocolate. They arrive there to find it had closed just five minutes earlier. The corporal in charge refuses to bend the rules and Douglas gets angry and suggests that "if the fighting troops were as finicky about their working hours as NAAFI employees* we shouldn't have begun a battle let alone won it." That doesn't make the corporal any more cooperative. Douglas's mood turns to one of impotent rage and a feeling he'd really like to shoot the corporal.

This contrast between the everyday life of a soldier at the front and that of the military bureaucracy with its petty regulations, inefficiency, bullying and insensitivity is a real cause of ill-feeling and irritation. Douglas has to return to his unit with his shopping trip incomplete. Like a dream, Alexandria soon fades away behind him and he hurries back through the monotony of the desert.

.   .   .

Willy Peter Reese reports, "The ground froze and the wind sometimes brought a hint of rime frost and snow." This day brings an interruption—both welcome and unwelcome—to everyday existence. His group receives orders to move their so-far-unused anti-tank gun back to the rear. That's good, in that things are a bit less risky there

---

* This was a British state-owned company that ran canteens and other services for all uniformed personnel. They were present everywhere and they were indispensable, but they were a constant target for the dissatisfaction and annoyance of fighting troops.

than in the front line. But first, it has to be dragged back there, which, being a dangerous procedure, is not so good.

Reese has to live with a general sense of ambivalence that troubles him. He is not a Nazi, and never has been one. His lack of enthusiasm for the regime came close to costing him his student entry exam—he was saved by one of his teachers, who was prepared to help and protect his gifted pupil. One of his close friends from that time was a young man with some Jewish ancestry and they had kept in close touch. At about this time, his friend is sent to what is said to be a big labor camp in the east and Reese has his prisoner number and his new address: "115613 / Block 2A / Konzentr. Lager Auschwitz / Oberschlesien, Postamt 2."

For many years, Reese's dislike of the regime remained passive and silent, but it has become more explicit over the last year. He has sabotaged all efforts to get him involved in the training of new recruits and he writes poems that could certainly lead to charges. Like this poem, composed earlier this year:

> *Murdered Jews,**
> *marched to Russia*
> *as a howling horde,*
> *oppressed the people,*
> *fought in blood,*
> *led by a clown,*
> *we are envoys*
> *and wade in blood.*
> *We carry the banners*
> *of our Aryan ancestors:*
> *they suit us well.*
> *We drink and whore,*
> *traces of vandalism*
> *mark our road.*
> *We rage and shriek*

* It is quite clear that Reese knew what was happening to the Jews as early as 1942. His posthumous papers do not tell us exactly how much he knew or where his information came from, but it is likely that he heard rumors at close quarters. He was transit marching through Kiev in 1941 when the Babi Yar massacre took place, and when he was at Kharkov the following summer, a similar atrocity occurred there.

and feast at the Witches' Sabbath
in the company of fools.

But he also perceives his own guilt in all this, in the contradiction of hating Hitler at the same time as fighting Hitler's war. Or as he puts it in another poem:

We are the war. Since we are soldiers.
I have burned all the towns,
throttled all women
killed all children
taken all the loot from the country.
I have shot millions of enemies,
destroyed all fields, destroyed churches,
laid waste human souls
spilled the blood and tears of all mothers.
I have done that.—I did nothing.
But I was a soldier.

At the same time, Reese would never even consider deserting.

He is decorated, proud of everything he has endured, and he scorns cowards—or, more accurately, he scorns those who allow fear to gain the upper hand. The whole time he is in the east, he longs for home, but once he is at home, he longs to be back at the front. This split is ripping him apart. Reese is trying to preserve the man he was before 1941, at the same time as recognizing that that man no longer exists. This is why he stands there as "a stranger to myself," as he expresses it. It is easy to understand why he drinks more and more, and more and more frequently. They are all doing that, of course.

Under fire, and with the help of a couple of horses, they drag the heavy gun—it weighs more than half a ton—from its emplacement, lever it across trench systems and shell craters. One of Reese's companions is hit, as is one of the horses; the man survives, but the horse dies the following day. Reese and the rest of them are glad to be a little farther from the front line, and the bunker they now have is better than the wet and muddy burrow they were living in before. "Our fighting spirit had long since turned into weary endurance."

. . .

John Parris, the American war reporter who sent such dramatic reports of the American landings in French North Africa, is not at what's called "the front." That is difficult to define at present anyway, being a zone that keeps time with the speedy advance of American and British troops towards the Algerian border, Tunisia and—Tunis. Parris, who is a quiet sort of man, has perhaps discovered that he isn't cut out to be a war reporter. Soon he'll be returning to the main office of United Press in London and will stay there.* Further coverage has been handed over to Ned Russell from California, who is the same age as Parris and from the same news bureau.

Russell and a number of other reporters are part of the same "pool," a system the American forces introduced in order to limit the number of journalists in one place. They are expected to share their reports with their colleagues. One of the advantages of this arrangement for the military is that it makes it significantly easier to control the reporters.

What they are permitted to witness is always limited, and the army censors then comb through everything they write—it is called "censoring at source," and there may be further cuts made before the material is published. In other words, there is a double filter, or even a triple filter, since the fact is that the war correspondents initially censor themselves. Quite justifiably, they see themselves as part of the war effort—they are all in uniform—and they want to avoid portraying the war in a manner that might make it more difficult to win. As a consequence, they end up producing an image that has been prettified, simplified, idealized and laden with clichés.

Stories of heroism, both on the grand scale and on the small scale, are popular topics, whether they deal with vain and publicity-hungry generals (who may have full-time PR people on their staff) or some local individual who has pulled off a heroic/remarkable/important deed/against all odds/in difficult circumstances/somewhere important. Many journalists are only technically "at the front." They use much of their time travelling between various headquarters, where they listen to uniformed people with pointers indicating this and that

---

* Once there, Parris attends press conferences and covers diplomacy and high politics. He makes no further attempt to report on the war. Being a reporter for United Press, however, was no small matter: at the start of the war, their material was distributed to 1,715 newspapers and radio stations in 52 countries.

on large maps; or they may simply spend their time rewriting official press communiqués into "reports from our man on the spot."

War for them is a rumble heard on the wind, smoke seen in the distance, worn phrases on freshly mimeographed slips of paper. Much of what they know or see can never be written about, not because it is secret, but because it is embarrassing, or quite simply does not fit in with the polished image of the war and consequently cannot be mentioned to the public at home. As another war correspondent put it, later:

> We knew that a certain very famous general officer constantly changed press agents because he felt he didn't get enough headlines. We knew the commander who broke a Signal Corps sergeant for photographing his wrong profile. Several fine field officers were removed from their commands by the jealousy of their superiors because they aroused too much admiration from the reporters. There were consistent sick leaves which were gigantic hangovers, spectacular liaisons between Army brass and WAACs,* medical discharges for stupidity, brutality, cowardice, and even sex deviation. I don't know a single reporter who made use of any of this information. Apart from wartime morals, it would have been professional suicide to have done it.†

On this day, Wednesday, November 18, Ned Russell and another American journalist are in Tabarka, a small and beautiful coastal town with many ancient ruins, just inside the Tunisian border. High on the expectation of the advances continuing to be as rapid as they have been ever since the landings, they travelled there by train and army truck. The landscape reminds Russell of Southern California or possibly Arizona. "We talked of Tunis and Bizerte as good as captured and some of us even wondered how long it would take us to get to Tripoli."

But this has all changed within less than two days. The earlier warm,

---

* Women's Army Auxiliary Corps. The women in WAAC worked on many staffs as telephonists, secretaries or personal chauffeurs.

† Words written by John Steinbeck, a future Nobel Prize winner, in his book *Once There Was a War*. Steinbeck accompanied the Allied forces during the invasion of Italy.

sunny weather has turned cold, with hail and lashing rain. Ever since the Allies landed and the French defenders laid down their arms after just a couple of days, everyone has been asking where the Germans are and what they are likely to do. Surely, they are likely to flee now that their situation in North Africa is so hopeless. The British forces leading the advance into Tunisia have now made their first armed contact and, unfortunately, the Germans they encountered show no great desire to run away. Rather the reverse, in fact: they seem to have been reinforced with tanks and with planes.

The two journalists are directed to an abandoned factory full of stacks of drying cork. The building is now the headquarters of the British 36th Brigade and a major briefs them on the new situation. There is hard fighting going on farther forward and the advance has been stopped. Travelling by road in daylight is dangerous as low-flying German planes swoop down under the low clouds and open fire on everything and everyone. Furthermore, Allied supply lines are now stretched to the breaking point and the rain has turned all the roads to sludge.*

Russell realizes that there isn't going to be a simple and rapid triumphal march to Tunis. He and the other journalist return that evening to Bône, the place they started from yesterday. He reports:

> The trip back was worse, if that was possible, than the trip to Tabarka had been. We huddled together under a canvas groundsheet on the back of an open truck with the rain and hail beating on our faces. Once, when the hail suddenly clattered down in unusually big chunks, I put my steel helmet over my face.

They reach Bône at midnight after five hours on the truck.

Russell knows that he ought to report something, but what? People back home need to hear that the advance on Tunis, hitherto depicted

---

* It wasn't only the roads. Allied air support had to operate from poor, muddy airstrips quite far away, whereas the German and Italian air forces had good bases close by. The major might also have mentioned that supply lines were not merely extended, but that a good deal of what actually reached the front was inessential—hair oil, for instance—whereas there was a severe shortage of shells and food.

as unstoppable, has now been stopped. But how? He knows that the simple, unvarnished truth that the British have been held up by German superiority in terms of firepower, armor and planes "would not pass the censors in Algiers."

So, instead, Russell writes a text in which the events are portrayed in as rosy a light as possible. Yes, Allied plans may have gone "completely haywire, but for the first time they had gone wrong in the right way!" The events were blamed on a sort of paradox of success: the advance had been so rapid that logistics had been unable to keep pace with it. The troops were days ahead of their timetable and now had to "sit tight in the soggy mud" and wait for "reinforcements and heavy equipment and air support" to arrive.

Russell sends off his report. Two months later, Ned Russell discovers that his euphemisms had not been successful: the military censors in Algiers had cut all of them.

. . .

Sophie Scholl can breathe easier. Fritz Hartnagel is still alive! She has received a letter from him at last, from Stalingrad. There is something slightly uptight and proper about Sophie's temperament and in her answering letter dated November 18 she can't stop herself showing the irritation that waiting for his letter had caused her quite unnecessary fears and dark fantasies.

She overcomes that, however, and, pointing to the faith they both embrace, she exhorts him to take Holy Communion and to pray. But as fast as her words flow across the paper, she seems to be seized by powerful emotions:

> Oh Fritz, if I can't write anything different to you, it's just because it is so utterly ridiculous when, instead of calling for help, someone on the point of drowning begins to pontificate on this or that of a scientific, philosophical or theological subject, while the gruesome tentacles of the creatures from the bottom of the sea grasp his legs and his arms and the waves close over him; it's just because I feel dread and nothing but dread and long for the one who can free me from this dread. I am still so far from God that I cannot feel his presence even when I pray. Sometimes when I utter the name of God, I want to sink down into nothingness. It is not frightening at all, not

dizzying, it is nothing at all—and that makes it even more unpleasant.

The following day, Sophie's father, Robert, receives the news that he is forbidden to practice—he is considered to be politically unreliable and so will no longer be permitted to work as a tax lawyer.* Will the family still be able to live in their large flat on Münsterplatz? Will the Scholl siblings be able to continue their studies at the university?

· · ·

It's the night between Wednesday and Thursday, November 19. John Bushby and the rest of the crew of the Lancaster bomber ED311 "K-King" have again made the long flight down to the south of France and over the Alps to northern Italy. The target this time is Turin.

Their unit, 83 Squadron, isn't just an ordinary unit, but part of PFF, Pathfinder Force. They have been picked out, given special training and special equipment to fly at the front of the dense swarm of bombers and mark the target with strong flares of different colors—red, green or yellow—which the following waves of planes only need to aim at. The K-King navigator is using a new radio navigation system, GEE (which Bushby and the rest of them always refer to as "the goon box"), which gives them and other Pathfinders enormously improved rates of locating the target at night—prior to this, accuracy was pretty well nil.

They find Turin without any problem. Its defenses, as usual, are lame. Bushby recalls: "On Turin the target marking went with textbook precision. I even had time to pick out the sprawl of the Fiat works and the circular outline of the car testing track acting as a giant bullseye for us to aim at."

As K-King and the other heavy bombers turn for home, they are able to see numerous fires in the factory areas but also in the center of the city: 121 tons of bombs have been dropped.† Their flight home

---

* Robert Scholl was a liberal and, after his experiences in the last world war, a pacifist. He was also a freethinker, and that could sometimes express itself as querulousness. Earlier this year he had served a short prison sentence for having made a disrespectful remark about *der Führer.*

† This was the first of seven raids during November and December, during which enormous four-ton bombs were used. The shock was so great that a

is undramatic, apart from the fact that Bushby's Lancaster flies into a thunderstorm over northern France. Bushby remembers:

> The heaped cumulo-nimbus clouds glowed and flared with internal light and for the first and only time we saw that phenomenon remembered from schoolbooks, St Elmo's fire. We watched, fascinated, as brilliant electric blue sparks flew continuously between gun-muzzles; and the propellers were four iridescent rings of shimmering blue. Glowing globules ran along each aerial wire like fluorescent raindrops. Then we were through the cloud and out into clear air on the far side.

. . .

In Mandalay, today is the day of the week when Mun Okchu and the other young Korean women in the field brothel are checked to ensure they aren't carrying a venereal disease. The examination takes several hours and provides a welcome break from servicing the seemingly never-diminishing waiting line of uniformed men outside the building.

The load is a heavy one, in spite of the fact that Mandalay will soon have nine field brothels. (One is reserved for officers, *Uminooya*, and only has Japanese girls; three have Korean girls, the Taegu Inn being one of them; one has Chinese girls; three have Burmese girls, and one of them, *Shinmenkan*, is being reserved for Burmese auxiliary troops who have chosen to fight for the Japanese against their former colonial overlords, the British.)* It's not unusual for the brothels to be run by civilians, as is the case with Mr. and Mrs. Matsumoto's business, but they are run under contract from the military. In an organizational sense, each business under this system is directly subordinate to a specific military detachment, regiment or army corps. The Taegu Inn is subordinate to a headquarters unit, Divisional Staff 8400, and it is their military police who supervise and keep order. It is the military unit in charge that has logistical responsibility for its own brothel and must provide it with everything from premises and condoms—this year

---

quarter of a million of the inhabitants of Turin would soon quit their homes and their city.

* At this time, the majority of Burmese did not view the Japanese as occupiers, hoping through them to achieve independence from the hated British.

alone, more than thirty-two million condoms are sent to the various units of the Japanese military—to bedclothes and food. As has already been noted, the comfort women are officially listed as "paramilitary functionaries" and are under military jurisdiction.*

Mun Okchu's route from Korea to Burma shows both the scale and the level of official organization involved in sex slavery. She and the other seventeen girls were recruited by the Matsumotos at the beginning of the summer under the pretext that they would be working in restaurants, retail outlets and the like overseas for good wages. That sounded attractive both because of the money Mun would be earning and because she didn't think "she had much to look forward to in Taegu." Her family is poverty-stricken, her mother left alone with four children and barely able to support her family by working as a seamstress and housemaid. Mun has a basic three years of schooling behind her and has worked as a housemaid and in a shoe factory. She gives everything she earns to her overworked mother—and is proud to do so. Her mother doesn't actually know how Mun earns her money.

What Mun and the other young women did not know when they were recruited was that the Matsumotos and a number of other civilian "operators" in Korea, many involved in organized crime, had been given a contract by the army. So on July 10 this year she was one of a party of 703 Korean women, all with identity papers issued by the military, who boarded a military transport vessel in Pusan harbor. They were accompanied by some ninety "operators" and their families, and a number of soldiers.

The ship sailed south as part of a convoy of six or seven vessels. During the lengthy voyage, the women were kept in small groups under their respective "operators." Mun remembers:

> Many women suffered from sea sickness. I wasn't sick throughout the long journey, maybe because I was so determined to earn money, or perhaps because I had very good health. I helped with the cooking of my group, I cleared away the mess

---

* The following year, Mun Okchu was brought before a military court for having killed an extremely intoxicated customer who threatened her with a samurai sword. It was something of a sensation when she was acquitted, quite a few Japanese testifying in her defense that the man had been an exceptionally vile troublemaker.

they made if they threw up, and I looked after anyone who lost consciousness. When I saw women from other groups, I would ask if they knew where we were going, and everyone replied that we would be working in restaurants. No one seemed to know what our impending fates were to be.

They did not know anything, perhaps because they did not want to, perhaps because they couldn't, since there was nothing that could be understood within the framework of their picture of the world other than that they had all been swallowed up by something bigger— enormously bigger—than them.

The convoy made a brief stop in Taiwan, where a further twenty-two women were picked up. When they arrived in Singapore (which the occupiers had rechristened Syonan), many of them were ordered to disembark. The vessel with Mun and about two hundred of the other young women and their operators continued on to Rangoon. That is where it began to dawn on them what their fate was to be. One of the women then took her own life by throwing herself into the water.

At the harbor there were trucks waiting to take the groups off in various directions. Mun knows that there are field brothels all over Burma: the system is expanded as and when Japanese forces take over more territory, and in the course of this year that has been unceasing.* Thus the "recruiting campaign" in Korea back in the summer, which resulted in her and the other girls being tricked out of the country and over the sea to Burma and Mandalay.

Today, Mun and the other women have been going through the health control, at the same time as their booths are being cleaned with powerful disinfectants. The examination provides welcome breathing space for a couple of hours, but it can also bring a longer break than that, though at a high price.

---

* In September of this year, in an official report to the Japanese war ministry, it was reported that what were euphemistically known as *comfort stations* for the use of the military existed in 400 places. In Hankou, now a part of Wuhan, the comfort station consisted of a cluster of 68 two-story buildings; in northern China there were 100; in central China 140; in southern China 40; in Nanto Bunto— the southern region, which included Burma—100; in the South Pacific 10; and 10 on Sachalin. There were approximately 3,200 comfort women, of which 2,800 were Koreans, in Burma. The total number of Korean comfort women was between 100,000 and 200,000.

There is actually only one way to get out of lying there legs apart and that is when the genital area has become so swollen and infected that it has started oozing whitish yellow pus, or when the woman is ill, especially if the disease is venereal. During treatment with various creams and painful and feared injections of something called "Compound 606" (Mun doesn't know what it is),[*] they have to remain in their booths, behind a closed curtain and hang up a sign saying "No entry this week."

·   ·   ·

It's a misty Thursday morning with the temperature somewhere around nineteen degrees. The snow that has been falling heavily all night is beginning to ease off. The explosions reach Mansur Abdulin's ears as a prolonged roar, reach his body as vibrations, vibrations that pass up from the soles of his feet into his body. His eardrums sting from the explosions and lumps of frozen earth tumble down on him from the walls of the trench. The date is November 19, the place a little south of the Kletskaya bridgehead, and Mansur Abdulin has never been through anything like it. His own side's artillery has been firing for almost an hour, since 7:30 a.m., and shows no sign of letting up.[†]

Abdulin and his fellow soldiers in the mortar group in the trench keep their heads down. They are wearing new white snowsuits and waiting for the order to go over the top. All they can see when they look straight up are low grey clouds. They have just attempted a collective "Hooray," but all that emerged from their frightened throats was a hacking, slightly foolish *a-a-a* sound, so they fall silent again, recognizing the impossibility of competing with the swish and crash and thunder of the artillery. In all probability Abdulin is slightly drunk—a few days earlier the Red Army had reintroduced the rule that each soldier would be issued around four ounces of vodka, roughly two shots, before combat—just enough to take the edge off fear, but not enough to blunt his judgment or physical functioning.

---

[*] Compound 606 was an arsenic compound used as an antibiotic around the world. It was effective against syphilis, among other diseases. The young women feared that repeated treatments would render them sterile, and that did indeed often happen.

[†] The unit was to attack across a front of just under two miles and support fire was provided by seventy-seven artillery pieces of various sorts and eight tanks.

At 8:30 a.m. the sounds change a little. The volume remains the same but something about the echo and rhythm of the explosions has changed. It continues for another fifteen minutes, before the firing ceases and is replaced by the long, drawn-out whine of Katyusha rockets arching over their heads and detonating with clattering cracks. In the midst of all this comes a growing, creaking roar as Soviet tanks begin to move forward. Several of them trundle right across Abdulin's trench and he and his companions lie flat while snow and earth pour down on them. The white-painted steel behemoths grind their way rapidly towards the enemy lines, unhindered by the almost two feet of snow.

The time has come.

One last deep breath before leaping out.

Abdulin gets to his feet and climbs out of the trench.

Looking over to the enemy lines he sees that the last of the rockets have landed and a haze of black dust is hanging in the air.

They advance. There are five of them: Suvorov, commander of the mortar crew, carries the sight; Fuat carries the support legs—forty-four pounds in weight; a third man carries the forty-four-pound baseplate; a fourth man carries the boxes with the mortar shells; and Abdulin himself carries the barrel—a yard long and weighing forty-two pounds. All of this in addition to their usual gear. They run, knees bent slightly by the weight. Alongside them and in front of them there are other groups of white-clad men hurrying forward. Some of them are already at the curtain of dust a couple of hundred yards or so ahead and disappear into it, firing as they go.

There are explosions still, but the sounds seem to be coming from far away. The tanks creak and drone. Abdulin is panting, heart pounding, as he runs into the slowly sinking curtain of dust. The world goes dark and is shut off for a moment.

He comes out the other side and they are all there: Suvorov, Fuat, the man with the baseplate, the one with the ammunition boxes. They pass a wrecked trench. It is empty, completely empty. Abdulin doesn't even see any corpses. The snow is a filthy black from the explosions.

. . .

One man's death is another man's boots. Vittorio Vallicella and his companions continue existing out on the fringes, still driving their truck on a slow and meandering journey westwards, still, for a while, living free and solitary lives on whatever they can find, steal or barter.

But even as they continue slipping past roadblocks, checkpoints, reorganization zones and vehicle columns, there is a growing feeling that their time is limited.

The worst chaos is over. Order is being restored. Sooner or later, they will be discovered and made a part of the army again. Sergeant Berrà is becoming more and more nervous, saying frequently that they need to locate a unit and make themselves known. Vallicella and the rest of them want to avoid that as long as possible. "We've done enough fighting" is his argument.

On this day, November 19,* they see four low-flying British fighter planes in the distance, sweeping in from the sea and attacking a long column of vehicles on the coast road. (The RAF is their great fear and, in spite of the heat and sharp sunlight, they have torn the roof off their truck in order to be able to spot planes in time.) They halt and watch in horror. There is no anti-aircraft defense so the four planes are able to shoot up the column precisely and systematically. The result, as Vallicella writes in his diary, is "a massacre." When the pilots fly off after about fifteen minutes, the air is full of plumes of thick, black, oily smoke.

Once the sun has set, Vallicella and a couple of his comrades slip down to the road, mainly on the hunt for fuel. They creep around among the wreckage in the darkness and siphon gasoline from one tank after another until they have gathered around twenty gallons. When it is time to return, they lose their way in the thick black of night and shout for Berrà and Doliman. No answer. They settle down and smoke and chat while waiting for dawn.

When the sun rises, they are horrified to discover they have spent the night together with many dead bodies. It takes them half an hour to find their own truck. They quickly fill the tank and drive away.

. . .

That same Thursday Abdulin meets some of the enemy for the first time. They are Romanian prisoners of war† and they seem almost

---

* According to the diary, this could possibly have been November 20. Vallicella says that, by this stage of their meandering, he was starting to lose his sense of time.

† They were soldiers of the 13th Romanian Infantry Division, which had been hammered on this first day. Abdulin's 293th Rifle Division was the most

relieved that it's all over. They repeat time after time, "*Antonescu kaput!*," "*Stalin gut! Rus Kamerad gut!*" One of them plays on his mouth organ, slightly ironically, the well-known, tuneful song about Katyusha, the girl who waits faithfully while her beloved defends the motherland. But Abdulin is most interested in the Romanians' horses: beautiful, well-groomed Thoroughbreds, with harnesses, bridles and reins all of creaking new leather. These were very different from their own small, hairy Mongolian horses with their coarse harnesses. He mounts one of them.

Abdulin and the others continue moving south-southwest across the milk-white winter landscape. The sounds of incessant gunfire and artillery barrages hang in the air the whole time. The temperature slowly starts to rise.

By lunchtime they have covered two and a half miles and are approaching the second Romanian line of defense. Before they have time to engage that line in combat, close columns of white-painted tanks, mainly T-34s, appear out of the mist behind them.* The tanks simply trundle through their ranks, snow and soil spurting up from their caterpillar tracks as they drive, all guns ablaze, into the Romanian line.

This looks to be going well.

.   .   .

From midnight to three in the morning on Thursday, November 19, Vera Brittain is on fire watch. She has gone through the training, taken part in practice exercises and dutifully performs her shift, which is not exactly onerous, it being a long time since London was raided. Given the new, more relaxed regulations for fire-watching, you are now allowed to stay at home in bed as long as you are fully dressed and have reported in. She has a special armband and an ugly helmet; she is also wearing trousers, which feels particularly strange.

---

successful rifle division in the 21st Army in this attack. The current image of the Romanians imploding at the first attack does not hold. Some of the units fought furiously and well—for instance, another of the rifle divisions of the 21st Army, the 96th, met such tough resistance that they had to break off their attack.

* This is the IVth Armored Corps. The army commander was taking a chance and sending his most powerful strike force into the hole the 293rd had punched in the Romanian lines—to great effect, as it would turn out.

George Catlin, Vera Brittain's husband, three years her junior and an academic prodigy, professor of political science and an unsuccessful Labour politician, sets off that day on yet another of his lecture tours. This doesn't bother her. The marriage may be characterized by mutual respect, but any eroticism is dormant.* What does trouble her, however, is the business of the children. Two years ago, she and her husband decided to send them unaccompanied to safety in the United States. It was probably the most difficult decision she had ever faced. (She decided she would commit suicide if the ship they were on was torpedoed.) Now, with the bombing over, she longs for them more than ever and not a day passes without her trying to find a way to bring them home. Flying home via Portugal, perhaps?

The only time she's happy is when she's working.

.   .   .

More reports (collected later) from the great famine in Henan:

A mother and father tie their six children to trees so that they can't follow them while they are searching for food.

A mother with a baby and two older children is unable to walk any farther and sends the two older children to a nearby village to beg for food while she sits down under a tree to breastfeed the baby. When they return, their mother is dead with the baby still sucking at her breast.

A mother and a father can no longer bear hearing their two small starving children crying for food, so they murder them.

A family sells everything they own, buys the biggest meal they can, eats it and commits suicide.

.   .   .

When dawn breaks on Savannah on Friday, November 20, a thick mist has moved in from the Atlantic. It would be a pity if it stayed all day, as today is the Great Day. Thousands of invitations have been sent out and the police have been put on alert to turn away nosy onlookers who haven't been invited. All work at the yard comes to a halt as so many people want to witness the launch of the first Liberty ship.

---

* A couple of years earlier, Vera Brittain had an affair with her American publisher and she'd been secretly and deeply in love with him ever since. Her love was not returned. She offered her husband a divorce, which he emphatically rejected.

One of the most iconic photographs of the war. It was taken by George Silk, an army photographer, during the battle for Buna and Gona on New Guinea toward the end of 1942. A barefoot and wounded Australian soldier is being led by a native New Guinean, Raphael Oimbari, along a path through tall cotton grass to a first aid station. The wounded Australian is George Whittington, and at the time of the photo he had just been injured by a bullet from a Japanese sniper. Whittington died of typhus a few weeks later. Oimbari died in 1996.

A similarly iconic photograph taken on December 28, also by George Silk. It shows Australian soldiers at a well-camouflaged, well-built Japanese bunker they have captured. Four of its dead defenders are lying outside.

Another photograph from the brutal war zone of New Guinea. The American soldier is standing over a Japanese man he has just shot. The dying man does not seem to have a weapon and the American is carrying a pair of gloves in his left hand; it seems likely that the American's task was to perform a routine check of the fallen (wearing gloves to avoid getting too bloodied) and that after finding one man still alive, he duly shot him.

On the Kokoda Trail in New Guinea: Australian soldiers of the 2/25th and 2/33rd infantry battalions are crossing a stream on an improvised bridge. In the background, a number of them are taking the chance to bathe and wash their clothes.

Dead Japanese from the final battle around Buna. In the background is a Japanese landing craft of the type used to ship in provisions and reinforcements for the bridgehead. This is likely to be the same beach as that shown in George Strock's famous photograph of three fallen Americans, published in *Life* in 1943. The beach was called Maggot Beach because of the large number of corpses there.

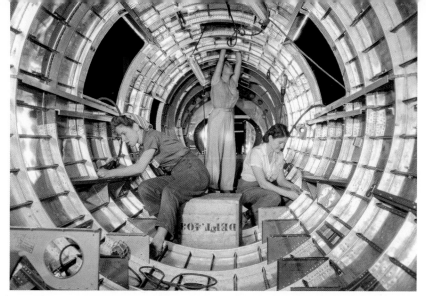

Three American women building a B-17 heavy bomber. Before the war, only 1 percent of the workforce of the aircraft industry were women; by 1943, they made up 65 percent.

Shirley Slade, a twenty-two-year-old transport pilot in 1943. She flew aircraft to waiting combat units—including the notoriously difficult B-26s.

Soviet soldiers making an attack at Rzhev—which they frequently did, and almost always unsuccessfully. The nickname of that section of the front was the "Meat Grinder." Tactics, conditions and losses were reminiscent of the Western Front in the First World War.

The 9th Company of the German 578th Infantry Regiment during the battle for Stalingrad is about to carry out an attack on a blood-soaked industrial complex—the tractor factory. By this stage, most infantry companies were reduced to roughly this size. On the left is an assault gun that will support their attack; the factory entrance is behind them. The photo was taken on the morning of October 15 by Hans Eckle, a soldier in the company. That day's attack went surprisingly well: the tractor factory was eventually captured and the unit reached the Volga.

At the same time as the battle of Stalingrad, there were also lengthy and pointless battles around what was known as the Rzhev bulge in the central Eastern Front. That was where Willy Peter Reese was located. The German look-out in his trench is an experienced front-line veteran, for he is smoking his pipe upside down so that the glow is not visible.

A dead horse lies in the endless, snow-covered waste of Russia.

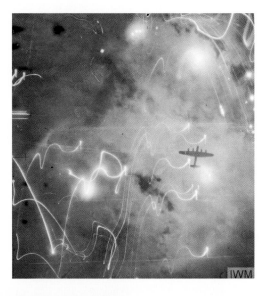

A Lancaster bomber over Hamburg on the night of January 30, 1943, photographed by the target camera in another bomber. This is what it looked like when Bomber Command mounted its increasingly powerful raids on various targets on the continent. The bigger, blurred lights are target markers—it was the job of John Bushby's unit to drop these; the snaking lines are tracers fired by anti-aircraft guns, distorted by the slow shutter speed of the camera and the movement of the aircraft.

This is what target markers and tracers looked like from the ground. This was Genoa in late autumn of 1942, and the photo may well be showing the raid of November 15–16, in which John Bushby took part.

Destruction on the ground after the major RAF raid on Turin on the night of November 18. John Bushby was also involved in this raid. The photograph shows the bomb damage to the Fiat-Ansaldo factory that Bushby mentions having seen and that his crew attempted to hit.

It took a lot of anti-aircraft cover to defend a city. Here, a Finnish anti-aircraft battery fires a Bofors gun at Soviet bombers outside Helsinki. Soviet air raids were few and small in the autumn of 1942, but they could cause losses nevertheless *(Försvarsmaktens bildarkiv JSdia285)*.

The Ostbahnhof (East Railway Station), Munich, July 22, 1942. Sophie Scholl is there to wave goodbye to her brother Hans (*on the left*) and other acquaintances who are on their way to the Eastern Front to serve as medical orderlies for a short period. The young man on the right is Christoph Probst. All of them are members of the secret anti-Nazi group known as the White Rose, and seven months later all three would be guillotined.

In the late summer of 1942, the SS assembly camp in Mechelen, to which Jews (and Roma) were brought from the whole country prior to subsequent transport to Auschwitz. Another group has obviously been brought to the camp during the night, and their luggage is lined up on both sides of the two trucks. In the second half of 1942, it began to dawn on the majority of Belgians that their hope of a painless end to the war and to the occupation was an illusion.

A Japanese camp for Allied prisoners of war on Java, after the end of the war in 1945. Weary Dunlop was in a virtually identical camp consisting of a cluster of low, fenced-in, white-painted buildings.

This drawing illustrates Dunlop's camp outside Bandung. It was drawn by Ray Parkin, a prisoner who survived.

The wind freshens and the mist over the river begins to disperse. A long, heavy, grey-painted shape emerges from the haze, its superstructure decorated for today with brightly colored pennants and its prow bedecked with layers of bunting in the American colors. A number of the town's dignitaries are gathered on a high podium that has been erected under the keel of the vessel and similarly decorated. On the scrubbed concrete below the podium there is a military band playing march music. A figure takes the microphone and asks for silence.

"The Star-Spangled Banner" rings out across the stocks and everyone sings along with it. The text is particularly suitable for this morning: "O say can you see by the dawn's early light / What so proudly we hailed at the twilight's last gleaming." A breeze from the river lifts the bunting hanging on the vessel.

It's time for speeches. The man who opened the ceremony speaks directly to the crowds of workmen following the launch from down in the stocks or up on the cranes, scaffolding or rooftops: "In celebrating Georgia's first Liberty Ship, the lion's share of the credit goes to the men and women of the yard. These fine results could not have been attained but for them." The fact that the speaker mentions the women, too, is something new. The audience can see that in among the helmeted men, there are many women in overalls with their welding visors raised.

The next man to take the microphone is a judge, who talks of this being a battle to "defend the ideals which…are so woven into the fabric of American life that if need be we will give all that we have, even our lives, before we surrender them, for without them life is not worth living." And this is all about "the right of men to be free, to set up governments to serve them rather than to become themselves servants to the state."

A man in an admiral's uniform steps up to the microphone. He, too, emphasizes the significance of these ships for victory, but is forced to cut his speech short, and the next man on the list of speakers simply has to put away his prepared speech. Something has happened. It turns out that the tidal waters have already risen, probably because of the wind from the Atlantic; and it is essential that the ship is launched when the water level is at its highest point.*

---

* There was some concern that, at launch, the ship would glide right across the river and run aground on long, thin Fig Island opposite.

Now there's no time to waste. One of the foremen gives a command to two welders, one on each side of the bow (one of them is named McNettles), and, in a carefully coordinated movement, they begin cutting away the firmly welded metal plate that is the only thing now holding the ship on the slipway.

When there is only one rivet left, Lucy Heard George, wife of Senator Walter F. George, steps forward on the podium to name the ship—SS *James Oglethorpe.** She swings a ribbon with a firmly attached bottle of Brut Cuvée of 1857 vintage, but the bottle misses. Maybe she is nervous, maybe a slight murmur runs through the crowd—an occurrence like this usually implies bad luck for the ship—but she gets a grip on herself, swings the bottle again and now it hits. The bottle shatters with a fizzing champagne crack and, at the same time, the last wedges are knocked away. The high, grey-painted shape immediately begins to move, slowly ... slowly ... and the thousands of onlookers break into a cheer so thunderous that it drowns out the military band. The cheering is accompanied by the pounding of numerous pneumatic hammers being fired simultaneously in tribute, this cacophony first mixing with and then fading into the dull, complaining sound of the SS *James Oglethorpe* sliding ever faster backwards down the greased slide rails before she finally, stern first, hits the muddy-green Savannah River with a growling splash.

The band packs away its instruments; the people on the podium leave the shipyard and go for lunch in the luxurious De Soto Hotel on East Liberty Street; the onlookers go home and the workers return to their work on the two ships left there. The decorations are folded and put away, ready for use at the next launch. Tomorrow, Saturday, or the day after tomorrow at the latest, a new keel will be laid down on the temporarily empty Slipway No. 2.

There is a category of people which is not mentioned either in the speeches or in the newspapers that reported on the launching of the SS *James Oglethorpe* at the Savannah shipyard, though their presence is quite obvious: Black workers.[†]

---

* James Oglethorpe, born in 1696, was a British officer considered to be the founder of the colony of Georgia—where, among other things, he introduced a ban on slavery.

[†] It's difficult to find Black faces on the photo of the event, so perhaps they weren't allowed down on the actual slipway.

They, too, were in demand. But whereas women had been allowed in, the Blacks still have to live in accordance with the race laws valid in the South, which, for instance, stipulate that whites and Blacks cannot eat in the same restaurants, use the same toilets, play on the same baseball teams, go to the same schools, bathe on the same beaches, occupy the same prison cell or, naturally, marry one another! When Blacks are travelling to the shipyard, they have to sit at the back of the bus and, when they arrive, they have to enter by a special gate solely for the use of Blacks. Without exception, they have the simplest, dirtiest and worst-paid jobs. It makes no difference that many of them are trained—as welders, for instance—and that as a rule they are more conscientious, drink less and take less sick leave than the white workers at the yard.*

But a simple job is better than no job at all—even though they recognize that victory over Germany is unlikely to improve their situation. The reverse is more likely.† Perhaps they are hanging on to the same wild hope as their fathers and their fathers' fathers before them—that by making a contribution to the U.S. winning, their lives will be better, even if it is only in terms of respect.

.   .   .

The storm hits them and there is no longer a horizon. The formless, raging sea is digging deep and then rising up in enormous, foaming embankments from which the froth of spindrift flies up and becomes one with the wind. The sea is everything, the vessel nothing. Time after time, the bow of HMS *Ulster Queen* digs down into the dark, deep, breaking waves that pound down along the whole length of the ship. Ice has begun to form white rings on the rigging and aerials.

No one is permitted up on the upper deck apart from members of

* Since 1941, there had actually been a national non-discrimination law that every shipyard involved in building Liberty ships was supposed to follow: time after time this led to violent protests on the part of white workers. In the shipyard in Mobile, Alabama, in May 1943, the promotion of twelve Blacks caused white workers to start serious race riots.

† Joe Louis, the heavyweight boxer who won the ideologically laden return match in 1938 against the German Max Schmeling, the Aryan star, was asked why he had volunteered to join the American army. He answered: "Might be a lot wrong with America, but nothing Hitler can fix"—a view no doubt shared by many Blacks.

the anti-aircraft crew, who are relieved every two hours or so. Leonard Thomas has caught glimpses of them, lashed fast to their guns, huddled close to each other for warmth, covered with layer upon layer of oilskins. Belowdecks, no one is eating. (They have stopped piping mealtimes. Almost all the crockery is smashed.) Hardly anyone is sleeping. Small groups can be seen here and there, bundled up and wet, exhausted by lack of sleep and seasickness. They slither around, half sitting or lying on the floor, in time with the uneven, unpredictable lurches of the vessel. The decks are slippery with vomit and bilge. It continues hour after hour, right through the raging black night. This is Friday, November 20.

By dawn the sea has calmed a little. Thomas and the rest of the crew venture up on the icy deck. When they look out over the chill, grey endlessness that surrounds them, they discover that the world is empty.

They are alone. The storm has scattered convoy QP15.*

. . .

It has taken Tohichi Wakabayashi's company two days to reach their new position on the hill. He is angry. He yells at his soldiers, but regrets it almost at once.

There can be no doubt how hard it is to hack, creep, push your way through the dense jungle on Guadalcanal, and no doubt that all the rain has turned paths and ravines into slippery tracks of mud, but he knows very well why it has actually taken so long. His soldiers cannot manage it. (The column is losing men. Men are falling out. Men are collapsing.) For the last few days they have survived on half rations, but now the rations have been cut to a third—at the most. A few days ago, his soldiers were hungry, now they are starving. "What used to be round faces of fellow comrades are now slender faces behind bandages." In his diary for November 20 he writes:

> Food, food, food. We are desperate for food. I want to see the
> soldiers eat until they are full so they can go out and fight

---

* The storm undoubtedly resulted in a number of damaged ships, with one sinking—a giant wave tore the stern off a Soviet destroyer. But it seems likely that the meteorological phenomenon was more of a help than a hindrance, since it made it impossible for German planes to fly and consequently the wolf pack of U-boats (code name *Boreas*) lying in wait couldn't find the convoy and attack it.

hard. That is all I wish for. Even if mortars fall on us like a
tropic storm, or the bombs completely level the ground into
something like a farming field, it doesn't affect me. But I cannot bear to watch the soldiers looking lifeless from starvation.
I do not want to see the soldiers in my company dead with
their head hanging low clutching their mess kits or firewood
in their hands, like I've seen in other places.

The cans of meat and the miso powder they had in their packs when
they landed just two weeks ago is all finished, as is most of the rice.
There are still some pickled plums. One of the platoons in the battalion
has been sent down to the shore to boil up seawater and produce salt.
(The need for salt was particularly great since the tropical heat made
them all sweat so much.) Such is the desperation.

The soldiers hunt for anything edible. They find palm shoots, sweet
potatoes, wild ginger and water celery, but none of these things are
common. Wakabayashi guesses that only one in a hundred men finds
anything. They eat snakes and lizards and someone is said to have
managed to make lizard teriyaki, but all the reptiles seem to have been
caught and eaten by this point.

The casual attitude that characterized the Japanese decision to go to
war in 1941 still characterizes their waging of the war and their planning
of operations on Guadalcanal. For a long time now, the Japanese army
has been an army with a small logistical tail—an astoundingly small
tail compared with the Americans, the champions in that field.* This
makes the Japanese army very mobile, but also vulnerable. This has not
been a great problem until now. On the whole, in this war and earlier
wars (like European wars in the seventeenth century), men have moved
through countries and territories where, when necessary, they have
been able to loot and plunder. But this is not possible on Guadalcanal.
As far as food for human beings goes, this island is a desert despite

---

* This can be measured using PTMD, which refers to how many tons of
provisions of various kinds are needed per one thousand men per day to enable
them to function and fight. At this stage, the Japanese army had a standard measure of four tons PTMD, though their troops on the island only received a
fraction of this amount. Their American adversaries on the island were receiving
something like twenty tons PTMD. On the Western Front in 1944, the American
logistics organization raised this to an almost unbelievable seventy tons PTMD.

its greenery. The calculations done by the leaders are incompetent, their plans are inflexible and their reliance on the selfless fighting spirit of their soldiers is characterized by thoughtlessness, cynicism even. Wakabayashi knows the slogans used, but he doesn't believe them. On that day he writes:

> Pretending to be unaffected by hunger by saying "A true sam-
> urai can go hungry but behave as if he has eaten plenty" is just
> plain foolish. Sure, there are ways to go without food for a day
> or two but having to tough it out for over a week, not knowing
> if provisions will ever be available, clearly takes a toll on the
> morale of the soldiers.

It is here on this island in the South Pacific that the gulf between Japan's grandiose imperial ambitions and the modest resources available to achieve them becomes clearly apparent. As evening approaches, the rain stops and Wakabayashi calms down and regains his composure. He watches the setting sun color the crowns of the trees above his head. "I am alone hearing only the sound of birds chirping." A little later he beds down in the dugout where he will spend the night.

· · ·

The God of War is singing now. The noises come together into a mighty chorus of explosions, cracks, swishes, whines, howls, crashes and thuds. Vasily Grossman has heard this many times before, but never at this volume and with such concentration. It's the thunder made by 1,077 mortars, field guns, howitzers and Katyusha rockets and their missiles raining down along the full length of a forty-mile front. It's impossible to tell whether the Romanians over there are shooting back. The ground is trembling. The colors of the wintry landscape are extinguished, veiled in a light mist.

Grossman peers out towards the curtain of smoke and dust and rapid flashes of light that seem to roll along the enemy lines. His position is a short distance from the village and lake Tsatsa, some forty miles south of Stalingrad, at a forward command post for the IVth Cavalry Corps. It's obvious that he was only told about this imminent attack at the last minute and given permission to accompany this unit positioned farthest out on the left flank of the attacking forces.* As far as can be judged, a major attack began in the north, up by the Don, yesterday (official news communiqués from Moscow neither confirm nor deny it), and today, Friday, November 20, it's the south's turn.

Grossman probably didn't have any great problem getting his request approved. He is a well-known and, more importantly, very respected reporter. His articles in *Krasnaja Zvezda* are read by almost everyone, especially at the front, where, as the Red Army's own paper, it is more widely read than either *Pravda* or *Izvestia*. Grossman's style, human interest and passion for the truth, along with his strong distaste for cheap propaganda, have made his articles popular with the ordinary soldiers as well as the higher command. During the summer, *Krasnaja Zvezda* published sections of a forthcoming novel by Grossman with motifs from 1941[†] and they bolstered his reputation among *frontoviki* (fighters at the front) as being the only one who tells it as it really is. And he isn't a member of the Communist Party.

In fact, everyone reads him. Rumor has it that Stalin, being suspicious of a Jew like Grossman, goes through all his texts assiduously; one of the reporter's friends says that the dictator is his most important reader—and his most dangerous. At the same time, the fact that Grossman's reports from the front have made him so famous offers a certain level of protection.

His texts are, of course, censored and often changed, which is a constant source of frustration to Grossman, but they remain in a class of their own. Given his psychological sensitivity, he is a perceptive interviewer who can get the most buttoned-up individual to open up during what seems to be an ordinary conversation. Since he has a phenomenal memory he doesn't take notes as he goes along, writing it all

---

* The IVth Mechanized Corps, their neighbors to the right, is meant to attack in a curve around the enemy lines and link up with those coming from the northwest and the Don (including Abdulin's rifle division, the 293rd) and so close the trap around the 6th Army. At the same time, the IVth Cavalry Corps has orders to attack in a slight outward curve to form the outer part of the trap.

† These later formed the basis of the novel *For a Just Cause*, published in 1952. It was nominated for the Stalin Prize, but was immediately withdrawn as a result of the anti-Semitic campaign underway at that point, which could have led to Grossman's death, were it not for Stalin's unexpected stroke in March 1953. (In English translation, the novel is better known as *Stalingrad*.)

up afterwards in almost illegible handwriting in small notebooks. And generals, in particular, whose vanity is frequently on a par with their brutality, like to be written about: Grossman knows how to exploit this weakness. Grossman can, in principle, go where he wants and talk to whom he wants.

The artillery barrage has been crashing and thundering for an hour now. Every so often a shoal of red streaks made by Katyusha rockets pass over their heads. At 8:30 a.m. Grossman notes a change in the sound of explosions north of them: they become more distant, more of an echo—a sure sign that the attack has started.

A quarter of an hour later, the barrage ceases where Grossman is. Soviet infantrymen climb out of their trenches and begin to advance into the smoke and mist. Grossman follows them on foot, dressed in a heavy uniform overcoat with a big sheepskin collar. He observes many soldiers holding their small infantry spades up in front of their faces as improvised protection when the bullets begin to fly.

There aren't any connected Romanian lines, just occasional strong-points. The last of them has been taken by lunchtime and Grossman writes in his notebook:

> An image: a strongpoint destroyed by a tank. There is a flat-tened Romanian. A tank has driven over him. His face has become a bas-relief. Next to him, there are two crushed Germans. There is one of our soldiers, too, lying in the trench half buried.
>
> Empty cans, grenades, hand grenades, a blanket stained with blood, pages from German magazines. Our soldiers are sitting among the corpses, cooking in a cauldron slices cut from a dead horse, and stretching their frozen hands towards the fire.

The mood among the infantrymen is good, optimistic. Grossman hears one of them say: "Oh, it would be wonderful to get to Kiev," to which another one answers, "Ah, I like to get to Berlin."

.   .   .

Berlin, the same day. Another day of wind and rain is coming to an end. It has become colder and yesterday sleety rain fell on the great city.

The newspaper headlines are monotonous, nothing but battles and more battles: in the Caucasus and Stalingrad, on the Solomon Islands and elsewhere in the Pacific, all around the Mediterranean and the Atlantic, on the various fronts in North Africa. They also report that Dr. Goebbels, Reichsminister für Volksaufklärung und Propaganda, has visited the Ruhr to see for himself "the damage done by British terror raids." In the afternoon, he made a speech ("received with a storm of applause") in Wuppertal town hall, where, among much else, he stated that "our final victory is just a matter of time."

Darkness is falling when the doorbell rings at the von Kardorffs' apartment at Rankestrasse 21. Ursula opens the door to find two people standing there. With some hesitation, they come in and under the light in the hall Ursula sees that both of them are wearing the yellow Jewish star. They are relatives of a businessman in Breslau, a man who owns a painting by Ursula's father. They have the painting with them and are hoping he will buy it back. After she has given them something to eat, their nervousness begins to ease and they start talking openly. Ursula von Kardorff writes: "The suffering these people are going through is indescribable. To avoid being picked up, they are trying to go underground, remove the stars and get a roof over their heads by claiming to have been bombed out in the Rhineland."

It's common knowledge that more and more Jews are removing their yellow stars, hiding and taking on false identities. They are called "U-boats" or Untertaucher (divers).* Ursula is clearly concerned by what is happening, by the whole situation, by how vulnerable these two individuals are. She knows that Jews are being transported east to be murdered *en masse,* and she is also aware that the majority of her countrymen "are indifferent to or even approving" of "the extermination of all Jews."† And she is concerned by the fact that "you can only help secretly, must not be seen with them in public unless you want to jeopardize your own freedom."

Even if the whole family dislikes the persecution of the Jews, they have different ways of dealing with what is happening. Whereas

---

* In Berlin alone, the number was estimated at between 6,000 and 7,000, of whom some 1,700 would survive the war.

† This is one of the many pieces that von Kardorff changed in her diary after the war. In the original entry for January 2, 1943, she wrote about "the extermination of all Jews, which leaves the great majority of people either indifferent or even approving." In the published version, the words "or even approving" are omitted.

her brother Klaus, a former SA man, finds it easy to shrug off all the unpleasantness, her youngest brother, Jürgen, a practicing Christian, is much more troubled. "Like our father, he has been unable to form a hard shell over his skin as so many people try to do nowadays." She finds herself in a kind of vague intermediate state: at times melancholic, lethargic, conscience-smitten, at other times full of sudden joy and cheer to the extent that she has begun to consider herself irresponsible, childish even. Her dreams tend to be dark and threatening.

Her father buys back the painting. Naturally. Her father must have been quite noticeably desperate, painfully awkward and embarrassed even, for when the transaction is over and the door closes behind the two visitors from Breslau, Ursula is clearly relieved, but—possibly to her surprise—mainly for the sake of her sensitive father. She is glad that the old Jewish family friends have emigrated because "in the long run, Daddy could not have endured it." She herself does not seem to understand the extent to which her own moral universe has shrunk.

At this point, she possibly sits down to flick through the newspaper. Fortunately, there is more there than just communiqués about the situation on the various fronts. On this day, Friday, November 20, she can read about the most recent recipients of the Knight's Cross, the fact that the Hitler Youth is planning to collect firewood on behalf of women whose husbands are at the front, that a man named Paul S. has been sentenced to seven months' imprisonment for the theft of two rabbits, that a wild boar attacked a cyclist in Landsberg, and the happy news that two wedding rings lost ten years ago have been found in a field in Jüterbog. In the lost-and-found section, a Mrs. Irma Koebe is looking for an umbrella she had with her on the 5:42 p.m. Berlin–Luckenwalde train the Friday before last. The Reichsprogramm channel on the radio is playing cheerful dance music, whereas the Deutschlandsender channel is offering Haydn. And the elegant common stair no longer echoes to the sound of footsteps.

·   ·   ·

That same Friday in Chicago turns out to be a grey but mild late autumn day with an occasional shower. Down under the west stands of the decommissioned football stadium, the building of CP-1 continues day and night without break. The work is being pushed forward with great determination, a core element of the mood. There is also, however, a level of anxiety in the air.

Going down through the dark corridors is like passing through a cacophony of whines, hums, rattles and creaks—through shafts of light and darkness. In one room wooden beams are being cut with a circular saw; in another they are working on long, black lengths of graphite, four inches thick. They are being cut to size, polished, and some are being drilled. The cutting and polishing is done with ordinary electric carpentry tools, such as planes and oscillating saws. Certain of the twenty-pound blocks are given round-bottomed holes. Precision is important—they must have a diameter of exactly eight centimeters—so the holes are made using a lathe. The cutters are made of steel, which are sharpened by hand when they get blunt. A newly sharpened cutter lasts about an hour, which means about sixty holes. They will need to drill an estimated nineteen thousand holes before CP-1 is ready for use.

Grey graphite dust hangs in the air and settles on everything—floors, walls, tools, clothes, hands and faces. The only external signs of the activity are two big, ugly, metal fan ducts on the neo-Gothic frontage of the stand to pump out the graphite dust. The dry dust makes the floor slippery and it's easy to fall over. Space is tight, and passing people in dirty clothes is a squeeze. Finished graphite bars are taken on small trolleys down to the squash court, where layer after layer is added to what will be CP-1. Men in overalls do the heavy lifting and sing work songs to pass the time.

Leona Woods suffers the same muted concern as the other physicists in the group, a concern that is made up of two related fears. The great fear that drives all of them, she reported later, was "that we were wrong (in our way of developing the bomb) and that the Germans were ahead of us. That was a persistent and ever-present fear." There lies the basis for the whole project: as a scientist, she knows that German physicists are the best in the world and that they are aware that it's theoretically possible to build such an enormously powerful bomb. Any moral qualms they may have about building a doomsday weapon of this kind are overcome by the thought of what Hitler could do armed with a weapon like that. Which is why the American project must get there first. But what if they don't?

And then there is their second fear—call it anxiety, rather. It's an anxiety that grows in time with the growth of the precisely interlocked pile down in the squash court. All the experts involved agree that the machine they are constructing shouldn't be able to explode, and that is some comfort. But there are other niggling unknowns: What, for instance, if their construction simply does not work? Would that mean that Hitler will win the race to build a bomb? Or, what if it does work but they are unable to stop the chain reaction? When the pile is fully loaded and a critical mass has been reached, it will contain over forty tons of radioactive material: What will happen then if they lose control and the process goes off the rails, here, in the middle of a city with a million inhabitants?*

Her boss, Enrico Fermi, made estimate after estimate on this issue, using the white slide rule he constantly carried with him. He thought the machine should be equipped with a triple-braking system, which would be sufficient.

Leona Woods was born on a farm in La Grange, Illinois, and she is used to hard work. She uses her leisure time helping her mother, who grows potatoes outside the city. One of the physicists leading the project is not keen on having a woman involved in the heavy, Sisyphus-like work of carrying, lifting and positioning the graphite blocks, so even though she is quite willing to pull her weight, her main involvement is with the boron trifluoride counter she has constructed and with two other instruments, all of which are essential to enable the CP-1 experiment. In order to calibrate her counter, she has built her own small pile of graphite and radioactive material. On this particular Friday, the fifteenth layer is laid and it is time to place the counter's sensor in the pile. Woods is able to confirm that neutron activity is increasing and that the increase is in line with Fermi's calculations.

·   ·   ·

Saturday, November 21, is an important day for Hélène Berr. Her great love, Jean, is to come to the flat on the Avenue Élisée-Reclus and meet her parents. That will make their relationship more or less official, a sort of informal engagement, in fact. In well-assimilated circles like the Berr family, the fact that Jean is a Catholic is of no importance.

---

* The location of the experiment was certainly not the best from the safety point of view. The intention had been to build the reactor in an isolated forest location southwest of Chicago, but when the building workers went on strike, and given the necessary haste, they decided to use the squash court—without bothering to inform the rector of the university. (Strikes were a common feature in the United States during the war years.)

Hélène spends the morning running various errands and writing a long letter to Jean. She is intending to give it to him later. She knows this will be the last time they see one another for a long time, as he is about to leave, secretly, and for the war. It is a long letter and, come lunchtime, she still hasn't changed and put on her makeup. She'll have to hurry.

At last the doorbell rings, and there he is: thin, well-dressed, slightly shy; his hair is quite long and swept back; he is very polite; he has serious eyes and an aquiline nose. Hélène's parents, Raymond and Antoinette, give Jean a very warm welcome.

Hélène is overjoyed. Her parents are extraordinarily important to her in everything. She is close to them both, particularly her mother, who is both affectionate and stylish; she never calls her anything but *Maman* and she shares many of her worries and her secrets with her. (*Maman*'s pet name for Hélène is Linlin.) Hélène's fifty-four-year-old father, however, is the central figure, not just for her but for all of them. He is the family's *bonus paterfamilias*, their undisputed protector and helper, the strong-willed and self-controlled figure whose intelligence, successes and influence made their affluent and protected existence possible.

The Raymond Berr who greets Jean Morawiecki so warmly is not, however, the same man he was just six months ago. Hélène has noticed the change and it pains her. She notices, too, how he tries in vain to hide his sufferings from his daughter and his wife.

What happened was this: last summer, at the end of June, Raymond Berr was arrested without any prior warning. It happened at his office at Établissements Kuhlmann, the major chemical conglomerate where he is one of the top bosses and most important innovators. The reason for the arrest was that his Jewish star was not sewn on with thread, as the regulations demanded, but attached with a press stud.

That same day, Hélène and her mother were called to a police station in order to give him what clothes and necessities he would need for his transfer to the huge transit camp at Drancy. It's difficult to tell what hurt Hélène most: seeing that it was only the French police who were running the operation, or seeing her proud father so humiliated, so exposed, with such a strange smile, obviously embarrassed—indeed, almost ashamed by the situation—and without a tie. She has hardly ever seen him without a waistcoat and tie.

Three weeks after that, *la grande rafle* took place, the great raid in

which thousands of French police—and not a single German soldier*
—carried out a carefully planned dawn raid all over Paris. They picked
up just over thirteen thousand Jews, most of a more or less foreign
background, many of them women and children, for transit to Drancy
and deportation. During the time her father was in the overcrowded
transit camp along with all those confused and desperate people,
Hélène and the Berr family lived in daily fear that he would be put on
one of the notorious trains to the east. She knew that many people were
being transported to what was said to be a big labor camp near Kraków.

That big raid has changed everything.[†] Even the most optimistic
Jews now recognize that all of them—without exception, irrespective
of sex and age, irrespective of wealth and contacts, irrespective of titles
and military decorations—are under threat and that their opponents
are completely without scruples. And many of the Christian French,
who had been prepared to look away during earlier arrests or actually willingly applauded the official propaganda that this was a matter
of deporting dangerous foreigners or potential terrorists, have now
recognized that there is something that doesn't add up. Why round
up women and children, too? What use could they be as forced labor
in the east?

Raymond Berr was freed at the end of September after the company paid a large (and secret) ransom. But something in him is broken.
Today, however, he seems to be trying to be at his best. Hélène, Jean
and her mother and father sit at the table, where *Maman* has prepared a
wonderful lunch. The signs of approval by her parents are quite unmistakeable and Hélène is overjoyed, "as in a dream." After lunch the
young couple listen to gramophone records.

Then it's time to say goodbye.

The apartment door closes.

---

* To be fair, it has to be said that the whole operation was the result of much
German pressure, but then, of course, the apparatus of the French state was
willing to follow Nazi directives and, in some cases, to go further than was being
demanded. As far as we know, not a single French policeman refused to take part
in the raids. And without the collaboration of the French police, the roundup
would have been impossible in a purely practical sense: the number of German
soldiers in France was too small.

† There is general agreement among historians that *la grande rafle* was a catastrophe in terms of public opinion about the Vichy regime. It did a great deal to
undermine the regime's legitimacy.

Footsteps on the staircase die away.

Hélène has invited a group of friends to join her, as a way of stilling the pain she knows she will feel. They arrive at her apartment and then, in the middle of it all, Jean returns. He got mixed up—so they still have some time to be together. Then more farewells. She writes in her diary: "I was *reckless** (because of the prohibition on going out) and went and accompanied him to the Métro. My friends were still there when I got back. It stopped me thinking."

. . .

Winter is approaching and it's getting colder outdoors. There are four of them now in the house on Warszawa Road in Międzyrzec Podlaski: Józek went to Warsaw and managed to convince Danuta's mother, Jasia, to come and live with them, and she came, bringing numerous possessions, not the least of which are warm clothes. Together they are working on setting up a small hairdresser's salon for Jasia to run in the room nearest the street. Danuta's strict and alcoholic father, Alek, is locked up in the notorious Mokotów Prison in Warsaw, ostensibly for sabotage at the mint where he has worked for years as an electrician. That particular accusation must be no more than some sort of excuse to hold him, since if the Germans really believed it, they would have shot him on the spot. The family is allowed to send Alek the occasional parcel.

Warsaw has become an increasingly dangerous city. Rarely a day passes without one of those random raids the Poles have come to call *łapanka,†* in which the Germans barricade a street and ship off—usually to slave labor in Germany—everyone who doesn't have the right papers. About four hundred people a day are taken in this way, sometimes as many as three thousand. It used to be that only people actually on the street were taken, but now the Germans have started going into cafés and restaurants and picking out customers. Law simply doesn't exist. The Germans need slave labor. Anyone who can avoids going out.

Not that Międzyrzec Podlaski and its surroundings are exactly a haven any longer. Even here, people get rounded up, shipped out and

---

* She uses the English word here. Every so often an English word pops up in her diary.

† From the Polish word for the children's game tag.

vanish. But, so far, the Germans have mainly targeted the local Jewish population. There are rumors of a number of mass shootings.

On this day Danuta is out shopping in the grey, autumnal town when she sees a woman coming in the opposite direction. Probably because of the yellow star, Danuta realizes she is Jewish and she also sees that she is carrying a baby in her arms. The significance of the scene suddenly changes when Danuta notices a big SS man a short distance behind the Jewish woman with the baby. And he is catching up with her.

Danuta now witnesses something that is both amazing and horrifying, and it happens quickly. It's obvious that the Jewish woman with the baby realizes she is being followed and she catches the eye of another woman walking immediately in front of Danuta. Some sort of wordless communication takes place—maybe no more than an almost invisible gesture or a glance or an eye movement—and the approaching woman spreads her arms a little and, without any sign of hesitation, the Jewish woman passes the baby across while hiding the movement with her body to prevent the SS man from seeing. Which he obviously doesn't.

A choice that no one should need to make, two different roads and an eternal loss, all in a couple of seconds, during which the absence of any hesitation on the part of the Jewish woman shows that she knows what awaits her. Her own life will soon be over, but not her baby's. Danuta turns around and watches: "One block later, the Jewish woman was rounded up and led to her death." Danuta is shaken. What she has just witnessed is totally incomprehensible.

She, Józek, Jędruś and her mother here in Międzyrzec Podlaski, her young brother Zbyszek in Warsaw and her father, Alek, in his prison cell are all trapped in this incomprehensible situation, where anything and everything may happen, and sometimes does—even things that were impossible earlier. The terror that is constantly present, almost as if it is an addition to the gravitational force of the earth, making everything heavier, more ponderous and sometimes cripplingly difficult, is ultimately a function of uncertainty. And it's no longer a matter of the uncertainty that arises from not knowing—the knowledge is there, because everything happens so openly and there are very few families that haven't been affected. They know *what* it is that happens; the uncertainty lies in *when* and *how* it will happen to them.

Uncertainty feeds silence, just as terror does. Talking is dangerous.

Who knows who is listening? And is the world listening? In addition to uncertainty about one's own fate, there is uncertainty about what is actually happening in the war. An underground news agency does exist and when they lived in Warsaw Danuta would sometimes read *Biuletyn Informacyjny*, one of many illegally circulating news sheets. They are often thin, simply mimeographed and usually well-worn from being passed from hand to hand, and possession can lead to a death sentence.

But what is truth and what is rumor, what is fact and what is hope—that is frequently impossible to know. What's happening at Stalingrad? What's happening in North Africa? (In any case, many people have stopped enquiring about the news since, as a rule, it's so awful.)

Poles are forbidden to possess radios, but her father had hidden a small set under the floor in the corner of the living room of their home in Warsaw. They could sometimes pick up a Russian news channel, but he was the only one who could understand the language. "The distant voices come and go, jumps louder and completely fades away in the whistling noise of outer space."

. . .

The waiting is over. The three-engine plane carrying Ernst Jünger takes off from the Lötzen airfield in light snow. It's about 9:00 a.m. They fly fairly low and Jünger carefully studies the landscape below: lakes, villages, isolated houses, winding rivers and winding roads. After a couple of hours, he falls asleep in spite of the cold and the noise that penetrates the thin corrugated metal of the fuselage.

Jünger is wakened by a sound or a movement. Something is not right. The plane's behavior has changed. When he looks out of the window he sees a pale-red flame fluttering like a long pennant from the round engine housing and whipping across the wing. The plane swings and lurches as the ground rises towards them. The crash seems to be no more than minutes away, maybe just seconds.

In this situation, Jünger is outside his element, both literally and metaphorically. He is trapped in the large but fragile fuselage of the plane, trapped in its rapid descent to the earth, and there is nothing he can do. And then, in this moment of enforced passivity, something both unexpected and logical happens to him: he, the fearless hero, with all his scars and medals, is so overcome with terror that he can't move. Jünger sits there petrified, staring out through a small, rectangular cabin window. And then, with a thump, but not a crash, the plane comes to earth and Jünger is amazed to see that they have landed at an airfield—the right airfield, in Kiev. It's Saturday, November 21.

Once in the city, he learns he will be quartered in the large Palace Hotel, reputed to be the best hotel in the occupied parts of the Soviet Union. The façade certainly promises luxury and imperial splendor, but the facilities are in complete disrepair. The magnificent marble staircase has missing steps and everywhere stinks of excrement. There are no towels in the room and no sink, the toilet refuses to flush, and however much he turns the bathroom taps, there is no water. The central heating doesn't seem to be functioning and there are rats running around. Jünger, moreover, has to share the room with a young captain of artillery, who fortunately turns out to be very friendly.

Jünger goes out for a walk, but quickly returns, disgusted by the place, its ruins and the megalomaniac Stalinist architecture. He writes in his diary: "Just as there are enchanted countries in our world, we get to know others in which the spell is broken, leaving nothing of the enchantment behind."

· · ·

That same Saturday, Elena Skrjabina is walking a tightrope over an abyss. She keeps her gaze fixed on a point in the distance, defending the fragile existence she has won for herself and for hers in Pyatigorsk. She cultivates her contacts within the occupying power, mainly within the powerful economics unit, but also elsewhere. She and her young relation Tanya have been courted by a friendly, helpful Luftwaffe officer by the name of Sulzbach. Elena has courteously stepped aside, but Tanya has allowed herself to be invited to parties. The town is full not just of the usual rumors, but also of suspicion, intrigue and informing. No one is to be relied on.

Skrjabina is worried about what might happen to her sister-in-law Lyalya and her half-Jewish daughter. She writes in her diary:

> These last days the rumors about the transportation of people
> of mixed marriages and children from such marriages have
> become more and more persistent. Some of Lyalya's friends
> advise her to take Vera and leave Pyatigorsk before someone
> reports to the authorities that Vera's father was Jewish. Lyalya
> is very worried about this. But where to go?

People are being transported away. To what? Elena tries to think her way through the rumors. Probably to forced labor. The Germans are short of people in their factories, everyone knows that.* Her sister-in-law, however, prepares for the worst—a hurried flight in the middle of winter, as soon as she can buy warm clothes for herself and Vera.

· · ·

On that Saturday, a number of trains arrive at Treblinka with forty or so cattle cars carrying somewhere between four thousand and six thousand Jews from the Bialystok area in northeastern Poland. All of them—men, women and children—are slaughtered before evening, with the exception of a small number spared to fill the constantly diminishing ranks of the Sonderkommando.

The wastage among the death Jews in the upper camp continues to be enormous. Given the slightest excuse, the SS men and the Ukrainians murder people, but there is also a high rate of suicide among the prisoners. The inmates here are not only living with the unceasing horror of knowing that the next hour or minute might be their last, they also witness daily atrocities that defy the imagination. The majority of those leaving the trains and waiting for selection on the platform have been separated from their wives, children, siblings, parents, relations, neighbors and friends. They know that all these have been murdered and they may even have seen their corpses, carried them, caught a glimpse of their half-recognizable forms in the tangle of arms, legs, thighs, mouths, penises, tousled hair and children's hands in the mass grave.

---

* Millions of people took comfort in asking why the Germans would do something as irrational as dispose of an easily available workforce at the critical point the war has reached. As English historian Adam Tooze has shown, there was an inbuilt tension in Nazi Germany between the economic aims and optimization of resources on the one hand and the ideological aims on the other—the latter encompassing first the annihilation of the Jews and then of the Slavs in the east as guiding principles. There were some situations, however, like the shortage of foodstuffs in Germany during the first half of 1942, when the slaughter of literally millions of potentially useful workers, whether Jewish or not, might appear rational both economically and ideologically. It was far better that they, rather than Germans, starved. The interplay of these factors gave rise to instability and uncertainty on a local level that led to wishful thinking on the part of potential victims.

Chil Rajchman is still working in the camp dentist squad. He arrived at the camp along with Rivka, his nineteen-year-old sister. He knows she is dead because he found her skirt in the mountain of clothes he was set to sort soon after their arrival. He tore off a strip of the material and he carries it with him at all times. He bears a sense of guilt for being alive when she is dead and because he wouldn't let her have something to eat from their common food bag. How was he to know? So she probably went to the gas chamber hungry. He carries that guilt with him all the time, and he will do so right up to his death on May 7, 2004, in Montevideo.

It would seem that the first day in a Sonderkommando is the worst. One either survives it and its complete cognitive and moral chaos or one goes out of one's mind. But even after that day, the erosion follows a virtually linear function: prisoners are broken down, morally, physically and psychologically. They all have a limit: "Every human being possesses a reserve of strength whose extent is unknown to him, be it large, small, or nonexistent, and only through extreme adversity can we evaluate it," wrote Primo Levi.

Suicide is a daily occurrence among the prisoners. Yankel Wiernik, a man in his fifties who sleeps in the same hut as Rajchman, works in the joinery where the dentist squad keeps its tables. He writes:

> The less resistant among us, especially the more intelligent, suffered nervous breakdowns and hanged themselves when they returned to the barracks at night after having handled the corpses all day, their ears still ringing with the cries and moans of the victims. Such suicides occurred at the rate of 15 to 20 a day.

And Rajchman himself writes in his diary:

> Immediately in front of me, I catch sight of a man who has hanged himself. I point it out to my neighbor who simply gestures and points to two others who have hanged themselves. There is nothing new about it here. There are fewer than usual today. He tells me that those who have hanged themselves are thrown out [of the hut] every day and that no one pays any attention to such trivial matters. I look at the hanged and am envious of the peace they have achieved.

For all its black desperation, committing suicide may be seen as a form of resistance—initially, many people were too crushed and too powerless even to take their own lives. "In this way they ceased to be complete slaves since they could choose between their death or continuing the struggle," wrote Jean-François Steiner. It was about this time that a significant change took place in the upper camp at Treblinka. The prisoners began to help one another hang themselves from the roof beams in the darkened barrack hut.

That is the first stage of their change from being an amorphous mass of broken, guilt-ridden and humiliated individuals to becoming a collective, capable of supporting each other and, in the long term, capable of offering resistance, organizing flight and perhaps even rising in revolt irrespective of how hopeless it may be.

·   ·   ·

Since Mansur Abdulin's rifle division broke through the Romanian lines up on the Don, they have constantly been on the move. It's been a hard march on foot and horseback,* curving south-southeastwards through the empty lands left behind by the armored columns that are preceding them but out of sight.

Every so often they come across the detritus of war: a burning house, shot-up trucks, burned-out tanks, corpses in ditches, corpses on the snow-covered road, now more or less erased after the passage of numerous vehicles has flattened them to a thickness of less than an inch. Most of it bears witness to a chaotic retreat: abandoned trucks and weapons, deserted artillery pieces, captured piles of ammunition and other stores, horses and carts—many of the horses either dead or standing on three legs—any uninjured beasts having been snapped up by the advancing troops.

Occasionally they encounter clusters of weary, demoralized Romanian soldiers in their characteristic tall sheepskin caps. They are usually the remnants of various signal and service units and they are eager to surrender. But the crews in the turrets of the passing T-34s, KV-1s and T-70s have simply waved them to the rear: the tank crews only have one aim at the moment—to reach the Don and Kalach-na-Donu as fast as possible.

How much does Abdulin know about what is going on? How much

---

* Sections of the division have been equipped with hastily acquired trucks.

have their superior officers told them? Secrecy was absolute before the offensive started, but it seems likely that he has started to understand that they have broken through the enemy front lines and are now moving far behind those lines. Among the things liberated during the day is a small airfield and twenty-five planes—a sure sign of how deep they have penetrated. He probably has some idea of what is at stake. But does he have any idea about the scale of the risk? The text he wrote when it was all over reveals no signs of any misgivings. (All accounts, of course, are written backwards, starting with how things ended and that means that anything that doesn't fit gets erased.) The Red Army has made this kind of attack a number of times before, but they have invariably ended in catastrophe. The Germans have always turned out to be too strong.

They push on. Onwards, onwards. The regiment is stretched out along the road like an uneven pearl necklace of white-clad men and horses and trucks. To the Don!

·   ·   ·

Ernst Jünger continues his journey early on Sunday, November 22. He flies to Stalino and then to Rostov. His destination is Voroshilovsk, but the weather takes a turn for the worse and he is forced to stay where he is, in the hope of eventually proceeding by train. Rostov offers a depressing image of distress, destruction and human misery. He is appalled by the mammoth Soviet building that he likens to the Tower of Babel after its destruction. ("The fearful destruction is always built in to these rational works. They emanate a chill that attracts fire, in the same way as iron attracts lightning.") Everything that creates life is absent from the city, not just light and warmth, but also joy and happiness.

Lost children root around in the ruins, using small hooks to hunt for pieces of wood or anything else that could be useful. The badly dressed people are often weighed down with a burden of some kind and they seem to be constantly on the move, but their movement appears to be random, like ants in a demolished anthill. The only respite from all the misery is the sight of some children playing happily on an ice rink. "It was like catching a glimpse of color in the midst of Hades."

·   ·   ·

Mansur Abdulin's regiment trudges on along the road that leads to the Don. That's when it happens. A cry goes up and spreads: "Air attack!"

Abdulin has just about enough time to think that it can't be happening. Since the offensive started, the weather has stayed more or less the same—low cloud and fog—and protected them from the dreaded German air raids. This thought has scarcely run through his mind before he hears the rapidly rising roar of aircraft engines and, looking back, he sees two twin-engine German bombers following the line of the road and approaching at no more than three hundred feet. The bomb doors are open and, as he watches, bombs begin to fall.

The bombers sweep noisily overhead and, with a slight delay, the dark, finned cylinders thud into the ground in front of and behind him. Instinctively he starts to run.

Time slows down.

Out of the corner of his eye, he sees his platoon commander dismounting from his horse. Abdulin leaps over people who have hurled themselves under cover and he leaps over bombs. Most of the projectiles are still moving, sliding, spinning, rolling, and there are a dozen or so more out in front of him. Why aren't they exploding?*

Then he hears the first explosion behind him, quickly followed by another and another. The detonations come closer and he feels earth peppering his back. It strikes him that he has to get away from the line of the road. He leaps off, but down in the ditch another bomb rolls over and over, while time slows down even more. Adrenaline is playing tricks on his mind and suddenly his movements seem so slow as he leaps over the rolling bomb—he feels as if he is "trapped by some gigantic magnet." This imaginary slowness is beginning to irritate him when something large comes flying past and lands just in front of him: it's a horse's head. Abdulin throws himself down flat at the same moment as there is a crack and the shock wave tears his rucksack from his back as he is swallowed up by dust and darkness.

He hears several explosions, then a couple more, and then one last one.

In the silence that follows he hears the fading roar of the aircraft engines. The dust disperses and Abdulin manages to get up on unsteady legs. His rucksack is gone, his ears are ringing and there is a smell of burning.

---

* The bombs had clearly been set for delayed detonation, which was a necessity when planes were attacking at low altitude; otherwise there was the risk the planes would be damaged by the explosions.

The snow is no longer white.

Abdulin looks over to the roadway. He sees severed arms and legs. He sees body parts. He sees guts. He sees blood. He looks down at the horse's head and recognizes the bridle. It's the platoon commander's horse. Abdulin begins to throw up, and he throws up again and again until he has no more to throw up.

.   .   .

Vera Inber is listening to a news report on the radio. Her excitement rises as she hears the reader announce that Soviet forces at Stalingrad have gone over to the offensive, from the northwest and south, and they have advanced thirty-five to forty miles and have taken Kalatj-na-Donu. Then come the words that excite her even more: "The advance continues." She writes in her diary: "Perhaps this is what they call the turning-point of the war?" The date is November 22.

.   .   .

On that day, Dorothy Robinson reads the front page of *The New York Times* with a degree of gloom. Her attention does not focus on news of the continued successes of the Allies in North Africa, or news that the RAF has bombed Turin again, or the article about advances on Guadalcanal, or that the German push on both Stalingrad and in the Caucasus have at last been stopped.

It is the two columns on the left of the front page that hold her attention. They deal with yet another extension of the rationing system on a variety of goods and groceries. Robinson writes in her diary:

> Gas ration to be cut to three gallons a week—coffee sales to be stopped for one week, starting next Sunday, and then rationed to one pound every five weeks—further cuts in oil for heating is likely on Eastern seaboard—heavy cream to be taken off the market soon and butter rationed—meat rationing to start early in new year—few vegetables to be shipped and fewer still to be canned—no raisins or chocolate or olive oil or bacon—less of everything including trains and buses and cars and telephones.

What Robinson chooses to pay attention to (or not) should not be thought of as insensitivity: with all its paradoxical contrasts, it has to do with what is at the top of her mind just then—like so many women everywhere, it's her responsibility to make everyday life work. (Ignore the fact that Lidiya Ginzburg, Vera Inber, Vera Brittain, Nella Last and all the rest would happily have swapped their problems with Dorothy Robinson. Surely, war, at least partly, is about the need—indeed, the right—to have a normal, even trivial, life in which the lack of chocolate is permitted to be a worry.)

It is above all in things like having to cope with unexpected restrictions and new shortages that makes the war real to Dorothy Robinson since, as yet, no one she knows has been wounded or killed. The colossal transition in the American economy over the last year from a fairly carefree consumption model to one that prioritizes the production of war materiel can be felt everywhere and seen everywhere, not least because the transition has been so rapid and so amazingly successful.*

These are good days for everyone working in the armaments industries, men and women, Blacks and whites, with rising wages and improved conditions, though the working weeks are longer. But housewives like Dorothy Robinson tend to see only the downside of the war economy—shortages, hassles, a lower temperature in the house, washing machines with no one to mend them. And that is what she writes about since that makes up such a large part of her everyday life. But she is not ignorant. Of course it was a pity that they couldn't take the car to the seaside even for one day last summer, and she knows full well why car ownership has to be registered, gasoline is rationed and new tires are impossible to get hold of.

But there are other things she doesn't write about—things beyond immediate news of the war. She makes no mention, for instance, of the waves of hoarding which housewives, in particular, have been guilty of in recent days, emptying the shelves of coffee and even butter, according to reports in today's *Times*. She doesn't write about all the cheats

---

* Many historians have noticed an interesting paradox here: Why were democracies like the United States and Great Britain far more successful in putting their industries on a war footing than the dictatorships they were fighting? In Hitler's Germany, in particular, with its partly parasitical economy built on slave labor and the plundering of conquered states, there was an unwillingness to carry through the transition. One reason for this was that a steady flow of consumer goods was seen as a guarantee against popular discontent; another reason was the existence of ideological barriers which led, for instance, to the long-term reluctance to mobilize women.

trying to evade military service or dealing on the black market. She doesn't write about the contradiction of investing everything in the defeat of Nazism and its absurd racial theories while racism is on the increase in the United States. She writes nothing about the increasing youth criminality and sexual promiscuity that follows the migration to the new war factories, nor about the dissolution of the institution of the family that some people see as a danger. But perhaps this apparent blindness is a way for her to defend her idyll.

"Less of everything," Robinson notes in her diary. But her thought doesn't stop there. She knows why it has to happen and that not everything that is happening is bad: people have come closer to one another and she writes: "But more of neighborliness and family loyalties and appreciation for the beauty and freedom and worth of the country we have so long taken for granted. We're all in it together and we'll all come out of it with colors flying."

. . .

Is it any cooler now? Probably not. Charles Walker has been on Guadalcanal for over a month and his body has begun to acclimatize to the damp heat and his senses to the sounds and smells of the jungle. And the mood has begun to change. They have left the uncertainty of that first period behind them, the period when the fear that this was going to turn into yet another defeat for the Allies was at its height. But the Japanese soldiers are by no means invincible, and the weight and sheer, raw power of the Allies' arsenal of weapons has begun to show.

Walker and his unit have been transferred to Point Cruz, a headland west of the airfield. Looking far up along the north coast with binoculars, he can pick out the oblong shapes of the stranded Japanese transport vessels. They are nothing more than shattered hulks now with numerous dead Japanese and fragments of matter drifting in the water and water's edge around them.

Their adversaries, however, are still unconquered and are formidably dangerous. Admittedly, no more than a couple of thousand men came ashore, without any heavy equipment and almost without provisions, but they are still lurking like predators in the jungle west of Point Cruz. The day before yesterday, Friday, the Japanese mounted a night attack on a battalion from the newly arrived 182nd Infantry Regiment. (The attackers belonged to Tohichi Wakabayashi's regiment and, at this point, Walker and Wakabayashi are only about six miles apart.)*

The newly arrived Americans threw down their weapons and fled head over heels back over the Matanikau River. Walker's battalion was sent in to replace them and traces of the panic were unmistakeable. Abandoned American equipment lay all round: "machine guns, mortars, packs, rifles and the prize, new sound-powered telephones, which didn't need external power to function." They handed over most of the things, but kept the fantastic telephones.

It is now the morning of Sunday, November 22. Everything is quiet and still. The only things to be heard are minor detonations, but they don't worry Walker. It's just the soldiers hunting the enormous shoals of glittering silver mullet that swim in the warm turquoise shallows. The men throw explosives into the water and after every explosion they can collect dead and stunned fish by the sackload. Then the fish are cleaned and fried. More and more men flock down to the beach.

·   ·   ·

Later that same Sunday the Germans commence an artillery bombardment of Leningrad. Many of the shells land in the Petrogradsky District, where Vera Inber and her husband live in their house on Pesochnaya Street. She hears an unusually powerful, swelling explosion and a moment later the earth begins to rock and the house to tremble. Artillery shelling this heavy targeting the northern islands of the city is fairly unusual. There have been rumors that the Germans have brought in one of those heavy long-range railway guns that they used earlier this year to pound their way into Sebastopol. A single shell from these monstrosities is capable of causing the collapse of half a block in a cloud of dust and stone splinters.

Inber and her husband leave their home—a smallish, tumbledown house she calls "our nest"—and run across to a neighborhood shelter. (Can we guess what she is wearing? Perhaps that black Persian fur and matching muff she is so proud of.) Even though there isn't a system, even though most things are a matter of luck, people's mental equipoise depends on the belief that they are not helpless in the face of

---

* A few days later someone informed Wakabayashi that they had examined the dead Americans and discovered them to be only from the army, not the Marines.

these blind forces, that there are safe zones, that there are tricks which can be used to outsmart death—though paradoxically enough they may be the same tricks that allow death to catch up with you. Lidiya Ginzburg explains:

> Confusion in the categories of space and time. The whistle of the shells overhead is more frightening but more comprehensible. It indicates a spatial presence—they are really here over your head at this moment—and temporal extension (the duration of the whistling). The noise of the distant explosion is something else altogether. What was the untrackable present had already become the past by the time it reached the consciousness. The reverse order: first the sound, then the fear at what had not by now happened. Then the silence and in that brief silence the question of the life and death of a man is decided. It is decided by the fact he has taken two extra steps towards the tram stop, or bent down to retrieve a dropped briefcase or stepped off the pavement into the roadway. Man thinks everything will happen in order—there'll be a whistling, then an explosion which he'll see from the side, then something will happen to him. He knows that's an aberration. This is an aberration of the link between cause and effect, but there is also the aberration of security—when a man speeds up his step under bombardment, so it doesn't catch up with him.

While Vera Inber is sitting in the shelter, someone arrives and reports that a heavy shell landed in her street and that someone in a neighboring house—No. 10—has been injured. A medical orderly is sent over, but he soon returns, having had nothing to do. A woman had been hit by a shell fragment flying in through the window and she has already died.

In what appears to be a way of trying to understand what is happening, but which may well be a ritual to keep her nerves in control, Vera times the intervals between explosions. She comes to the conclusion that they come at fifteen- to twenty-minute intervals, which backs up the theory that it's likely to be one of those huge, heavy railway guns. There is no possible protection against the enormous projectiles—if they strike, you are unlikely to know anything about it.

After the landing of twelve to fifteen shells that make the earth tremble, the gun falls silent. By then it's 4:00 a.m. Vera Inber makes her way out and finds an indescribably lovely winter night, in which the blue light of the moon creates a pink reflection on the pure white snow.

·   ·   ·

At this time, too, there is a meeting taking place at the *Deutsche Allgemeine Zeitung* on Ritterstrasse in Berlin, and since it's Sunday, this would appear to be an extraordinary meeting. The mood is bleak. Flurries of snow hang in the air outside the windows. Ursula von Kardorff's diary doesn't reveal the exact reasons for the mood in the room. They are talking about the situation in North Africa, that much we know.

Fritz Dettmann, who is the same age as Ursula and one of the paper's star reporters, has just returned from that war zone and he "gives very pessimistic reports. The Allied landings have been successful in four places." The report is given special weight by the fact that it's Dettmann who delivers it. No one could suspect him of being a defeatist in any way: he is a member both of the NSDAP and the NSKK, as well as holding the formal rank of lieutenant in the Luftwaffe, the latter enabling him to function as a much-praised front-line reporter since the outbreak of war—his speciality being stirring and exciting stories about the war in the air.* (We should probably picture him sitting there in a lieutenant's uniform, desert version even.) Dettmann is probably confirming what they've all heard already, but doing so with the inescapable force of an eyewitness.

The diary makes it apparent that the mood is as it is partly because they have been admonished by the propaganda ministry. Ursula von Kardorff writes: "The politicians' attempt to hint at things in their comments usually has the opposite effect. The reader doesn't understand a thing, but Promi reads too much into it."†

---

* By this stage, he had already contributed to several anthologies of war reporting, as well as having written two successful books: *Unser Kampf in Norwegen* (Our Battles in Norway) and *40,000 Kilometer Feindflug* (40,000 Kilometers of Combat Flight). He had also started working on a biography of the air ace Hans-Joachim Marseille, who had been killed in North Africa in September of that year. NSDAP = National Socialist German Workers' Party; NSKK = National Socialist Motor Corps.

† Promi is "Propaganda Ministry." And by "politicians" she means the staff on the editorial committee, i.e., the lead writers.

To work as a journalist in Nazi Germany as Ursula von Kardorff does is both complicated and dangerous, particularly when you write for a paper like *DAZ,* which calls itself right-wing conservative but wants to appear slightly independent of NSDAP. (If you step over the line, you can be fined, lose your job or even get a visit from Gestapo gorillas. Promi might even pronounce a temporary ban on the publication of the paper as a whole, something that is not uncommon.) So there is a need to be adaptable, to have a rubberized backbone and an elastic conscience.* And it's essential to be able to maneuver your way through the psychotic jungle of language rules, which is the regime's most important method of controlling the image of reality—indeed, of controlling reality itself.

The linguistic terrain never stays the same. Virtually every day, Promi issues new directives on which words may be used and which avoided, which concepts replace others, what may not be depicted and what may be—and, if so, how.† Most people have no difficulty understanding, for instance, why the term "realignment" should be used rather than "retreat," or why the deportation of Jews and others to an uncertain fate should be referred to as "relocation to the east," or why enemy soldiers should never be called "brave." But it's a bit more problematic to understand why referring to British bomber crews as "cowardly" is not permitted,‡ and the term "air-raid shelter" should be used rather than "air-raid cellar," and civilians from bombed towns should be "rehoused" rather than "evacuated."§

The editorial meeting on this Sunday focuses mainly on the deterioration of the situation in North Africa. Dettmann also mentions, rather *en passant* it seems, another piece of news he has picked up: some sort of enemy breakthrough has occurred on the Don.

---

* The various directives were humiliating, both in number and in detail. As far as Goebbels was concerned, this seems to have been at least part of the point. He is supposed to have said that "in the future, anyone with any honor left in their body should think very carefully before becoming a journalist."

† The flood of linguistic rules started in 1933, and by the time the Nazi saga was over, somewhere between 80,000 and 100,000 directives had been issued.

‡ The thinking was that use of the pejorative might lead to questions being asked: If they were so cowardly and the Luftwaffe so competent, how could they bring themselves to return night after night?

§ Eventually even the word *Katastrophe* was banned and had to be replaced by using *Grossnotstand,* "situation of great need."

For the last two months both journalists and the general public have been hearing that Stalingrad will soon be in German hands—soon— *der Führer* himself says so. It was only a month ago when Promi gave detailed directives on how news of the fall of the city should be presented. As part of it, the intention is to fly a number of highly decorated soldiers who fought in the triumphant battle to Berlin, where they will be interviewed on the radio, appear in the weekly newsreels in the cinema, and feature in the press in newspapers like *DAZ*. Perhaps all that won't happen now.

· · ·

Back to Dorothy Robinson on Long Island, where a great deal has changed, and quite significantly, not always for the worse. She is living in a new community of women. Men are for the most part absent, so female relations, neighbors and friends help one another in new ways—with cooking and baking, with clothes, with childcare, shopping, repairs, by going together to the maternity ward when the time comes, and by sharing, supporting and comforting. They go to the cinema together and the cinemas are almost always full. Never have so many people attended as they do now: eighty million or more tickets are sold every week. Just recently, she and Sally, the relative who lives with her, went to see *Mrs. Miniver,* the most popular film of the year. It has stayed in her mind—after all, it is sort of about her.

As the title implies, the main character is a woman, the matriarch Kay Miniver, who, at the outbreak of war, is living with her middle-class family in an idyllic village by the Thames outside London. She is fond of her comforts and pretty clothes, but her life changes completely. Her eldest son volunteers to be a fighter pilot in the RAF; her husband takes his small boat and helps with the Dunkirk evacuation. Mrs. Miniver finds a wounded yet anything but defeated Nazi pilot in her garden; the family home is blown up by a bomb. But life goes on and people form ever closer bonds with one another.

The key scene for Dorothy Robinson, however, is not the famous finale when the vicar makes a speech in his bombed-out church—"This is not only a war of soldiers in uniform. It is a war of the people, all of the people. And it must be fought not only on the battlefield but in the towns and villages, in the factories and on the farms, in the home and in the heart of every man, woman and child who loves freedom"— but when someone says that the war will put an end to the traditional village flower competition—a core theme of the film—and Mr. Ballard, the stationmaster and an amateur gardener, answers: "Don't talk silly. You might as well say goodbye to England. There will always be roses."*

"That line," Dorothy Robinson writes in her diary, "is one to remember when the headlines in the papers make you feel that nothing will ever be the same." Sunday, November 22, started cold, with a temperature about thirty-two degrees, but it slowly gets a little warmer. Dorothy often knits herself to sleep. Does she do so this evening, too?

. . .

Everything is on the move, and that's how it should be. Vasily Grossman is accompanying the 81st Cavalry Division of the IVth Cavalry Corps—some five thousand men and about four thousand horses—on the chase to the west-southwest. After the breakthrough and the sudden collapse of the 4th Romanian Army, a noticeable vacuum has arisen. The steppe is empty and white, like a clean sheet of paper. There is no longer any organized resistance.

Every so often they bump into scattered groups of Romanians who haven't managed to escape or, perhaps, haven't even found out what happened. Their adversaries usually lay down their weapons, though sometimes there is a brief, confused exchange of fire that ends quickly. From Grossman's notebook:

> A killed Romanian and a killed Russian were lying next to each other on the battlefield. The Romanian had a sheet of paper and a child's drawing of a hare and a boat. Our soldier had a letter: "Good Afternoon, or maybe Good Evening. Hello, Daddy. . . ." And the end of the letter: "Come and visit us, because when you aren't here, I come back home as if to a rented apartment. I miss you very much. Come and visit, I

* MGM started filming *Mrs. Miniver* in Los Angeles in the autumn of 1940 while the U.S. was still neutral. But as the wartime situation worsened, William Wyler, the German-born Jewish director of the film, sharpened the script in spite of resistance from MGM. The tone became increasingly pro-British and anti-German and a number of scenes were refilmed. The vicar's speech, for instance, was revised repeatedly, the final version only being agreed upon by Wyler and the actor playing the vicar on the evening before the scene was filmed. Later, the speech was frequently reused in Allied propaganda.

wish I could see you, if only for an hour. I am writing this and
tears are pouring. That was your daughter Nina writing."

The situation is fluid, changing by the hour. That is not all good—no
one knows where the front is any longer. When evening comes, Grossman and a reporter colleague by the name of Kapler decide to stop
and spend the night in a deserted house. After a while, they hear noises
and several soldiers enter the house. From the shadows on the ceiling
Grossman sees that they don't have Soviet helmets. They are Romanians. The two Russians huddle down, silent and afraid. Grossman has
a pistol and is a pretty good shot. Should he take it out now? Then the
Romanians disappear as quickly as they came, and the two Russians
remain undiscovered.

.   .   .

It's late on Sunday and the editorial meeting at the *DAZ* is over. Ursula
von Kardorff is walking through the dark, chilly streets of Berlin. (Or
perhaps she takes a streetcar part of the way. Details of that sort rarely
get recorded in diaries.) Just now she is on her way to join a Swiss
diplomat by the name of Obersteg for dinner. She is a happy, sociable
woman who usually loves occasions like this—they cheer her up, in
spite of the increasing darkness that surrounds her.

Ursula is neither stupid nor blind. As a journalist, she frequently
knows more than the average German, paradoxically enough thanks
to the linguistic rules and the petty directives issued by Promi. The
silences, the bans and the erasures allow her and her colleagues to
glimpse a vague and different reality as though in a distorting mirror. And she sees and knows and feels what the regime is capable of,
but has chosen to conform. It's not all about living a double life with
double standards, however; the question is whether there is still some
part of her that survives from the days when she greeted the Nazi
Machtübernahme (accession to power) with satisfaction. The desire
for order, predictability, unity, or, in her case, perhaps, an existence
in which she can feel safe in spite of it all—an existence in which the
inescapable, everyday taste of subservience is sweetened by privileges
and consumption is, in itself, sufficient.

Material matters are important to her, as for many of her countrymen. Wages have continued to rise, and in spite of various sorts of

rationing, the shops are still reasonably well-stocked, including goods from the occupied countries. The regime is still proving adept at giving an appearance of abundance: the shop windows often display items that can be displayed but not sold.*

There is no shortage of makeup, and beauty parlors, hairdressers and manicurists are all well-frequented. Von Kardorff enjoys going to the hairdresser and having her hair permed in spite of her mother's disapproval. Other distractions are provided by holidays (winter sport resorts will soon be open for the season), outdoor activities and pleasures and, of course, the movies. Everyone goes to the cinema in Germany, now even more than ever before.[†] (She is well aware of this since one of her time-consuming duties at *DAZ* is to review new light-entertainment films.) And then there are the parties and other events, like this one at the diplomat's residence.

But there is something that doesn't feel quite right about this evening. Perhaps something of the dark mood of the editorial meeting is still with her. Whatever it is, her usual cheerfulness is absent. Afterwards, clearly disappointed, she writes in her diary:

> It's the last time I shall go to something like that, however much the material pleasures are attractive. The risk of giving away information at receptions with foreigners is too great, and I'm no longer capable of pure conversation.

. . .

It's night on Guadalcanal. John McEniry sleeps in a small tent with three other pilots—or tries to sleep, rather. It's never quiet here at the Henderson Field. The front line is so close that not only do they hear

---

* The sense of increasing abundance that characterized Germany in the years before the war was not false—not when compared to the years of the Depression. A variety of desirable consumer goods such as watches, radios and private cars became more accessible. Ownership of private cars increased threefold and production continued right through to this year, unlike the United States, where all such production ceased when the United States entered the war. The expectation of a rise in the standard of living was, as British historian Richard Grunberger has pointed out, just as important as real improvements. (Many goods actually became scarcer and worse even before 1939.)

[†] Cinema attendance in Germany quadrupled in the nine years between 1933 and 1942. In 1942 one billion tickets were sold in Germany.

every shot and exploding hand grenade, but also the voices. Japanese snipers or patrols sometimes manage to slip through the lines over on the ridge, causing confused, nocturnal firefights to break out. McEniry is in the habit of sleeping with a loaded .45 pistol under his pillow. Every so often a shell lands somewhere nearby, fired by long-range Japanese artillery in the jungle-clad distance. It's never safe. Fear is a constant factor. You can put it out of your mind, but it's always there, like tinnitus.

They get a visit every night from lone enemy planes that drone around up in the starry sky, "Washing Machine Charlie,"* dropping an occasional bomb without any precision or doing any material damage worthy of the name, but doing enough to wake people up, drive them out of their sleeping bags and send them scuttling to their muddy, sodden dugouts.

McEniry is no longer as frightened by these nocturnal visitors as he was during his first weeks on Guadalcanal. These days, he and his companions stand peering up at the pillars of light from the searchlights and the glittering necklace of tracers and try to pick out the intruders as if the planes were bats attracted to a lamp. He hasn't seen a single one of them shot down so far, but on top of everything else, the effect is to keep them awake the whole time.

They get too little sleep and the sleeplessness makes them red-eyed, slovenly and irritable.

Despite all that, McEniry still looks forward to darkness and nightfall with its more or less illusory promise of rest, recovery and dreams. Flying back to Guadalcanal when the sun has started to go down and you've managed to evade death for another day is a special experience. McEniry has noticed that, viewed from a high altitude, you can clearly see that twilight does not *fall*: the darkness actually rises up from the ground.

---

* The nickname refers to the fact that some of these two-engine aircraft have consciously non-synchronized engines, which results in a more disruptive engine noise.

NOVEMBER 23–30

This Time Our Side Will Win

"To trust anyone or to admit to hope of a better world is criminally foolish, as foolish as it is to stop working for it. It sounds silly to say work without hope, but it can be done."

"We could dream of our youth when the war robbed us of it; we could longingly paint a picture of our unlived lives. Once upon a time there was a night of drinking, singing, dancing and much kissing, and there were a thousand other nights full of music, magic, intoxication, laughter and thoughts, wanderings and blissful melancholy. But they never belonged to us."

"I am condemned to absolute isolation from the moment I refrained from killing. It's the others who will create history. I also know that I obviously cannot condemn these others."

This is how a defeat looks. And a victory. Vasily Grossman has continued to follow the 81st Cavalry Division in its sweep west-southwest through the snow. There is still no enemy resistance to speak of, except occasionally. Time after time he passes groups of Romanian prisoners of war coming in the opposite direction. They are usually in columns of a couple of hundred limping and silent men guarded by no more than two or three Soviet soldiers. The tramp of their boots blends with the jingle of the flasks and mess tins that dangle from their belts on pieces of string or wire. They don't look very soldierly, given that many of them have wrapped colorful blankets around their shoulders to keep out the cold.

Grossman approaches the scene of a battle. He writes:

Romanian corpses are lying along the roads; abandoned cannon camouflaged with dry steppe grass point eastwards. Horses wander about in *balkas* dragging behind them broken harnesses, vehicles hit by shellfire are giving off blue-grey smoke. On the roads lie helmets decorated with the Romanian royal coat of arms, thousands of cartridges, grenades, rifles. A Romanian strongpoint. A mountain of empty, sooty cartridges by the machine-gun nest. White sheets of writing paper are lying in the communication trench. The brown winter steppe has turned brick red from blood. There are rifles with butts splintered by Russian bullets. And crowds of prisoners are moving toward us all the time. They are searched before being sent off to the rear. Heaps of peasant women's belongings that were found in Romanian rucksacks and pockets look comical and pitiful. There are old women's shawls, women's earrings, underwear, skirts, and swaddling clothes.

A little farther on Grossman sees more abandoned cannon, trucks, staff cars and even some armored vehicles. The Romanian collapse appears to be total.

.   .   .

The evening has been grey, cold and rainy and Vittorio Vallicella is just on the point of creeping into his dugout and going to sleep when he gets an order to go to his battery commander. He is to take part in a night patrol. Night patrol? Vallicella can scarcely believe his ears.

It was to avoid stupidity of this sort that he and his companions had stayed out of the way for as long as possible. But just a couple of days ago the inevitable had happened: they were rounded up at an Italian *carabinieri* checkpoint, weary, depressed and in shock. They had just been attacked by a low-flying British fighter; "the Greek" had been wounded by a bullet through the calf and was in need of care. Their boys' own adventure was over.

As survivors of the Trento Division they were now formally transferred to the remnants of the Trieste Division, to which the 21st Artillery was attached. A friendly captain has ensured that the little group can remain together. Vallicella has shown the typewriter he kept with them on the truck throughout their whole odyssey and got a half-promise of work as a quartermaster's assistant—fetching and distributing the mail, paying the wages, and whatever else. It's a good, safe job, all the more so as the rumor is going around that they are to dig in and attempt to stop the British. But where on earth are they? Vallicella frequently finds himself slipping into some wishful thinking: maybe they, too, have gotten tired of all this.

.   .   .

The sun is setting over the North Atlantic on Monday, November 23. In the softly fading light, Leonard Thomas and his fellow crewmen on board HMS *Ulster Queen* see a dark landmass begin to emerge. "No lights, nothing bar that luminous glow off a glacier, an unreal light, somewhat eerie, yet we knew that where it was, there would be some kind of life, habitation, and safety."

It is Iceland, occupied by American troops since 1941. What they see is the east coast of the island and soon they are sailing into the deep, long Seyðisfjörður, where there is an Allied supply base. Once between the high, steep sides of the fjord everything is suddenly "unbelievably calm." The still, mirror waters of the fjord reflect his own mood. It is 192 hours since they left Archangel and now the worst is behind them.

Their vessel heaves to alongside a huge anchored oil tanker and begins to take on fuel. Suddenly one of the crewmen rushes up out of breath and tells them that there is an American coast-guard cutter on the other side of the tanker and they have a canteen that will sell anything to anyone! They flood across, climb on board, push their way past amazed but amused American seamen and rush into what Thomas himself calls an "Aladdin's Cave." They come from a Great Britain that is just entering its fourth winter of war, a land of rationing, greyness and shortages, and they have just left the Soviet Union, a country where shortages aren't just a sad fact that lead to inequality, but a form of privation, sometimes famine even. What they now see is something they hardly believed still existed—an abundance!

Everything is there, *everything*. And the American standing behind the counter with a cigar in his mouth even offers them a really favorable exchange rate. Thomas's eyes sweep over the bewildering, bewitching array of goods, some of which he hasn't seen for years (possibly never in some cases). There are sweets, including the famous Hershey chocolate bars;* top-quality cigarettes, both Marlboro and Chesterfield, as well as boxes of Henry Clay cigars; cosmetics produced by Max Factor; a rack of women's underwear; perfumes, aftershave and talcum powder; and perhaps most desirable and iconic of all, there are nylon stockings.

It is, of course, possible to judge the immense power and almost immeasurable heft of the American wartime economy from all those new ships, military aircraft, armored vehicles and so on, but a PX like

---

* They are famous because they were part of the American forces' personal emergency ration packs and consequently could be found everywhere: it's estimated that three billion bars were produced during the war. They were not famous for their taste, however, which was purposely bitter and tasteless to discourage gorging. Later on, the American forces introduced an emergency ration pack that consisted solely of sweet things—what was called the "Candy Assault Ration"—which was issued before difficult landings and similar operations, where there was a great risk that the men would initially be unable to access normal food.

this, full of half-forgotten luxury goods, shows that power and heft in a much more recognizable form, at least to a sailor born and brought up in Portsmouth. Thomas and his companions quickly spend virtually all their money. And all of them are pleased.

*   *   *

Vittorio Vallicella has no desire to go out on night patrol. He is unhappy right from the start and he shows it. They get lost and that new lieutenant becomes unsure of himself and produces a pocket flashlight every now and again. Vallicella frowns and tells him to be more careful—if you have to put on a torch, you should do so in your pocket, and preferably not even then. You shouldn't even light a cigarette. The lieutenant gets angry and threatens Vallicella, who sticks to his guns. This is a serious business, you have to be smart and absolutely disciplined about noise and light and the like. And how many times has the lieutenant been out on night patrol? He is forced to admit that this is the first time. Likely to be your last, too, Vallicella snorts.

The rain has stopped and the moon disappears behind a thick blanket of cloud. The night is pitch-black. In the darkness their argument escalates and the lieutenant raises his rifle to hit Vallicella with the butt, but manages to stop himself. Instead, he breaks down and starts crying "like a little boy," and to his own surprise Vallicella begins to cry with him. It ends with the two men falling into one another's arms. They dry away their tears and the little group carries on into the darkness.

A little while later, the group comes across an empty bunker and they all creep into it and carefully cover the opening. They sit there for the rest of the night, smoking, chatting and drinking a bottle of brandy the lieutenant has brought with him. Nothing happens. No shooting, no engine noises, no flares. And when the stars above them begin to fade and the grey of dawn appears, they return to the battery. The brandy is long since finished. It's Monday, November 23.

*   *   *

At 11:40 a.m. on that same Monday, two torpedoes from a German U-boat hit the SS *Benlomond* in the South Atlantic. She is a 420-foot civilian freighter that had sailed from Cape Town in South Africa thirteen days before with Paramaribo, Dutch Guiana, as her destination. There, she was to pick up a cargo to be taken to New York. The ship was sailing alone, but she can do twelve knots, and ships that can do that speed are sometimes allowed to sail unescorted in the hope they can outpace danger. The captain is a forty-four-year-old Scot named John Maul.

Since the hold is empty and the hull shattered by the explosions, it does not take long for water to flood in and fill the SS *Benlomond*. The hull twists, shudders and cracks and the crew begin to abandon ship. One of them is Poon Lim, a twenty-four-year-old Chinese mess steward on board. Poon grabs a life jacket and rushes to the rail. Roughly two minutes after the torpedoes struck, the inflow of water reaches the boilers, causing them to explode in clouds of steam, smoke and flying debris. That moment is probably when many of the crew die, almost certainly including Captain Maul. The pressure wave hurls Poon Lim overboard and he flies through the air and disappears beneath the surface.

Poon resurfaces among the waves to find that all that remains of SS *Benlomond* is floating wreckage.

· · ·

At dawn, when the 1034st Rifle Regiment marches into a small place on the Don,[*] the battle is long over. Tramping through the muddy streets Mansur Abdulin is amazed and more than a little impressed by the chaos caused by the tanks. By this time he is well aware that battlefields are among the messiest places you can find, but since this place is (was)—like so many other villages and small towns out here on the flat steppe—the location for staff or workshops or depots, there was unusually much to destroy, plunder and scatter.

The Germans seem to have been taken by surprise and left the place at great speed. The panic was such that some of them jumped out through closed windows and Abdulin sees a dead German hanging from a window ledge, still in his nightshirt.

· · ·

The cavalrymen have reached Abganerovo, a slightly larger village by the railway that runs all the way from Rostov and Salsk up to Stalingrad. Vasily Grossman talks to a couple of civilians and they are happy to have been liberated. Many of them weep. Grossman writes:

---

[*] Abdulin names the place as Kalatj-na-Donu, but it is more likely to have been some other small town or village on the Don.

An old peasant woman told us about the three months of the occupation. "It became empty here. Not a single hen to cackle, not a single cock to sing. There isn't a single cow left to let out in the morning and let in in the evening. Romanians have pinched everything. They whipped almost all our old men: one didn't report for work, another one failed to hand in his grain. The *starosta* [community elder] in Plodovitaya was whipped four times. They took away my son, a cripple, and with him a girl and a nine-year-old boy. We've been crying for four days, waiting for them to return."

Could he not be thinking of his own mother, Ekaterina, at this moment? This is surely the fate Grossman would have wanted for his mother—an old woman trapped somewhere behind the enemy lines being freed by the advance of the Red Army. But it didn't happen.

At the outbreak of war, seventy-year-old Ekaterina Grossman was still living and teaching French in the small town of Berdychiv in northern Ukraine where Grossman was born. The thought had been to move his mother to Moscow, but Grossman's wife managed to convince him otherwise—she thought there wasn't enough room in their small flat. And a couple of weeks later it was too late. Berdychiv and northern Ukraine had been swallowed up by the advancing German army. Grossman is convinced she is dead. As a reporter he is not only aware of all the rumors and stories, but he has also seen enough for himself to know that Hitler's talk of exterminating the Jewish race is not just metaphorical.

Grossman has had a dream—possibly a recurring dream—in which he enters an empty room in which there is an armchair of the kind Ekaterina used to sleep on. On it lies a shawl that he recognizes as hers—she used to put it over her legs when she went to bed for the night. He stares at the empty armchair for a long time and when he wakes up he is convinced that his mother is dead.*

---

* She *was* dead. In the middle of September 1941 one of the German mobile Einsatzgruppen carried out a major massacre in Berdychiv, shooting twelve thousand of the town's Jews at the airfield. Ekaterina was one of those murdered. Grossman didn't learn the exact details until much later. In 1950, he writes: "I have tried dozens, perhaps hundreds of times to imagine how you died, how you walked to your death. I have tried to imagine the man who killed you. He

Grossman leaves the old woman and moves on.

There are rows of goods wagons at the railway station. Grossman walks around and notes that they come from all over Europe: Germany, of course, but also wagons stolen from Poland, France and Belgium. They are all fully loaded with everything from sacks of flour and maize and big, square tins of cooking fat to ammunition, fur caps and strange winter shoes with wooden soles.

Darkness falls. Early tomorrow they will continue along the railway. The farther southwest they get, the greater the distance to Stalingrad— and the more difficult it will be for the Germans to relieve those trapped there. They hope to reach the small town of Aksai before evening. It is more than seven miles away. The wind is cold and sharp.

· · ·

Poon Lim was one of twenty-two Chinese crewmen on board the SS *Benlomond*—almost half the crew came from China. That, in fact, is the situation on many of the British merchant ships, as there is a great shortage of white seamen. Even though they accept anyone who volunteers (people from neutral countries such as Sweden or Portugal, for instance), many of those who end up serving on these ships tend to be from British or other colonies—Chinese, Indians, West Africans, Vietnamese.*

Poon comes from Hainan, a big island off the south coast of China, and he is no stranger to the sea. One of his brothers has already gone to sea and Poon's father considers it a better alternative than to be forcibly conscripted as cannon fodder in one of the anonymous and rapidly depleted divisions of the Chinese army in its unequal battles with the Japanese.

Poon started work as a cabin boy on a British ship while only sixteen, but he was on the receiving end of so much bullying and humiliation from the whites on board that he jumped ship in Hong Kong in 1937 and tried instead to learn to be a mechanic. About a year ago, however, he signed on again, along with his cousin; they wanted to get out of

---

was the last person to see you. I know that you were thinking about me a great deal—all this time."

* Roughly 40,000 of the 185,000 seamen in the British merchant navy had that sort of background. About one in four of these civilian seamen lost their lives in the service, which was a higher proportion than some uniformed fighting units.

the Crown Colony, which was about to fall into Japanese hands, and the needs of war by then had compelled the British to make many improvements to the conditions for non-white seamen.

Most of his clothes have been torn off by the explosion. In the distance, he catches a glimpse of five men huddled on a life raft. That's all. No one else. Then the waves break over him again and they disappear from sight. Two hours pass. Poon sees a life raft drifting nearby that must have floated free when the ship went down. It's square, about eight feet by eight feet, made of wood, built around several empty oil drums. He approaches it, or it approaches him—Poon is not a good swimmer. He climbs up onto it and finds it empty. He is naked. The hours pass and darkness is falling.

His exact position when this happens is latitude 0°30'N, longitude 38°45'W. To put it in simpler geographical terms, he is 752 miles east of the mouth of the Amazon. All around Poon there is sea, more sea and yet more sea, and a sky stretching from horizon to horizon.

.   .   .

It may seem surprising that Keith Douglas can sleep at all, but what's even more surprising is that he has slept well. (One of the things the army teaches you is to sleep wherever you can and whenever you can.) He is lying on an air mattress which is resting on the engine cover of a tank which, in turn, is firmly chained on the back of a heavy transporter which is clanking and bouncing its way along the main coast road. He wakes up and opens one eye. He notes that the sun has risen.

It is Monday, November 23,* and since night fell the whole of Douglas's regiment is heading west towards Benghazi and the retreating enemy army. Nothing has come of the colonel's promise that they would be pulled out of the front line after the battle and allowed to go to Cairo and have a bath. Nor was there any truth in the rumors— actually disguised desires—that they were soon to be sent to Syria or India or Great Britain or elsewhere. Douglas, however, is not surprised, as he suspected this would happen. Nor is he particularly disappointed. Ever since they received the news of the American landings somewhere in French North Africa he and almost all the rest of his unit are

---

* This might actually have been November 24. According to Stanley Christopherson's diary, the move began on the twenty-third; according to Desmond Graham, Douglas's biographer, on the twenty-fourth.

convinced that all that remains is a couple of weeks of straightforward
fighting, not much more than mopping up. After that, the campaign
should be over.

Douglas looks at his wristwatch. The hands are pointing to five past
eight. The air is warm and he decides to stay on his airbed and watch
the empty, sunburned desert landscape sweep past at a ninety-degree
angle. Every so often they travel past the imploded and chaotic remains
of the enemy retreat: clusters of burned-out wrecks, abandoned vehicles and graves marked with crosses.

He is interested in the graves, not least because they correspond to
his prejudices about the Germans and the Italians. He thinks it is easy
to see which contain Italians and which Germans. The German graves
are neater, with the name and rank carefully stated on the cross and
each crowned with a steel helmet. The Italian graves are often more
slovenly dug, and they are decorated with those tropical helmets that
Douglas finds so hideous. He writes:

> There is something impressive in the hanging steel helmet
> that links those dead with knights buried under their shields
> and weapons. But how pathetically logical and human—one
> of those touches of unconscious comedy which makes it dif-
> ficult to be angry with them—that the Italians should have
> supplemented the steel cap with a ridiculous battered cut-
> price topee [*sic*]. The steel helmet is an impressive tombstone,
> and is its own epitaph. But the cardboard topee [*sic*] seemed
> only to say there is some junk buried here, and we may as well
> leave a piece of rubbish to mark the spot.

The column of transporters comes to a halt. The dust settles. They
climb down from the sun-warmed tanks and eat breakfast. Douglas is
in good humor. He is looking forward to getting to their distant destination, Benghazi, where the landscape is said to be really green. And
he is also looking forward to more looting, more plunder. They have
a journey of six hundred miles in front of them and they have no idea
what awaits them.

It is sometime around now that Keith Douglas begins to change, to
get harder. It would be wrong to say that he loses hope—it's more that
he disposes of it. He has perhaps discovered, as many others did, that
anxiety lessens if you allow your mind to harden up and start accepting

that you aren't actually going to survive. (Douglas said to several people in several circumstances that he doesn't believe he will survive the war.) Later, in a letter, he writes the following: "To be sentimental or emotional now is dangerous to oneself and to others. To trust anyone or to admit to hope of a better world is criminally foolish, as foolish as it is to stop working for it. It sounds silly to say work without hope, but it can be done; it's only a form of insurance. It doesn't mean work hopelessly."

·   ·   ·

Today Tohichi Wakabayashi on Guadalcanal is more bored than afraid, despite the fact that showers of American shells continue to rain down over his position up on the jungle-covered hill, making the earth tremble and filling the air with dust and smoke, and despite the swarms of American fighter planes firing on anything that dares move. But the Japanese foxholes and bunkers have been built with the usual Japanese care, and if they keep their heads down there, they are more or less safe.

So that is exactly what he and his men are doing. Keeping their heads down. Waiting. (Often in the rain. Not today, though, as the skies are blue for once.) It's what they do most of the time. Keep their heads down and wait. Wait for the mess patrols or the water carriers to come back. Wait for orders to go on the attack—Wakabayashi is assuming they will soon go on the attack. The primacy of attacking is imprinted in him, as it is in all the Japanese army's rules, images and culture: when there is a problem, solution number one is to attack.

Today's order of the day arrives from the divisional commander: its fussy vagueness expresses the particular mentality of the Japanese army. Wakabayashi reads it:

> With consideration to the severity of the state of the war on Guadalcanal Island, as the common decency of a warrior, each and every soldier should make sure their weapons and equipment are properly maintained, and be ready to quickly respond to any situation when the time comes.

Orders on paper are rarely crystal-clear, reports likewise. Euphemisms are the norm. People want to avoid putting down undesired or problematic facts in print. Important decisions may sometimes be imparted non-verbally, with gestures, facial expressions and sounds. Emanating as they do from a culture that shrinks from open conflict, objections frequently take the form of *mokusatsu*—meaningful silence. There is almost always a subtext.

Wakabayashi interprets this most recent order as meaning that the final battle is approaching. And he is ready. He notes in his diary: "We have been prepared for this from the very beginning. We will fall as the glorious blossoms of the Greater East-Asian War and lay down our lives on Guadalcanal." But they are not there yet. They still have to wait before they can face their deaths as heroes.

Waiting and tedium are concepts that overlap. His soldiers are bored, too. When there isn't too much crashing, banging and exploding, Wakabayashi sometimes eavesdrops on the soldiers in the adjacent foxholes. The topics that used to dominate their conversations—women and sex—no longer do. "It's highly unlikely that lust would be on anyone's mind on Guadalcanal," he writes in his diary. (That's a universal phenomenon. Libido and mortal danger don't go together: desire dies at the front.) Earlier in the autumn, during their time in East Java, he began a relationship with a young Muslim woman. It wasn't without passion, but when it became clear the regiment was moving on, he broke it off with some bittersweet feelings. It's a long time since he mentioned her in his diary.* Wakabayashi notes that when the young soldiers talk about their wives at home, the stories almost invariably end "with their wives feeding them plenty of delicious meals." The calls of the stomach triumph over those of sex.

Wakabayashi passes the time in his foxhole this Monday, November 23, working on another poem. He writes in his diary, of course. He eavesdrops on his soldiers' conversations. He daydreams about heroic deeds and the coming final victory. He takes out his compass and works out the direction of his homeland. He studies maps, one of all of Asia, one of the area round Australia, and he "boldly [lets] my imagination run wild." He observes the insects crawling down there with him and he writes a *tanka* about it:

---

* It's interesting to note that neither her ethnic nor her religious background seems to have been any barrier for Wakabayashi, in conscious defiance perhaps of the axiom that the Japanese were racially superior to all other races. And the relationship was not without an element of seriousness: he got to know her family.

A fly crawled
into the trench during a brief break
from the roaring of the cannons
and I watched him
rub his hands together

.   .   .

That same Monday, Sophie Scholl's brother Hans and Alexander Schmorell, another member of their circle and one for whom she'd felt a painful and unrequited love for a while, take the train back to Munich in order to resume their studies.* She will be doing the same within a few days.

Sophie has been enrolled at the university since the beginning of May and she is reading philosophy and biology. This reflects both the breadth of her interests and her intelligence. She had originally intended to study art but refrained from doing so as she has doubts about her own talent.† Sophie is ambitious and demands high standards of herself. She cannot bear the thought of being mediocre—she would rather just abstain. She has had a frustratingly long wait before being allowed to start university studies. As the current system in Nazi Germany now functions, young women, as well as young men, must first be at the disposal of the state.

For Sophie Scholl that meant that after she had taken her university entrance exam in the spring of 1941 she had been obliged to enroll for compulsory service in RAD, the quasi-military Reichsarbeitsdienst (Reich Labor Service), somewhere outside Sigmaringen. There, along with other young women, she had been housed in a camp where their time was spent partly on being drilled ideologically and partly on clearing weeds and shovelling dung at the farms of the area. (Private books were forbidden, so she read in secret; smoking was forbidden—everyone knew what the Führer thought of that vice, particularly when practiced by women—so she smoked secretly; her letter-writing was secret, too.) That had been followed by six months of what was called

---

* The date is uncertain. It is often stated as being December, but there are indications that suggest the journey was undertaken on November 23 or the days immediately around then.

† As well as her music-making, this multitalented young woman also draws remarkably well.

Kriegsarbeitsdienst (War Labor Service) as a pre-school teacher in the small town of Blumberg close to the Black Forest. Only then had Sophie Scholl been able to start her studies. She had scarcely begun when she received orders to pack herself off to Ulm for another period in the RAD, this time in the Constantin Rauch screw factory, northeast of the city.

This last period of service is the one that has the most effect on her, not so much because ten hours at a stretch on the factory assembly line was both tiring and utterly boring, but because it literally placed her alongside forced laborers from the east. The experience has filled her with pity and rage—and also with disappointment at what she sees as indifference on the part of most people in the factory, particularly the ordinary German workers, but even to some extent among the Russians ordered to be there. In a letter to her father, she describes how she "looked out over the big hall of the factory and saw a hundred or so people standing by the machines as if they were naively suffering under a power they themselves had created but then elevated to be their tyrant."*

Sophie Scholl will soon be returning to her studies. Nominally. She is the only one who knows that her brother and her friend are not on the way to Munich. The journey they are making is a longer one and they will be visiting several towns, including Stuttgart and Chemnitz, as far as we know—much is still unclear even today. Their purpose is to meet contacts and recruit members for their small resistance group. Travelling is risky in itself. All travellers, especially those going to a border city like Chemnitz, can expect to be checked at any time by the ordinary police, by the secret police or by the military police, who sometimes board the trains and go from compartment to compartment checking everyone's papers.

While the others were still on the Eastern Front, Sophie compiled a list of names of people it might be worthwhile for them to approach. One of those names is an old friend and business partner of Scholl's father, a man she hopes will help finance the group. This man is one of those Hans Scholl and Alexander Schmorell will be approaching.†

---

* It is experiences like this that lead her and the rest of the group to give up any hope for "the ordinary people" and turn instead to those who shared their views.
† He is Eugen Grimminger, a silent anti-Nazi. They were to meet Falk Harnack in Chemnitz as well; he was the brother of one of the members of what the

Their next action is going to be bigger, much bigger. More graffiti and more flyers targeting more places is no longer sufficient: it is time for them to start building an organized network, and Scholl and Schmorell's journey is an important first step.

Back at home everything is as normal, and that's how it must stay. Certain conversations only take place behind carefully closed doors or out in the open air. Certain conversations immediately change tone and content when anyone else enters the room. Neither Sophie's mother nor her big sister, Inge, suspect anything. As far as they can see, Sophie ought to be glowingly happy but, instead, she comes across as distant and reserved.

·   ·   ·

John Bushby sees the cliffs of the Normandy coast getting nearer and beyond them there is a glimpse of the water of the English Channel, metallic black in the strong moonlight. ED311 "K-King," the Lancaster bomber, is on its way now, and it looks as if it has survived the night's experiment. In the far distance, lines of tracer bullets wink in the darkness and then die out. That's all.

To Bushby and the others there is something incomprehensible about the nature of the war. A few hours ago they were hovering in the night sky above a burning German city without any contact with the reality they had created twenty thousand feet below, their moral universe reduced to an extremely vulnerable tube of duralumin and steel just seventy feet long and built at a unit cost of £42,000, roughly $2.8 million today. For the uniformed, faceless bureaucrats who man the RAF staff offices, the men who thought up the experiment that Bushby and his crew—Bill, Wally, Charley, Davey, Bish and Tommy— are taking part in, the whole thing is little more than an abstract idea.

K-King and its crew took off from its home field at 6:10 p.m. yesterday, Sunday. It's after midnight now and along with 220 other bombers they have attacked Stuttgart as best they could, given that there was

_____

Gestapo called the Red Orchestra, a wide-ranging resistance network with links to Moscow. Scholl and her friends had learned of the existence of this group by listening to the broadcasts of the BBC. (To be more precise, it "had existed": the network was broken up during the autumn and most of its members executed during December.)

a lot of cloud over the city.* The experiment consists of them flying both ways at as low an altitude as possible. At the prior briefing they are given an explanation why: "What Command wants to find out is the ratio between what happens from light flak at low level and the loss we would normally expect from fighter attacks higher up in full moonlight." So the desk experts are just sitting waiting with their slide rules, ready to produce more figures, tables and graphs.

So Bushby and the crew of K-King had to give up what they considered the best protection of all: height—the possibility of flying as high as possible, higher than the norm, higher than the manufacturer of Lancasters, Avro, recommends. This has earned them the nickname the Stratosphere Kids. The squadron leader noticed their misgivings during the briefing and tried to make a joke of it. He slapped Bill, their pilot, on the shoulder and laughed: "Guess this just isn't your night!"

John Bushby would remember those words long afterwards, just as he would remember with absolute precision all the other small details from that fateful night—such as the fact the Sunday morning was sunny, clear and unusually cold; that the mechanics working on their plane were wearing gloves and "their breath rose in cloudy vapour"; that they flew so low he could see doors opening and see the silhouettes of people looking up outlined in the bright rectangles.

· · ·

Ernst Jünger already knows enough. He is still in Rostov, waiting for a train to take him to Voroshilovsk. During the evenings he can hear the sounds of shooting coming from the empty industrial area close to the railway station. His diary does not say so directly, but the implication is clear: executions are being carried out under cover of darkness.

This simple observation made *en passant* is, however, in no way decisive as far as Jünger is concerned. (It could be deserters being shot, or saboteurs, looters, partisans, people like Nikolai Obrynba.) His knowledge precedes his journey to the Eastern Front. To some extent, we could say that it precedes the war, in that his early distancing himself

---

* As a result of poor visibility, the bombs were spread across a fairly wide area, hitting mainly the southern and southwestern districts of Stuttgart. The result was 88 houses destroyed, 334 seriously damaged, 28 people killed and 71 injured. The old railway station was burned down.

from Nazism reveals a recognition that these people stand for something new and brutal. To turn away and leave the places where things were happening; to move from Berlin to Kirchhorst in the country; to leave public life and write such a subtle allegory of the threat of the breakdown of civilization as *On the Marble Cliffs* (published in 1939)*; to fall silent—that was Jünger's way of offering resistance, resistance via distance. And then, when the time came to don his uniform again, he did so without enthusiasm, mainly with a sense of distaste and hopelessness, as if he could recognize his own prophecy becoming reality.

Not even his exile in uniform in the elegance of Paris was able to protect him from further insights. He already knows that the mentally ill are being exterminated. Officers he has met, those returning from the east, have brought not just vague rumors but detailed, eyewitness accounts of mass murder, mass executions and unlimited bestiality, accounts that darken the brightness of day for him and actually make him contemplate suicide.

In addition to all that, he has seen with his own eyes the beginning of the persecution of Jews in the capital of France. On June 7, for the first time, he saw people wearing the yellow Jewish star—three young women he encountered on Rue Royale. He was so shaken that he was ashamed of his German uniform. When deportations struck people he knew for the first time—the wife of Silberberg, the chemist on the corner, for instance—he wrote in his diary: "I must never forget that I am surrounded by suffering people. That is far more important than all military or intellectual honor or the empty applause of young people, who take a fancy to one thing or another." He had actually tried to help several persecuted individuals—when the risks were reasonable, that is.

Without any doubt, this explains Ernst Jünger's sleep problems,

---

* The work was noticed even outside Germany. The following month, December 1942, the British journalist F. A. Voigt wrote this about *Auf den Marmorklippen:* "It is astonishing by reason of its audacious and trenchant attack on modern tyrannies and on the cold intellectualism that makes them possible. The nightmare figure of the tyrant and the catastrophe which he brings upon himself and upon his fellow men, the liberating power of the inspired word, and the final triumph of the spirit, are drawn with a daring and an intensity of vision that makes Jünger's book one of the masterpieces of the world's literature." Göring wanted the book banned—the book's evil genius, the head forester, could be seen as a caricature of him. Hitler said no.

nightmares, depression and loss of weight. His keeping company with the anti-Nazi officers on the staff in Paris and then this strange journey can all be seen as a kind of penance.

This man with his sharp intellect and his cold, penetrating gaze must, of course, have understood that, for all of his earlier distancing, his texts had helped in a certain sense to pave the way for the regime he now scorns so profoundly. He finds it hugely disturbing to be courted by young readers who admire him for the wrong reasons. They wear the same uniform as he does and are not ashamed of their hardness and brutality, calling it the absence of sentimentality; they seem to assume that Jünger is cut from the same cloth, as if he had been transformed into all the things he once detested.

In the afternoon of Monday, November 23, Jünger visits a café that a number of Russian civilians had been allowed to run close to the railway station in Rostov—it's not unlike the kind of establishment Elena Skrjabina is running in the not-too-distant Pyatigorsk. The prices are extremely high. For instance, a small piece of cake costs three marks, an egg two. What he finds really depressing, though, is the appearance of the people, who are just sitting there passively wasting time while waiting for "departure to some awful destination."

A little later, the military police turn up and start combing through the café and everywhere nearby, looking for soldiers waiting for transport home to Germany. These and others going on leave are then formed up and forced to climb aboard a train taking them back to the front. All leave has been cancelled. Someone tells Jünger that the Russians have broken through north of Stalingrad.

. . .

Back to John Bushby and his crew in the Lancaster bomber ED311, "K-King." The low-altitude flight across France has been a "wild, exhilarating, moonlit ride over rooftops and valleys," and now, with the coast in sight, they can return to cruising altitude. Bushby sees, feels and hears that Bill is beginning to carefully edge the great machine upwards to win a little height. "Instinctively we relaxed, knowing that we were almost home and dry. Then it happened." One solitary burst of light flak, no more than half a dozen tracer shells, came up into the dark night from below.

And a couple of them hit.

No system can guarantee survival—nor can skill, nor courage.

(Particularly not courage: many people die because they are courageous.) In the end, it's luck that decides.

Afterwards, just a series of images and memories.

There is the steadiness of Dick's voice calling for a fire extinguisher,
with perhaps just a tone of mild irritation; Wally crawling towards
him on all fours; remembering that the two handles he hung on to
were painted yellow; the tearing, crashing roar dissolving into darkness; the taste of salt on his lips and the recognition it was seawater;
the rectangle of grey light above his head and instinct telling him it
was the open escape hatch, followed by the confused thought "Now
who had done that?"; the sound of waves; the shout from somewhere
outside that jerked him awake; realizing that yellow shape floating by
the wing was the life raft; how dreadfully cold the sea was; the feeling
of heaviness and numbness and weakness and the fear that he wouldn't
have the strength, in spite of feeling the rubber of the raft rubbing his
face, in spite of someone grabbing hold of his arm; Dick's desperate
shout for a knife to cut the raft free from the sinking wreck, followed
by the confused thought that "They've got to pull me in and save me.
They've got to. I've got the knife!"; sitting up in the raft and seeing the
others "coughing and retching" from the smoke they had breathed or
from the cold salt water or whatever it was; noticing that Dick's big
moustache was half burned off; the moment he and the others noticed
that Tommy was missing.

What followed was the worst part of all, not least because Bushby
was alone in it. He writes:

> We began calling his name, voices echoing over the water.
> Then I, and I alone, heard him answer. Afterwards the others
> swore they heard nothing but as there is a sun in the sky I
> heard him and know he was alive at that moment in the cold
> black water in front of us. He answered from somewhere out
> there in the sea with a clear cry which showed that he must
> have been at the ultimate moment in a man's life; a moment
> when the instinctive, despairing cry of a little boy afraid in the
> dark comes to his lips and when once again he is a child afraid
> and lonely and cries the same thing in his last moment as in
> his first. "Mother!" That was all.

It was still dark when the German boat picked them up.

.   .   .

That same Monday in Berlin and the week has started with unusually miserable weather. There is a strong wind and cold, sleety rain
is blowing through the streets. Ursula von Kardorff is meeting Martin Raschke, an old acquaintance. Raschke, stylish and charismatic, is
a well-known and celebrated author among the younger generation,
something of a prodigy during the 1920s, gifted, productive and with
a powerful voice. Now married and with two children, he is still very
productive.

The two of them are friends and members of the same generation.
Both of them welcomed Hitler's rise to power and, just like her, he
holds an attitude towards the regime and its henchmen that might, at
best, be called ambivalent. Like her, he is an opportunist and since 1933
has been able to live well on well-paid commissions for the radio, particularly plays about life in the country, about blood, soil and Volksge-
meinschaft (national community).*

Raschke was called up last year and has served as a uniformed
war correspondent. It is very obvious that, just like von Kardorff's
two brothers or Sophie Scholl's big brother, he has been more than
affected by the experience; it has changed him. Whereas the 1940 war
in the west seemed to reinforce the regime's propagandistic image of
the excellence of Germany and war, what has happened—and is still
happening—in the east is unparalleled in terms of scale and brutality.†
Reality has begun to change focus for Raschke, just as it has for Ursula
von Kardorff. But how will he deal with it?

Today, Raschke is reading aloud to her from his latest work, a small,

---

* Those artists, actors, playwrights and authors who were approved of by the
regime could reckon on high—in some cases very high—incomes. For instance,
Arno Breker, Hitler's favorite sculptor, had an annual income three times that of
Goebbels.

† German losses from the start of the attack on the Soviet Union are without
parallel: they averaged somewhere between 40,000 and 50,000 dead a month,
frequently more. (The whole of the successful campaign in the west in 1940,
including the occupation of Norway and Denmark, cost almost exactly 50,000
dead.) In addition to those losses, we should add the wounded and the missing:
the failure to take Moscow and the following winter crisis led to losses of about
700,000 men when all categories are included. It was impossible to keep losses
on that shocking scale secret or to veil them in propaganda platitudes.

thin volume, *Zwiegespräche im Osten,* "Dialogues in the East," based on notes he had made in the barracks and at the front. It's not a matter of cheap propaganda effects but of something which, in its own way, can be just as bad. The book's elevated literary, internal dialogue between "I" and "he" offers reflections on war, sparked by something seen or a situation—a newly dug grave or a burning village or some shot-up tanks—but all presented in abstract, highly aestheticized terms.

The reception has been good and the book is achieving excellent sales, going into its twelfth printing, probably thanks to, rather than in spite of, its experimental and stylized pseudo-philosophical content; it will be welcomed by those who need some subtle phrasing to justify their actions. Ursula von Kardorff is impressed. The pieces are intelligent and stylistically polished, but for some reason they do not move her—perhaps because she already knows enough to suspect that, at heart, they are untrue.

. . .

Mansur Abdulin is one of the reliable ones. His parents are party members and he himself has been a member of the Young Communists. His role in battle has already led to the award of a medal and it's little wonder that he has recently been made a member of the Communist Party, and that's not easy.* It has undoubtedly become more common for soldiers and officers to apply for party membership, for ideological reasons or simple opportunism or because of the advantages it brings. But you have to have distinguished yourself at the front. Soldiers are expected to keep a book of how many Germans they have killed, of tanks they have knocked out—the so-called vengeance record. Without accomplishments of that sort, it is virtually impossible to be accepted into the party.†

This is not a problem for Abdulin. He has a little notebook and on

---

* Mansur Abdulin became what was called a *partorg,* party organizer, and his main responsibility involved recruiting new party members.

† Paradoxical as it may sound, this flow of new party members was one aspect of the relative political softening that was introduced during the war and which served to close the gulf between party and society a little. Many people were accepted simply because they were good soldiers, even if their ideological education and real conviction was often no more than nominal. Towards 1945 the party leadership began to perceive this trend as dangerous and made it more

the first page the battalion commissar has signed a testimonial that Abdulin was the first in the newly raised regiment to kill an enemy soldier. That was the man with the hay bale on November 6, 1942. He is by no means a fanatic, but he considers Stalin's famous Order No. 227 to be good. ("Not one step backwards... those who panic and useless cowards will be annihilated on the spot....") If he is ever at risk of being taken prisoner by the Germans, Abdulin intends to commit suicide.

But there are a number of unpleasant tasks that come along with party membership, such as searching for the Soviet dead and taking charge of their papers. That is what he is doing at the moment. Several soldiers of the mortar company are missing after the most recent battle. Abdulin noted where one of them fell, a Siberian from Bodaibo, an acquaintance who had worked in the same mine as Abdulin and his father before the war. Abdulin finds the body. There is no sign of blood. Abdulin kneels in the snow and eases off the man's rucksack. It's unusually heavy. Abdulin turns the body over. There don't seem to be any wounds from bullets or shrapnel, but the back of the skull is damaged. When Abdulin opens the rucksack to search for documents, he finds... a sewing machine. The man stumbled and the full weight of the heavy sewing machine hit him at the base of the skull. Abdulin recoils:

> I felt sick. What a cause of death! The Siberian was an excellent soldier: brave, cool-headed and tough. As a civilian, he was a fine worker and a decent family man. For him a sewing machine was a symbol of prosperity. He wanted to bring it back from the war and present it to his wife.

Should he tell the company about this? It's such a meaningless death, so absurd. People will come up with stupid jokes or say the dead man was an idiot. Abdulin decides to say nothing. The man will remain one of those fallen for the motherland.

· · ·

Winter is approaching in Barrow-in-Furness, too. November has been unusually sunny, but yesterday saw the first frost. This Monday

---

difficult to become a party member again, and they tightened up supervision within the party.

morning when Nella Last opens the delayed local paper, *Barrow News,* she sees something that almost makes her feel sick. Another of Cliff's schoolfriends has been killed: it's Michael Hockey this time, and it happened in North Africa a fortnight ago.*

Nella Last knows the boy and the family very well. He is . . . was the couple's only son and everyone knows how frugally the family lived in their small house so that they would be able to afford to send him to Cambridge. She likes his mother, one of "the sweetest, nicest women I'd ever known." The woman usually comes to the Red Cross center "and last Thursday we all laughed and joked together." Mrs. Hockey had brought a bunch of chrysanthemums with her—frost had recently taken all the flowers in the garden.

By this stage, Nella Last knows many who have been killed or are missing, children of acquaintances, old friends of her sons, young men she had gotten to know in her work at the canteen. And she has been through this before: opening the paper and seeing tiny, grainy photos of "bright-faced boys I'd watched grow up from babies who were reported 'missing.'" She describes in her diary how seeing the old Christmas decorations again made her fall down a rabbit hole back in time, and she thought of "Ken and Laurie killed in the Air Force, Bill and Ted lost at Dunkirk, and gay Dorothy a sad widow."

Nella Last doesn't usually take news of deaths so badly, not these days. She herself has noticed—and been unhappy about—the way she has grown harder, particularly when it comes to more superficial acquaintances. Just three weeks ago they buried an Australian pilot who was a frequent visitor to their canteen: they all liked him because he was so nice and chatty and told them about surfing and warmth and tropical fruits. She wrote in her diary at the time: "How hard—or is it philosophical?—we are growing. Beyond a 'Poor lad, I thought he was late' [in visiting the canteen] and pity for the wasted lives, no remarks were passed. Things that would have shocked us to our heart's core now receive no more than a passing remark."

Her strong reaction on this occasion is interesting. It must have to do with knowing both the young man and his parents so well (also,

---

* In the records, the date of Hockey's death is given as November 11. He is buried in the big military cemetery in Fayid, Egypt, which was created to serve the many military hospitals in the area. All the evidence suggests he was wounded at the battle of el-Alamein and then died of his injuries.

that two other boys she knows of have been reported as "seriously wounded"). And all this, of course, makes her constant worry about Cliff even more acute. But there is more to it than that, and it is rather complicated.

Back at the start of the year, Nella Last and her husband had a big argument, caused by Cliff's decision to volunteer for service abroad. Nella's husband thought it was a stupid decision and that their son should exploit his chances of finding a safe occupation at home. Nella, however, thought he was doing the right thing by volunteering. She said: "What about honor and duty?" And he said: "You always did talk damned daft—I want MY boy to be safe." That did it! Something burst in her and years of frustration and repressed anger poured out. This selfish man, so lacking in enterprise and so afraid of life, had ruled *her* life for so long and now he was trying to rule their son's. She had responded loudly—possibly shouting; for her diary records she "shook with rage":

> If I knew my baby was going to his death, I'd not hold him back, even if I could. We must all play our own game as the cards are dealt, no trying to sneak aces from another. Cliff must LIVE—not shun life, and always be afraid of things and people and ideas, and be an old man before he has had the fire and endeavour of youth.*

He was the one who had tears in his eyes at the thought of losing his son, whereas *she* was the one who said, Go! Is it that Nella Last, when reading about Second Lieutenant Michael Hockey in the local paper, perhaps feels a sting of regret? For the thought going through her head is the same as must have occurred to millions of other mothers—and will occur to many more—in similar situations: "Why should children be born at all, if they are to be mown down in the early morning of their bright lives?" And for the rest of the day she has the image of the young man in her mind, his "smile, his little excited stutter, his too thin, boyish shoulders, in his blazer when he came back from Cambridge, his ridiculous swathings of scarf instead of wearing his good overcoat."

---

* That last sentence summarizes what she thinks is lacking in her sad and unimaginative husband—and why she has become so indifferent to him.

. . .

Ursula von Kardorff spends the evening of that day packing Christmas parcels to be sent to friends and acquaintances who are in uniform. Ever since the outbreak of war, this has become a ritual in the run-up to the final great festivals of the year. It is one of many rituals under this ritual-mad regime—like, for instance, the Eintopf dinners—any kind of stew—on Sundays, like the swarms of people with their red boxes collecting for winter relief (and God help anyone who doesn't contribute, even if just a couple of pfennigs), like the obligatory Hitler salute performed with everything from enthusiasm to no enthusiasm at all, like the mandatory silence in restaurants and cafés when *der Führer* is making a speech on the radio, or when that well-known fanfare rings out on the radio to signal that High Command Wehrmacht is about to announce another great victory.

The government substantially increased the food ration last month and, in the same spirit, there has been an increase in consumer goods ready for Christmas, with extra allowances of spirits, sweets and what are called Führer parcels to soldiers on leave. The German people must be kept happy. The coming Sunday will be the first Sunday in Advent.

Ursula's little brother, Jürgen, and her old flame Eberhard Urach will each get a box of cigarettes "with a photo of me pasted on the lid. It will maybe amuse them since it's unexpected." She is seriously concerned for Urach, as she knows he is somewhere on the Caucasus front, "where things are looking bad." She stays up wrapping these parcels well into the night.

. . .

It is cold and clear in Stalingrad that Monday. Snow has begun to blanket the endless chaos of ruins in the city. Adelbert Holl, like many other people, compares it to a shroud, which conceals much that is ugly, blackened and smashed, but simultaneously emphasizes how dead the city is, with street after street of silent, broken buildings, some of them hardly more than façades or grotesquely sculpted outlines. There are empty, blown-out windows everywhere.

Holl knows that the 6th Army has been surrounded in Stalingrad for the last two days. It shows in practical ways. They have started rationing ammunition and today Holl learned that food rations are to be restricted. All their own attacks have been called off, and now the constant grind of shots and explosions that has hung like a curtain of sound over the city since September has thinned out. At times it is silent. It is usually possible to tell exactly where the front line lies from the flares and signal rockets being fired by both sides, but, from Sunday on, darkness once again became darkness. It is quite obvious that both sides are taking a deep breath.

An order reaches Holl at lunchtime—Order No. 118. It takes him by surprise. All vehicles that still have fuel should be made start-ready. Only absolute essentials should be loaded, particularly ammunition. Everything that cannot be taken with them must be destroyed, above all abandoned cars and heavy weapons that don't have tractors. All important documents are to be burned.

The army is going to break out, heading southwest.

Holl bristles at the thought. Given their tight situation and massive shortage of equipment he finds the idea of a general retreat terrifying; moreover, at a single stroke, it will wipe out all their efforts. Wasn't this the place where the war was to be decided? Holl writes:

> With what energy and offensive elan had we foot-soldiers fought forward to this point, and with what casualties! And now back? My comrades—as far as I'd been able to speak to them—were of the same opinion. We didn't like the idea.

As mentioned earlier, Holl had been an enthusiastic and loyal supporter of the regime ever since 1933. Along with many other ordinary soldiers in Stalingrad, he shares the regime's distorted picture of the war. If the Führer says it is a battle for Lebensraum, then that's what it is. They are here "to prevent the red flood known as bolshevism from reaching Europe and our own country," as he writes. They are "soldiers who must obey orders." *Befehl ist befehl.* So he and the rest of them obediently follow the directive, load the trucks that are still drivable and begin to destroy unnecessary gear and burn the documents.

·   ·   ·

It's Tuesday, November 24, in Chicago. Yesterday was a day of sleety rain over the city, but today has cleared up a little. The temperature is in the thirties. Winter is approaching and the sun has only just risen as Leona Woods walks the short distance from her apartment to her work in the basement beneath Stagg Field.

The building of CP-1 is proceeding at a rapid pace. The night shift has just signed off and the day shift taken over. The pile is now so tall that they have had to install a small elevator to raise the material up. The careful jigsaw puzzle work continues. Everyone knows the system now: a layer solely consisting of graphite blocks is followed by two layers of graphite blocks in which each block has two holes drilled, into which cylinders of uranium metal are sunk. Then comes another layer of graphite, followed by two layers of graphite with uranium, and so on. Woods measures the neutron activity in the pile several times a day using a boron trifluoride counter: it is rising more and more, faster in fact than predicted. The physicists agree that the reason for this is probably that the graphite they are using is purer than what they were using for the tests, and the uranium supplied to them recently is a good deal purer than anything they have seen earlier.

This is good news. (Progress is clearly being made with other parts of the project.) According to Enrico Fermi's calculations—and all of his calculations have proved to be exactly right so far—the pile would need to be 76 layers high in order to achieve critical mass. After consulting his slide rule once more, the quiet Italian says that 57 layers will now be enough.* They will be finished in time. Layers 27, 28 and 29 are added today, so they have reached the mid-point. And since there will be almost 20 layers fewer, it will not have the shape of a sphere as was originally intended, but of a 6.5-yard-tall ellipsoid—a slightly flattened bun, if you will.

At the end of the day Leona Woods returns to the apartment she shares with her sister. She washes off the graphite dust that hangs in the air around the pile and, as usual, she has to take a long shower. The first greasy, greyish-black layer comes off fairly quickly, but there is still graphite seeping out of her pores even after a further half hour under the hot water.

If she has the energy to read the daily paper before falling asleep, and if she only skims the main war headlines and looks instead at the

---

* The higher neutron activity also meant that the pile would not need to be airtight—that had been the intended function of the balloon material.

small notices: she will see that the city of Chicago is contemplating the introduction of parking meters; that a big meeting has been held at Palmer House to discuss the wave of youth crime; that the famous violinist Jascha Heifetz has had to cancel a concert because of influenza; that an eighty-five-year-old widow was set alight and killed in her kitchen by an unknown robber; that a Los Angeles court acquitted the famous film star Errol Flynn in a rape case; that Charlie Chaplin took afternoon tea at the Ambassador East today as part of an event arranged by the Russian War Relief Society.

· · ·

The night before November 24 is a night of nervous waiting for Adelbert Holl. When will the order to move arrive? Neither he nor the other staff officers are able to sleep. They just doze and mostly pass the time chatting. Holl, who has always paid almost doglike attention to the senior officers, notes carefully everything they say, what tone of voice they use, what they look like, what their handshake feels like. He notes that the colonel of the regiment goes over to the field telephone at regular intervals, winds the handle a couple of times, asks a question and listens.

At midnight they are given the news that those parts of the division in the front line have begun to withdraw. Holl's regiment must wait. Renewed sounds of fighting can be heard north of them. (Where are the Russians getting all of their tanks?) Day breaks and nothing happens. They wait and wait. At lunchtime they receive a counterorder: there is not to be a breakout and the 6th Army is to defend its present position.* Holl thinks that's the best way. The only problem from his point of view

---

* On November 22, Paulus, the commander of the army, had already asked Hitler for "freedom of action," which could have been used for an immediate breakout: that would have been the only sensible thing to do given that supply lines were already strained and most people believed that supplies from the air would not work. (Göring had promised just that, as usual with no backing in reality.) The whole of November 23 was spent waiting in vain for a response from the Führer's headquarters. General Walter von Seydlitz, the clear-sighted commander of the corps that Holl's 94th Division belonged to, decided for himself to start a retreat, in the hope that it would prompt the dilatory Paulus to do the same with the whole army. The moment Hitler got wind of this, he forbade all withdrawals, Stalingrad being a matter of prestige for him. The retreat led to

is that his journey home was supposed to start tomorrow. It is unlikely to happen now and he is probably stuck here in Stalingrad for a while yet. And he has already started dreaming of home and of Germany.

.   .   .

An ordinary day in besieged Leningrad. Winter has arrived. Lidiya Ginzburg reports:

> We have once more attained something unknown to modern man—the reality of city distances, long ago swallowed up by trams, buses, cars and taxis. A city plan has appeared, with the islands, the branching Neva, a visual system of regions, because in winter, without trams, telephones, friends who lived in Vasilievsky, the Vyborg side or the Petrograd side didn't meet for months on end and died unnoticed by one another. The various regions took on new qualities. There were regions which were fired on and regions which were favorite targets for air raids. Sometime, crossing a bridge meant entering a zone of altered possibilities. There were border regions which had prepare themselves to withstand the storm. Thus the significance of short distances increased.

There is no wind, but a small amount of snow is still falling. The date is November 25.

.   .   .

What decides who will survive and who will die? A reminder: the holy geometry of chance. Nothing can save you from the play of circumstances—a fact that gives rise to different reactions in different people: denial, negotiation, depression, fatalism. Physical condition has a role to play, of course, but not necessarily physical strength—not the raw kind of strength given divine status in the illusory, vulgar-Darwinist world of the Nazis. Poon Lim out there on his raft in the South Atlantic is slim and quite short—no more than five feet five inches—but he is persevering. That, perhaps, is his most important inheritance: the ability of the poor to find a way, to endure.

---

major losses for the 94th Infantry Division and proved to be a mistake, since they were giving up a well-constructed defensive line in the north.

Up to now the geometry of chance has been on his side. He could have died in the explosion that sank the SS *Benlomond,* but he was hurled free. He would certainly have drowned if the life raft had not happened to float past him. And the fact that the raft was empty, that, too, was a piece of luck. There are several boxes of ship's biscuits, a container with ten gallons of water, chocolates, cans of meat, dried milk tablets and a bag of sugar loafs made up of compressed sugar. The fact that Poon is alone means that these provisions will last long enough for him to be found and rescued. That should be quite simple as the waters are heavily trafficked and the raft has the necessary equipment to attract attention: there is a flashlight, two flares and a number of emergency rockets.

The sun begins to sink and the sea grows calm. The raft lies where it lies, motionless in the endless nothingness of water. As the daylight rapidly fades, Poon begins to think of home, of Hainan, of his parents and his wife, and he begins to doubt whether he will ever see them again.

The Atlantic night closes around him. Poon has lost all his clothes in the shipwreck, but there is a big tarpaulin sheet in the raft and he can use that both as shade from the sun and to give him some protection against the cold.

Morning comes and when the warm balloon of the sun rises above the horizon, Poon shakes off his dark thoughts. He has no intention of giving up. Without strength of spirit, physical strength is of little value. Poon Lim ties another knot in the rope he is using to keep track of the days.

．　　．　　．

The work of repairing the Japanese destroyer *Amatsukaze* is continuing on the atoll, Truk. On this day, at last, letters arrive from Japan. (Mail to the South Pacific is irregular and uncertain.) Two of the letters are for Tameichi Hara, one of which is from his mother. He reads it: "I pray each morning and night at the family altar that our ancestors and the Merciful Buddha will protect you. Take care of yourself and come back alive."

The other letter is from his wife:

Little Mikito awakened suddenly last night and cried loud and long. I thought at first he was sick, but he finally explained that he had dreamed you were in danger. He said you looked pale and frightened. I wonder where you were last night and what you were doing. The newspapers tell of bitter battles in the south. I am worried about you.

The letter is dated November 13.

Hara weeps, not least because the letter makes him think of his forty-three dead crewmen. And he is reminded of a task that he has neglected, or forgotten in his low spirits: as commander of the vessel he must write letters of condolence to the families of the fallen. Of course he must. He shuts himself in his cabin, takes out pen and paper. It takes Hara eight hours to write the letters and by the time he goes back on deck, the sun has started to sink behind the steep, jungle-clad slopes of the volcanic island.

.   .   .

The weather is better on Guadalcanal today—which means it is raining less. This certainly increases the risk of being attacked by the American warplanes that are constantly circling high above the treetops. (It's more than likely that John McEniry in his bluish-grey dive-bomber has flown over Tohichi Wakabayashi's head more than once.) Wakabayashi wonders how the men in the machines have the energy for hour after hour. He is reluctantly impressed by the enemy pilots' endurance.

Even such a simple thing as cooking rice is now dangerous. It has to be done in special small huts, well-covered with palm leaves, because if as little as a single wisp of smoke shows above the rain forest the response is almost immediate in the form of bombs, shells and other missiles. Last night Wakabayashi's soldiers were able to cook under the protection of darkness as the moon is waning and is no more than a thin silver sliver in the pitch-black sky.

Nevertheless, today, Wednesday, November 25, Wakabayashi welcomes the splash of sunlight that finds its way down through the high foliage. The constant rain makes all forms of transportation more difficult, all movement slower. He has observed how the wet has an impact on the mood and health of his troops. At lunchtime he climbs to the top of the hill, from where—in clear weather—there is no problem in seeing what is happening behind the enemy lines. He can see two American freighters, escorted by four destroyers, in the process of unloading stores; he can see American soldiers digging fortifications; he can see the airfield and planes taking off in clouds of dust. He notes bitterly: "If we had shells, how easy it would be to take control of the airfield. The enemy fires at least 10,000 shots a day, compared to our 100 a month."

Wakabayashi has also noted with amazement and a touch of fear the immense scale of American firepower: the stream of shells that seems endless. One of his men jokingly likened the noise to twenty badly trained geishas drumming out of time. He has never before seen such a number of automatic weapons, certainly not in China, nor during the fighting with the British or the Dutch. He has recognized that the Japanese are now fighting "a country that has it all."

Does it mean that they don't stand a chance? No! Wakabayashi believes in the primacy of the will, on the victory of the spirit over matter—on *seishin,* that hard-to-define but fundamental concept that describes the superior spirit and willingness to self-sacrifice of the Japanese warrior. He believes in this not just because it is an undisputed doctrine of his country and his army, but probably also because he must believe it if he is to endure and to hope. Aren't resources actually the only thing the enemy has? Otherwise, why are they so afraid of close combat? He wrote in his diary yesterday: "Those of you who rely solely on resources, just wait and see. We will show you. The time will come soon when they face the full force of the Japanese spirit. Be prepared to see how powerless the power of money is against the power of our spirit."

.   .   .

Well, everyone has a limit, and Major Paolo Caccia Dominioni has reached his. His exhaustion is partly physical: he has lost a lot of weight, sometimes finding it difficult to walk. (Isn't he a bit old for all this?) But surely his exhaustion must be psychological, too. He is bitter and angry and his anger is not directed at the enemy but at those in power in Rome—all the fascist commissars, cheerleaders and ideologues, with Mussolini at their head, who are ultimately responsible for this catastrophe.

For twenty years they have been locked into Mussolini's hypernationalist and militarist world of illusions. Many of Caccia Dominioni's young soldiers have grown up with fascism, known nothing other than the world of fascism with its synthesis of the grandiose and the banal: they have been led astray by its dream of war as hope, desire and intoxication. It has long been possible to catch a glimpse of the gulf between rhetoric and reality, but the gulf has never been as enormous as in the present humiliation. One of these young men, one of the long-term believers, says that scarcely anyone "had understood before that this, and this alone, was what he himself had been calling for with all the force that his throat could muster in the piazzas and in the streets," and only now, for the very first time, had he realized that it was "purely words repeated as to be heard, names without objects."

But Caccia Dominioni's anger against fascism is not about the gulf between appearance and reality. He knows that already; being a veteran of the last world war, he has no illusions. To some extent, it is no doubt linked to his aristocratic background. (His formal title is 14th Baron of Sillavengo.) Caccia Dominioni describes a senior officer he comes in contact with as "a survivor from an era that disappeared with the pressure gauge, pistons, working class dictators and Hertz waves," a man who—like so many of his class—found fascism and Nazism vulgar and unpleasant, but who chose not to protest but to wear their uniforms as an act of loyalty to some other object such as the king, the nation or history. (As if it was possible to make such a distinction.) And it is by no means difficult to imagine that Caccia Dominioni, in describing that senior officer, is also describing himself.

And to some extent it undoubtedly has to do with the acute insights he gained in his earlier position in the army information unit in Rome, where he sat at his desk for fourteen months reading reports stamped "Most Secret" as well as uncensored newspapers from overseas. Not only did it make him aware of the absurd caricature of reality the Italian people were being fed, but he could also see the truth about the "political corruption, military incompetence, speculation and dirty swindles" the regime was guilty of. This is the reason why he applied for active service—it represented a flight back to reality.

But people react in different ways. Not all of Caccia Dominioni's men are losing their faith in the regime.* A good many of them retain it, because fascism, just like its German cousin, has succeeded in convincing them that loyalty and unconditional obedience are the foundations of existence; or it may be that they have already invested so much for

---

* This manifests itself in particular after Italy capitulates just a year later: some members of the battalion choose to become partisans, some remain passive civilians and some choose to fight to the end in the service of the notorious Saló Republic.

so long in its world view; or it may just be that they need something (anything?) to hold on to in this crisis, like a drowning man clinging to a life buoy. Illusions are frequently the most durable aspects of all.

But when Paolo Caccia Dominioni attempts now and in the future to find a meaning in this catastrophe, he falls back on something we might perhaps call the dignity of the victim. In the heroic stance he cultivates in the face of Armageddon, the sacrifice is in no sense diminished by being performed for a lost cause and with no hope of success. Rather the reverse. For him, the sacrifice, the heroism, has a value in itself, a value beyond the context. For what he wants to remember is the heroism and nothing but the heroism, not those who were cowardly, not those who refused to fight, who willingly surrendered, who ran away pissing in their pants in terror, or broke down and lost their minds.

Dominioni is carried aboard the hospital ship *La Gradisca* on a stretcher. The vessel had been a luxury liner on the South America route until the Italian navy took it over and painted it white, with a green stripe the length of the hull and with red crosses on the sides and on the funnels.

On board, as the ship is steaming northwards across the Mediterranean for Italy, he feels shame. He has always looked down on people who left the front line with anything less than "a respectable bullet wound," and now he is doing it himself. He is surrounded by numerous officers in excellent health who are running off home "for reasons of health." A thought strikes him: What if people assume he is one of them? Caccia Dominioni regrets leaving his battalion.

. . .

Snow has now come to the front at Rzhev. Winter has been mild so far. Unlike last year the German soldiers now have proper winter clothing: bulky, lined white jackets with a hood and matching lined trousers, to be worn on top of their usual uniforms. And thick gloves and felt boots. The bunker occupied by Willy Peter Reese and the rest of his group is cramped, but it's warm and contains everything they could reasonably ask for: somewhere to sleep, a bench to sit on and a table. They drink schnapps mixed with hot lemon water and toast bread on the stove.

A short while ago it looked as if the front was coming to life again. The night was filled with noise and flashes, flares of various colors and swaying, curving necklaces of tracer bullets. They all felt uneasy—were the Russians about to attack again? But nothing happened. Everything

calmed down, and as the tension eased, the group went back to quarrel-
ling. One of Reese's many disappointments was that the famed cama-
raderie at the front almost inevitably collapses when external strain
grows too great. The group becomes atomized. Members disappear
into their own thoughts. That was something Reese observed already
last winter:

> The ceaseless longing for sleep and oblivion was a fruit of
> death. Only a few people were able to pull themselves together,
> the majority anaesthetized themselves with superficiality, with
> gambling, with cruelty and hate, or they masturbated.

But now that the immediate danger has eased off, the atmosphere
eases with it. And the weather is fine. For once, Reese is satisfied. He
writes: "A clear, blue sky. A filigree of snow on the branches and grass,
rime frost glistening in the morning light, and the front is calm. That's
the way we wanted our world."

·   ·   ·

For Hélène Berr, yesterday was dark in every sort of way. She had sat
at home "struggling with J. M. Murry the whole afternoon, gloomy."*
But today is Wednesday, November 25, and the day is bright in every
sort of way. The sun is shining over Paris, she has received a letter from
Jean and when she returns home to Avenue Élisée-Reclus from her voluntary work with orphans there is a bouquet of carnations waiting for
her from him. (Pink? Red?) They come from a florist they have visited
together in the past on one of the side streets off Avenue de l'Opéra.
It's a reminder of their walk on Monday, the ninth. Certain moments
never come to an end. She writes in her diary: "I was overwhelmed
with joy, and yesterday seemed no more than a bad dream. Went to
the Sorbonne to register."

·   ·   ·

What does a heroic action spring from? After the attack outside Klet-
skaja on November 19, Mansur Abdulin's regiment was on the march

---

* It's impossible to tell from her diary which of the British Keats scholar and
critic's texts was giving her so much trouble, but as a guess it was *God, Being an
Introduction to the Science of Metabiology*, 1929.

for five days, pushing into the rapidly growing split that had arisen in the German lines. The split has been widened to a gap as the armored corps ploughed on into the distance and an attacking unit from the northwest joined up with an attacking unit from the southeast. In places, the gap is now forty to fifty miles wide. The German 6th Army is surrounded in Stalingrad. This is a sensation, a piece of news of the kind they have been waiting for. And it looks fantastic on the maps in the newspapers.

The situation on the ground, however, is still uncertain. The Germans, true to themselves, won't take this dangerous threat lying down. Yesterday evening, Abdulin and his weary companions reached the front and today, Wednesday, November 25, they will immediately go on the attack, pushing eastwards towards the huge pocket that has been formed.*

It is not going to be easy. That's something that Abdulin recognizes quickly. The terrain is flat and open, offering little protection from bullets or from the biting wind. And they are no longer facing Romanians; now it is Germans, who put up their usual brutally efficient defense. You can *hear* that they are Germans from the volume and rhythm of the gunfire and from their ever-present, quick-firing machine guns that make a tearing, sawing noise (*pup-turrrr, pup-turrrr*). The sound alone is terrifying. (Soldiers in the Red Army call it "the lino ripper" or "the bone saw" or "the electric machine gun.") And from the repeated, sharp, high detonations he recognizes that the enemy still has plenty of direct-fire anti-tank guns, and perhaps even armored pieces of some kind.† No, it's not going to be easy.

They do have the support of a number of tanks and Abdulin's company follows a white-painted colossus as it rattles and creaks through the snow towards the enemy position. What they are facing is not a connected system of trenches, but a number of strongpoints, clearly established in haste but defended with vigor. Here, there is Illarionov, a slightly larger village; there, a *balka,* one of those long, deep rainwater

---

* Fearing a relief operation or a breakout, the leadership of the Red Army wanted to eradicate the pocket as quickly as possible. But they made a gross underestimate of the number of troops trapped in the forty-by-twenty-five-mile "cauldron."

† They are facing the German 3rd Motorized Division, soon to be reinforced with elements of the 14th Armored Division—taken together, a substantial force.

ravines that can be found all over the steppe. Both have to be taken, and from both there comes the rattle and crash of gunfire.

There is a characteristic tinkling sound when an armor-piercing shell hits the tank, which immediately comes to a halt as smoke and flames start pouring from it. Abdulin sees a man on fire jump out of the tank. Abdulin sees that the soldiers in front of him move away. They all know that it's only a matter of time before the heat causes the ammunition in the smoking vehicle to explode, and no one wants to be in the immediate vicinity.

The burning man rolls in the snow to douse the flames. He shrieks time after time: "Comrades, save the colonel!" Abdulin's first impulse is to follow the rest of them away from the burning vehicle and the big explosion that could come at any moment. A heroic act can arise from two very different impulses—one selfish (but disguised), one unselfish. The disguised selfish urge has to do with a desire to stand out, to win approval and praise; the unselfish urge is more of an impulse, a sudden and virtually irresistible need to intervene, to rescue someone or something, irrespective of the circumstances. The end result is, however, the same.

The two voices rapidly crisscross in Abdulin's mind. First: "Those who ran past the tank had time to save the man in it." Next: "Help him now—there isn't a second to waste!" Then: "No, that's not smart! There's not enough time!" Finally: "But you have to try!" This last voice got the upper hand.

Abdulin clambers up on the tank and there is a hissing sound as his frozen gloves touch the rough steel. It's already really hot. He has difficulty holding on, slips, can't find anything to catch hold of; he takes a run at the tank, jumps and slips again; jumps at it again, gets hold of something and heaves himself up to the turret where the hatch is open and choking smoke is pouring out. He can see nothing, but two hands desperately grip Abdulin's clothes. He stretches his arms down into the hot fog that's pouring out and feels around—he can't look since he has to turn his head away and shut his tear-filled eyes because of the hot smoke. He feels a body, takes hold and starts pulling slowly, slowly. Never has a body felt this heavy, but eventually he manages to raise this sooty piece of life up to the turret and out through the hatch. One more heave and they both tumble down the battered sides of the tank and land heavily in the snow, bruised.

Once he's caught his breath, Abdulin drags the man a couple of dozen yards and only then does he notice that the man's legs are just hanging there uselessly. Then the explosion comes and the turret is blown twenty feet in the air and fragments of metal rain down everywhere. The man, the colonel, embraces Abdulin and says: "My dear boy! I'll never forget this!" He hands him his pistol as a gesture of gratitude. A couple of medical orderlies arrive and take the colonel away on a *pulka*.

. . .

The mood is good among the men surrounded in Stalingrad. Adelbert Holl is not worried—they won't be surrounded for long. It will be sorted out. "Our leadership wasn't born yesterday." Commander-in-Chief Paulus's latest order of the day was read out yesterday and it informed them that the aim was now to defend themselves where they were and to wait for relief from outside; in the meantime, they will be provisioned from the air. It concluded with a snappy slogan that sounded good to many of them and which they frequently repeated from man to man, without any irony: *"Drum haltet aus, der Führer haut uns raus!"* Hold out now, the Führer will get us out.

And hold out is what they do. The remnants of Holl's regiment along with the survivors of the decimated 94th Infantry Division are defending an improvised line that runs due west from the northern suburbs of the city along a series of heights and a railway embankment. Soviet units have been making repeated efforts to break through. Today, Wednesday, November 25, is no exception.

The alarm sounds the moment day breaks. The Russians are coming. Holl emerges from the subterranean hole in which he sleeps. The steadily rising noise of battle can be heard from the snow-covered heights that can be glimpsed about a mile and a half away. It sounds serious. To judge by the noise, every weapon available is being fired. Holl sets off for the regimental staff headquarters.

No one has received winter gear yet, so instead of white smocks the men have wrapped white sheets around themselves, with a hole cut for the head. At about ten o'clock two tanks roll up. The regimental commander, Colonel Erich Grosse, gives Holl an order to "personally" direct them to the most threatened spot, Hill 135.4. The sky hangs blue and chilly above the flat, snow-covered landscape.

Holl gestures to the armored vehicles to follow him and sets off flat out, puffing and panting. He passes the village of Orlovka to his left and begins to approach the hills. The tanks roar along behind him, their caterpillar tracks throwing up snow and frozen soil. Holl runs down into a ravine and then up onto a hill before eventually coming to a breathless halt immediately behind Hill 135.4. After pointing out to the tank commander the place from which they will get a good view out over the plain beyond the heights, Holl turns on his heel and sets off back to the distant staff. Over his shoulder, he soon hears the first characteristic cracks of the German tank guns opening fire. "Bravo, boys," he thinks to himself, "take care of yourselves now."

· · ·

Back to Mansur Abdulin and the attack he takes part in that day. While he was rescuing the colonel from the burning tank, Abdulin's company had moved on. He collects himself and runs after them.

He catches sight of a soldier crawling rapidly towards him. It looks almost as if the man is bouncing along but, in fact, it's because his body is shaking convulsively as he heaves himself along on his elbows and one knee, like some sort of three-legged animal. As the soldier passes, Abdulin sees that the man's felt-booted trailing leg is almost severed. Every time it hits the ground it sends a shock of pain through his whole body. Then Abdulin hears a howl; he turns and comes to a halt.

The soldier has pulled the damaged leg in close to him and, with a knife, started cutting through the strands of muscle and sinew that are still attaching it to him. The knife is small and clearly blunt. Abdulin thinks, Should I help?, but he is paralyzed and can do nothing but stand and stare. The man cuts through the last of the leg and places his fur cap over the bleeding stump, before tying it with his belt. "Then he lifts the severed leg, and holds it close to his breast, as if it were a small child."

· · ·

Adalbert Holl is on his way back from Hill 135.4 after showing two tanks the way there. He is returning on the same route. Holl is on the far side of a small mound when he hears the noise, the dreadful howl he has learned to fear in recent months. Stalin's organ. (Where are the Russians getting all their artillery from?) When he turns around he can see the first rockets detonating in a cloud of dust and smoke behind him. Everything moves very quickly now. He looks around. Is there anywhere at all to shelter. Here is Holl's own description:

> There, a small hole! It was about 40 centimeters wide and 10 centimeters deep. It was practically nothing. I had never tried to make myself so small in my entire life. My legs were pressed close to the ground, face downwards, arms stretched out to the front. Then there was one explosion after another. I lay there unprotected, a helpless bundle of humanity submitting himself to this concentrated show of force produced by the hand of man. Rockets constantly exploded around me, one time here and the next time there. Would this never end? Shell splinters hissed through the air. I waited and didn't know whether I'd been dreaming. I lay still for several minutes, completely stunned by this "morning blessing."

Eventually he gathers himself and gets up, shocked but miraculously unhurt.*

He gets back to the staff location without further incident, where he reports to Colonel Grosse and then starts going down into the bunker. Holl tells him it is dangerous above ground now and asks whether the colonel is coming down, but the latter wants to wait awhile. Holl has only just gone down the six steps when the sound of a dull crack is heard and air pressure blows the door open. Someone comes running: "The boss is wounded!"

Colonel Grosse is carried down, bleeding and in severe pain. A big piece of a rocket has penetrated his stomach. Holl hurries over to the seriously wounded officer, but even in this extreme situation, he is careful to use the proper forms of address: "Colonel, sir, why didn't you listen to my advice?" They anesthetize Grosse with morphine and send him to a field hospital in Stalingrad, which is already overloaded, but a colonel will no doubt be given priority.†

A little later they receive a report from the front line. The Soviet attack has been repulsed. Two T-34s have been shot to pieces and the

---

* Survival was possible because the thin-shelled rockets fired by Stalin's organ did not have the same splinter effect as ordinary artillery shells; most of the splinter actually went upwards. Ricocheting rockets were the most dangerous of all.

† Capacity was already under pressure because previously all serious cases could be immediately evacuated; that required flights, which have now become problematical.

bodies of some thirty enemy troops are lying dead in front of the position. Eighty others have surrendered.

The truth is that Holl is more concerned about food shortages than enemy attacks. The daily ration has now been set at 14 ounces of bread (virtually a half ration), 4 ounces of meat (usually horse), 4.4 ounces of vegetables and 1 ounce of fat (that represents a 50 percent cut in both cases), 5.6 ounces of preserves (usually 7 ounces) and .25 ounce of salt (usually a half ounce).* This is bad news, particularly in winter. Holl comments: "In the cold, our bodies required a higher calorie intake." But they will hold out. Rescue will soon be arriving.

.   .   .

In the afternoon Lieutenant Tohichi Wakabayashi leaves his lookout post on the hill and walks down towards the small Matanikau River, where he is intending to have his first wash in two weeks. The location is well-chosen, being a hundred-yard stretch of the river concealed by cliffs on both sides. The gently flowing water is bright and clean, and the bottom is clearly visible. Shoals of what appear to be carp are swimming around and there are crayfish creeping among the rocks—unfortunately, like the carp, they are notoriously difficult to catch. There are also freshwater snails, which are collected, cooked and eaten by the hungry soldiers. Slivers and fragments of sunlight filter down through the surrounding rain forest. For Wakabayashi the place is a paradise, and the fact that dead bodies are said to be floating around both upstream and downstream is something he chooses to put out of mind: "It doesn't bother me."

Wakabayashi wades out in the shallow stream, dips his head underwater and then soaps himself from head to toe. "The chill of the water felt really good and I was beginning to feel refreshed," but then comes a warning of enemy aircraft—yet again. More irritated than frightened, he jumps out and, still naked, hides among the trees.

On his way back from the river Wakabayashi calls in at divisional headquarters, which is carefully concealed in the rain forest. He wants to pay his respects to Major General Takeo Itō, commander of the regiment. In spite of the notably strong hierarchy in the Japanese army,

---

* The allocation of cigarettes and cigars has also been more than halved—from seven a day to two. The only item that hasn't been cut is sugar, which remains at 1.4 ounces a day.

its demand for unconditional obedience and its harsh and often brutal discipline, its social boundaries are paradoxically low, especially when compared with the British army, for instance. A strong sense of family is cultivated within companies from basic training onwards. (From Wakabayashi's diary, we gain a picture of a man who has a strong and real concern for his soldiers.) A lieutenant can simply go and visit his regimental commander just for a chat.

It is obvious that Wakabayashi looks up to Itō. Is it in spite of his ruthlessness?* Is it because it is unusual to find a major general this close to the front line? (Senior Japanese commanders frequently stay well away from the front, at a comfortable distance from the reality being experienced by their troops.)† Or is it because Itō inspires a real sense of confidence? Wakabayashi writes in his diary about that afternoon, which he spent listening to Itō's stories: "I started to feel like we had already won the war. I enjoyed those moments."

But something remarkable occurs there, something that actually should have shattered that sense of confidence, but which strangely enough seems to have reinforced it.

As they talk, Itō is rummaging through his things and a small packet of white folded paper falls out. It is hardly accidental. It is probably yet another example of the non-verbal communication within the Japanese army mentioned earlier. Itō is slightly embarrassed, hesitates a moment and then explains: "I shaved my head today. My hair had gotten really long so I saved some." Wakabayashi understands immediately what this implies. Obviously moved, he writes in his diary afterwards: "None of us is expected to survive the Battle of Guadalcanal. We cannot expect our bones to be brought home. It is only natural that we would wish for at least our hair to be brought back."‡

---

* As already mentioned, soldiers of the 38th Division, to which the 228th Regiment belonged, were guilty of a series of atrocities at the start of the war in the Pacific. After the war, Itō was found guilty of war crimes at Rabaul (1946)—charged with the murder of Chinese civilians—and in Hong Kong (1948), where he was partly responsible for the many massacres of civilians and prisoners of war that were perpetrated there in December 1941.

† This is the background to many of the Japanese military's most costly operations, particularly during the second half of the war. There was a culture and thinking among Japanese generals which is reminiscent of that of commanders on the Western Front during the First World War.

‡ The return of the fallen to Japan was (and is) particularly important and, for

The absolute and unconditional willingness to sacrifice oneself—
that is ultimately what Wakabayashi himself is referring to when he
considers the issue of the superior "spirit" of the Japanese army. During
the long voyage to Guadalcanal, he clearly did a great deal of thinking about the fact that he and his soldiers might never return home.
He seems to have become reconciled to the thought: his diary entry
for October 11 refers to Socrates. The insight that "we're going to die
anyway" offers a kind of freedom, for if we are all going to die "then
giving it your all, right to the bitter end, is supreme."

Perhaps that moment is now approaching. Wakabayashi is moved by
the seriousness of the moment, of the major general's silent gesture—
they will face death together. His eyes fill with tears. Itō takes out a
bottle of spirits (clearly something stronger than *sake*), fills the mug
from his canteen and passes it to his lieutenant, who swigs it down.
Itō pours another drink and Wakabayashi swigs that down, too. The
alcohol puts him "in a good mood." His diary entry for Wednesday,
November 25, concludes with these words: "I sweat a lot while climbing the mountain after drinking."

The death pact these two men sealed with a couple of drams was
only kept by one of them. Major General Takeo Itō was evacuated
from Guadalcanal two months later. He survived the war and a death
sentence for war crimes and passed away at home in Japan in 1964 at
the age of seventy-five.

·   ·   ·

It is Thursday, November 26. U-604 has been serviced, its tanks and
stores are full and every available space, such as empty cabins and
one of the toilets, has been packed full of provisions. The crew, clean-
shaven and smart, is back from ten days of loose living at Château de
Trévarez. But the time has come and the sea awaits.

Most of them are volunteers. There might be a level of
impatience—the fighting spirit among the men of the U-boat service
was at a peak. What they were doing, the risks they took and the sac-

---

religious and practical reasons, was done in the form of cremated ashes—in the
worst cases, of just a single limb or hair. It wasn't unusual for Japanese soldiers,
when they realized they were going to die, to place locks of hair in their mess
tins along with their identity tags, in the hope that these would then find their
way home.

rifices demanded of them were not at all meaningless in their eyes; rather the reverse—they were making an important (their commander, Admiral Dönitz, would say decisive) contribution to Germany's final victory. We can assume that the majority of these young men still believed that, and even believed it was coming soon. As far as they can see, they are currently winning the Battle of the Atlantic.

November will soon be over and it has been the German military's most successful month in terms of the Battle of the Atlantic. In total, 126 Allied ships have been sent to the bottom, with a combined gross tonnage of 802,150. And during 1942, German U-boats have sunk more vessels than during the three preceding years put together.

For a short time yet they will still be able to feel themselves superior, technically and mythically. Those low, slim, fast-moving shapes that slice seemingly unhindered through the restless waves of the Atlantic are not just an image of a threat that is everywhere and nowhere and seems unstoppable, but it is also evidence of the superiority of German engineering skill. The notion that superior technology together with superior courage can outweigh inferior numbers derives from the last war, but has achieved fullness under the Nazi regime with its worship of modernity. And in the future there beckons something that will become more and more important in propaganda terms—the talk of a Wunderwaffe (wonder weapon).

For a while yet, the constantly growing problems of locating convoys while simultaneously avoiding being located by enemy aircraft can be explained away.* For a while yet, they can continue to sail on waves of superlatives and propagandistic exaggerations, on eloquent

---

* The success of the U-boats in the autumn of 1942 was partly because the German navy had won an important but temporary cryptographic advantage. The German naval intelligence service had broken several British and American naval codes, whereas British code breakers at Bletchley Park could no longer read the traffic between the U-boats and their headquarters because the Germans were now using a new, advanced version of the Enigma machine. But in December 1942 the British also broke that code—"Triton"—and could then, as before, begin to direct convoys away from the voraciously waiting wolf packs. And despite all the heroic posturing, it was at about this time that the Allies achieved such technical superiority—aircraft, ASDIC (sonar), code breaking, advanced radar, radio location—that it was just a matter of time before they won the Battle of the Atlantic.

words on *Deutsche Wochenschau* (German Weekly Review), because they
have official statistics on their side: German U-boats are sinking more
and more vessels.

There is, however, another statistic that is not shared with the young
crew members on U-604. Dönitz's staff has calculated that most U-boats
will not make more than three voyages. The reason why their time
ashore is mainly used for leave, pleasure, drinking and fornication—
Kraft durch Freude (Strength through Joy)—is not because their *pater
familias* Dönitz has recognized the importance of reward and recovery, but because concentrated training and further education for the
crews is rather pointless. Most of them will never do more than these
three trips. A contemporary estimate made by the Allies states that,
on average, a U-boat crew during this period survived sixty-two days
of service at sea.

This will be U-604's third voyage.

.   .   .

Voroshilovsk, in the Caucasus, the same day. Yesterday's rain has turned
into squalls of snow, wind and freezing temperatures. Ernst Jünger is
out exploring. The town has a large number of older buildings and
is the first he has seen in the east that he finds in the least appealing.
"The barbaric generally always shines through in older buildings, but
still makes a more pleasing impression than the abstract vacuity of
new construction." Curious to get some sort of overview, he climbs up
a half-demolished church tower only to discover that the top part of
the staircase is burned out. He doesn't see much.

Yesterday—Wednesday—Jünger dined with Colonel General
Ewald von Kleist, commander of Army Group A, the German forces
in the Caucasus. He is someone Jünger knows from earlier and is probably one of the officers he has been sent to "sound out."*

Afternoon comes and Jünger is given an injection against typhus,
which sets off his constantly enquiring mind again. Isn't this an action
that resembles the holy sacrament? "We utilize the living experience
that others gathered for us, through sacrifice, through sickness, through

---

* Von Kleist, like Jünger's commander, Stülpnagel, was critical of the Nazis even
before 1939, though not from a particularly democratic perspective. His critical
stance led to his being pensioned, but he returned to service when war broke
out.

snake bites. The lymph from the lamb that suffered for us. The miracles are anticipated and enclosed in the matter—they are its highest actualization." (Rather like the historical memory of a catastrophe, one might think.)

In the evening Jünger meets several senior officers. A lieutenant colonel produces a map and shows what has happened at Stalingrad. Unless it is possible to break through to them, the surrounded forces will have to be provisioned via an air bridge. Jünger, obviously worried, thinks this is like the great sieges of antiquity he has read about "in which no mercy is to be expected."

·   ·   ·

At 4:21 p.m. that day U-604 leaves the great U-boat bunker in Brest and heads out to a leaden Atlantic. At 10:17 p.m. they signal farewell to the minesweeper that has escorted them out of the harbor. Twelve minutes later their radar system warns them that an enemy aircraft has located them and is approaching. They do a rapid dive which, as usual, takes between 25 and 30 seconds before the U-boat begins to disappear beneath the surface. They remain underwater for 41 minutes and then the captain orders them to surface. There is another alarm almost immediately and they have to dive once more.

This pattern continues all night, until morning.

Five days later U-604 torpedoes an American troop transport, which sinks within five minutes. Then the U-boat surfaces. The waves are high and running from the southwest. The men in the conning tower catch sight of a raft with three survivors and the U-boat is ordered to approach them in the hope that the men on the raft will state the vessel's name.

Höltring, up on the conning tower, shouts to the men and asks time after time for the ship's size and name, but the survivors' answers are impossible to understand. The U-boat approaches closer. Are they saying "Ceoui"?* The survivors misunderstand the situation or, given the endless, empty, icy waters of the indifferent sea, they are so desperate

---

* The ship was SS *Coamo*, which pre-war had sailed between Puerto Rico and New York with tourists. At the start of 1942 it was chartered by the American forces as a troopship. The captain was a Norwegian by the name of Nils Helgesen. The 186 on board had no chance given the cold winter weather, all of them vanishing without a trace.

they start crawling up onto the slippery hull of U-604. Höltring gives the order to shoot them.*

U-604 then ploughs on through the waves, staying on the surface to charge its batteries. Its course is 353°N and a cold front is moving in.

.   .   .

Twenty-five miles separates Ernst Jünger in Voroshilovsk and Elena Skrjabina in Pyatigorsk, as well as a growing degree of disillusion. Many of the people in Pyatigorsk are still hanging on to their hopes about the Germans. Elena Skrjabina is one of them. She is still sticking with the fragile and dangerous notion that my enemy's enemy is my friend—a notion that millions had already been forced to relinquish in late summer last year. The advancing columns that many of them believed would liberate them from a relentless dictatorship turned out to have come to set up an even more unrelenting order, one in which they are slaves without a future, whose lives are worth nothing at all.[†]

This self-delusion is to some extent based on the fact that the people of Pyatigorsk have only been occupied for a few months and the Germans have been fully occupied achieving the real purpose of this campaign—capturing the oilfields in Majkop, Groznyj and ultimately Baku. Moreover, there is only a relatively small Jewish element in the population,[‡] and that has limited the scale of mass murder, which,

---

* In September Dönitz had issued an order categorically forbidding U-boats from rescuing survivors from torpedoed vessels—"this includes pulling people out of the water and placing them in lifeboats, righting capsized lifeboats and distributing food and water." The order encouraged "harshness" but said nothing about killing survivors.

† As far as the majority of people in the occupied areas of the Soviet Union was concerned, this was something they encountered mainly in the form of what was called (with quite unbelievable cynicism) the Hunger Plan, established by a variety of German state agencies before the German invasion in June 1941. Its aim was to feed the German military and Germany itself without regard to the occupied civilian populations: the cold and brutal calculation was that somewhere between 20 and 30 million Soviet citizens would die of hunger. As Adam Tooze has shown, this plan could not be fully carried out, not for any lack of will, but for practical and pragmatic reasons. Nevertheless, millions of Soviet citizens starved to death as a result of the plan. All of this went on in parallel with the mass murder of the Jews.

‡ There were approximately 45,000 Jews widely dispersed in a population of

in turn, has made it possible for Elena Skrjabina to retreat into ignorance. Furthermore, the partisan movement has not become active here, which means that the local population has not yet experienced the draconian repressions that have become everyday events in the Ukraine and White Russia. (There are, of course, Chechen guerrillas up in the hills, but they are anti-Soviet and thus collaborating with the Germans.)

Elena has met several Russians in German uniforms, people who have been living in exile for a long time, opponents of the Bolsheviks, people who are still convinced that the Germans have come to free Russia. The fragile normality that exists in Pyatigorsk acts as partial confirmation: consider, for instance, the opening of the churches and the fact that they have started celebrating weddings and baptisms again.

On that Thursday, Elena Skrjabina is actually invited to a church wedding. She has a sense of uplift as she steps into the church and sees the floral decorations, the lighted candles and the guests in their fine clothes. She remembers her own wedding seventeen years earlier, which had to be celebrated in secret, behind closed doors and with the lights turned down for fear of being discovered. But that is all in the past now, or so it seems. She writes in her diary: "It was as though we were in some different, fairy-tale world." People believe what they need to believe.

.　.　.

True to habit, Vasily Grossman has set off to visit one of the most dangerous places, or, to be more accurate, one of the places where the most important events are likely to occur. He is accompanying one of the units which, like Mansur Abdulin's, is attacking the surrounded 6th Army, with the hope of quickly causing the huge encirclement to implode. All in vain. Grossman jots down some lapidary notes in his notebook: "A happy, bright day. Preliminary bombardment. *Katyushas.*

---

roughly 7.5 million. It was the job of Walther Bierkamp, head of Einsatzgruppe D and a doctor of jurisprudence, to decide which of the various special ethnic groups in the Caucasus belonged to the right—or wrong—category. This mainly concerned the population known as Mountain Jews, which Bierkamp concluded were Jews in name only and could therefore be spared. (He reached this conclusion as a result of his interest in anthropology.)

Ivan the Terrible.* Roaring. Smoke. And failure. The Germans have
dug themselves in, we couldn't hunt them out."

.   .   .

Camp No. 5, outside Batavia, on Java. The mood among the prisoners is deteriorating. There is more irritation and many more quarrels.
Even Weary Dunlop is feeling low: "The squalor and oppression of this
life stirs a streak of bitter perversity in one." The number of sick men
is rising, most of them suffering from various diseases of deficiency,
which result mainly from inadequate diet. And it has become hotter,
which makes it more difficult to sleep at night in the cramped space
they have, with rats and other vermin skittering around in the darkness. In addition to all that, they know they will soon be moving on.
The paperwork is being done and a typewritten card being produced
for every prisoner. (Dunlop's card still exists.) But where are they to be
sent? The uncertainty eats away at them.

On this Thursday, November 25, he and the other prisoners of war
are forced yet again to parade in the heat, twice in fact, notionally
for checks and to be counted. Dunlop is sick of these interminable
parades, sick of the two Japanese NCOs in charge of it all who constantly keep them waiting, irritated that the two NCOs are always so
sloppily dressed. The Japanese perform their inspections while wearing
tennis shoes! "Dreadful slovenliness," he writes in his diary, annoyed.

Enmity is imitative. In general, Dunlop hates the Japanese, intensely.
But some of them he respects, and a couple of them he actually likes.
He also notices how the Japanese are having an influence on him.

Early on, he and the other Australians learned to greet and exercise in the correct Japanese manner simply to placate the guards and
reduce the level of screaming, shouting and beating. It's just the same
with personal hygiene: keeping clean, shaving carefully, having your
hair cut very short as the Japanese do, all these are approved of by the
camp guards. Once, on seeing a group of newly arrived white prisoners, his spontaneous reaction was how scruffy they looked with their
wild beards and uncut hair. And afterwards he finds himself thinking
about it and writing in his diary—not without concern: "Am I becoming Nipponised?"

---

* Probably a variety of Soviet heavy mortar.

.   .   .

In New York that same Thursday *Casablanca* is being given its world premiere at Warner Bros.' main cinema, the Hollywood Theatre, at 237 West 51st Street. The building is a peculiar hybrid. The external frontage is restrained Art Deco, the entrance flanked by two pilasters formed as statues. The interior with its double balcony, high boxes and seating for 1,603 is Neo-Rococo—a shock of gold and red, with ornamentation, wall paintings, engaged columns and rosettes in stucco, all of which gives the visitor a confusing sense of suddenly being hurled back a couple of hundred years—a time machine taking them away from an insecure present. But the premiere is actually taking place here and now.

The company is making every possible effort to link the film to the war and to the landings in Morocco. In the morning, the premiere is introduced by a small parade along Fifth Avenue with both civilians and people in uniform (including that of the Foreign Legion), most of the participants being linked to various Free French groups. The parade swings into West 51st Street and proceeds to the cinema, where they all line up for the photographers, open a banner of the Cross of Lorraine and then join in singing the "Marseillaise."

The box offices open at 11:30 a.m. Tables are laid out in the magnificent rotunda, some of them selling souvenirs, others signing up volunteers for the Free French Forces. The whole event, which according to one reporter "took the tone of a patriotic rally rather than the premiere of a timely motion picture," was also broadcast on the radio.

The reviews are consistently good, some of them glowing. *The New York Times:* "One of the year's most exciting and trenchant films." *Time* magazine: "Nothing short of an invasion could add much to *Casablanca*." *Variety:* "*Casablanca* will take the box offices of America just as swiftly and certainly as the American Expeditionary Force took North Africa." *The Hollywood Reporter:* "Smashing melodrama of timely import should click heavily at box-offices everywhere."

Casablanca arrives at precisely the right moment. The film is an allegory of the United States' road from isolationism to engagement. It is simultaneously a manifesto aiming to make people recognize that the war is something that will have an impact on them whether they like it or not and that they must be ready for the sacrifices that will come in its train. Few people in the audience could miss that. But the film is also a romantic story about lost love; a tragedy that speaks of impossible choices and inevitable loss; a psychological drama about the need for reconciliation with the past; a thriller full of threat, tension and uncertain, insecure alliances; a comedy in that there are many pieces of dialogue that make one laugh aloud; a melodrama about how a disillusioned hero finds a way back to himself; a morality tale as clearly black-and-white as its visual style.

The fact that the film has remained popular is partly because it leaves room for all these readings. It also possesses a certain dark energy, which in all probability was immediately and clearly recognizable to all those sitting there in that darkened auditorium and which still grips us today in a manner we perhaps feel but don't really understand.

Casablanca remembers something we ourselves have forgotten. Its tone is set by the fact that the film was made at a stage when it actually looked as if the Axis powers were capable of winning the war. Most of the people we see on the screen, whether in major or minor roles or simply as extras, are refugees from Europe, who have fled the war or Nazism or both,* and in playing their roles they reveal a desperation that is not merely acted.

And when the final music fades, the curtain falls, the audience leaves the theatre's dream of velvet and gilded rococo and emerges onto West 51st Street under a grey November sky, what is it that stays with them? Given that the film is open to so many readings, it is, of course, impossible to know, but it is not difficult to point to the passage that was absolutely central at that time and in that place, both to those who created the film and probably to many of the people who had just watched it. It isn't one of the smart one-liners that have since become immortal; it is Lazlo's words of farewell to Rick at the airfield: "Welcome back to the fight. This time I know our side will win." The words are accompanied by a sudden surge in the music and a dramatic cut to an aircraft engine starting up.

---

* Paul Henreid (Victor Laszlo) fled Germany as an outspoken anti-Nazi; Peter Lorre (Guillermo Ugarte) came from a Jewish family; Conrad Veidt, who plays Major Strasser, left Germany because his wife was Jewish. (Ironically, he ended up typecast as a Nazi in Hollywood.) Both parents of Marcel Dalio (the club croupier) died in concentration camps and the three sisters of S. Z. Sakall (the waiter Carl) suffered the same fate.

A few months earlier, those words would have merely been an invocation. Now they are a promise.

· · ·

Just for once, Mun Okchu of the Taegu Inn in Mandalay is free from her usual routines. Today is her single day off every month. She can stay at the inn or she can go into the city. In the latter case she must have a stamped and signed leave pass from divisional staff. The girls from the "inn" are only allowed out in groups of five or six and one of the group has to be responsible for the others. Mun is the one with that responsibility today.

Mun is considered to be particularly reliable, possibly because, superficially anyway, she shows signs of becoming Japanese in the way that Japanese policy desires in the areas under occupation. The leave pass uses the Japanese name she has taken and states: "Fumihara Yoshiko and a group consisting of..." It goes on to state the time for which it is valid and when the young women must return to the inn. Mun knows their return time will be checked—very precisely.

The little group is not supervised by an armed guard or even by Mr. Matsumoto or his wife. Where could they run away to, anyway? They are outcasts, two months' sea voyage from home, in an unknown country, in a city surrounded by mountains and jungle, among a foreign, unfriendly people who speak a language they don't understand. She says: "Wherever we went we were taunted and despised for becoming comfort women and for being Korean."

Mun Okchu has a dark secret. She has found herself in this situation before. One evening when she was sixteen and on her way home from visiting a friend, she was kidnapped by a Japanese officer and after many twists and turns ended up in a military brothel in northeast China. She was kept captive there and compelled to have sex with up to thirty soldiers a day. "On the day I lost my virginity, everything seemed to black out before my eyes," she writes. "I wept and wept.")

She did, however, manage to escape. She formed a relationship with another Japanese officer and he provided her with the travel documents she needed to get home to Korea.

Did Mun allow herself to be recruited by the Matsumotos against her better judgment? Was it a matter of naivety, the victory of hope over experience, or was it something worse? (Money is important to her.) Any hopes or plans she may have nourished are, however, doomed to come to nothing. Mun Okchu may be physically tough beyond measure, but her mental health is declining badly. In the account she composed after the war, we see that she will later attempt to commit suicide.

In Mun and in many of her sisters in misfortune we can see elements of fatalism that reflect the arbitrary and violent power they have to live under, particularly as women and even more so as poor women. It's the numbing kind of fatalism that makes things easier to endure, but simultaneously makes it more difficult to cut oneself free.

The little group walks towards Mandalay with its tall pagodas and scorched black stone elephants, its sunshine, palm trees and delicately tinkling temple bells. The greater part of the city is in ruins. Lush green grass has started to sprout here and there among the piles of stones, cement and twisted, rusty sheets of corrugated iron.

·   ·   ·

An ordinary day in Leningrad. The ever-present waiting lines wind their way forward through the snow and cold. Forward? Well, it's virtually impossible to see any movement. Lidiya Ginzburg writes:

> A waiting line is an assembly of people, doomed to a compulsory idle and internally isolated communality. Idleness, unless it be given point by way of recreation or diversion, is just misery, a punishment (prison, waiting in line or to be received). A queue is complete idleness coupled with a grievous expenditure of physical energy. Men cope particularly badly with waiting lines, since they are used to the idea that their time is valuable. The point is not even in the objective situation, it's simply a matter of inherited habits. Working women have inherited from their grandmothers and mothers time which is not taken into account. Their everyday lives do not allow that atavism to lapse. A man considers that after work he is entitled to rest or amuse himself; when a working woman comes home, she works. The siege lines were inscribed into an age-old background of things being issued or available, into the normal female irritation and the normal female patience.
>
> On the other hand, almost every one of the men who turned up in a shop tried to get to the counter before his turn.

Men can't explain the origin of this feeling of inner rightness despite the outward unfairness of their action. But one thing they do know—a waiting line is women's business.

The temperature is falling. The houses take on a slightly pink color in the weak winter sunlight.

.   .   .

Vera Brittain has another shift as fire-watcher, fully dressed but sleeping in her own bed, from 3:00 a.m. to 6:00 a.m. She spends a lot of time thinking about her children in the United States, especially John, who will be fifteen next month. "John must certainly be a grand looking boy by now," she writes in her diary for Friday, November 27. "I shall hardly know him again. By my reckoning, he is now 5 foot 7 inches tall. Trying not to feel too grieved because he is growing so tall and handsome and I am missing it all. But the years pass & the war gets nearer to him without my having his attractive youth at all."

.   .   .

About a week has passed since the SS *Oglethorpe* was launched. Tugs towed her a couple of hundred yards up along the Savannah River. That's where she is now, in a big wet dock, part of the same shipyard.

She is not yet ready for service at sea. Various pieces of heavy equipment still have to be mounted—anti-aircraft guns, lifeboats, life rafts, radio equipment, deck machinery and stoves. And she still has to be fitted with the sorts of things the crew will need during her coming voyage—everything "from furniture, medicines and cooking utensils to navigational instruments." She will carry 2,160 sheets, 2,160 bath towels, 2,780 hand towels, 1,380 pillow cases and 118 blankets.[*]

The first trials of the ship's big steam turbines will start soon, and the first members of the crew will come aboard. The hope is that SS *Oglethorpe* will be ready to put to sea in the second half of January, when she will take on a cargo and join a convoy crossing the Atlantic from New York to Great Britain.

.   .   .

[*] There were no laundry facilities aboard these ships: all dirty linen was to be dealt with when the vessels returned to the United States.

From attack to defense. Mansur Abdulin is digging down into the frozen earth, inch by inch. All around him, his comrades are doing the same thing. Clods of frozen soil and snow fly in the air as a line of holes are dug. The air is filled with the dull clank of spades at work. It's heavy going. They have to get down into the frozen earth, but can't manage more than is absolutely necessary, so each of them digs a hole just big enough for himself. In a certain sense, each foxhole thus bears the imprint of an individual body. And some of them will, indeed, be buried in the womb they have dug. "Dig or die," the saying goes. But sometimes you die anyway.

The attacks on the large village of Illarionov and the long ravine continued for many days. Unsuccessfully. German resistance was too strong and the Soviet forces too weary, exhausted even. Abdulin and his fellow soldiers had the support of the IVth Tank Corps, which was famous by that time, but when the attacks around Illarionov began only 30 of the 143 tanks the corps had at the start of the offensive remained, and they were now spread across a front that was perhaps six miles wide. The rest had been damaged, knocked out or had mechanical problems.* The 293rd Rifle Division Abdulin belongs to started Operation Uranus at full strength with 10,420 men, but just a week later only 6,000 of these remain—Russians, White Russians, Ukrainians, Jews, Kazakhs, Tartars and other Central Asians.

So they are now preparing for defense, both because they have to and because it is the only thing they are capable of doing just now. The most rational action for their encircled opponents would be to smash their way out—everyone recognizes that—and that's the reason Abdulin and the rest of them are digging in.

Gradually their energy returns and they dig more. Digging is also a way of keeping busy and staying warm in the cold. The dugouts grow slowly, with small niches for weapons and ammunition, and others for cooking gear. There is no fighting going on. Every so often they hear the dull sound of a mortar being fired, followed a few seconds later by the muffled thud as it strikes. And every now and again comes the echo of a single shot fired by a sniper. After dark, the usual curving

---

* In addition, many of the artillery units that had provided them with considerable support at the time of the breakthrough on November 19 had been left behind. It's true that they have taken the big village and the long ravine, but that was only after the Germans themselves beat a retreat.

necklaces of tracers can be seen in the distance. Both sides are waiting and watchful. What's going to happen next?

Abdulin is keeping a careful watch on the German line. They do not seem to have dug themselves in as deep. Their battlement seems to consist of no more than two or three layers of frozen corpses, mostly their own dead, that they have shovelled snow over. It might be a sign of desperation, but it might equally be a worrying sign that their breakout is coming so soon that they don't think it's worth digging themselves in too deep.

. . .

They have been on the way to Benghazi for the best part of a week now and Keith Douglas is bored, tired and irritable. All of them seem to be bored, tired and irritable. It's not just that the journey has taken an unexpectedly long time; it has also turned out to be unexpectedly uncomfortable. There is no suspension on the trailers transporting their tanks, so, on the bad stretches, they have literally bumped along for mile after mile. There have been squabbles over seats in the greater comfort of the tractor units; those in charge of transport have squabbled with those in charge of the squadron over the order of march; and sandstorms have been replaced by cloudbursts.

One good thing is that they have put the Libyan desert behind them and reached greener, inhabited areas. Douglas makes a note of the graffiti on the whitewashed walls of the buildings: "*W il Duce W il re*," "*Vinceremo Duce Vinceremo*," and—a touch ironic—"*Ritorneremo*."* One night they made camp on a tree-clad slope among empty champagne and chianti bottles, chocolate wrappers and empty cans of cherries left behind by their retreating adversaries.

Later, several Bedouin approach Douglas and his companions, give them the fascist salute (again a touch ironic in the context) and show them eggs they have for sale. Not that they are keen on the British: they dislike them at least as much as they disliked the Italians—in their view, they are the same kind of unwelcome colonial overlords who happen to be fighting one another in front of them. Interestingly enough, it is only the Germans who have gained widespread approval among the Bedouin. During the war in the desert, the Germans have

---

* "Long live the Duce, Long live the King," "The Duce Will Be Victorious," "We Shall Return."

found themselves cast in the role of liberator, a rather unusual position for them.*

This war is following the logic of all major wars in that, like some greedy black hole, it grows by sucking in other apparently unrelated conflicts. Thus roles can change depending on circumstances, and unholy alliances can arise.

It is this mechanism that led many Egyptians to hope for an Axis victory in North Africa. This showed clearly just under six months ago at the time of "the Flap," the widespread panic that arose in Cairo when Rommel's seemingly invincible forces crossed the border into Egypt. Many Egyptians, along with the tens of thousands of Italians interned in the city, looked on with ill-concealed delight as the British lined up to take out all their savings before squeezing onto overcrowded trains heading for Sudan or Palestine. At that point, local shopkeepers began changing the language of their display windows to German.†

But the Bedouin Douglas meets have survived the same way they have survived all the various conquerors that have come and gone throughout the ages: they have stood to the side and observed the grand narrative of history as if it were a natural catastrophe— incomprehensible, destructive and transient. Nor were the Bedouin interested in money, particularly not in the British pound. They wanted tea or sugar in exchange for their eggs or, if need be, canned meat or biscuits.

This is the end of November and the column—now in possession of eggs—trundles on through the small town of Barce. After all the time he has spent in the monochrome landscape of the desert, Douglas now finds himself in a world of color for the first time since leaving Alexandria. There are three colors in particular that his eyes are unaccustomed to: white, red and green. The walls of the houses are chalky white, the roofs tiled red and the trees green. And there are chickens and goats and children who wave to them. Patches and flickers of

---

* It's superficial. There was already an Einsatzgruppe Ägypten ready and waiting to undertake the massacre of the Jewish population in Egypt and then in Palestine once the Africa Corps was victorious and had occupied those territories. In July 1942, the head of that group, SS-Obersturmbannführer Walter Rauff, was sent to Tobruk to confer with Rommel.

† There was one group for which this panic was completely understandable: the Jews of Cairo, both those who had lived there since time immemorial and those who had arrived more recently as refugees from Nazism.

sunlight play through the leaves of the trees lining the street. The town seems undamaged and, as far as he can see, the only sign of the war is a blown-up bridge. Beneath the bridge lies an overturned truck with a load of crosses to mark German graves: they are empty, gleaming, still waiting for names.

.   .   .

Yesterday, Friday, the Germans executed eight Belgians, individuals who had been held hostage in an attempt to discourage armed attacks by the resistance movement.* But they haven't stopped; attacks began seriously last spring and they have increased more and more as the year goes on. There have been some sixty violent attacks in the last six months, the targets not primarily being Germans but Belgian collaborators. Nine of them have been assassinated between the end of October and the end of this month, many of them extreme right-wing Rexists whom the Germans appointed as mayors in place of those elected democratically. The most recent assassination was on November 19 when Prosper Teughels, the mayor of Charleroi, was gunned down outside the city hall.† The response came yesterday, when those eight hostages were shot.‡ They were shot in Fort Breendonk, outside Mechelen, where the Germans use an old army fort as a transit camp

---

* The use of the singular here is actually wrong. As in all the occupied countries, we should be talking about resistance movements, across a wide spectrum from communists on the left to conservatives and monarchists on the right. The communist groups were usually the most successful, since they were used to working undercover—and they were the most violent.

† Teughels was not an extreme collaborator. In fact, he was known as a reasonably competent mayor, but the fact that he had been a well-known Rexist before the war was sufficient to make him a target.

‡ The Germans responsible for the execution hesitated to the last, as they considered it to be counterproductive. The decision was taken mainly to appease the Rexists and other collaborators who were terrified by the wave of assassinations. Just as in France, there were conservative German military men in Belgium who were anything but pro-Nazi, but, as the author Werner Warmbrunn has pointed out: "Their misfortune was that they did not see, as given the limitations of their own political culture, they indeed hardly could, that cooperating with the absolute evil represented by Nazi Germany was bound to corrupt and contaminate the best intentions of those trying to 'work from within.' And that such cooperation was bound to turn all persons in positions of authority into accomplices of crime."

for political prisoners, resistance men and Jews. (The place is awash with rumors of torture and brutality.)

Today is Saturday, November 28, and Anne Somerhausen is reading about the execution on one of the green posters that the occupation authority has had stuck up around Brussels. They also proclaim further threats. She reads: "The military commander reserves the right to sentence those who commit political crimes to be hanged after they have been sentenced to death by a military court, if the crime in question has been carried out in a particularly brutal or insidious manner."

This is clearly an escalation. The Germans have executed people earlier, but it has only affected those directly involved in perpetrating sabotage or those taken with a weapon in hand. (The sentences will have been countersigned by Belgian judges.) There has always been an appearance of legality, but now it's all about hostages, of people being executed for deeds they have had nothing to do with. The atmosphere is changing, in Brussels and in Belgium, and it is doing so in a way that is major, complicated and seriously worrying.

It seems that the war is on the point of turning. Even Anne Somerhausen now listens secretly to foreign radio broadcasts, and information about what has happened and is happening in North Africa, on the Eastern Front and in Southeast Asia is actually getting through. There is also a growing number of underground newspapers. Most of the people she knows are pleased with the news: the joyful reception of the news of the American landings was both genuine and widespread.

At the same time, however, it has started to dawn on most people that any hope of the occupation coming to a sudden end as the result of compromise or negotiation is an illusion. And the notion that has carried Somerhausen thus far, the notion that says that everything will return to normal in, say, six months, now looks to be no more than banal wishful thinking.

There is the horrifying thought that Belgium, as so often in history, might once again become a battlefield. The country has, to a certain extent, already become that. During the current year, the British air force has become more and more aggressive and air-raid warnings much more common even in Brussels. The wail of the sirens frightens Anne Somerhausen, even though she knows there isn't usually any danger. Not yet, anyway. The city has been left untouched for a long time, apart from a couple of bombs that fell on one of the suburbs at the beginning of the summer. But the coast, Ostende in particular, is said to have been badly hit. She notes in her diary: "The general impression here is that we would be safe if the English could strike their targets with greater precision. Most people feel that certain weapons factories and certain airfields should be bombed, but what concerns us is that the surrounding residential areas usually have to pay for it."

Something new is becoming apparent to Anne Somerhausen and her fellow countrymen: the "numerous shades of grey that have dominated recent years," as British author Martin Conway wrote, are beginning to shade over into black and white. A simpler and more brutal world is becoming visible. The war will end and the Germans will be defeated, but the road to achieve that will be a long one. Brussels is grey, dark and cold. The chestnut trees along Avenue Louise have lost their leaves.

.   .   .

Danuta Fijalkowska can't forget that picture of the Jewish woman on the street who, quickly and without any hesitation, passed her baby over to a passer-by. She wonders whether her husband, Józek, can imagine being so certain of his own imminent death that he would do something like that. He, a devout Christian and former Auschwitz inmate, says that yes, he does understand that act, but simultaneously he attempts to comfort her: "Many things are beyond our comprehension. But try to think about it this way. Death brings liberation from earthly suffering. This woman may be happier now, up there, with God." The argument does not convince Danuta. She, the skeptic, lacking all illusions, becomes argumentative: "I don't believe it. I just don't! I don't believe in eternal life. Look what happens to us after death. We turn into dust, just mere dust! And all those thousands and millions of people that are being killed every day in Poland! What's left of them? Just dust, nothing else." He tries once more, and there is a pleading tone bordering on desperation in his voice: "Danus, there is eternal life, I know that for certain. You must believe that." But that's as far as they get.

That is more or less all she remembers of the conversation later. And that snow was falling outside, on the other side of the frost flowers on the window. The fact that she remembers all this so clearly implies, perhaps, that the conversation had a meaning that was hidden from her at the time. But it took on a meaning afterwards. At this point Józek has only a couple of months left to live.

.   .   .

Another reprieve for Willy Peter Reese. Twice before he has been in the hospital and spent long periods as a convalescent. The first time was after last year's catastrophic winter campaign on Moscow, when he was seriously affected by frostbite in his legs; then in July he suffered a collapse of some sort after long marches in the oppressive heat. And now luck or a kindhearted officer has excused him from a new and dangerous posting. The fatalism that Reese and so many other soldiers subscribe to—soldiers in different armies and different parts of the world—is a calming and in its way rational reaction to being trapped in a situation in which they can do very little to avoid injury or death.

A few days ago, on Wednesday, November 25, yet another Soviet offensive began at Rzhev. How many had come before is difficult to say. The growl of distant, heavy artillery fire is once more hanging in the winter air. The fighting is not affecting the sector in which Reese is, but his company with its armor-piercing guns has been sent off to provide any support needed at Olenino, one of the threatened points. This all happened in haste and the unit has left much of its personal gear behind. Reese has been ordered to stay back and "guard the bunker and keep things in order."

So he is spending most of his time sitting there on his own in the increasingly snow-covered bunker, keeping the fire in the stove going, chopping wood for it, making ersatz coffee, writing in the light of a small oil lamp, dreaming, thinking, listening to the crackling of the stove and staring into the glow. This is as close to happiness that Reese can come. The only times he meets anyone is when he goes out to fetch food or when someone else who has been left behind drops in and they talk of "their lives in peace time, war experiences and hopes for the future." "I kept myself going on a storehouse from past times," he writes.

> We could dream of our youth when war robbed us of it; we could longingly paint a picture of our unlived lives. Once upon a time there was a night of drinking, singing, dancing and much kissing, and there were a thousand other nights full of music, magic, intoxication, laughter and thoughts, wanderings and blissful melancholy. But they never belonged to us. We saw snow: God had formed it, just as he had also created us. We thought of home, of the books we would have to burn with all their lies.

The most dramatic thing that happens is that he gets lost in a snow-storm when going out to fetch food. But tonight he is back, sleeping in his bunker.

A sound wakes him. Not a crack or a loud explosion, but something much, much quieter, something that is different from the norm and immediately makes him pay frightened attention. It is the crunch of cautious footsteps in the cold snow. He reaches for his pistol. The steps come closer and he hears voices whispering. Russians. He gets ready to shoot, but the steps disappear. Only later does he understand that the entrance to his bunker is so covered with snow that the Russian patrol couldn't see it. One more reprieve.

.   .   .

November, so far, has been a reasonably warm month in Shanghai, but a strong stream of cold air has now swept down over the city from the north. Winter is here. When twelve-year-old Ursula Blomberg leaves the walled garden of the house at Place de Fleurs 475 this morning, she can see the silver of the first frost on the grass. Another winter in Shanghai. What was supposed to be a temporary stop for her and her family, an exotic interlude, has now lasted for three and a half years. They are stuck here for as long as the war lasts. And how long will that be? In spite of time and uncertainty, Ursula Blomberg neither wishes to nor can make herself at home here in this great city, which is both familiar and exotic, safe and threatening, distant and incomprehensible and yet part of herself. She writes:

> Ever since my very first day in Shanghai, I never lost the odd sensation of living a dream-like experience—that I was just a casual visitor, a sort of uninvolved observer to my life in China. My past lay in Europe, my future in America, and the present was merely the passage that led from yesterday to tomorrow. I kept myself somewhat detached from my surroundings—not looking for roots in China soil. I had places to go—faraway places.

She holds on to that feeling, or maybe it's a case of that feeling holding on to her. Perhaps it's a way of shutting discouragement out? And not just for a child. And maybe the worst of despair is behind them.

·   ·   ·

An ordinary day in Leningrad. It is becoming colder. The time when
people undressed at night is long past. Lidiya Ginzburg writes:

> For months on end people—the greater part of the citizens—
> used to sleep without undressing. They lost sight of their body.
> It disappeared into an abyss, immured in clothing, and there
> in the depths it changed and degenerated. A person knew
> it was turning into something horrible. He wanted to forget
> that somewhere far away, under the quilted jacket, under the
> sweater, under the vest, under the felt boots and the puttees,
> he had an unclean body. But the body advertised its pres-
> ence through pain and itching. The most vital people washed
> themselves sometimes and changed their underclothes. Then
> an encounter with the body could not be avoided. They would
> examine it with grim curiosity, conquering their desire to
> remain ignorant. It was unfamiliar, with new hollows and
> angles every time, bruised and rough. The skin was a blotchy
> sack, too big for its contents.

German air raids and artillery bombardments continue, randomly,
irregularly. The front around the city is calm. And that is not a good
thing. The citizens know that as long as the front is calm, they will
continue to be trapped.

·   ·   ·

It's a scene worthy of a Christmas card: a sledge pulled by a grey horse
and carrying two well-blanketed passengers is gliding through a dark
wood, heavy with snow. Snowflakes are spinning in the air and the
runners of the sledge squeak. One of the two passengers is Nikolai
Obrynba, the partisan. He, an aesthete whose thoughts are usually open
to beauty and the picturesque, now finds his thoughts elsewhere.

Once again he has to execute someone. Last time, when he shot that
Polizei deserter, it was unpleasant, but now, as if that wasn't enough,
it's a woman, a refugee from Leningrad who had found accommoda-
tion in a village outside Antunovo. The woman has started a relationship with a White Russian collaborator, a Polizei, in Lepel, a small
town nearby. The other inhabitants of the village suspect that she has

possibly become an informer and consequently they are no longer willing to cooperate with the partisans, as they are afraid that the woman might report them. Ergo, the woman must go, even though there is little more than suspicion and gossip to go on. That's what headquarters has decided.

They are approaching the village. No lights are visible. The houses emerge as black silhouettes against the snow-covered spruce trees. The other man in the sledge, Obrynba's guide, a man by the name of Pavel Khotko, points out the broken-down house in which the woman lives.

Khotko clearly senses Obrynba's reluctance and so he emphasizes the importance of the mission and what a traitor the woman is. "He was trying to embitter me, harden me, knowing it would be difficult to do the deed." In an attempt to get support, Obrynba asks the guide to accompany him to the house, which he does. Obrynba has his Nagant revolver. They knock on the door. Obrynba takes up the narrative:

> An old man opened the door. Walking ahead of us, he led us into the shack and lowered the light in a kerosene lamp hanging on the wall. The light was weak, but seemed bright because of the darkness. It lit up a plank partition covered by pink wallpaper. Through an aperture without a door, we saw an aging woman lying on two chairs pushed together. I asked the old man: "Who are you lot?" He replied that he and his wife were evacuees from Leningrad. He stood looking at us helplessly, wearing a woman's knitted jersey, his neck wrapped in a rag. "And where is the other tenant here?" I was speaking loudly, trying to sound stern in an effort to arouse indignation against the traitor-woman: but it felt strange, awkward and annoyed me even more. "Nadezjda? She's here…" said the old man, pointing at another aperture screened by a curtain.

Obrynba pulls the hanging aside. Lying there on an iron bed is a young woman and beside her she has two sleeping children, a girl who is maybe three years old and a boy just a little older. Obrynba hadn't been reckoning on the presence of children. His thoughts and feelings are all over the place.

Nadezjda gets out of the bed, pale and silent. She is wearing a man's white shirt. Obrynba informs her why he is there and that she has been sentenced to death for associating with the enemy. She just stands there, head lowered and arms hanging down, as if turned to stone. He raises his voice, uses foul language, calls her scum, hoping to get some sort of reaction, anything that might make his deed easier. She remains silent and passive. He is thinking of the children the whole time—what is he to do with the children, what will happen to the children? She is not showing any emotion, perhaps she has already given up. He snarls at her: "Get dressed! We're going out." She sits down at once. All her movements are mechanical, robotic, dull, as they tend to be when someone knows they are about to die. She shoves her feet into a pair of army boots that are much too big for her. She drapes a padded woollen jacket over her shoulders in the way you do when you are just going outdoors into the cold for a moment and don't want to go to the trouble of putting your arms in the sleeves. (The gesture implies that this will be over quickly.) He says to her: "Bring a spade with you. You will have to dig a hole for yourself." She takes a spade.

They go out into the dark backyard. Obrynba is still thinking of those two children and what will become of them; the old couple are in such a bad way that it will be impossible for them to take on the children, and the people of the village won't care. She follows him through the snowy kitchen garden with shuffling steps. He points to a spot and says in an intentionally dull voice: "Now, dig there!" She drives the spade down into the frozen soil and now, at last, everything cracks, her body shudders and she begins to weep and wail.

He orders her back into the house and the two of them sit down at a table. The boy and the girl are still asleep. Khotko is becoming impatient at all the delays. The young woman sits there, her face buried in her hands, weeping uncontrollably, her shoulders shaking, but she keeps the noise down, obviously not wanting to wake the children. Which, in itself, is profoundly human behavior.

What Obrynba had initially taken to be defiance or resignation proves to be shame, shame so deep as to be almost more powerful than death. In answer to a direct question she starts telling him what the situation really is:

> I went to the bazaar...my dress...the blue crêpe de Chine one...I wanted to sell it...to feed the kids. He came up and said, "Come with me, I'll buy your dress." I did...he said, "I'll give you a bucket of rye, I like you." We came inside and he

dragged me to the bed ... he gave me grain. I went home. They were hungry back at home, after all.

What looked like treachery or conceivably informing turns out to be just another case of predatory behavior on the part of someone who had gained extraordinary power in these exceptional circumstances and who exploited that power to extort sexual services from a vulnerable individual. It's happening all the time, everywhere, on all sides. And this young woman's aim, both for herself and for her children, was the same as everyone else's—survival.

As far as Obrynba is concerned, Nadezjda's innocence is self-evident.

In spite of his guide's protests, he decides to spare her, on the condition that she promises never to meet that man again and never to go anywhere near Lepel. He writes a voucher for her, a requisition for half a sack of rye that she can collect from the partisans' store in Antunovo. And he advises her to talk to one of the partisans about getting work in one of the workshops there. Her hands tremble as she takes the paper from him. Before leaving he tells the two old people to keep an eye on her for the sake of the children.

Obrynba and the guide go out into the winter night. The temperature has started to rise and the falling snow is now mixed with rain. They climb into the sledge and leave.

. . .

A pure, white landscape, the trees covered in snow, the bare branches of the bushes clad in crystals of frost. The observation post periscope is steamed up and Kurt West is bored out of his mind, just standing there, his breath quietly steaming from his mouth. It is quiet along the whole length of the line, and it has been like this for a couple of weeks. Every so often a shot can be heard, or an explosion, far off or nearby. And that's all. It is winter at the Orren strongpoint on the Svir Front, which is where Kurt West is still stationed.

The mood is good in the warmth of Camp Bunker No. 2. This isn't just because of the calm and the lull and the fact that they have started to put what happened at Kako out of their minds, as young men will. It's also because they no longer feel quite so forgotten, and that is largely thanks to the new officer in command of the regiment.

Lieutenant Colonel Alpo Kullervo Marttinen is small in stature and can be hard, abrupt and difficult to warm to—Kurt West both admires him and is afraid of him—but he has seen to it that all the worn-out uniforms are replaced and he is generous with leave for those who carry out their duties properly or show the right attitude.* Hygiene has also begun to get much better. Lice are less of a problem in the severe cold and, behind the line, anyone who wants to can take a sauna. West's own frame of mind is easier. After the fighting at Kako he has won the respect of the veterans and can no longer be considered a greenhorn.

The only thing that disturbs him and his comrades is that they have been given a new platoon leader, a second lieutenant from Helsingfors named Rosberg, who is a replacement for their popular Lieutenant Kurtén, who has been posted to a training center. Rosberg's big-city manners irritates these farm boys: such things, for instance, as wearing gloves with fingers, using a flashlight in the trench and insisting they should sweep up even outdoors. They have simply ignored the order about sweeping up, and one of his gloves has vanished, as has his flashlight.

There is a party going on in the company commander's bunker this evening, for officers only, of course. The field telephone rings at about ten o'clock and they are told to bring a stretcher and come and collect their platoon commander, so "we understood that they had drunk Rosberg under the table." West and three others help to carry the second lieutenant out under the stars and away to their main Orren bunker, where they play a trick on him.

One of the soldiers has a couple of pin-on officer's stars, which he attaches to Rosberg's collar while he is unconscious. (We can assume this is accompanied by a good deal of sniggering.) When the second lieutenant eventually comes round, eyes red and bleary, they congratulate him on his promotion. Initially he refuses to believe them, but when he sees the extra stars, he leaps to the telephone and calls his company commander: "Lieutenant, Sir, is it true that I've been promoted?" They can hear the roasting Rosberg is given over the telephone.

---

* Marttinen also doled out many more punishments than his predecessor, so there is a clear symmetry in his regime. The fears that Marttinen, being a Finnish speaker, could not function as commander of a Swedish-speaking regiment proved unfounded. Rather the reverse, in fact: he was strongly supportive of his subordinates on the language issue. Respect for Marttinen grew even more when it became public knowledge how, at a critical point in the fighting at Kako, he had personally led a counterattack, pistol in hand.

The following morning the half-platoon is formed up in the presence of the lieutenant of the company. "And what a bawling out we then got—we'd never had one like that before!" Apart from that, there is nothing to say about the situation at Orren. A great deal of West's time is spent transporting firewood by horse. When the occasional shell lands at random, great sheets of snow crash down from the trees.

. . .

Mansur Abdulin is going around to his comrades and asking them what the words "*Gott mit uns*" mean. (God [is] with us.) It is written on every German soldier's belt buckle. Their belts are so substantial, made of real leather, and Abdulin has often looked at a fallen German and wondered whether to take his belt and use it. But first he wants to know the meaning of those words.

It's towards the end of November and things are still quiet here at the western end of the trap. For some inexplicable reason the encircled Germans have not made any effort to break out.

Every so often German transport flights fly over on the way to or from Stalingrad, sometimes at night, sometimes in the day. If it's dark, they fire off captured German signal flares and it's not unknown for a plane to drop them large containers of provisions. These might contain everything from cigarettes, woollen socks and big, useless overshoes made of plaited straw to sausages, bread and canned food. (Food is particularly desirable as provisioning is still not working as it should and they often go hungry.) Abdulin and his comrades are continuing to dig themselves in. Their foxholes have gradually grown, some of them now offering enough space for two or three men. That's good—it means they can huddle up close to one another and share the warmth of their bodies.

Abdulin wants to know what those words mean, because he is not keen on the idea of taking things from dead bodies. It might be bad luck. He suspects there is a pattern: a soldier who, for instance, takes a watch from a dead German will soon die himself, sometimes within a matter of hours. One of his friends acquired a German pistol and accidentally shot himself in the hand with it—this could technically have been considered self-inflicted, an offense that may be punished by execution on the spot. Moreover, Abdulin feels he possesses a sixth sense that allows him to feel whose turn it is to die: those people usually begin to be exaggeratedly fearful, to lose self-control or become withdrawn and lose themselves in transparent attempts to toughen themselves up. There are signs.

"*Gott.*" He knows that means God. He has seen more than one German prisoner sitting, rocking back and forth, head in hands, mechanically repeating, "*Oh, mein Gott! Oh, mein Gott!*" But what about the other two words? He goes around asking people, most of whom simply cut him short. They are all tired, hungry, at the end of their tether. Eventually he finds someone willing to help—a man who used to be a village schoolteacher. "It means 'God is with us,'" he says. "It's probably not a good idea to take a belt with that on it. The buckle with the inscription resembles a gravestone, doesn't it?"

Abdulin hasn't been out of his clothes for weeks, let alone washed. He is dirty. He has lice. They all have lice. He itches all over. Their only comfort is that the weather is milder.

·   ·   ·

Poon Lim is still drifting around on his life raft. He has put up the large tarpaulin to protect himself from the sun and the rain. He still has plenty of foodstuffs: biscuits, water, sugar and tablets of dried milk. A rough estimate suggests he has enough to last two months at least, so there's plenty of time. He knows he isn't a good swimmer and he is frightened of falling in and being unable to climb back onto the raft, particularly when there is a rough sea. Which is why he has tied himself to the raft with a rope around his waist.

Poon uses the sun to count the hours, a knotted rope to count the days and the moon to count the weeks. Gulls hover over the raft and every so often sharks swim around it. To help pass the time, he sings the songs he learned as a child.

·   ·   ·

Albert Camus is still living and writing at the small *pension* in the Massif Central. He is starting to be really sick of Le Panelier and the increasingly severe winter weather, which is particularly harsh at this altitude. He wants to get away from here. But where to go? And how?

He toys with the idea of returning to Algeria by crossing the Pyrenees and going via Spain. The idea is more romantic than practicable, especially for someone in such poor health as Camus. A number of friends and contacts are working hard to help him get away from Le Panelier, either to some decent sanatorium or individual care. Camus himself is still waiting for a pass from the German occupation authorities that will permit him to go to Paris and the renown that awaits him there.

Meanwhile, he is writing, page after page. The working title of his new novel is *La Peste*—The Plague—and, as usual, he feels dissatisfied with what he has written.

．　．　．

"Action stations!" is piped aboard HMS *Ulster Queen,* but Leonard Thomas doesn't take it too seriously. The same thing happened yesterday evening and nothing happened. He and the rest of the crew feel safer with every passing hour, and if it hadn't been for the strong westerlies, they would possibly already have sighted Cape Wrath and the Scottish mainland. But then comes the order for full steam and the ship is put into a fast turn.

The whole ship vibrates and keels over hard and Thomas feels the stern lift almost clear. Then comes the sound he has learned to hate— the dull blast of depth charges, followed by the shock waves that cause everything not tied down to rattle and bounce. The dull explosions continue, one after another, until there comes a sudden order to stop. Thomas and his colleagues go through the familiar routine they have done so often before, checking "pumps, circulators, generators, compressors, bilge pumps, air pressure, fuel filters, heat, sprays, bearings, fans."

The noise and the roaring fade away and everyone listens.

It's clear now that the vessel has doubled back in its own tracks and dropped depth charges. And now they have stopped in order to see the results. Someone tries to make a joke, saying, "No doubt the Wardroom wanted fish." It falls flat: "Then the buzz—a U-boat."

After a while, the ship continues on her earlier course, at a slightly increased speed. Down below in the noisy engine room, Thomas and his mates continue their half-blind existence. It's a while later before someone bothers to inform them that it wasn't a U-boat that the echo-sounder picked up, but an old shipwreck. The danger is over—one more time.

At last! Land! Northern Scotland.

It is Sunday, November 29. Thomas puts on his outside clothes and goes up on deck, where more and more of the crew are gathering. The ship is steering into a wide sound. The mood lightens noticeably, faces change, smiles are exchanged, relief becomes happiness, happiness becomes euphoria. Land and home. "The colour of the water was a welcome bluey-green, clear where it had been so grim and iron-grey at our last connection with the shore ... somehow we felt we were important, looked-for and expected."

·   ·   ·

Camus is still working on his book. What else is there to do in Le Panelier? In his own words, what he is trying to do in the book is "to express the suffocation we have all suffered and the atmosphere of danger and exile in which we have all lived." It concerns a town that is suddenly afflicted by a deadly danger from outside in the form of a plague that begins to ravage the inhabitants. As the town becomes ever more isolated from the outside world, the sense of powerlessness grows and more and more people lose their lives, and this threatens to bring about a breakdown of what is usually called civilization.

What Camus is writing is an allegory, of course, but it's an allegory with many layers. One of these deals with the way different people react to extreme situations. Some people lose themselves in denial or submission or indifference; others attempt to abscond or to numb themselves with empty pleasures; many reveal their cowardice, selfishness, even cruelty; whereas others try to help, try to hold back the plague, even putting their own lives at risk. Yet, paradoxically, their efforts may also cost the lives of others, and how are we to deal with that contradiction? What morality is possible in a world without God?

Towards the end of the book, one of the main characters speaks a monologue:

> I am sentenced to eternal exile from the moment I abstained from killing. It will be the others who create history. But I know, too, that I really cannot condemn these others. I lack some trait that would enable me to be a rational murderer. It's not something to be proud of. But now I accept being the man I am; I've learned to be modest. All I would say is that here on earth there are scourges and there are victims and, if at all possible, we should refuse to be on the same side as the scourges.

Camus is feeling a bit better. His isolation is coming to an end. He has, for instance, begun to socialize both with a man by the name

of Pierre Fayol and with Fayol's wife. They are newcomers to the
district. Fayol is an alias: he sometimes calls himself Simon and at
other times Roux or Vallin. His real name, however, is Lévy and he
comes from Marseille. Camus soon sees that he is an active member
of the resistance, a member of Combat, one of the first armed underground groups. Fayol/Simon/Roux/Vallin/Lévy shows him how to
go about sending letters to Francine in Algeria via Portugal. Lévy's
wife, Marianne, who considers Camus to be just one of those typical
egocentric authors who don't care much about anything apart from
his writing, gives him German lessons. Camus helps their son with
his homework.

The atmosphere is good. The weather is crisp and cold. Someone
has taken pity on the shivering French-Algerian and made him a pair
of pajamas out of old curtains.

·   ·   ·

The sun is shining down from a cold, blue sky and the reflection of the
light off the gleaming new snow that covers the city in a thin blanket
is almost dazzling. Munich is rarely this beautiful in winter. It's the
first day of Advent and Sophie Scholl arrived here by train from Ulm
two days ago. She and her brother, Hans, have found somewhere new
to live. They can be found today in a room off the courtyard of Josef-
strasse 13B, as lodgers of Frau Schmidt, a doctor's wife. Their landlord
moved out to the country after the city was bombed for the first time
in September.* They have permission to use the kitchen and also—for
an extra payment—the telephone and the bath (1 Reichsmark each
time). The latter is particularly pleasing to Sophie, who loves lying and
soaking in a bath of hot water.

Sophie Scholl has two closely interlinked lives.

On Sunday evening, she and her brother host a small party. Among
those invited are a couple of the other conspirators, Christoph Probst
and Willi Graf, the latter having been away on a secret recruiting

---

* The air raid on the night of September 19–20 was a fairly small one (eighty-
nine aircraft) and the damage was minor. The RAF had attempted to hit the
center but, as usual, the bombs were spread across the whole city, most of them
landing in the suburbs. However, as has already been mentioned, this autumn the
RAF has started to attack cities all over western Germany and the population is
becoming increasingly nervous.

journey. Graf's younger sister Anneliese is also present, but she knows nothing of their secrets.

It's a pleasant evening with a great deal of light gossip about people and talk about books. Only occasionally does politics or the war come up, and even then it is fleetingly, *en passant*, as if no one wants to spend time on such depressing things. They smoke, of course, and drink wine. (Beaujolais perhaps? Someone served that on a similar occasion a while ago.) There must have been music, played on the gramophone, but it's unlikely to have been the forbidden swing that cliché would have liked it to be, since no one in this circle is into jazz. It would have been various classical pieces—to make some wild guesses, Sibelius's *Finlandia* and Beethoven's Third; perhaps one of the rich but melancholy works by their contemporary Karl Höller.*

The little we know about this evening comes mainly from Anneliese Graf. She was much taken with Hans Scholl, who she thought was one of the most delightful men she had ever met. (And he certainly was good-looking, with sculpted features, a naturally wavy mane of hair and warm but piercing eyes. At this point, he had a well-deserved reputation as a ladies' man.) Anneliese fell for him in a flash and, although too shy to speak, all of her attention was focused on him; he, however, ignored her.

What Anneliese does not know is that her presence causes a change in the atmosphere and topics of conversation. This is one of the things that Sophie Scholl finds burdensome, having to jump between two lives and always having to be on one's guard. As she wrote to Fritz Hartnagel a few weeks ago: "Every word has to be examined from every direction before it is uttered, in order to ensure that there isn't the tiniest suggestion of ambivalence. Trust in other people has to be replaced by mistrust and cautiousness. Oh, how wearying it is—and sometimes depressing." This is particularly difficult when socializing with family and friends, who mean so much to them and with whom they all have close bonds.

---

* The names are not chosen at random. Earlier in the month, Graf and several of the others had attended what they described as a fantastic concert with *Finlandia*, Beethoven's Third and Höller's Cello Concerto. Classical music was revered in Nazi Germany and Höller, like a number of other gifted German composers such as Carl Orff and Paul Höffer, was considered controversial from the start as being slightly "too modern." Nevertheless, at this point he was enjoying the regime's approval and consequent rich rewards.

We should not, however, imagine the mood that evening as being heavy. The various attempts to make connections with other groups in opposition has worked out well. Sophie herself has recruited a small group in Ulm and a cell of like-minded students in Hamburg has been formed. They now have contacts in Freiburg, Berlin, Saarbrücken and Stuttgart and they think they have found channels both to a group of centrally placed anti-Nazis in the army and to an unknown but long-established opposition group that is said to include a number of highly placed individuals.* (And intellectual and political stability in the group has increased considerably, since just a few days ago they managed to recruit Kurt Huber to their group; Huber is a respected professor of psychology and musicology, and a mentor of Hans Scholl's.) Things are looking promising.†

They have their plan and in just a few days they will activate it.

The text of the flyers will be formulated; paper, printing matrices and ink are being accessed: Sophie's tasks are to purchase envelopes and stamps—in small quantities here and there, so as not to arouse suspicion; gather addresses from telephone books at the library (the intention is once again to send out some of the flyers to random addresses); stencils for painting slogans on walls have to be produced; and so on. The activity is to be on a large scale this time, with at least ten thousand flyers sent out from a series of different locations.

.   .   .

It's the first day of Advent in the home of Nella and Will Last at 9 Ilkley Road in Barrow-in-Furness. She is sitting on the living room sofa, doing what she does most evenings—handicraft work. At the moment she is making a little cloth rabbit. She often makes dolls and things like that to be sold in the Red Cross shop. The manufacture of all toys stopped in Great Britain very soon after the outbreak of war, so there is a good market for her work. And Nella's work is good quality. She

---

* This is what's known as the Kreisau Circle, a wide-ranging group that included army officers, aristocrats, socialists and Christians, among others. These, in turn, thought they had found channels to anti-fascist groups in Italy.

† With the emphasis on "looking." Miriam Gebhardt in her history of the group thinks that all the new contacts created an impression that opposition was more widespread than it really was and that this false perception encouraged them to take unnecessarily big risks.

doesn't mention it in her diary, but her husband, Will, is probably sitting in his armchair, silent as usual, maybe reading his paper, maybe just staring into space as he frequently does. And it is very likely that the room is lit by the flames from the open fire in the hearth.

It's late autumn and there is a crack in the wall by the bay window that lets cold air in—it's one of the results of bomb damage still waiting to be repaired. (Nella put up her heavy winter curtains a month ago.) Their Morrison Shelter is also located in the bay window—it resembles a table but it's a miniature bomb shelter made of steel.* Perhaps the chicken-wire sides have been removed, and possibly the airbeds they used to sleep on, too. We can also imagine that the grey top surface is now covered with one of Nella's many handsewn cloths. It's a long time since they needed it as protection. The last time the air-raid sirens went off was back in March, and no bombs fell then.

The wireless is on and Winston Churchill's confident but slightly drawling voice fills the room.† He is talking of the victories in North Africa and what is happening on other fronts; he talks of the setbacks that have been suffered; he talks of the pride of being those who held out alone; he says that things have begun to get brighter; he says that there is still much to do; he quotes Kipling; he speaks at length; he says that they must not start to ease off, to take anything for granted, to believe in a quick victory; and, finally, he says they can go into the next year "with the assurance of ever growing strength and as a nation with strong will, a bold heart and a good conscience."

.   .   .

* The Morrison Shelter was yet another British improvisation, invented when they were struck late in the day by the realization that only a fraction of the population had access to shelters. (For reasons of economy, many newer British houses had been built without cellars.) Only 5 percent of the population in Barrow-in-Furness had shelters, so during air raids people took shelter anywhere they could—in hedges on the outskirts of the town, for example. It goes without saying that this increased civilian losses. Households earning less than £400 could order a Morrison Shelter free; others had to buy them. They came in the form of Ikea-like parts that you had to bolt together yourself.

† This speech, written specifically for the radio, was also broadcast to listeners in the United States. It should not be confused with the famous speech Churchill gave in the Mansion House on November 10, in which he uttered the often-quoted words: "Now this is not the end. It is not even the beginning of the end. But it is, perhaps, the end of the beginning."

There is an interesting double-sidedness to Nella Last. She shows increasing levels of self-confidence and strength, that's for sure, but there are also the beginnings of doubt. As she wrote in her diary a few months before this:

> I feel I'm dividing more into two people: the quiet, brooding woman who, when alone, likes to draw the quiet round her like a healing cloak; and the gay, lively woman who "keeps all going," who "never worries about anything."

This doubleness is also apparent in the way she looks at the war. Nella Last is fifty-three years old and, exactly like many of her generation, she is marked by the First World War. (She remembers all of those young men marching off so happily and then never coming back; she remembers details such as the time she saw the oblong shape of a zeppelin outlined against the moon and how that sighting filled her with horror; she really dislikes nights when there is a full moon—not for nothing is it known as a "bomber's moon.") But things aren't simple. She can sometimes have doubts about the war as such. She can doubt whether the war is being pursued sufficiently forcefully. She can feel great joy at victories.

The wireless is on and it isn't the prime minister's message of confidence, new strength and the turning point that Nella Last focuses on; it is his emphasis on everything that still awaits them. For, as Churchill says towards the end, 1943 will be starting soon "and we must brace ourselves to cope with the trials and problems of what must be a stern and terrible year." It's as if she stops listening then.* She writes in her diary:

> I listened to Churchill with a shadow on my heart. It's bad enough to think privately all that he said, without hearing it on the wireless—to see the long, hard and bitter road, to feel the shadows deepen rather than lighten, to envy the ones who think that Germany will collapse in the spring, to have

---

* Further to Nella Last's double-sided nature: there can be no doubt that she genuinely detested Hitler, but she thought the German euthanasia program seemed sensible. It's also worth mentioning that her eldest son held anti-Semitic views, and that worried her.

in mind always the slave labour, the resources of rich Europe,
to remember Goebbels' words that whoever starved, it would
not be Germany. I thought of all the boys and men out East.
How long will it be before they come home? It's bad enough
for mothers—but what of the young wives?

Nella Last feels her hands go "clammy and damp." She stops sewing,
puts the toy rabbit down in her lap and looks at it.

.   .   .

There are times when Mansur Abdulin dreams he is dead. In one of
these dreams, he finds himself inside what seems to be the famous
painting *After Prince Igor's Battle with the Polovtsy* by the historical romantic Vasnetsov. The painting, inspired by Pushkin, portrays the scattered
corpses after a whole Russian army suffered ignominious defeat and
annihilation during the early Middle Ages.* On one level, Abdulin's
dream is an expression of his fear that they will fail, that the Germans
will yet again be victorious. On another and perhaps more profound
level, it suggests that some sort of dark death wish is growing in him.
    This is one of the last days in November and pretty well every sec-
ond soldier in his division has been killed, wounded or gone missing
in the last two weeks. (Those serving in rifle companies have suffered
even more.)† And the guilt often felt by survivors has begun to work
on him. Abdulin finds himself dwelling on it: "Why am I still safe and
sound in this hell, when most of my comrades are dead or wounded?"
He is beginning to get a reputation as being absolutely fearless, some
have even started calling him a hero,‡ but within himself he bears the

---

* The tale is possibly apocryphal. The authenticity of the Lay of Igor, in which
the defeat is mentioned, has frequently been questioned.
† It's of some comfort that they now have plenty of weapons. They have been
able to collect them on the battlefield, including an MG-34:a, one of those German rapid-fire machine guns.
‡ Abdulin was expected to receive a medal for helping that officer out of the
burning tank, but nothing came of it. Not until long after the war did Abdulin
discover that the colonel, whose name was Provanov, disappeared without a trace
immediately after being rescued. He was possibly the victim of a direct hit with a
shell and consequently the people in his unit never heard about Abdulin's brave
act.

shame that soon he will be the only one to have survived. There are occasions when he has charged straight into German fire, and there can be no doubt that it looks very courageous, but he himself was almost hoping to be hit.

But a wound alone would not absolve him from his guilt, it would merely mean that he'd be withdrawn from the front for a while, away from this loathsome and exhausting existence in a variety of trenches and foxholes half filled with snow. You only have to look at Abdulin and his fellow soldiers to see their state: their snowsuits, once so clean, are filthy and torn, trousers and coats ragged and coated with dried mud. There are times when they look at their comrades and laugh, because they can scarcely recognize one another. Most of them have grown unkempt beards and their faces are covered with soot. Abdulin, himself, is plagued by lice worse than ever: the troops are actually issued a powder that is supposed to kill off vermin, but it doesn't seem to work. Worse still, he has begun to suffer from incontinence and needs to urinate every five minutes or so. He constantly walks around with his fly open so as not to wet himself.

Abdulin tells an older Siberian infantryman about his nightmare. The Siberian doesn't see it as a bad omen—rather the reverse: "You will return home from the war, so don't be afraid of such a dream!"

The encircled Germans are still not showing any sign of wanting to break out. And the transport flights on their way to and from Stalingrad have continued to fly over, sometimes in the darkness, sometimes in the lightest hours of the day, and sometimes Abdulin and his fellows shoot at them. The mild weather has continued. The flat, anonymous steppe is white, but it's no longer dazzling white. The snow has begun to pack down.

.   .   .

The first day of Advent at Tabakovo. New Russian attacks have started some distance away, but everything is still calm here. Willy Peter Reese has been made the machine-gunner in a redoubt that also holds a mortar crew and their weapon. The troops in the 279th Regiment have continued digging themselves in and a kind of "underground town" has taken shape with a long line of bunkers. This town has everything they need for the moment: protection, warmth, food and places to sleep. For once, the space underground is quite generous, as is food and sleep. He has to stand guard now and then, and that's all. But, as often in the past, Reese's mood is unstable. He does, however, remind himself of the first day of Advent a year ago. Surely, nothing can be that bad.

He found the battles during the winter campaign outside Moscow deeply disturbing, not just because they marked his baptism of fire in appalling circumstances, but because there was nothing about them that corresponded with his expectations. When he thinks back on the hard fighting he was involved in, he feels "an uncertain mixture of fear and disappointment." In some sense, it felt neither sufficiently horrifying nor sufficiently involving. Reese writes:

> War could break a man, millions suffered and died, and neither conquest nor crusade was worth its shameful madness. The war revealed apocalyptic aspects and, through them, its cosmic necessity became clear to me. I had experienced something great and heroic—the death struggle of our soldiers. But there was no comradeship, no willingness to become a sacrifice, no fighting spirit, no heroic courage or fulfilment of duty. No. Each and every one died at the right moment and died their own death. When many people desire death in war—then war must happen.

After all, Advent means "arrival," but what is it they are waiting for? They know that Russian reinforcements are gathering out there. Is it going to be their turn next? It's continuing to get warmer. Maybe it will start thawing soon.

·   ·   ·

Everyone has a limit and Sergeant Bede Thongs of the 10th Platoon, 3rd Battalion, has reached his. It's the morning of Sunday, November 29, and he's going to see the regimental doctor. The average soldier in New Guinea doesn't meet his fate in the form of an enemy bullet, but as a result of disease and deprivation. That's how primitive the conditions along the Kokoda Trail are, how onerous the climate is and how inhospitable nature is.

Every sort of disease is present: malaria, of course, beriberi, jungle rot, dengue fever, fungal infections and typhoid fever. The greatest scourge for the Australian troops is dysentery, largely as a result of the notoriously poor field hygiene—one of the military doctors has called it "amazingly bad," "a disgrace."

To walk, scramble, tramp, stumble along the trail is to progress through a never-ending stench of human excrement. Whenever nature calls, the troops take no more than a couple of steps to the side of the trail and drop their trousers. And it usually has to be done quickly, because many of them suffer from diarrhea. The constant rainfall washes the excrement into the watercourses, the same watercourses from which the soldiers collect their drinking water. Initially, the Japanese, whose field hygiene is very obviously superior to that of their adversaries, suffered mainly from malaria, but when, at the start of the campaign, they began moving through the bacterial miasma the Australians had left behind them, they too began to suffer the same misery of dysentery as their opponents.

The doctor didn't need long to examine Thongs. He is showing symptoms of malaria, typhoid fever and yellow fever, and his temperature is above 102 degrees. Anything lower than that means you remain in the ranks. The doctor writes a slip and pins it on Thongs's shirt: Sergeant Bede Thongs is too sick for further service and should be evacuated.

Three days ago Thongs and the 10th Platoon returned from patrolling up along the Kumusi River, hunting for any "stray Japanese." How many they found and killed, if any, can't be found in his account. When they returned and rejoined their comrades in the 3rd Battalion, the latter was in Gona.

Gona is a former mission station right by the sea and is the westernmost outpost of the twelve-mile-long, semi-circular and well-fortified bridgehead along the coast to which the Japanese have withdrawn. In spite of the fact that the slogan "Kokoda or Bust!" has been changed to the similar sounding "Gona or Bust," it signals, sadly, that very little has changed. Simultaneously, however, they might get the feeling that they have tumbled through a hole in the space-time continuum, departed from creeping nerve-rackingly along steep, jungle-lined mountain paths and suddenly—via a chute a couple of miles long that one eye-witness has called "arkadian," all "blue hills, green fields and grass waving in the soft breeze... a midsummer day in England"—landed in a landscape from the last war, a sort of tropical Passchendaele.

Within just a week, Gona will be turned into a wasteland of craters, shattered trees and rain-filled trenches, where young Australians, just like their fathers barely thirty years earlier, will storm forward time after time, bayonets fixed, straight into the gaping maw of machine-gun fire. And where Japanese soldiers in their bunkers will fight on while wearing gas masks in order to endure the stench of their unburied dead comrades, whose bodies they are standing on to reach up to the loopholes to fire.

·   ·   ·

Recent days have been monotonous for Lieutenant Tohichi Wakabayashi and his men in the Guadalcanal jungle. They have been building bunkers and digging foxholes,* an occupation that they frequently have to cut short at breakneck speed because of American shells crashing down at odd intervals, apparently randomly and to no great effect, but in steadily increasing numbers.

The ground is hard and it's slow and heavy work, because the soldiers are weak from lack of food. The day before yesterday someone told Wakabayashi that half the men in one of the companies in the regiment had died of starvation. His company has managed better than that, so far anyway, and it looks as if that's because of the closeness of the small Matanikau River, where the soldiers are still catching freshwater snails and sometimes even managing to catch fish, though the situation is steadily getting worse. Food is probably the most common topic of conversation.

Today, Sunday, November 29, Wakabayashi orders a group of soldiers to stop digging, bring their spades and come with him. The aim is to locate the bodies of some of their own men, who are thought to be just a little south of them and close to the river. Wakabayashi and his men go down the slope of the hill and enter an unusually dense and dark patch of jungle. They clamber over big, fallen trees, hear strange birds, note that the jungle is thinning out and enter groups of palm trees. They see that there is more light showing between the trunks and they reach a flat, grassy opening.

They can smell the stench now.

A small army tent has been erected there and they can see two pairs

---

* An interesting cultural difference: the one-man holes the Americans call foxholes are known by the Japanese soldiers as octopus pots. A fox can hide in a den and even slip away, but once an octopus is in the pot, that's where it stays.

of feet sticking out. Wakabayashi looks in. The boots and the puttees appear to be intact, but there is little more than bones left of the rest of the bodies, which had rotted quickly in the tropical heat and then been eaten clean by ants and birds. He tries to work it out. This pair had obviously been wounded and there seem to be traces of blood on the puttees; moreover, something that looks like an improvised stretcher is lying there. Wakabayashi writes in his diary: "We bid them a last farewell, collected their ID-tags, buried them and made a note of the event."

They carry on down towards the river, clambering down a high cliff with considerable difficulty, and approach the river, where they come to a stretch of flat ground. And there, once again, they smell the stench.

Wakabayashi notices the bodies immediately. It's a strange, almost bizarre sight. He makes a note in his diary: "They are mostly bones now—even their rib cages have collapsed. Their clothes have half decomposed but were enough for us to count the number of men. Their equipment [was] all placed neatly in one area; their ammunition also gathered into one area and [the] ammunition pouches were half-burnt." The hollowed-out skeletons are lying in a perfect line, carefully arranged side-by-side with their heads pointing north—towards Japan. So Wakabayashi understands what he is seeing here: the soldiers have committed ritual suicide, as a group.

The willingness to sacrifice themselves which has been indoctrinated into the soldiers of the Japanese army reveals itself in manic courage that scorns death and is sometimes so theatrically exaggerated that it shocks their Western adversaries. But it does have a downside. A preparedness to give your life is one thing, but to elevate that willingness to the level that death becomes something sublime and beautiful—desirable even—means that it has been perverted into a death wish. And that, however you look at it, is irrational.*

Wakabayashi finds himself in the twilight zone between these things. In his diary and also in a letter to his mother dated September 25, he uses the same metaphor: "I would rather fall as glorious blossoms than become a large flower." To this, we should add another idea, linked to

---

* It might be thought that this has its roots in the Japanese tradition of *bushido*. Like the Nazi and fascist continual referencing of the past, however, the *bushido* referenced by Japanese militarists is a distorted picture, a newly created tradition (like the samurai swords worn by officers) introduced as recently as the 1930s.

the concept of self-sacrifice and equally emphatically drummed into all the soldiers: that is the notion that nothing is more humiliating than to give up and be taken prisoner—it brings shame on yourself, on your family, on your village. Far better to die by your own hand.* In this context, suicide is less an act of dark desperation than an honorable, even heroic, act that elevates the individual above the circumstances and atones for everything.†

Wakabayashi does, however, find himself somewhat at a loss. On one level, he is gripped, even impressed—he writes in his diary that "this commitment would make anyone search their soul"; at the same time, he cannot really understand what can have led these soldiers to act in this way, seemingly unprovoked. He fantasizes about what might have happened: the Americans attack, the group suffers losses—the corpses in the tent are two of those losses; the rest then retreat; perhaps it is at night and perhaps it is raining and possibly they are hungry, injured and exhausted; their way back is blocked and there are aircraft hovering above them. "Did they accept that it is impossible to advance and decided to commit ritual suicide here?"

Wakabayashi and his men dig shallow graves, lay the disintegrating corpses in them and shovel the earth back. Then they erect some simple, temporary markers. Wakabayashi prays: "Spirits of the great men of war, please wait. In one month more we will annihilate the enemy and avenge you all." Their task done, the group returns to the company position up on the hill.

That night, the American artillery bombards them more heavily than ever, but apparently still without any particular plan. The following day, Monday, November 30, Wakabayashi writes in his diary: "I suspect that the enemy is going for the 'starving' tactic and completely cut off our food supply from the rear and wait for us to reach our limits at which time they will go on the offensive. If so, bring it on. That is exactly what I am waiting for."

.   .   .

* This partly explains why the Japanese army treated prisoners so badly and why it underestimated its Western enemies for so long: the Western preparedness to surrender was seen as proof of how weak and degenerate they were.

† The unwillingness to be taken prisoner wasn't a new thing: the Japanese prisoners returning to Japan after the Russo-Japanese War of 1904–1905 were socially ostracized.

An express train is drilling through the winter night. The British defector John Amery and his French mistress, Jeanine Barde, are sitting in the restaurant car, accompanied—as always—by a fixer and watchdog from the German foreign ministry. Today, it's a young Austrian SS man and diplomat named Reinhard Spitzy. The three of them are eating sandwiches and drinking champagne—copious quantities of champagne. Spirits are high and there is much talking and toasting and laughter.

The Austrian is charmed by the happy, attractive Frenchwoman and, at his request, she sings "*Sur le Pont d'Avignon*." The party breaks up when Amery and his mistress withdraw to their sleeping compartment, "from whence," the Austrian writes, "they emerged after a short while, she evidently refreshed and he looking rather exhausted."

Amery is in a great mood, and it is not just the alcohol talking. His broadcasts to Great Britain are finished and, to some extent, he is feeling relieved—the sort of relief one feels on finishing a task one has been worrying about and ended up discovering it wasn't so hard after all. But it also has to do with the fact that Amery, who has a string of fiascos and crashed projects behind him, now feels that he has really been successful, having at last found a project that provides stability and meaning to his otherwise aimless existence. To crown it all, it's a grandiose project that blows new life into the dormant megalomania in his personality. There is no doubt that what he has been up to is treasonable, but what does that matter given that he is on the side of the victors.* They'll be the ones to write the history, won't they?

The SS man is reluctantly impressed by the thin, intelligent Englishman, at the same time as recognizing the selfishness inherent in his personality and his motives. Spitzy writes: "For him there was no turning back. Perhaps the whole thing would not last very much longer and come to a bitter end. His own conscience was clear. Whichever way things might turn out he intended to stick at it and enjoy life to the full."

---

* What was happening in Stalingrad, among other places, was carefully concealed from the German public. After his speech of November 9, when Hitler declared that Stalingrad was mainly in German hands, all reports had been drastically curtailed. The fact that the Red Army had encircled the 6th Army was kept a secret, and when anything was written at all, it consisted of short, vague notices about "hard defensive operations" and the like.

The party continues toasting and chatting and laughing.

The white landscape with its slumbering angels flits past unseen on the other side of the window. Early tomorrow morning they will arrive in Paris.

.   .   .

Camp No. 5, outside Batavia, on Java. The heat is not easing its hold. Signs that Weary Dunlop and the other Australian prisoners of war will soon be moved are becoming increasingly common. They are forever being formed up and counted, and then formed up and counted again; long typewritten lists of names are circulated; those who've fallen sick are checked off; questions are asked about equipment. In addition to all that, some of the guards have said they'll be returning to Japan "in a day or two." But there've been no orders, no information, and so all they can do is wait—yet again. Dunlop spends the last couple of days of November in the shade of coconut palms. He sits there reading Harold Lamb's 1927 biography of Genghis Khan, with great pleasure.

.   .   .

How we experience a war is influenced by pictures and mental images acquired in peace, and that often leads to battles playing up to their own myth even while they are still being fought. The reason for the repeat action at Gona on New Guinea is the same as the reason for the horrors of the First War: uninspired orders from a distance, the whims of ill-informed commanders for whom reality is largely cartographic reality.*

On this last Sunday in November, new attacks are mounted at Gona, the first of them immediately after eleven in the morning, but as Peter Brune writes: "The 29th was to be a day of duplication of the slaughter of the preceding evening." What is left of the 3rd Battalion is at the front. They are pushing on into a bushy area and have very little

---

* The one ultimately responsible was none other than "Dugout Doug," General Douglas MacArthur. He was as always located well away, in Port Moresby on the other side of New Guinea, whereas he was shameless enough to let it be known to the press, to which, given his monumental vanity, he always played up, that he was at the scene and led the troops in battle. It's typical that his reasons for pushing the senseless attacks on the north coast were political, not military: he wanted to ensure *his* victory before the Battle of Guadalcanal was decided, so as to gain more attention, to impress Roosevelt, and so be allocated more resources.

contact with the enemy. (It is only later that Thongs learns that his "very best friend," a sergeant named Bob Taylor, was killed on this day.) Everyone in the unit is weary, and most of them are ill. The next day the 3rd Battalion are expected to make an attack in order to support another battalion, but in fact they do not move from where they are. The official explanation is that they didn't see the others attack and therefore remained where they were.

At the time this happens, Bede Thongs is already on one of those precious American transport planes on his way to the field hospital in Koitaki. Somewhere along the way he notes that the crew have painted a name on their plane: "Chattanooga Choo Choo," a massive Glenn Miller hit from the previous year. The 3rd Battalion is withdrawn from Gona a couple of days later. At the start of September there had been 560 men in its ranks; only 110 remain.*

. . .

It is possible to see whether an individual's nerves are beginning to crack by studying the way he drinks his coffee. If he can lift the mug with just one hand, there's nothing to worry about. If he needs two hands to get the mug to his mouth, he is on the way to cracking. If the shakes are so great that even two hands are not enough, it's already too late. In the last days of November, John McEniry has to use both hands—and the same is true for most of his colleagues.

Different people react in different ways to mortal danger and extreme stress. Some go to pieces at the mere thought that they could be injured or die. Some, on the other hand, appear to be perked up by danger—at least initially. Most people seem able to deal with it, able to bring themselves to face up to it, at least for a time. The absolutely unshakeable rule, however, is that everyone has a limit. And the question at the present time is whether the men in McEniry's dive-bomber squadron, VMSB-132, are approaching that limit.

Their sense of solidarity is still holding up well, as is their faith in Major Sailer, the squadron commander they worship. And they believe in what they are doing, know that it matters, that it matters a great deal.

---

* Studies carried out separately by Australian, American and Japanese army experts came to almost identical conclusions: after three months in the jungle in a tropical climate, a unit's effectiveness is radically reduced, even if it is not involved in any combat.

And now, for the very first time, there is a sense of being on the winning side. The situation is nothing like as desperate as at the beginning of the month. McEniry: "Things were slowly improving." This can be seen in such things as improvements in the food—they have even been given a bit of ice cream! And there are more and more new pilots, new aircraft and new, rested mechanics. It's ages since they had to siphon fuel from an old wreck in order to keep the aircraft in the air. At the same time, the Japanese in the jungle are strangely passive.

But, as said earlier, people react in different ways. One of the pilots who was most self-confident on the voyage from the States—he was given to boasting that he "could not wait to get there so that he could start sinking ships and killing Japs"—has come up with ways of avoiding combat missions by forever discovering new faults in his plane, being unavailable, visiting the dentist and so on. Another of them can be guaranteed to be ill when a combat mission looms: he throws up all night and is unfit to fly when the time comes. (The same man has also developed a fear of the dark.) A not unexpected pattern that has become evident is that married pilots seem to be more careful, more cautious than those who don't have a family.* And maybe not just these men.

McEniry himself has continued to fly mission after mission, but there can be no doubt that he is increasingly worn down, irritable, bitter even, and wrapped in the misty vagueness brought on by lack of sleep. He has noticed himself how much his hands shake and how many mistakes he makes. Even their squadron leader, the indefatigable Major Sailer, is showing signs of no longer being so indefatigable: they can all see how thin and worn he has become. (Sailer has no more than a week left to live. He will be shot down and killed by Japanese fighter planes during a bombing mission off New Georgia on December 7.) Everyone has a limit.†

---

* It's been shown that, irrespective of experiences in uniform, stress coupled with worries about civilian life cause an individual to be at greater risk of developing combat fatigue or similar psychiatric problems. (It's common knowledge that stress is a cumulative phenomenon.) We can see the role played by the individual's disposition from the fact that a significant proportion of those who crack mentally do so *before* their first combat experience.

† There are differing ideas as to exactly where that limit lies. A man who commanded a squadron of fighter aircraft on Guadalcanal said that a pilot can manage five days of very intense combat, with proper rest. An estimate that appears to have widespread support is that a soldier's "emotional lifespan" is

. . .

A while later, McEniry is on the return flight from a mission when his engine cuts out and he prepares to make an emergency landing in the sea. The aircraft, its propeller locked, is gliding down towards the deep-blue surface with no sound but its slipstream. Then, suddenly, the engine restarts, as inexplicably as when it stopped, and McEniry is able to fly back to Guadalcanal. His own reaction to the knowledge that he was about to make a crash landing surprises him. He writes in his diary: "I was as calm as could be. In fact, there was a sigh of relief. I'm tired and disgusted."

Two days later, the unit medic bans him from flying.

. . .

Vera Brittain was up half the night yesterday, vomiting. (She guesses it was caused by one of these new synthetic foodstuffs that has replaced pre-war food.) Nevertheless, she forced herself to go out to yet another meeting—a meeting with a small but well-disposed audience where she managed to sell several copies of *Humiliation with Honour.* The audiences Vera Brittain attracts are becoming much sparser and, on a personal level, she is becoming more and more isolated. Many of her old acquaintances have started avoiding her, or even become unfriendly, and it is almost invariably because of her stubborn promotion of pacifism. (And, of course, her husband, George, is often away travelling and her children are still in the United States.) Vera suspects, with some justification, that MI5 is opening her mail.

When she wakes up on the morning of Monday, November 30, she feels "sick, tired and wobbly." When Amy, the home help, arrives, she attends to Vera. Brittain has always appreciated her help, but given her increasing isolation Amy has also started to be important to her as company. They talk. Amy tells her how reluctant her husband has been to do military service: "Always meant to wait until he was fetched and

---

between eighty and ninety days of combat. Something like 30 percent of the non-combat-related losses among American airmen in the Pacific had to do with battle fatigue and other mental problems. On Guadalcanal, the number of psychiatric diagnoses among all combatants was significantly higher than that and, at one stage, threatened to overwhelm the medical system, necessitating reforms and rethinking.

rather despised those who didn't." Brittain thinks that the loss of illusions that affected the soldiers of 1914–1918 "has lasted on even among those who were only children at the time."

Later she reads the most recent issue of the left-liberal journal *The New Statesman*. It includes a review of a new novel by Margaret Storm Jameson, *Then We Shall Hear Singing*. Storm Jameson is one of the close friends she has lost, perhaps the most important one.

The two authors are of the same generation, come from the same background and have the same fearless temperament. Both of them are feminists and socialists. Both of them were converted to pacifism by bitter experiences in the First World War, but whereas Brittain has stuck firmly and consistently to her pacifism, Storm Jameson reevaluated hers. The crunch question was a simple one: Which is worse— fight the war or allow Nazism to win? Vera Brittain insists: "I don't think Hitler's victory would be worse for humanity in the long run … than recurrent war." Disagreements, quarrels, misunderstandings and reproaches pushed the two of them apart. Since the start of the year they have no longer spoken to one another.

Storm Jameson's *Then We Shall Hear Singing* is a dystopia set in an unspecified European country after a German victory. A scientist there is experimenting on how to erase human memory and turn people into easily controlled robots. This is Storm Jameson's second work in the dystopian genre. Her earlier one was set in a future, fascist Great Britain. Vera Brittain comments that the new work seems "completely sterile" and dismisses the book as "another of her obsessive studies of Nazi frightfulness."

In that Monday's newspapers there are small items to inform the readers that the prime minister (sixty-eight this Monday) has had lunch this weekend with General Charles de Gaulle, leader of the Free French; the king and queen and their two daughters, Elizabeth and Margaret, have been to the movies to see the highly praised film *In Which We Serve*, starring Noël Coward; occasional German fighter planes, flying at low altitude, continue to raid places on the south coast apparently haphazardly, and a thirty-one-year-old woman was shot and killed; cases of sexually transmitted disease continue to rise— there has been an increase of 50 percent among the civilian population since the start of the war, and a 70 percent increase among those in the services.

Vera Brittain stays in bed all day.

. . .

That same day, Ned Russell and three journalist colleagues (including Drew Middleton, an experienced journalist from *The New York Times*) are walking along a dirt road in the eastern outskirts of the small Tunisian town of Tebourba. Since the British and the Americans captured the place, little is left but a collection of ruins. Russell hasn't seen this level of destruction before and, with a mild sense of unreality, it reminds him of "Hollywood movie scenes."

Almost all the population has fled. The only living things he has encountered in the town, apart from a pig, an ass and some chickens and rabbits, are a half-dozen Arabs, "ostensibly indifferent to the spectacle of destruction around them," and three Italian civilians, recently arrived to work on a reservoir. The Italians are sociable and treat them to wine and beer. It's just possible to catch a glimpse of the minarets of Tunis from the summit of a high, bare ridge that rises steeply a mile or so outside Tebourba. The high command has yet again been bursting with optimism and, yet again, this optimism has proved to be overhasty.

When Russell and his colleagues arrived yesterday, they interviewed a number of soldiers. It is obvious that the bombastic official communiqués have very little to do with reality. The attack on Tunis has been checked. A British infantry lieutenant, "one of the few surviving officers from his battalion," described to Russell the effect of close-range machine-gun fire. ("Men were falling all over the place. It was horrible.") Someone else told them how the American tanks that were supposed to be giving support to the British infantry were knocked out one by one by concealed German anti-tank guns. ("Eighty-eight millimeter shells had crashed through their turrets. One, at least, beheaded an American officer.")

It is Monday afternoon and the two reporters are hunting for American tank personnel who can give them more information about the failed attack. They stop a jeep and ask if they are going in the right direction. There is an "excited, young" American officer at the wheel who confirms that they are, but also warns them: "You better get out of here—quick. German tanks have got us surrounded.... He jerked the jeep gears and sped off down the road."

Russell and his companions don't really know what to believe, but they start going back towards the town. They see a British anti-tank battery in the process of packing up. They hear the rattle of a machine gun unexpectedly close by. They hide in a ditch and wonder what to do. They start running—across a couple of fields, up a small hill, past a churchyard, through a ravine, and then another ravine. Up on a ridge, they stop to catch their breath and they hear someone shouting to them from a foxhole: "Don't stand on top of the hill like that. You'll be seen." They crouch down, hesitantly. They hear British field artillery opening fire down in the valley below them. And in the distance, hardly visible against the bushes and dark olive trees, they pick out dark, angular shapes moving slowly out of the woods—German tanks. They start running again.

The sun is going down by the time they eventually catch sight of the small farm where they left their gear and their car (1934 Ford V-8 bought in Algiers for $450). The plan is to wait for darkness and then try to drive out of the small town—assuming they can get the Ford going. Russell and Middleton start talking about sports, which helps calm their nerves. Middleton speaks of his football stardom and Russell of his years playing high-level tennis.

·   ·   ·

It is late evening of the same Monday and pitch-black, tropical darkness blankets land and sea at Guadalcanal. It has been another quiet day for Lieutenant Charles Walker and his men, dug in on the little headland, Point Cruz. The Japanese in the jungle to the west are strangely inactive. They are said to be starving.

Towards midnight, he and his men can see flashes over the water, far away to the northwest, in the direction of Savo Island. The roll and echo of explosions take longer to reach them. Searchlight beams play up and down along the sound. Flares spark and blaze across the dark sky. Another nocturnal sea battle. The bombardment, however, is not as heavy as it was in a battle just a couple of weeks ago, though at one point they see an enormous flame-red explosion in the distance. The whole business is over in about half an hour. It's impossible to say what has happened. As usual.

At dawn, the outlines of jungle and shoreline become clear and the water regains its color. Looking at the turquoise breakers, Charles Walker and his men can see numerous casks and drums being washed ashore, most of them a long way off, behind the Japanese lines to the west. In the weak morning light, they can pick out small figures trying to drag the barrels ashore, and they recognize immediately what is going on. During the night, Japanese destroyers have made another desperate attempt to supply provisions to their troops on the island.*

This gives Walker's company an opportunity to use their heavy machine guns. They fire away and keep firing, first of all at the Japanese trying to salvage the barrels and then at the barrels themselves. One by one, they hit and shatter the barrels and sink them. One of the barrels drifts ashore close to their own position and they salvage it for themselves. It turns out to contain rice, matches and candles.

For several days afterwards, the bodies of dead seamen are washed up on the long, sandy Point Cruz beach on Guadalcanal. They are probably both Japanese and Americans, though it's hard to tell which is which: as usual, the bodies have been ripped apart by the sharks.

. . .

Meanwhile, Ernst Jünger is still in Voroshilovsk in the Caucasus. The weather is mild. There is so much in this war that is new and difficult to comprehend compared with the old war. What he has seen in the east is more like the apocalyptic landscape of the Thirty Years War than anything he encountered during the years 1914–1918. Visiting the places that Jünger has heard rumors about—places "where violence is used on defenseless people" or where collective reprisals occur (as he phrases it cautiously in his diary)—has turned out to be more difficult than he thought. However whispered and distorted, the rumors, images and evidence continue to reach him. There can be no doubt that something horrific in its brutality, appalling in its intent and colossal in its scale is going on here.

He tries to keep it at a distance. He thinks of it as being ultimately a part of the spirit of the age, its Zeitgeist, and consequently something external to himself, something that is part of the "now" that he detests,

* Historical accounts have named that night's sea battle the Battle of Tassafaronga. The Japanese navy demonstrated once again its superiority over the Americans when it came to nocturnal combat. The numerically inferior Japanese force inflicted what is regarded as the worst tactical defeat of the whole war on the American fleet by sinking one American heavy cruiser and damaging three, all for the price of one destroyer. This was in spite of the fact that the Americans were forewarned by intercepted communications and assisted by radar. From the strategic point of view, however, the battle was an important success for the Americans, since the Japanese attempt to resupply their starving troops on the island once again came to nothing.

the "now" that has been shanghaied by technocrats and corrupted by ideologues. (And aren't both sides guilty of the horrors?) Jünger attempts to formulate a moral imperative, but it is an individual one, not to say an individualistic one: what matters is not to allow oneself to become hard, not to allow the brutalization to contaminate one's own character, not to forget that one is surrounded by suffering.

For some days now, Jünger has begun to contemplate writing a new allegory, something like *On the Marble Cliffs*, but not so difficult to interpret. He has already come up with the opening: the narrator is a traveller, one of a group leaving the desert on their way to the sea. The land has been laid waste and is deserted. They pass empty ruined towns and abandoned machines of war. The narrator possesses an obscure but important map, which shows the route to a secret cave that is full of precious stones. But once they have managed to decode the hieroglyphics on the map, the hardest part still remains—how to get there. They cross a precipice high above the sea, on a ledge so narrow that passing anyone would be impossible, as would turning back. Another party is approaching them in the opposite direction—will this lead to one of the parties being wiped out, or will both parties meet their doom?

Jünger spends this Monday exploring Voroshilovsk independently. He visits an old churchyard. Everything there is overgrown with scrub; dry stands of thistle and withered weeds cling onto the crosses and gravestones with their indecipherable inscriptions. In the midst of this picture of decay and disappearance, Jünger comes across several new unmarked graves. The gravediggers, with little sign of reverence, have scattered the bleached bones they encountered when digging out new resting places in the earth. Jünger sees vertebrae, ribs, thigh bones lying there "like parts of a puzzle." Up on the wall, he notices the green-colored cranium of a child.

·   ·   ·

At last, what Poon Lim has been waiting for happens. It's a week since SS *Benlomond* was torpedoed and now a dot is visible on the horizon, and it grows and takes shape. Poon lights one of his smoke flares as the cargo ship approaches.

Finally! Rescue!

The ship approaches so close that Poon Lim can see the white officers moving around on the bridge. The ship's swell reaches the little raft and makes it rock and bob. Poon calls out and yells at them in his broken English. They just look at him, and don't wave back. The ship moves on past without slowing down. It becomes a dot on the horizon again before disappearing. Poon is devastated. He doesn't understand. Why? Did they think he was Japanese and therefore not worth rescuing? But a Japanese, here in the South Atlantic? Unlikely. His own explanation is that they turned away as soon as they could see he wasn't white. Poon himself said a long time later: "The ocean sees no difference between a yellow man and a white man."*

This, too, happened on Monday, November 30. Poon Lim had been shipwrecked for 7 days. He didn't realize at that point that he would spend another 126 days alone on the raft.

. . .

Nothing new at Stalingrad. The encircled defenders in the huge trap hold their positions, and those encircling them do the same. The white-painted German transport planes continue to fly over, often solitary and often at low altitude. Vasily Grossman was weary and at the end of his tether back at the beginning of the month, and he is even more so now at the end. Three long months in Stalingrad have taken their toll. He feels "overloaded with impressions," as anyone can understand. And like every other fighter who has recognized that it is actually fate or luck that decides, Grossman has developed smalls tics and superstitions. For instance, he considers it unlucky to seal his letters himself and always wants someone else to do it.

Grossman is back by the Volga.† His intention is to make one last visit to the mass of ruins that had been Stalingrad, to talk to some members of the highest command, and to visit a number of combat units. It is not an easy journey to make. It's true that the German attacks within the city have ceased, and the earlier firing both night and day has moderated noticeably. The problem now is the ice. The great river

---

* There has been an attempt to explain this away by suggesting that U-boats used people in life rafts as "bait"; apart from the fact that I have never seen any examples in sources or literature of this being done, it wouldn't actually make sense. If the cargo ship was afraid of U-boats, it would immediately have sailed away rather than approach the raft first.

† I have assumed that this description actually originates from the time after the end of the offensive, not from the period before it: the latter would be illogical.

is not yet frozen over, but an endless flood of broken pieces and ice floes makes crossing the river problematical. And Grossman needs to cross the Volga twice: first from west to east from his current location south of the city, and then to move north and repeat the crossing, this time from east to west. He writes:

> Ice is moving down the Volga. Ice floes are rustling, crumbling, crushing against one another. The river is almost wholly covered with ice. Only from time to time can one see patches of water in this wide, white ribbon, floating between the dark snowless banks. The white ice of the Volga is carrying tree trunks, wood. A big raven is sitting sulkily on an ice floe. A dead Red Fleet soldier in a striped shirt floats past. Men from a freight steamer take him from the ice. It is difficult to tear the dead man out of the ice. He is rooted in it. It is as if he doesn't want to leave the Volga where he has fought and died.

Grossman is revisiting Stalingrad to collect further material, in the first place for an extended version for *Krasnaja Zvezda*—that, anyway, is the reason he gives his superior. At the same time, the idea of writing a big novel about the war is forming in his mind, a novel that will tell the whole of the "ruthless truth." By this point, Grossman is becoming increasingly frustrated by the way the newspaper edits his texts, both cutting pieces and making additions. He is aiming high within the novel. His model is an obvious one: his rucksack contains a well-thumbed copy of the only book he can bring himself to read these days—Tolstoy's *War and Peace.**

Grossman's contributions to *Krasnaja Zvezda* had made him

---

* He was not alone in this. Never before had *War and Peace* had such a large readership, not least because the authorities considered its message and motifs—victory over the foreign invaders—were beneficial to the country's fighting spirit. They therefore did all they could to spread the book. It was read on the radio, and pamphlets were distributed in which the novel was abridged and explained. Two of the most important commanders in Stalingrad, Chuikov and Rodimtsev, read it. Lidiya Ginzburg observed that it was much read in Leningrad under siege, and people compared the way they dealt with the war with how Tolstoy's characters had done so. And during the weeks before Grossman's mother was murdered, she had been teaching her students from a French translation of the novel.

famous—he, the man who had done so much to create a sort of everyday legend out of the ordinary men and women he met at the front. But
more significant than that is the fact that Grossman's experiences and
his efforts to capture them in words has made real something within
himself and made him a great author rather than just a good one.

Grossman watches a barge loaded with Romanian prisoners of war
move past. They are freezing cold in their thin brown overcoats and
they are stamping their feet and rubbing their hands.

·   ·   ·

Winter weather has arrived in Chicago. Yesterday, Sunday, it snowed,
and the temperature remains a couple of degrees below zero. Down
in the unheated basements under the west stand at Stagg Field, it feels
even colder than that. It is the armed security guards who are suffering
worst from the cold, as they have to remain at their posts all day. They
have now been given the full-length, coonskin fur coats that used to be
worn by the now defunct football team. One of the supervisors jokes
that they have "by far the best dressed security men in the business."

By this Monday there are not many layers left to go before CP-1 is
ready. Once the mid-point is passed and the number of graphite blocks
decreases, the outer framework of heavy timbers becomes unnecessary. CP-1 looks nothing like a piece of high technology: Enrico Fermi
described it later as "a crude pile of black bricks and wooden timbers."
The only moveable parts of the whole arrangement are visible at the
top and on the side facing the viewing gallery of the squash courts:
three wooden sticks, each pushed into a separate hole. These are the
control rods. They are covered with cadmium foil because cadmium
is a very powerful absorber of neutrons and can thus prevent a chain
reaction.

Together with Herb Anderson, a physicist and her shift supervisor,
Leona Woods is able to use her boron trifluoride counter to confirm
that the pile is now very close to the critical mass needed for a spontaneous nuclear chain reaction to occur.

Two days later, the time has come. Leona Woods writes:

> The next morning it was terribly cold—below zero. Fermi
> and I crunched over to the stands in creaking, blue-shadowed
> snow and repeated Herb's flux measurement with the standard
> boron trifluoride counter.... We agreed to meet again at two

o'clock. Herb, Fermi and I went over to the apartment I shared with my sister (it was close to the stands) for something to eat. I made pancakes, mixing the batter so fast there were bubbles of dry flour in it. When fried, these were somewhat crunchy between the teeth, and Herb thought I had put nuts in the batter. And back we mushed through the cold, creaking snow.

The streets are strangely empty and someone remembers that gasoline rationing has just been introduced. They go into the chilly stand and put on their lab coats, which are now black with graphite dust. Woods accompanies the group up to the viewing balcony overlooking the squash courts—the balcony is currently "filled with control equipment and read-out circuits glowing and winking and radiating some gratefully received heat."

There are a number of prominent onlookers, including Professor Léo Szilárd, small and round. Szilárd is the Hungarian-American physicist who did much of the early theoretical work about nuclear chain reactions and who nourished wonderful dreams of the peaceful possibilities of atomic energy. But, in 1939, along with Albert Einstein, he was involved in writing the decisive letter to President Franklin Roosevelt warning that it was possible to construct a bomb of immense destructive power and that Hitler's Germany was likely to be working on it, which was why they—reluctantly—were pushing for the United States to do the same thing.

The majority of those present were not, however, mere onlookers; they each had their own specific functions. In case the chain reaction goes out of control, one is standing ready with an axe to cut the rope that holds up the vertical control rod hanging over the pile; someone else is standing by with a bucket of concentrated cadmium nitrate solution to slosh over the pile to quickly stop the chain reaction in an emergency; a third person is standing ready to pull out the sole remaining control rod foot by foot on Fermi's command. Leona Woods's job is to read out the counts of the boron trifluoride counter in a loud voice.

So they start, with Fermi controlling every step. On a command from him, the last control rod is pulled out, slowly, foot by foot. After each foot the counter is checked and Fermi double-checks with his slide rule. The numbers match.

Woods writes: "You could hear the sound of the clicking boron trifluoride counter increase. I called, 'Eight, sixteen, twenty-eight, sixty-four...,' then the clicks merged into a roar too fast to read." Fermi allows the simple chain reaction to run for four and a half minutes. The intensity continues to increase and the chain reaction is self-supporting. Eventually the intensity reaches half a watt, sufficient to power a flashlight.* Then Fermi gives the order to push the control rod back into the structure and the intensity rapidly drops. The roar of the counter subsides to a clicking and the clicking slows and comes to a stop. The pile is turned off.

The system functions. A decisive barrier on the way to producing an atomic bomb has been pushed aside.

They switch off all the equipment, secure the control rods and tidy up. Leona Woods gets ready to leave. She has already taken off her dirty lab coat when someone produces a bottle of chianti in its straw basket, in honor of Fermi. The bottle is opened, the wine poured into paper cups and they drink a toast. All eyes look silently at Fermi. Then they all leave the squash courts, satisfied and happy, and go out into the crunching snow. There are only two men who stay behind up on the viewing gallery, Fermi and Léo Szilárd. Szilárd goes over to Fermi, shakes his hand and says: "This will go down as a black day in the history of mankind."

. . .

On Monday, November 30, a train of cattle cars arrives in Treblinka carrying about 1,700 Jews from Siedlice. They are among the last people from what was known as the town's small ghetto, which has been cleared and transported to Treblinka in batches since last Wednesday. With the exception of a small number spared to replenish the constantly diminishing number of workers in the camp Sonderkommando, all of them—men, women and children—will have been murdered before evening.

Chil Rajchman is still working in the camp dental squad.

Winter has arrived, but everything continues as it has been.[†] People

---

* At this point, the flow of neutrons is doubling every second minute and, as Pulitzer Prize winner Richard Rhodes writes, if it had been allowed to continue, "given that rate of increase for an hour and a half, it would have reached an intensity of a million kilowatts. Long before that, it would have taken the lives of all those remaining in the location and also melted itself down."

[†] Thanks to what's known as the Höfle Telegram, which the British code

stand naked and trembling from cold in the hosepipe while waiting their turn. Bowls of bloody teeth are taken into the dentists' hut for cleaning. The sub-zero temperatures make things difficult. Rajchman writes:

> It's worth mentioning that extracting teeth is much more diffi-cult in winter. The corpses had either stiffened after the open-ing of the door or people had been frozen by the frost before they even went into the chambers. We had all the trouble in the world trying to open the clamped mouths.

There seems to be a procedural change taking place. A blond SS man in his thirties has arrived; he has a gentle expression, a childlike face, and he is given to laughing.* The prisoners call him the Artist. He is said to be an expert on cremation, and for some reason the dead are no longer to be buried; they are to be cremated instead. A later order stipulates that the cadavers already buried should also be dug up and cremated. And the ashes are to be ground down to powder. Why?

.   .   .

The Scholl siblings' group has great determination, great courage and the firm idea that they *must* do this, that they *must* go through with it. They all agree on this. At the same time, however, they differ on how best to deal with the pressure. Some of them are frightened almost the whole time; they have difficulty sleeping, seek anything to take their

---

breakers in Bletchley Park intercepted, we have a very exact figure for how many people were murdered in Treblinka by year's end: 713,555. Rajchman's account tells us that there were fewer transports during December, and that is confirmed by the telegram: the number of victims in the two weeks preceding December 31, 1942, was 335.

* This was Herbert Floss. It's not absolutely clear when he arrived at the camp—according to Rajchman it was in January 1943, but according to the witness state-ment Heinrich Matthes gave to the Treblinka trial in Düsseldorf in 1964–1965 it was November 1942. The latter coincides with the decision already made in the summer of 1942 to remove all traces of mass murder. The process—known as Sonderaktion 1005—began that autumn. An important meeting was held that November in Adolf Eichmann's office in Berlin and Paul Blobel, head of Sonder-aktion 1005, described the methods decided on. Work on exhuming and burning the corpses had already started at Sobibor and Belzec.

minds off things; have nightmares, easily interpreted nightmares, such as being met and knocked down by skeletons obviously derived from Holbein's *Dance of Death* woodcuts. Others, on the other hand, react to the increasing danger by embracing everything that life has to offer. In a couple of weeks, Hans Scholl will fall in love yet again.

And Sophie Scholl will be happy skiing on the gleaming white snow of the Englischer Garten and no one she encounters will suspect her secret. We shouldn't imagine, however, that her carefreeness is just put on, as a mask or cover; life can actually be multilayered like this, not in spite of extreme times but thanks to them. There is not a different young woman within her—both are in there, the two of them utterly entwined.

.   .   .

It is now the last days of November and the nights are getting really cold in Shanghai. There have been changes on the maps pinned up in the hall of the Blomberg house in Place de Fleurs. The colorful flags are being moved again, and now, for the first time, the areas controlled by Japan and Germany have begun to shrink, not to any dramatic degree, but nevertheless. Ursula, her family and the other European refugees are still living in a bubble, in a world where it is impossible to know what is fixed and what is shifting, where news still reaches them in fragments that are sometimes confirmed and sometimes contradicted by someone who knows someone who owns one of those well-concealed shortwave radios. And they pore over official information sheets, hunting for the tiny, easily missed fragments of fact in the stream of propaganda phrases.

In this ongoing ebb and flow of ignorance and guesses, speculation about the SS officer Meisinger seems to have surfaced again.* The rumor that a ship carrying a cargo of poison gas has landed in Shanghai doesn't seem to bear scrutiny.† It seems, however, the Americans have

---

* In Poland in 1946, Meisinger was charged and sentenced for atrocities committed there in 1939–1940. He was executed the following year.

† The rumor of poison gas was false, but what is true is that Meisinger attempted to get the Japanese to gather all the Jews in the city into a concentration camp, or alternatively organize a pogrom, or alternatively lock them in a ship in the harbor in order to starve them to death. The Japanese authorities were not interested, paradoxically because, although they had accepted some elements of anti-Semitic propaganda, they had come to the conclusion that a group so powerful

won control of the island they landed on and, in doing so, inflicted a first major defeat on the Japanese army. And everything suggests, too, that Allied forces have landed in North Africa and set up some sort of Free French regime there; and Egypt is no longer threatened; and it also seems that the German armies on the Volga and in the Caucasus have run into problems, major problems.

The Japanese have become more nervous now. One of the things they have done is to proclaim a general ban on all news outlets and rumormongering in western Shanghai in order "to preserve Peace and Order." Moreover, they stress that "OFFENDERS WILL BE SEVERELY PUNISHED," employing capital letters for emphasis. As if a ban was likely or able to silence rumors. As if rumors, obscurity, lies and ignorance were not to a great extent part of the essence of war.

If one reads the memoir Ursula Blomberg wrote when she was a grown woman, one suspects that she, her family and her friends breathed a little easier at this point. She has been thinking of arranging a small Christmas celebration this year with "the sisters," the three young Chinese girls she is teaching English to. She is intending to have an exchange of Christmas presents and sing traditional Christmas songs—someone has managed to find the music. And Ursula has noticed that something in her is changing. Living in one and the same room as her parents no longer feels secure and uncomplicated. She has started longing for quiet and to be on her own, for something as simple as being able to lock the bathroom door. "For me, the end of the war would mean a room of my own."

---

and resourceful as the Jews should be exploited in some way rather than exterminated. Before 1941, there were a number of Japanese civil servants who had played with the idea of allowing large groups of Jews to migrate to Manchuria and contribute to its modernization.

Epilogue

What Happened to Them Afterwards

Abdulin, Mansur After the battle for Stalingrad, Abdulin fought in the great conflict of Kursk in 1943. He survived that, too. When the Red Army struck across the Dnieper later the same year, he was badly wounded then demobilized. After the war he returned to his work in the mining industry. He died in 2007 in the same district where he was born, on the border of Kazakhstan.

Amery, John Amery continued working for the Nazi propaganda apparatus until the end of 1944. He left Berlin then in order to link up instead with the fascist Saló Republic in northern Italy. He was taken prisoner there in 1945 and sent to Great Britain, where he was tried and sentenced for high treason. In December of that year he was hanged in Wandsworth Prison.

Berr, Hélène Hélène and her parents were seized in March 1944 and deported later the same month. Her mother was gassed on arrival in Auschwitz; her father was killed after six months at the IG Farben sub-camp, Buna. In November of the same year Hélène was transferred to Bergen-Belsen, where, sick with typhus, she was beaten to death just five days before the camp was liberated in 1945. Her boyfriend, Jean, survived the war and became a diplomat.

Blomberg, Ursula Ursula and her parents did get to America, in 1947. She married another young refugee and her married name was Bacon. They all settled in Denver, where she had two children. She wrote a memoir of her time in Shanghai and a number of other books, including *The Nervous Hostess Cookbook*. She died in 2013.

Brittain, Vera After the war Vera Brittain continued to follow the voice of conscience. She was involved in campaigns against apartheid and for nuclear disarmament. She aged prematurely, both physically and mentally, after an accidental fall in 1966. She died in 1970. In accordance with her last wishes she was cremated and her ashes scattered on her brother's grave in northern Italy, where he had been killed in 1918.

Bushby, John Bushby spent the rest of the war as a prisoner of war in the famous camp Stalag Luft III in eastern Germany (now Poland).* On his return home, he remained in the RAF. During the Cold War he became a specialist in air defense and during the 1960s was involved in operations intended to prevent Soviet intrusions into British airspace.

Caccia Dominioni, Paolo On his return to Italy he joined the anti-fascist resistance movement. He devoted twenty years after the war to the gathering of the fallen from the el-Alamein battlefield and he was involved in the design and construction of the ossuary that now functions as a memorial to the Italian dead. He died in Rome in 1992.

Camus, Albert Camus was later active as a journalist in the resistance. After the war he and Francine settled in Paris and had two children. He went on to become one of the leading figures in twentieth-century literature and in 1957, at the age of forty-four, he was awarded the Nobel Prize for Literature. He died in a car accident three years later.

Douglas, Keith Having fought in the battles in Tunisia, Douglas returned to Great Britain in December 1943. He took part in the D-day landings in Normandy on June 6, 1944, and three days later he was killed by a shell from a German mortar after leaving his tank to scout ahead. His body was buried under a hedge on the battlefield.

Dunlop, Edward "Weary" Dunlop and most of his fellow prisoners ended up on the notorious Railway of Death in Thailand, where a great many men died. The number of deaths would have been far greater had it not been for Dunlop's work. After liberation in 1945 he married Helen and went on to forge a successful career in medicine in a variety of functions. He also worked for reconciliation between Australia and Japan. Dunlop died in 1993 and his funeral was attended by over ten thousand people.

Fijalkowska, Danuta Danuta's husband, Józek Fijalkowski, was killed by the German military police in February 1943 while attempting to avoid arrest. After the war was over, Danuta completed her education and became a teacher. She remarried in 1951 and had two more children. She and her new husband moved to the U.S. in the 1970s and she died there in April 2002.

---

* Famous after the war, that is to say: the camp was the scene of two daring and spectacular escapes, which later inspired action films and later still computer games.

Ginzburg, Lidiya Ginzburg survived the war and also the anti-Semitic campaign in the Soviet Union at the end of the 1940s. She remained at the university and during the thaw that followed the death of Stalin she was able to publish a number of well-received works of literary criticism. She died in Leningrad in 1990.

Grossman, Vasily Grossman continued reporting on the war until 1945, and he was the first person to report on Treblinka. After the peace, he found himself more and more out in the cold. When he completed *Life and Fate* (1959), his great novel about the war, it was confiscated by the KGB: in fact, they took everything associated with the book, even the typewriter ribbon he had used, and it was stated on the highest authority that it couldn't be published for three hundred years. Grossman died of stomach cancer in 1964.

Hara, Tameichi Hara took part in many more sea battles and was the only Japanese destroyer captain to survive the entire war. He became more and more pessimistic about its outcome and wrote a letter to the emperor in 1943 appealing to him to make peace. After 1945 he continued working as a ship's captain, but now on civilian cargo ships transporting salt. Hara died in 1980.

Hartnagel, Fritz After the execution of Sophie Scholl and her brother Hans, Hartnagel—who'd been evacuated from Stalingrad in January 1943—attempted to support the family in a variety of ways. On his release from an American prisoner-of-war camp in 1945, he married Sophie's sister, Elisabeth, and they had four children together. He worked as a lawyer and became a member of the Social Democrats. He was a committed supporter of the German peace movement throughout the 1980s. He died in Stuttgart in April 2001.

Holl, Adelbert Hardly surprisingly, Holl was one of those who fought to the last at Stalingrad. He was taken prisoner there on February 2, 1943. The majority of those German POWs did not survive, but Holl did. He returned to what by then was West Germany in 1950 after seven years in a Soviet camp. He died in June 1980.

Inber, Vera Vera Inber became a member of the Communist Party in 1943 and her career as a writer continued to flourish after the war. She won the Stalin Prize in 1946 and *The Pulkovo Meridian*, the long narrative cycle of poems about the siege of Leningrad she began in 1942, won great and justified praise. She died in Moscow in 1972.

Jünger, Ernst Although peripherally involved in the July 20 plot against Hitler, Jünger, whether by luck or skill, avoided punishment, but was dismissed from the army in August of that year. (His eldest son, however, was found to be in possession of subversive speeches and was sent to a punishment battalion in northern Italy, where he fell in November 1944.) Jünger continued to write after the war and regained his position in the literary sphere. He died in February 1998 at the age of 102.

Kardorff, Ursula von After the death of her younger brother, Jürgen, on the Eastern Front in February 1943, Ursula became increasingly critical of the regime. The house at Rankestrasse 21 was completely destroyed by the RAF bomber offensive of late 1943. Faced with the threat of the Red Army, she fled Berlin in March 1945. She continued working as a journalist after the war, now with the *Süddeutsche Zeitung*. She became well-known for her fine depictions of Paris. She died in Munich in January 1988.

Last, Nella Nella continued to keep her diary until 1966 and its twelve million words make it one of the longest in the English language. In other respects her life did not change much, and she remained unhappily married. Her youngest son was wounded but survived the war and emigrated to Australia, where he became a sculptor. By the mid-1960s, Nella's health began to fade and she was afflicted by dementia. She died in June 1968.

Lim, Poon He was rescued by Brazilian fishermen on April 5, 1943, after 133 days alone on his raft. When his story became known, he was sent to Great Britain by ship and awarded a medal by the king. He emigrated to the U.S. after the war and died in Brooklyn on January 4, 1991.

McEniry, John McEniry remained active as a pilot with the Marine Corps in the Pacific until the end of the war, by which stage he'd been awarded many medals. Apart from a short period when he was recalled to service during the Korean War, he worked as a lawyer in Bessemer, his hometown in Alabama, and continued to do so until retiring in 1982. He died in 1993.

Mun, Okchu Mun was moved around from one field brothel to another in Burma and Thailand. She spent the last months of the war nursing the wounded. When the war was over, she returned to Korea, where she was treated as an outcast. She supported herself by working as a *kisaeng*, a kind of geisha. She married, but six years later her husband took his own life. Her time as a comfort woman left her plagued by disease, insomnia and shame. She never had children of her own. She died in 1996.

Obrynba, Nikolai Obrynba fought on as a partisan until the autumn of 1943, when the Germans were forced to fall back from the area. He then returned to Moscow, where he was reunited with his wife. After the war he continued working as an artist, painting many works in the socialist realist style of the time. He died in 1996.

Oglethorpe, **SS** The Liberty ship SS *Oglethorpe,* built with so much effort, had a short life. She was sunk by German U-boats in March 1943 on her very first convoy to Great Britain. She was carrying a cargo that consisted mainly of steel, cotton and foodstuffs. Her captain and forty-four of her seventy-four-man crew disappeared. She is now resting at the bottom of the North Atlantic, at roughly 50°38' north, 34°46' west, almost exactly the halfway point of her voyage.

Parris, John Parris returned to the U.S. and carried on working as a journalist, mainly for the *Citizen Times* in Asheville, North Carolina. From the 1950s on he was much appreciated as a chronicler with a folkloristic approach, portraying the people and culture of the old Appalachians. He died in 1996.

Rajchman, Chil Rajchman was one of those who escaped from Treblinka during the camp uprising in August 1943. He made it to Warsaw, where he adopted a Christian alias and joined the Polish resistance movement. Immediately after the war he married another survivor and the couple emigrated to Uruguay. He had a successful career there in the textile industry and had three sons and eleven grandchildren. He served as a witness in several trials, including the trial of John Demjanjuk. Rajchman died in Montevideo in May 2004.

Reese, Willy Peter Reese carried on writing his poetry and prose and ensured it came into the care of his parents in Duisburg. He served at the Eastern Front until he disappeared at Vitebsk during the big Russian summer offensive at the end of June 1944. His final fate remains unknown.

Robinson, Dorothy Robinson's post-war life seems to have been as undramatic as it was during it. There is no sign that she went back to writing. She and her husband remained together. He died in 1966 and she died in 1977. They are buried together in a churchyard in Saratoga, New York.

Russell, Ned After the war Russell continued working as a journalist, with London as his base, covering mainly economic topics. He also had commissions for the Marshall Plan. He was involved in a serious car crash in Los Angeles in 1954 and died in 1958, having been in a coma for four years.

Scholl, Sophie Sophie was arrested along with her brother Hans on February 18, 1943, after being discovered distributing oppositional flyers in one of the Munich University buildings. After a very quick trial, sentence was passed on February 22 and both were executed by guillotine within hours. She is said to have shown courage to the end.

Skrjabina, Elena Together with her two children, Elena fled again in 1943, this time westwards. Through further dangers and complications, she yet again demonstrated her incontestable skills as a survivor. She ended the war doing German forced labor in the Rhineland. When peace returned, she emigrated with her children to the U.S., undertook further studies and eventually became a professor of French at the University of Ohio. She died in 1996.

Somerhausen, Anne As time passed, Anne became more and more involved in resistance activity of one sort or another, and on a number of occasions she hid Jewish refugees in her house. In spite of increased risks, she and her boys survived the war and in May 1945 her husband, Marc, returned from being a prisoner of war. He returned to his career in politics and law and she returned to life as a housewife. She died in 1986.

Thomas, Leonard Thomas remained in the navy and sailed on two more Arctic convoys. After he was demobilized in 1946, he settled in Edinburgh with a woman he had met before the war. He had two children and eventually became an electrical engineer. He retired in 1977 and died, still in Edinburgh, in April 2000.

Thongs, Bede Thongs recovered from severe illness and later took part in the continued fighting in New Guinea. He was promoted in the field to captain and awarded a prestigious medal. Much of Thongs's later life was played out in the long afterglow of the war: he returned to the old battlefields nine times and often took part in a variety of memorial projects. He died peacefully in 2015. His coffin was draped with the flag of the 3rd Battalion.

U-604 U-604 set out on her last voyage in June 1943. On August 11 she was badly damaged by American aircraft and was scuttled by her crew. Thirteen of the crewmen died, including the captain, Horst Höltring, who took his own life after shooting two wounded crewmen who were trapped in the sinking, chlorine-gas-filled vessel. The U-boat now lies on the bed of the South Atlantic at about 4°15' south, 21°20' west, more or less halfway between Brazil and West Africa.

Vallicella, Vittorio After a long and sometimes harsh time as a prisoner of war in French hands, Vallicella returned to his home province of Verona in 1947. He went back to farming, was involved in political and trade union affairs, married in 1950 and had two sons. Energetic, inquisitive and with a hunger for knowledge, he set up a newspaper kiosk and then later a small bookshop. He died in 2005.

Wakabayashi, Tohichi Wakabayashi was badly wounded on Guadalcanal on January 12, 1943, during the defense of the group of hills known to the Americans as Galloping Horse and to the Japanese as Miharishi Highlands. He rejected the offer of evacuation and remained with his men. He was killed two days later (January 14), probably in the river ravine to which the rest of his battalion had retired and where they were cut down almost to the last man. By this stage, Wakabayashi had ensured that his diary had been taken to safety.

Walker, Charles After Guadalcanal Walker took part in the prolonged fighting for the Philippines and he belonged to one of the units that landed in Japan after the capitulation. At war's end he worked in agriculture, and then spent ten years flying light cargo planes in rural Canada. In the 1970s he moved home to Pembina, North Dakota, and died there in 2009.

West, Kurt West remained in the service and took part in the hard fighting in the Karelian Isthmus in the summer of 1944 when a major Red Army offensive was stopped. After being demobilized, he returned to Esse, the place of his birth, and worked first in agriculture before setting up an electrical business in 1948. In the 1960s he specialized in installing television sets. He was an active Baptist. In his old age he made several visits to the old battlefields. West died in Esse in 2007, leaving a large family.

Woods, Leona Leona worked on the Manhattan Project until the end of the war and then returned to her studies. She enjoyed a fine academic career as a physicist, writing some two hundred papers and becoming a professor, first at New York University and then at the University of Colorado. She divorced her first husband in 1966 and married Willard Libby, winner of the Nobel Prize. In later years she became interested in environmental questions and developed a method of measuring climatic changes with the help of isotopes in wood. She died of a stroke in 1986.

Sources

Abdulin, M: *Red Road from Stalingrad: Recollections of a Soviet Infantryman.* Barnsley 2004.

Adam, W & Rühle, O: *With Paulus at Stalingrad.* Barnsley 2015.

Aldridge, J: *Cairo: Biography of a City.* New York 1969.

Alman, K: *Angriff, ran, versenken: Die U-Boot-Schlacht im Atlantik.* Rastatt 1965.

Amery, J: *John Amery Speaks / England and Europe.* Uckfield 2007.

Anderson, N: *To Kokoda* (Australian Army Campaign, Series 14). Canberra 2014.

Arad, Y: *The Holocaust in the Soviet Union.* Lincoln 2009.

Arendt, H: *The Origins of Totalitarianism.* New York 1976.

Atkinson, R: *An Army at Dawn: The War in North Africa, 1942–1943.* London 2003.

Bacon, U: *Shanghai Diary: A Young Girl's Journey from Hitler's Hate to War-Torn China.* Milwaukee 2004.

Barton, D: "Rewriting the Reich: German Women Journalists as Transnational Mediators for Germany's Rehabilitation," in *Central European History,* vol. 51, no. 4 (2018).

Bartsch, WH: *Victory Fever on Guadalcanal: Japan's First Land Defeat of WWII.* College Station 2014.

Bastable, J (ed.): *Voices from Stalingrad.* Cincinnati 2006.

Battistelli, PP: *El Alamein 1942.* Stroud 2015.

Beevor, A & Vinovgradova, L: *A Writer at War: Vasily Grossman with the Red Army 1941–1945.* London 2006.

Bergerud, EM: *Fire in the Sky: The Air War in the South Pacific.* Boulder 2000.

Berr, H: *Journal.* Paris 2008.

Berr, H: *The Journal of Hélène Berr.* New York 2008.

Berry, P & Bostridge, M: *Vera Brittain: A Life.* London 2008.

Bowman, MW: *Bomber Command: Reflections of War. Volume 2: Live to Die Another Day (June 1942–Summer 1943).* Barnsley 2012.

Brittain, V: *Humiliation with Honour.* New York 1943.

Brittain, V: *Wartime Chronicle: Vera Brittain's Diary 1939–1945.* London 1989.

Brune, P: *Those Ragged Bloody Heroes: From the Kokoda Trail to Gona Beach 1942*. Sydney 1992.

Brustat-Naval, F: *Ali Cremer U 333: Ein U-Boot Buch über den authentische Lebensgeschichte des U-Boot-Kommandanten Peter E. Cremer und seiner Mannschaft*. Berlin 1994.

Busch, R (ed.): *Stalingrad: Der Untergang der 6. Armee: Überlebende berichten*. Graz 2012.

Bushby, J: *Gunner's Moon: A Memoir of the RAF Night Assault on Germany*. London 1974.

Caccia Dominioni, P: *El Alamein 1932–1962*. Milan 1966.

Calvocoressi, P, Wint, G & Pritchard, J: *Total War: The Causes and Courses of the Second World War*. London 1995.

Camus, A: *Carnets, Janvier 1942–Mars 1951*. Paris 1964.

Camus, A: *Pesten*. Stockholm 1983.

Casdorph, PD: *Let the Good Times Roll: Life at Home in America During World War II*. New York 1991.

Chandler, R: "Mother and Son—Life and Fate," in *Granta*, June 2019.

Christopherson, S: *An Englishman at War: The Wartime Diaries of Stanley Christopherson 1939–45*. London 2014.

Conway, M: *Collaboration in Belgium: Léon Degrelle and the Rexist Movement 1940–1944*. New Haven 1993.

Cope, Tony: *On the Swing Shift: Building Liberty Ships in Savannah*. Annapolis 2009.

Costello, J: *Love, Sex and War: Changing Values 1939–45*. London 1985.

Craig, W: *Enemy at the Gates: The Battle for Stalingrad*. London 2000.

De Jonghe, A: "La Lutte Himmler-Reeder pour la nomination d'un HSSPF à Bruxelles (1942–1944)—Troisième partie: Evolution d'octobre 1942 à octobre 1943," in *Cahiers d'histoire de la seconde guerre mondiale*, no. 5, December 1978.

De Launay, J & Offergeld, J: *La vie quotidienne des Belges sous l'occupation 1940–1945*. Brussels 1982.

Denkler, H: *Werkruinen, Lebenstrümmer: Literarischen Spuren der "verloreren Generation" des Dritten Reiches*. Tübingen 2006.

Douglas, K: *Alamein to Zem Zem*. Oxford 1979.

Douglas, K: *The Complete Poems*. Oxford 1978.

Duggan, C: *Fascist Voices: An Intimate History of Mussolini's Italy*. London 2013.

Dumbach, A & Newborg, J: *Sophie Scholl and the White Rose*. London 2007.

Dunlop, EE: *The War Diaries of Weary Dunlop: Java and the Burma–Thailand Railway 1942–1945*. Victoria 1990.

Ebury, S: *Weary: The Life of Sir Edward Dunlop*. Victoria 1994.

Ellis, J: *World War II: The Sharp End*. London 1990.

Enstad, JD: *Soviet Russians under Nazi Occupation: Fragile Loyalties in World War II*. Cambridge 2019.

Facos, M: *An Introduction to Nineteenth Century Art*. London 2011.

Fest, JC: *Das Gesicht des Dritten Reiches: Profile einer totalitären Herrschaft*. Munich 1993.

Findahl, T: *Ögonvittne Berlin 1939–45.* Stockholm 1946.

Forczyk, R: *The Caucasus 1942–43: Kleist's Race for Oil.* London 2015.

Forster, EM: *Alexandria: A History and a Guide.* Alexandria 1922.

Fredborg, A: *Bakom stålvallen.* Stockholm 1995.

Frei, N & Schmitz, J: *Journalismus im Dritten Reich.* Munich 1989.

Fussell, P: *Wartime: Understanding and Behaviour in the Second World War.* Oxford 1989.

Gasperi, R: *La grande illusione: Diario di guerra.* Rovereto 1991.

Gebhardt, M: *Die Weiße Rose: Wie aus ganz normalen Deutschen Widerstandskämpfer wurden.* Munich 2017.

Gerasimova, S: *The Rzhev Slaughterhouse: The Red Army's Forgotten 15-Month Campaign Against Army Group Center, 1942–1943.* Warwick 2016.

Gillies, M: *The Barbed-Wire University: The Real Lives of Allied Prisoners of War in the Second World War.* London 2011.

Ginzburg, L: *Blockade Diary.* London 1995.

Glantz, DM: *Armageddon in Stalingrad: September–November 1942.* Lawrence 2009.

Glantz, DM: *Endgame at Stalingrad: Book One: November 1942.* Lawrence 2014.

Glantz, DM: *Endgame at Stalingrad: Companion.* Lawrence 2014.

Gogun, A: *Stalin's Commandos: Ukrainian Partisan Forces on the Eastern Front.* London 2016.

Golomstock, I: *Totalitarian Art in the Soviet Union, the Third Reich, Fascist Italy and the People's Republic of China.* London 1990.

Graham, D: *Keith Douglas 1920–1944: A Biography.* Oxford 1974.

Grossman, D: *On Killing: The Psychological Cost of Learning to Kill in War and Society.* Boston 1996.

Grossman, V: *Liv och öde.* Falun 2007.

Grossman, V: *Stalingrad.* London 2019.

Grossman, V: "The Treblinka Hell," in *The Years of War (1941–1945).* Moscow 1946.

Grunberger, R: *A Social History of the Third Reich.* London 1971.

Guéhenno, J: *Journal des années noires.* Paris 2014.

Gustavsson, H: *Sino-Japanese Air War 1937–1945.* Croydon 2016.

Hara, T: *Japanese Destroyer Captain: Pearl Harbor, Guadalcanal, Midway—The Great Naval Battles as Seen Through Japanese Eyes.* Annapolis 2011.

Harmetz, A: *Round Up the Usual Suspects: The Making of Casablanca: Bogart, Bergman, and World War II.* London 1993.

Harries, M & Harris, S: *Soldiers of the Sun: The Rise and Fall of the Imperial Japanese Army.* New York 1991.

Hartmann, SM: *The Home Front and Beyond: American Women in the 1940s.* Boston 1982.

Hastings, M: *Bomber Command.* London 2007.

Heckmann, W: *Rommels Krieg in Afrika: Wüstenfüchse gegen Wüstenratten.* Bergisch-Gladbach 1976.

Hellbeck, J: *Die Stalingrad-Protokolle: Sowjetische Augenzeugen berichten aus der Schlacht.* Frankfurt am Main 2012.

Helmus, TC & Glenn, RW: *Steeling the Mind: Combat Stress Reaction and Their Implication for Urban Warfare.* Santa Monica 2005.

Hicks, G: *The Comfort Women: Sex Slaves of the Japanese Imperial Forces.* London 1995.

Holl, A: *After Stalingrad: Seven Years as a Soviet Prisoner of War.* Barnsley 2019.

Holl, A: *An Infantryman in Stalingrad: From 24 September 1942 to 2 February 1943.* Sydney 2005.

Höss, R: *Kommendant i Auschwitz.* Eskilstuna 1979.

Howard, K (ed.): *True Stories of the Korean Comfort Women: Testimonies Compiled by the Korean Council for Women Drafted for Military Sexual Slavery by Japan.* London 1995.

Inber, V: *Leningrad Diary.* London 1971.

Ireland, J: *The Traitors: A True Story of Blood, Betrayal and Deceit.* London 2018.

James, C: *Cultural Amnesia: Notes in the Margin of My Time.* London 2007.

Johansson, G: *Soldater: Frontbrev 1940–1942.* Helsinki 1942.

Johnston, GH: *New Guinea Diary.* London 1946.

Jünger, E: *Dagböcker från Tyskland och Frankrike under krig och occupation* (ed. Jonasson, S). Lund 1975.

Jünger, E: *Leben und Werk in Bildern und Texten.* Stuttgart 1988.

Jünger, Ernst: *På marmorklipporna.* Lund 1976.

Jünger, E: *Strahlungen I: Gärten und Straßen / Das erste Pariser Tagebuch / Kaukasische Aufzeichungen.* Munich 1998.

Kardorff, U von: *Berliner Aufzeichnungen 1942–1945: Unter Verwendung der Original-Tagebücher neu herausgeben und kommentiert von Peter Hartl.* Munich 1992.

Kater, MH: *The Twisted Muse: Musicians and Their Music in the Third Reich.* Oxford 1997.

Keene, J: *Treason on the Airwaves: Three Allied Broadcasters on Axis Radio during World War II.* Lincoln 2010.

Knightley, P: *The First Casualty: The War Correspondent as Hero and Myth-Maker from the Crimea to Kosovo.* London 2001.

Kolganov, KS (ed.): *Taktikens utveckling i Sovjetarmén under det Stora Fosterländska kriget 1941–1945.* Stockholm 1960.

Krasno, R: *Strangers Always: A Jewish Family in Wartime Shanghai.* Berkeley 1992.

Kuussaari, E & Niitemaa, V: *Finlands krig 1941–1945: Landstridskrafternas operationer.* Helsinki 1949.

Leckie, R: *Challenge for the Pacific: Guadalcanal: The Turning Point of the War.* New York 1965.

Levi, P: *The Drowned and the Saved.* London 1995.

Liu, Z: *Remembering 1942.* New York 2016.

Lucas Phillips, CE: *Alamein.* London 1965.

Lutjens Jr., RN: "Jews in Hiding in Nazi Berlin, 1941–1945: A Demographic Survey," in *Holocaust and Genocide Studies,* vol. 31, no. 2 (2017).

MacArthur, B: *Surviving the Sword: Prisoners of the Japanese, 1942–45.* London 2005.

MacKenzie, SP: "Beating the Odds: Superstition and Human Agency in RAF Bomber Command 1942–45," in *War in History,* vol. 22, no. 3 (2015).

Mansergh, R: *Cumbria at War 1939–45.* Croydon 2019.

Mark, JD: *Death of the Leaping Horseman: The 24th Panzer Division in Stalingrad.* Mechanicsburg 2003.

Mark, JD: *Into Oblivion: Kharkov to Stalingrad: The Story of Pionier-Bataillon 305.* Sydney 2013.

Mark, JD: *Island of Fire: The Battle for the Barrikady Gun Factory in Stalingrad.* Guildford 2018.

Marshall Libby, L: *The Uranium People: The Human Story of the Manhattan Project by the Woman Who Was the Youngest Member of the Original Scientific Team.* New York 1979.

Marshall, SLA: *Men Against Fire: The Problem of Battle Command.* Oklahoma 2017.

Marutani, H & Collie, C: *The Path of Infinite Sorrow: The Japanese on the Kokoda Track.* Adelaide 2009.

McEniry Jr, JH: *A Marine Dive-Bomber Pilot at Guadalcanal.* Tuscaloosa 1987.

Merillat, HB: *Guadalcanal Remembered.* New York 1982.

Merridale, C: *Ivan's War: Life and Death in the Red Army, 1939–1945.* New York 2006.

Metzler, J: *The Laughing Cow: A U-Boat Captain's Story.* London 1960.

Middlebrook, M: *Convoy: The Battle for Convoys SC.122 and HX.229.* London 1976.

Middlebrook, M & Everitt, C (eds.): *The Bomber Command War Diaries: An Operational Reference Book.* Leicester 1996.

Mitter, R: *China's War with Japan 1937–1945: The Struggle for Survival.* London 2013.

Monelli, P: *Mussolini, Piccolo Borghese.* Milan 1970.

Morris, M: *South Pacific Diary 1942–43.* Lexington 1996.

Motadel, D: *Islam and Nazi Germany's War.* Cambridge, Mass. 2018.

Neitzel, S & Welzer, H: *Soldaten: Protokolle vom Kämpfen, Töten und Sterben.* Frankfurt am Main 2011.

Nevin, T: *Ernst Jünger and Germany: Into the Abyss 1914–1945.* London 1997.

Noack, P: *Ernst Jünger: Eine Biographie.* Berlin 1998.

Nykvist, N-E: *Sextiettan: Infanteriregemente 61 1941–1944.* Pieksämäki 2005.

O'Connor, VCS: *Mandalay and Other Cities of the Past in Burma.* London 1907.

Pack, SWC: *Invasion North Africa 1942.* New York 1978.

Parris, JA, Russell, N, Disher, L & Ault, P: *Springboard to Berlin.* New York 1943.

Paull, R: *Retreat from Kokoda: The Australian Campaign in New Guinea 1942.* London 1983.

Peri, A: *The War Within: Diaries from the Siege of Leningrad.* London 2017.

Piotrowski, T: *Poland's Holocaust: Ethnic Strife, Collaboration with Occupying Forces and Genocide in the Second Republic, 1918–1947.* Jefferson 1998.

Poirer, RG & Conner, AZ: *The Red Army Order of Battle in the Great Patriotic War.* Novato 1985.

Pope, D: *73 North: The Defeat of Hitler's Navy.* New York 1959.

Pope, T: *Good Scripts, Bad Scripts.* New York 1998.

Poulsen, NB: *Dödskampen: Kriget på östfronten 1941–1945.* Lund 2018.

Prag, C: *No Ordinary War: The Eventful Career of U-604.* Barnsley 2009.

Pugsley, AF: *Destroyer Man.* London 1957.

Rajchman, C: *The Last Jew of Treblinka: A Survivor's Memory, 1942–1943.* New York 2011.

Reese, WP: *Mir selber seltsam fremd: Russland 1941–44.* Berlin 2004.

Rhodes, R: *The Making of the Atom Bomb.* New York 1986.

Rhodes, R: *The Masters of Death: The SS-Einsatzgruppen and the Invention of the Holocaust.* New York 2003.

Rosbottom, R: *When Paris Went Dark: The City of Light Under German Occupation 1940–44.* London 2015.

Rudakova, D: *Civilian Collaboration in Ukraine and Crimea, 1941–1944: A Study of Motivation.* Perth 2018.

Rutherford, J: *Combat and Genocide on the Eastern Front: The German Infantry's War, 1941–1944.* Cambridge 2014.

Rybicki, F: *The Rhetorical Dimensions of Radio Propaganda in Nazi Germany, 1933–1945.* Duquesne 2004.

Sachs, RH: *White Rose History, Volume 1: Coming Together.* Lehi 2002.

Sachs, RH (ed.): *Gestapo Interrogation Transcripts: Willi Graf, Alexander Schmorell, Hans Scholl, and Sophie Scholl,* NJ 1704, vols. 1–33. Phoenixville 2002.

Salisbury, H: *The 900 Days: The Siege of Leningrad.* New York 1970.

Scheibert, H: *Nach Stalingrad: 48 Kilometer! Der Entsatzvorstoss der 6. Panzerdivsion Dezember 1942.* Heidelberg 1956.

Scholl, H & Scholl, S: *Briefe und Aufzeichnungen.* Frankfurt am Main 1984.

Schwilk, H: *Ernst Jünger: Ein Jahrhundertleben.* Munich 2010.

Sebba, A: *Les Parisiennes: How the Women of Paris Lived, Loved and Died Under Nazi Occupation.* New York 2016.

Seidler, F: *Prostitution, Homosexualität, Selbstverstümmelung: Probleme der deutschen Sanitätsführung 1939–1945.* Neckargemünd 1977.

Sennerteg, N: *"Allt jag känner är att mina fötter gör ont": Förhören med Rudolf Höss.* Stockholm 2020.

Sereny, G: *Into That Darkness: From Mercy Killings to Mass Murder.* London 1995.

Shay, J: *Achilles in Vietnam: Combat Trauma and the Undoing of Character.* New York 2003.

Shimoyamada, I: *Glory Forever: The Life of Captain Wakabayashi.* Tokyo 1963.

Silver, E: *The Book of the Just: The Silent Heroes Who Saved Jews from Hitler.* London 1992.

Simonsson, I: *Fransk-algeriern Albert Camus.* Falun 2013.

Skrjabina, E: *After Leningrad: From the Caucasus to the Rhein, August 9, 1942–March 22, 1945.* Carbondale 1978.

Skrjabina, E: *Siege and Survival: The Odyssey of a Leningrader.* Carbondale 1971.

Somerhausen, A: *Journal d'une femme occupée: Relatée jour après jour, la vie d'une femme de prisonnier de guerre à Bruxelles du 10 mai 1940 au 10 mai 1945.* Brussels 1988.

Steinbeck, J: *Once There Was a War.* London 1973.

Steiner, JF: *Treblinka: Revolt i ett utrotningsläger.* Stockholm 1966.

Szejnmann, CCW & Umbach, M (eds.): *Heimat, Region, and Empire: Spatial Identities Under National Socialism.* London 2014.

Szonert, MB: *World War II Through Polish Eyes: In the Nazi-Soviet Grip.* New York 2002.

Tanaka, Y: *Hidden Horrors: Japanese War Crimes in World War II.* Boulder 1998.

Tetsuo, A: *From Shanghai to Shanghai: The War Diary of an Imperial Japanese Army Medical Officer 1937–1942.* Manchester 2017.

Thomas, LJ: *Through Ice and Fire: A Russian Convoy Diary 1942.* Croydon 2015.

Todd, O: *Albert Camus: A Life.* London 1997.

Tooze, A: *The Wages of Destruction: The Making and Breaking of the Nazi Economy.* London 2006.

Troyan, M: *A Rose for Mrs. Miniver: The Life of Greer Garson.* Lexington 2005.

Villanella, V: *Diario di Guerra: Da El Alamein alla tragica ritirata 1942–1943.* Varese 2009.

Wakabayashi, H: *The Diary of Commander Tohichi Wakabayashi, Died in the Battle of Guadalcanal* (The 52nd Graduations Students from the Military Academy). Tokyo 2008.

Walker, CH: *Combat Officer: A Memoir of the War in the South Pacific.* New York 2004.

Warmbrunn, W: *The German Occupation of Belgium 1940–1944.* New York 1993.

Werner, HA: *Die eisernen Särge.* Stuttgart 1970.

West, K: *Vi slogs och blödde: Ung finlandssvensk soldat i IR61.* Otalampi 2003.

Westkaemper, E: *Selling Women's History: Packaging Feminism in Twentieth-Century American Popular Culture.* New Brunswick 2017.

White, AS: *Dauntless Marine: Joseph Sailer Jr., Dive-Bombing Ace of Guadalcanal.* Fairfax Station 1996.

White, TH & Annalee, J: *Thunder out of China.* New York 1946.

Wiernik, Y: *A Year in Treblinka.* New York 1945.

Willet, P: *Armoured Horseman: With the Bays and the Eighth Army in North Africa and Italy.* Barnsley 2015.

Williams, P: *The Kokoda Campaign 1942: Myth and Reality.* Cambridge 2012.

Worrall, R: *The Italian Blitz 1940–43: Bomber Command's War Against Mussolini's Cities, Docks and Factories.* Oxford 2020.

Wüster, W: *An Artilleryman in Stalingrad.* Sydney 2007.

Yoshiaki, Y: *Comfort Women: Sexual Slavery in the Japanese Military During World War II.* New York 2000.

Zank, H: *Stalingrad: Kessel und Gefangenschaft.* Hamburg 2001.

Züchner, E: *Der verschwundene Journalist: Eine deutsche Geschichte.* Berlin 2010.

INTERNET

Material concerning U-604, including its war diary and interviews with crewmen:
http://www.uboatarchive.net/U-604A/U-604.htm
http://www.uboatarchive.net/U-185A/U-185INT.htm

http://www.uboatarchive.net/U-604/KTB604-2.htm
http://www.uboatarchive.net/U-604/KTB604-3.htm

Material concerning the U.S. 164th Infantry Division:
https://commons.und.edu/infantry-documents/index.3.html

Report concerning Guadalcanal, previously listed as secret:
https://www.history.navy.mil/research/library/online
-readingroom/title-list-alphabetically/g/guadalcanal
-campaign.html#crit

Material concerning the Guadalcanal naval battle, November 12–13:
https://www.history.navy.mil/research/library/online
-readingroom/title-list-alphabetically/b/battle-of-guadalcanal
.html#phase2

The Pacific War Online Encyclopedia:
https://pwencycl.kgbudge.com/Table_Of_Contents.htm

Interrogation report, Burma 1944, concerning sex slavery:
https://en.wikisource.org/wiki/
Japanese_Prisoner_of_War_Interrogation_Report_49

Official publication with regard to the fortieth anniversary of CP-1:
https://digital.library.unt.edu/ark:/67531/metadc718175/

Concerning *Frankfurter Zeitung* and its closure:
https://www.faz.net/aktuell/politik/inland/31-august-1943
-dasende-der-frankfurter-zeitung-15728028.html

Concerning Ursula von Kardorff and her diary:
https://www.zeit.de/1992/28/
geschoent-und-darum-kaum-mehrauthentisch

Concerning the Jewish colony in Shanghai and its relations with the Japanese
and Chinese:
http://history.emory.edu/home/documents/endeavors
/volume1/Ians.pdf

Weather data, Shanghai 1942:
https://library.noaa.gov/Collections/Digital-Docs
/Foreign-Climate-Data/China-Climate-Data#o18201879

Documents concerning Weary Dunlop's service and time as prisoner of war:
https://recordsearch.naa.gov.au/SearchNRetrieve/NAAMedia
/ViewPDF.aspx?B=6231386&D=D
https://recordsearch.naa.gov.au/SearchNRetrieve/NAAMedia
/ViewPDF.aspx?B=31830190&D=D

Interview with Charles Walker, made in 2007:
    https://digitalarchive.pacificwarmuseum.org/digital/collection
    /p16769coll1/id/8520

Material, diary and interviews concerning Bede Thongs:
    https://3rdbattalion1942.com/

Concerning German radio, propaganda, etc.:
    Rybicki, F. (2004). The Rhetorical Dimensions of Radio
    Propaganda in Nazi Germany, 1933–1945. https://dsc.duq.edu
    /etd/1137

Information concerning the Japanese 38th Division and the 228th Infantry
    Regiment:
    https://www.fireandfury.com/orbats/pachongkong1941japanese
    .pdf

Concerning the trial of Takeo Itō for war crimes:
    https://www.online.uni-marburg.de/icwc/australien/81030.pdf

Index

Note: Page numbers in *italics* reference photographs and captions.

A Note About the Author

Peter Englund, an academic and journalist, is a member of the Swedish Academy, which chooses the winners of the Nobel Prize. He is the recipient of a number of literary awards, including the August Prize, for the best Swedish book of the year, and the Selma Lagerlöf Prize. He is the author of ten previous books. He also worked as a war correspondent in the Balkans during the nineties, in Afghanistan and Iraq, and has recently been covering the war in Ukraine.

A Note on the Type

This book was set in Janson, a typeface long thought to have been made by the Dutchman Anton Janson, who was a practicing typefounder in Leipzig during the years 1668–1687. However, it has been conclusively demonstrated that these types are actually the work of Nicholas Kis (1650–1702), a Hungarian, who most probably learned his trade from the master Dutch typefounder Dirk Voskens.

Composed by North Market Street Graphics
Lancaster, Pennsylvania

Printed and bound by Berryville Graphics
Berryville, Virginia

Designed by Betty Lew